W9-CKU-778

WICCA
The Complete Craft

D. J. Conway

THE CROSSING PRESS

Text copyright © 2001 by D. J. Conway

All rights reserved. No part of this book may be reproduced in any form, except brief excerpts for the purpose of review, without written permission of the publisher.

The Crossing Press
www.crossingpress.com

A division of Ten Speed Press
P.O. Box 7123
Berkeley, California 94707
www.tenspeed.com

Library of Congress Cataloging-in-Publication Data
Conway, D. J. (D. J.)
    Wicca : the complete craft / by D. J. Conway.
       p. cm.
   ISBN 1-58091-092-0 (pbk.)
  1. Witchcraft. I. Title.
  BF1566.C59   2001
  299—dc21   2001042121

Cover design by Coulson Design

First printing, 2001
Printed in the U.S.A.

   4 5 6 7 8 9 10—06 05 04 03

TABLE OF CONTENTS

PART III: THE BOOK OF RITUALS

FOREWORD

Being an ordinary person made me think that writing a foreword for such a well-known author in the Pagan community was a farce. However, that's exactly who this book is for—ordinary people who want to know more about the Craft.

What is being a witch? It certainly is not the Hollywood stereotype that most people continue to believe—the wizened old hag or the pleasantly plump fairy god-mother. No, sorry, you can't just wave your magic wand and have all your wishes come true—I wish! Being Wiccan, or a witch as I prefer, is the hardest path anyone could choose to follow. It is certainly not, as my mother has so aptly put it, for the faint of heart. It is scrutinizing every part of your life even when you do not have the desire to do so—the Lady will do it for you; owning when you screw up, which is often; letting go of paths that She does not want you to follow; being patient beyond what you think you can endure, and knowing a joy and peacefulness beyond anything you thought was possible. Sound contradictory? It is that and much more.

I have been struggling on the path for twenty years, I initiated myself, and have been a part of a formal coven. It doesn't matter which path you choose—solitary or group work—being a witch is not just magic, it is life. It is doing New and Full Moon ritual even when you're exhausted from the trials of working and parenting. It is choosing not to spray the dandelions in your yard, even though it pisses off the neighbor with the perfect lawn. It is rejoicing in the changes of the seasons and sharing that beauty with others. It is anguishing with heartache in the senseless killing of animals. Magic is all around us—being a witch just gives you a clearer lens to see and experience it.

May your path be full of wonder and magic—Blessed Be.

—Jeanne McLarney

INTRODUCTION

This book reflects my personal approach to, beliefs in, and practice of the religion of Wicca. I do not pretend to have the ultimate word on Wicca, nor the only views available. My views and opinions will not necessarily be those of other Witches or Pagans, nor should they be. The primary reason that Wicca and Paganism have survived and continue to be the chosen path of so many people is that these religions are adaptable to our individual spiritual needs, as well as open to change to fit the changing times. The people who follow these religions tend to be highly independent individualists.

Wicca/Paganism is a path I have studied for forty years. I still consider myself a student even after all this time. I realize that to grow spiritually one must always be open to learning something new. According to some definitions in the Pagan community, I would be called an Eclectic Witch. Such classifications ceased to be of much interest to me long ago, as I found I never fit into accepted classifications. I use the magical method that applies to a given desire and works for me. I have only one set of unbendable rules: I will not include in my rituals, spellworking, or healing, deities or names that are part of Christianity or any other orthodox religion. I am not opposed to being open, but being too complacent or too trusting is not synonymous with having an open mind. These male-god dominant religions were, and still are, opposed to independent-minded humans and any unique ideas about spiritual growth, particularly if you are female. Members of orthodox religions still are prone to constant efforts to condemn, control, and eradicate any other religion. Fanatics in any form and for any reason are dangerous to human life and spirituality. I believe in the two admonitions of Apollo, written on his temple at Delphi: Know thyself and moderation in all things. Besides, when you commit to a new spiritual path, you cannot hang on to old religious ideas and expect to progress by dabbling in new ones.

To all newcomers to the Wiccan/Pagan fields, please realize that you do not have to belong to a coven to learn. You can do quite well on your own. Belonging to a coven does not guarantee that you will learn and grow, just as not belonging to one does not cancel out your being a Witch. A strong desire, commitment to the Path, persistence, practice, and patience are all that are needed to establish oneself on this spiritual path. Read with discrimination as many books on the subject as you can, realizing that there is as much trash as treasure available. Set up a regular monthly and yearly routine of ritual. Do meditations and visualizations at least once a week. Control your urge to run out and buy every magical tool listed in these books. Rituals can be performed with a minimum of items borrowed from the kitchen as they are needed; the old Witches, especially during the Burning Times, used ordinary implements. Also, expensive, fancy tools work no better than simple, inexpensive ones. The power is within you, not the tools.

I do not encourage teens to become involved in Wicca or practice magic without the explicit approval of their parents. However, many writers do. Magic is not a part of the Wiccan religion, but more of a sideline to the practice of Wicca and some adults can be unscrupulous when using magic to fulfill desires, regardless of whom it might hurt. Indiscriminately teaching teens this power compounds the evil. The vast majority of teenagers do not have the life experience or emotional maturity to deal correctly with the ethics involved in magic. When karma backlashes and negative things come home to roost, these young people panic and, instead of blaming their own lack of ethics or personal greed, they point a finger at Wicca in general and start babbling about the devil and how evil Wiccans are. If you are a teenager thinking of studying Wicca, but your parents object, please wait until you are of age and on your own. If your desire to become Wiccan is sincere, neither time nor circumstances will kill it. It still will be there when you establish your own household.

The spiritual path of Wicca/Paganism is not an easy one. It is still misunderstood by many people, and many cities and states still have anti-Witch laws on their books, regardless of Constitutional rights or the fact that Wicca is recognized as a legitimate religion by both the United States military and the United States government. Depending upon the tolerance level of your town or the kind of job you hold, you may find it more expedient to remain quiet about your choice of religion. I am a firm believer that religion of any kind should remain home where it belongs, and never talked about in public. The way people live their lives should express the purity of the spiritual path they follow. Besides, religion and spirituality are not the same thing.

If you are sincere and determined to follow the Wiccan/Pagan path, I hope this book will open a few inner doors for you. May you find only enlightenment and spiritual growth within.

D. J. Conway

Part I

WHAT IS WICCA?

CHAPTER 1

What Is Wicca?

In this chapter, I will try to explain the general beliefs, philosophy, and ethics of Wiccan and Pagan groups. Most groups will agree with all or most of what I say, although there will be a few groups that disagree vehemently.

There is a large amount of misinformation about Wicca and Paganism floating around in our society, most of it the wild imaginings of non-Wiccan/Pagan folk. These erroneous ideas are fueled by lurid movies, television, the scandal magazines, and the anti-everything-not-orthodox fanatics. So, before I discuss what Wicca or Witchcraft is, I will discuss what it is not.

Wicca is not a cult, for cults actively recruit members, isolate them from friends and family, brainwash their members to be totally obedient to the cult leader, punish members who try to leave, and teach that their way is the only way. You will find that most true cults are offshoots of an orthodox religion.

A true Wiccan group never proselytizes for members. Those drawn to Wicca find others of like mind; no proselytizing is necessary. Witches do not stand on street corners with pamphlets, nor do they ring your doorbell. By the same token, a Wiccan group will carefully screen applicants for those who are sincere and who will enrich the group. They do not want those interested in the latest fad of black clothing, weird makeup, and tons of clanking jewelry, nor do they want fence sitters who will inevitably become troublemakers. Careful selection of applicants avoids the problem of members leaving. However, members who become uncomfortable with others in the group are free to leave and join another Wiccan group or begin to practice by themselves.

Wiccan folk have a strong sense of family and respect for elders (providing that respect is merited), and will not advocate breaking familial ties. If you should encounter the rare group that has leaders demanding obedience, leave quickly.

Dictatorship is not part of the usual Wiccan philosophy. Although there needs to be a leader or leaders in a Wiccan group to coordinate activities and lead rituals, they do not demand obedience. To avoid this situation, many groups have experienced, qualified members rotate in the roles of High Priestess and High Priest. They also do not encourage any members to call themselves "guru" or "master," although they may vote to bestow the title of "elder" on an older, experienced member.

Wiccan/Pagan folk do not believe that their spiritual path is right for everyone. Witchcraft is a self-demanding path, not suited to those who need to be told what to do and when to do it. Witches firmly believe that all responsibility for actions or inactions falls directly on the shoulders of each person. Since we object to other religions attempting to dictate our spiritual paths, most Wiccans go out of their way to avoid perpetrating this "sin" on others.

One of the vilest accusations against Wiccans or Witches is that we worship the devil and are Satanists performing blood sacrifices and having wild sexual orgies spiced with drugs. First, we do not believe in the Christian devil and would never consider worshipping such a foul, negative entity. The devil is a creation of orthodox religions, which seem to know far more about this creature than Witches do.

We do not kill animals or humans in our rites, as we believe the life force and life itself to be very sacred. Witches believe that everything in the universe has great value and is worthy of respect, whether it is animate or inanimate. We do not consider that humans have more value than animals.

As for the sexual orgies, Wiccans are far more apt to avoid sexual promiscuity than other religions, probably because there are few if any sexual taboos. Female Witches know their value as humans and are unlikely to believe that their life is meaningless without a man, even on a casual basis. Male Witches also realize the sanctity of sexual union, believe that the Goddess can be manifested within every woman, and are less likely to engage in meaningless sex. On rare occasions so-called High Priests demand sexual rites before an initiate is allowed to join the group. If you should have the misfortune of encountering such a group or leader, remove yourself from their influence at once. This is not the normal Wiccan practice.

Most Wiccan groups or solitaries avoid illegal drugs and seldom overindulge in alcohol, if they drink at all. It is impossible for anyone to remain rational and alert—necessary qualities for practicing magic—while under the influence of drugs or alcohol. A Witch cannot fully experience spiritual truth while under the influence of anything.

So what exactly is the truth behind Wicca or Witchcraft? Witchcraft is an ancient nature religion that dates back to the Neolithic times. These religions were not called Wicca, but were generally referred to by archaeologists and historians as Goddess religions. Witch and Wicca were used much later, during the European Middle Ages. Before that, Witches were known as shamans or wise men and wise women, or followers of the Old Way.

The name Wicca comes from the Old English word *wicce*, which means "wise" or "wisdom." The name may also have connections to the Indo-European word *wic*, which means "to bend, turn, or shape." Witches do bend and shape energy whenever they perform magic.

Witchcraft is only a very small part of the large religious community called Paganism. The words Wicca, Witchcraft, and the Craft are actually interchangeable. Some followers prefer to call themselves Wiccan and thus avoid the stereotyped mental image of the ugly, evil Witch. Others use the name Witch, hoping to remold that stereotyped image in modern minds. Being eclectic, I call myself Pagan, since I am not a follower of any orthodox religion. However, Paganism also includes a wide variety of names of other groups besides Wicca.

In modern usage, the word Witch or Wiccan is applied to both female and male members of this religion. Very few groups use the term Warlock for males. Warlock was not used until medieval times in Scotland and was then primarily used to denote a malicious sorcerer. Some groups use the old definitions of Wicca for males and Wicce for females.

Basically, Wicca or Witchcraft is an ancient nature religion with a belief in the duality of deity: that is, there is both a Goddess and a God. Usually, the Goddess holds the prime place in Wicca, with the God acknowledged as Her consort, helper, and co-creator. This acknowledgment and worship of the Goddess or goddesses set Witchcraft apart from orthodox religions. However, some Pagan groups are more male god-oriented than those in Wicca.

Wiccan groups, or covens as they are often called, are led by a High Priestess and a High Priest. These leaders do not have absolute power in the group (or coven), but represent the Goddess and the God during rituals. They are also responsible for coordinating the group activities. They hold their positions by consensus of the group members and because of their experience and knowledge. The High Priestess and High Priest of any coven may step down in favor of others, rotate the responsibility with other experienced members, or be voted out by the members. There is no absolute hierarchy of power in Witchcraft, just as it is rare to find a Wiccan church building.

We believe in reincarnation; that everyone has lived many lives and will live many more lives in the future. Witches are not alone in this belief, as many other of the world's religions believe the same thing.

We believe that karma, or cause and effect, operates in every life, whether a person believes in it or not. Every true Witch knows that we do not have the luxury of pointing a finger at someone else as responsible for our breaking any spiritual, ethical, or universal law. People are responsible when they do things that they shouldn't, and when they don't do things that they should. No one pays the penalty but the person who committed the acts. However, we also know that not every negative thing that happens to a person is connected with "bad" karma.

Witches celebrate the changing seasons of the year through the observation of eight ancient holy days: Imbolc, Spring Equinox, Beltane, Summer Solstice, Lughnasadh, Autumn Equinox, Samhain, and Winter Solstice. They also acknowledge and celebrate the New and Full Moons every month, as well as rites of passage.

Witches acknowledge the existence of psychic powers, among them healing, foretelling, and magic (the casting of spells). Magic is not a religious belief, but simply a sideline to better the lives of Witches and their extended families. Using magic also carries an admonition not to interfere with or control others. Deliberate interference or causing harm will bring the law of karma into action.

Like many in the New Age groups, Witches believe that each person has spiritual or astral guides and teachers. We also acknowledge the existence of nature spirits and other non-earthly beings, such as Fairies, dragons, Elementals, and other mythical creatures. Communication with the dead is possible, although whether one wishes to do so is a personal decision.

The primary difference between Witches and the orthodox religions is of ancient origin: we recognize the existence and power of goddesses and worship the Goddess as well as a God. We do not acknowledge the erasure of "sins" by a one supreme male god or his representative, priest or otherwise; we are each responsible for paying for our own mistakes. We do not believe that women are of lesser quality and value than men; after all, we are each born of a woman, and women are a physical manifestation of the Goddess Herself. We do not believe in hierarchies that dictate decisions. We do believe that each woman can be a priestess and each man a priest, and each person is a free individual responsible for their actions. Our chalice of wine or juice existed long before the Christian ceremony; it represents a joining of male and female, not someone's blood. Our rite of "baptism," or its equivalent, was once part of the ancient Mystery Religions and represents a conscious decision by an adult initiate to undertake a new path in life. It is not a "saving" from "sin." We do not believe in the devil or in hell, although we acknowledge the goddess Hel, who rules over the land of the dead, according to the ancient Norse. We do not sacrifice animals or humans. We believe that all life, animate and inanimate, is sacred and should be used wisely and treated with respect. And, perhaps the greatest obstacle (beside the Goddess) that stands between Witches and the orthodox religions is we believe in and practice magic to improve our lives.

If you can accept all of these beliefs and have turned away from orthodox religions because you feel they don't offer you what you seek in a spiritual path, then Witchcraft may be for you. If, however, you don't want to let go of the orthodox deity, but want to practice magic, I suggest that you delve into ceremonial magic, whose practitioners believe in a one male god and call upon angels and demons in their work. Ceremonial magic arose in the Middle Ages as an acceptable method of working magic. It uses the Hebrew names of God, plus the names of angels and demons. Because it was practiced by scholars and churchmen alike (all males), the orthodox Church turned a blind eye to it.

Wicca is the most satisfying way to live my life. I cannot envision living any other way. If your heart and soul draw you to this path, then I say, "Welcome." If not, may you continue your search until you find the path you seek.

CHAPTER 2

The History of Wicca

The fundamental roots of Wicca lie in the very beginning of spiritual seeking on this planet. Although there are no written records to confirm this, statues and wall paintings portray scenes of ceremonies that are very similar to the ceremonies used by later Pagan cultures and by Witches today.

The earliest deity sculptures are from the Stone Age. Of the sixty sculptures uncovered by archaeologists, only five are male. These five are very small and poorly executed. The remaining fifty-five are larger and female; they have great detail, in comparison to the male figures. They represent the Goddess or Great Mother and Her consort.

Most of these first cultures were matriarchal, in that they primarily worshipped the Goddess and the women in these cultures were free of male domination. Many of their religious ceremonies were attended by women only with a priestess officiating.

Matriarchies, however, held that men and women were equal. Creative endeavors held a high priority, while war was practically unknown. Archaeologists, digging in the matriarchal ruins of Catal Huyuk in Turkey, found no evidence of defensive walls for at least one thousand years. Women owned the property, and children took their mother's name. Marriage was based on mother right.[1] The man moved to his wife's family, not vice versa, when he married. After all, he and the other men hunted, and came and went in these societies. The only stable figure was the woman.

When patriarchal societies began to encroach on these peaceful matriarchies, the evidence of defensive walls, weapons, and war arises. Men took control of the government and religion of the culture. The importance of deities changed from the Great Mother and goddesses to the War God or All-Powerful God and gods in general. Traces of the Goddess religions were cloaked in the Mystery Religions and sacred oracle sites, until these, too, were taken over and converted to the worship of male deities.

Many of the ancient goddesses became connected with black magic under the patriarchies. Male rulers condemned Goddess worship by women as Witchcraft and evil, against the declared natural order of spirituality. Patriarchy began to rewrite spiritual history, connecting a great many goddesses with dark magic. Some of these were Isis, Neith, Nephthys, Cerridwen, Anat, Ashtart, Ereshkigal, Lilith, Nanshe, Circe, Cybele, Gaea, Hecate, the Morrigan, Freyja, Holda, Ilmatar, Rauni, Diana/Artemis, Diiwica, Kali, Ch'ang-O, and Inari.

As the Mysteries were forbidden, destroyed, or rewritten for male deities, some women privately rebelled. They established secret groups for only women. They met at night in out-of-the-way places where men seldom came. They celebrated the old holy days. They embraced the term "Witchcraft" as a badge of honor, and successfully hid their religious rites from men for centuries. Later, when the men who were dissatisfied with patriarchy sought out these groups, the Witches allowed selected ones to join them.

In the very beginning of Christianity, this new religion gave Witches little trouble. In fact, Christianity taught that Witches and Witchcraft did not exist. By the thirteenth century, however, Christianity was in trouble. The number of wars was increasing, due in most part to Christian rulers conquering new areas and forcing their religion on the inhabitants. A number of things were going wrong, from famines and disease to crop loss and poverty. The Church began to look for a scapegoat and settled on Witchcraft. At that time, the word "Witch" was used by the Church to describe any believer in a Pagan faith, especially women.

There was another reason for this persecution. Since the best healers were the Witches and wise women of any area, the male doctors backed this Christian-inspired idea that Witches were evil. After all, a good Witch healer with a high success rate in her profession as healer could successfully put male doctors out of business in her community.

Also, during the thirteenth century, Pope Gregory IX issued edicts that marked the beginning of the infamous Witch hunts. He attacked both the Cathars (breakaway Christians) and the Knights Templar. Both of these groups had great wealth and property that was confiscated by the Church and their followers were tortured and killed. Both Cathars and Knights Templar were Christians. The Cathars refused to acknowledge the Pope as ultimate authority while the Templars, who fought holy wars for the Pope, had vast wealth which the Church wanted.

Seeing the possibility to gain further wealth and control over people's minds, the Church created an office of Inquisition, which still exists today. This action also gave the Church greater leverage to extend its field of domination over spiritual matters. During this period, Witches still had not been targeted.

The gates of terror swung wide when, in 1489, Pope Innocent VIII issued an order to rid the lands of all Witches and to kill all cats; cats were said by the Church to be minions of the devil and the companions of Witches. This was a declaration of open warfare against Witches or any Pagan followers. Pope Innocent VIII commissioned the writing of the *Malleus Maleficarium* (Hammer for Witches). Two German Dominican priests, Jakob Sprenger and Prior Heinrich Kramer, did the actual writing. This became the "bible" for all Witch hunters, describing in detail how to torture people to obtain confessions. The expense for every form of torture was billed directly to the victim, a way for the Church to justify stealing the victim's property.

The Church immediately appointed Inquisitors (all men) who had total authority over which accused persons to convict, torture, murder, or set free. It was rare that a person accused of Witchcraft ever was freed, and even those who were freed had to endure the most horrendous tortures.[2] All property was confiscated immediately upon accusation and never returned, even in the rare cases when people were found innocent. After all, the Inquisitor of each region and all his helpers were paid out of the property and belongings of anyone upon accusation of Witchcraft. Being an Inquisitor and Witch hunter was big business and made many men very wealthy. Of course, the Church got its cut also. After all, the Church had invented this murder/extortion racket.

The male doctors heartily approved of all this, as it removed their female competition. Any female healer who attended a childbirth was automatically branded as a Witch, for she knew which herbs to use to kill pain, and, worse yet, which ones could be used as contraceptives. This attitude that women should suffer during childbirth continued into the mid-1900s, long after anesthetics were available. If a woman miscarried for any reason, including a beating from her husband, the Church considered her guilty of deliberate murder, which carried a death penalty. In the clergy's mind, all women were guilty of something evil until they were dead.[3]

Using fear as a major weapon, the Witch hunters coerced many good churchgoers and priests to take an active part in the accusations, tortures, and murders of their fellow countrymen. However, some people spoke up against this injustice and were murdered along with the others. In 1126, a man named Pierre de Bruys was burned for saying that God no longer was in the Church. Frere Raymond Jean preached against the Church's abuses of power and was executed. When a Franciscan splinter group preached that the Pope and priests abused God's laws, the entire group plus every person in the village of Magnalata was murdered.

Children as young as three years old were tortured until they gave evidence against their mothers. The Church gave its blessing and absolution of sin to all who helped.[4] As a consequence, accused women were frequently raped by their torturers and their assistants; all women were gagged on their way to execution to keep them from revealing this crime.[5]

For the next three centuries, the European Christian churches hunted and murdered so-called Witches from the Scandinavian countries in the north to Spain in the south.[6] All the women and girls in entire villages were wiped out.[7] Strasbourg, Germany, burned five thousand victims in twenty years. A thousand so-called Witches were killed at Como in 1524. Some historians estimate that as many as nine million died during the cruel Witch hunts in Europe. Eventually, the paranoid practice spread even to the Americas. Countries outside the influence of the Christian Church did not participate.

Because cats suffered the same fate as Witches during this time, there was no protection against the rats that carried the black plague into Europe. At first, the Church did not care about the growing population of rats, as they considered it part of the torture for packs of rats to attack prisoners. By the time anyone paused long enough to consider the connection between the plague and the lack of cats, it was too late.

The terrible Witch hunts continued into the seventeenth century, until King Louis XIII ordered the persecutions stopped in France. However, both the Catholic and Protestant Church officials of England and Scotland were making far too much money and widening their control to stop. One of the most enthusiastic and fanatical of the English Witch hunters was Matthew Hopkins, the Witch Finder General (1644–1646), who was responsible for more executions than anyone else; he did it all for money.

The last so-called Witch was hanged in Scotland in 1727. The last Scottish law against Witchcraft was repealed in 1736, but the last of the Witchcraft Acts in Britain wasn't removed from the books until 1951.

Because of the millions of people slain, true Witches went underground, revealing themselves and their groups to no one. Few groups had contacts with other similar groups. Nothing was written down for fear of being discovered. The Old Ways became garbled and distorted over the centuries, until most of what survived was thought of as superstition and folklore.

It was not until World War II was on the horizon that Gerald Gardner, a retired British civil servant, discovered that little pockets of Witchcraft did survive. He wrote that he contacted the remains of a Witch group in New Forest and was initiated into the Craft. However, Gardner's and the group's fear of persecution kept him from writing about Witchcraft until after 1951. Even then, the group did not agree with Gardner about making public the practices of Witches.

After Gardner's books reached the public, hundreds, then thousands, of people began to consider Witchcraft as a viable, fulfilling spiritual path. They walked away from orthodox religions without a backward glance, feeling as if they had come home when they stepped inside a consecrated circle. They based their new groups on Gardner's work for the most part, but departed from the rest of his ideas to conceive and write their own rituals. Slowly but surely, Witchcraft began to spread. Today many thousands of followers of this ancient path stretch around the globe.

Yet most Witches still must face periodic, if not daily, persecution by members of orthodox churches, whether these persecutors are family, neighbors, or members of the United States Congress. Lest Witches become too complacent, please remember that the Office of Inquisition was still active in Central and South America as late as 1834, and that the Church has always maintained that its reign of terror and murder was fully justified. In fact, the Office of Inquisition is still an active part of the Catholic Church, and was used to justify certain negative actions as late as 1969.[8] As one can plainly see from the recent attempts to make Witchcraft and Paganism illegal by Christian-influenced Congressmen, and by the harassment and menacing of Wiccan/Pagan folk while the law looks the other way, the Burning Times could happen once more if all those who believe in religious freedom are not vigilant.

Witches, however, are resilient people who believe firmly and steadfastly in their religion. They will continue to survive, whatever comes.

Endnotes

1   Bachofen, *Myth, Religion & Mother Right.*

2   Lea, *The Inquisition of the Middle Ages.* In Pagan societies, people were considered innocent of a crime until proven guilty.

3   Sjoo & Mor, *The Great Cosmic Mother.*

4   Coulton, *Inquisition and Liberty.*

5   Robbins, *Encyclopedia of Witchcraft and Demonology.*

6   Most of the millions of men, women, and children tortured and condemned as Witches actually were not Witches, but people who had jealous, hateful, and/or fearful neighbors. Still, they were tortured, burned, hanged, and flayed alive, all in the excuse of saving souls.

7   Robbins.

8   Ronald Holmes, *Witchcraft in History.*

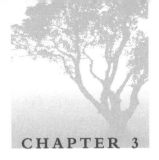

CHAPTER 3

Modern Wicca

Division between Paganism and Wicca was defined long ago when the patriarchal cultures overran the earlier matriarchies. However, the two groups managed finally to live side by side with a minimum of friction until Christianity began its bid to take over the world.

The word Pagan is derived from the Latin word *paganus,* which means "a country dweller," just as the word *heathen* means "one living on the heath," or in remote spots. Christians began to apply these labels to believers in other gods when the country people refused to be intimidated into joining the then new Christian religion. To Christians, the word Pagan came to mean someone who was backward and uncivilized.

The Pagans, however, were anything but backward. They recognized a forceful takeover when they saw it, wanted no part of this control, nor did they want to be told how to live their lives. Besides, their pantheons of gods and goddesses had always met their spiritual needs. They saw nothing logical or practical in a one, male god, who seemed to enjoy having his priests tell people how ignorant and spiritually wrong they were, while holding out a hand for money at the same time.

Another point of contention was that Pagans had women priestesses and healers, both of whom were highly respected for their knowledge and skills. These women often were part of secret, women-only groups that we would recognize as the ancestresses of today's Witches.[1]

Both the Pagan priests and priestesses did not hesitate to point out the dangers of Christianity to the less educated commoners. They taught that people could communicate directly with the deities of their cultural pantheon, an anathema to the Christians who dictated that people could communicate to their deities only through one of their male priests, and that there was only one god, and that god was male.

The last straw for Pagans and Witches was the Christian condemnation of, and attempts to destroy, all goddesses. However, religious history, as well as regular history, is always rewritten by the fanatics with the most military power. When kings and rulers joined Christianity in an attempt to absolve themselves of negative past actions and in an attempt to escape the law of karma, the ordinary person had to follow suit. Pagan and Wiccan practices went underground for centuries.

Beginning in the 1950s, there was a resurgence of interest in old religions in Britain and the United States. Some people who had held on to bits of the Old Ways began to be more open about their beliefs. Some of them taught people outside their close family group. Paganism and Wicca began to grow again, providing other avenues for spiritual growth for independent thinkers.

There are a few differences between Wicca and Paganism, besides the difference in their ages: Wicca dates to the Stone Age, and authentic Paganism arose much later under the patriarchal systems and cultures.

Paganism is primarily based upon a specific ancient pantheon of deities, such as Norse, Celtic, Egyptian, Roman, et cetera, as are some Wiccan groups. Some Pagan groups do rituals within a cast circle, some do not. Like those in Wicca, few Pagan groups claim to practice authentic ancient rituals, because historic details are too sketchy to make such claims. Pagan groups frequently incorporate aspects of both Wicca and ceremonial magic into their teachings, as do some Wiccan groups. Perhaps the greatest difference between these two religious systems is that Paganism does not usually hold the Goddess in higher esteem than the God.

Wicca is very likely the oldest Western religion.[2] It is usually both a nature-oriented religion and a magical system. It focuses on the Goddess and Her consort, and is not based on a human leader, a dogma, or a sacred book. Most Wiccan rituals and spellworkings are performed within a consecrated circle. However, there is more to Wicca than this simple explanation. It becomes a way of life, a way of viewing everything around you, of seeing and knowing deep within that everything in the universe is connected to and is part of a supreme creating power, frequently referred to as the Great Mother or Great Goddess.

It would be more semantically correct to call adherents of these modern versions of ancient religions Neo-Pagans and Neo-Wiccans, for they are not exact duplicates of ancient religions. It is obvious from research into the subject that neither Paganism nor Wicca can claim an authentic, direct, unbroken link to ancient practices.[3]

However, Witches and Pagans are independent rebels and do not care about being semantically correct. They are far more interested in expanding their spiritual growth, exploring their connection with the Goddess and the God, and being allowed to practice their religion as they see fit.

Modern-day Wicca, or Witchcraft, although based on ancient Pagan ideas and deities, is very flexible. A solitary practitioner or a group may graft parts of ancient traditions onto what they already practice, or may base their entire religious system on a particular ancient culture. Since someone had to create the original practices of every religion, there is no stigma attached to creating modern rituals and following them. In addition, the ancient rituals we are familiar with are all written in a language few modern people, if any, can understand or correctly speak and they are not really applicable to the needs of modern worshippers. Witches have had to move with the times in order to survive, and are quite good at changing rituals to meet their present needs.

However, Witchcraft, as with Paganism, is not a one-size-fits-all religion. There are many branches of it that have arisen to suit the needs of various groups of people. The Wiccan response to this is much the same as the inscription over an ancient lamasery in Tibet: "A thousand monks, a thousand religions." Every group does it their way. If outside Wiccans are invited to join a particular group for a ritual, they consider it common courtesy to follow the procedures of that group. When groups do hold large regional gatherings, the rituals are a joint effort. These gatherings rarely result in any major friction, which is an amazing thing, since Witches most often agree to disagree on points of rituals.

In 1973, a Council of American Witches met in Minneapolis, Minnesota, to talk about, and perhaps come up with, the definition of Wicca and a creed of beliefs.[4] Since Witches do not recognize any authoritarian hierarchy, drafting one set of rules, or even one creed, was difficult and the resulting articles of belief was short. They decided that to call oneself a Witch does not make one a Witch; there has to be a total commitment to that religion. Neither does the fact that one may have been born into a particular family with bits and pieces of the Old Ways make one a Witch. Witches should not collect titles or degrees, or grant themselves special positions because of the number of initiations they might have. No Witch believes in absolute evil, although they believe in general evil and evil entities. No Witch worships the Christian Satan.

In 1975, two years after the Minneapolis gathering, another group met in northern California. This gathering was called the Covenant of the Goddess. A few more beliefs were added to the Council's articles. All members should worship the Goddess and be autonomous. Money should not be made through initiations or the teaching of the Craft. All members should respect the secrecy of their group, and of the Craft in general.

Even though there are varying differences within Witchcraft itself, Witches instantly pull together whenever their religious freedom is threatened. Not long ago, a southern Congressman tried to force bills through Congress that would declare that Wicca and Paganism were not religions and should be outlawed. The Wiccan/Pagan community fought back successfully. Today, Wicca and Paganism are considered legitimate religions recognized by the United States government, and are listed in the books of military chaplains.

Although it is impossible to cover all the branches of Wicca, the following is a brief list of the types of Witchcraft being practiced today. The deities and ideas of any ancient culture except Christianity can be grafted onto Wicca, thus forming a legitimate form of Witchcraft.

Alexandrian Tradition: a branch of Wicca started in Britain during the 1960s. It is based on Gardnerian Witchcraft, and named after its founder, Alex Sanders.

British Traditional Witchcraft: a branch of British Witchcraft based on a blend of Celtic and Gardnerian ideas.

Caledonii Tradition: a tradition that originated in Scotland and is blended with ancient Scottish lore. It was once called the Hecatine Tradition.

Celtic Witchcraft: a branch of Gardnerian Witchcraft mixed with Celtic and Druidic ideas.

Ceremonial Witchcraft: a form of Witchcraft that uses Qabalistic magic.

Christian Witch: this name is an oxymoron, meaning two conflicting words have been joined, thus canceling out each other. In other words, this is an impossibility. True Witches do not believe in the Christian god, nor do they meld their religion with an orthodox religion that tried to exterminate them.

Dianic Witches: a feminist branch of Witchcraft practiced by all-female groups worshipping the Goddess in Her Triple form only. These groups may use a mixture of various traditions. They use the Goddess of the Four Directions in circle work, and all tools have a Goddess symbolism.

Eclectic Witch: a Witch who practices or uses no particular Wiccan or magical tradition. It can be a group or a solitary Witch who uses whatever works, excluding orthodox ideas.

Egyptian Witchcraft: a branch of Witchcraft using ancient Egyptian deities and ideas.

Gardnerian Tradition: a branch of Witchcraft founded in Britain by Gerald Gardner in the early 1950s.

Greek Witchcraft: a branch of Witchcraft using ancient Greek deities and ideas.

Green Witch: usually a solitary Witch who bases her magic on the uses of herbs and plants. Often, there is little or no religion involved.

Hecatine Tradition: the original name for the Caledonii Tradition.

Hereditary Tradition: a specific family tradition of Witchcraft and/or magic that has survived through several generations of a particular family and is taught by living relatives. Sometimes this branch of Wicca is call Family Traditions or Fam Trads.

Kitchen Witch: a name not often used, it describes a Witch who practices practical magic using earth power, earth objects, herbs, and the Elements. These Witches do most of their work in the kitchen at the hearth or stove. There may or may not be religious ideas incorporated.

Mesopotamian Witchcraft: a branch of Witchcraft using ancient Mesopotamian deities and ideas.

Natural Witch: the same as a solitary Witch.

Nordic Witchcraft: the same as Teutonic Witchcraft.

Pictish Witchcraft: based on the Picts who inhabited England and Scotland before the arrival of the Celts. This usually describes a solitary Witch, rarely a group. There is little religion in this branch of Wicca, as the Witch deals primarily with nature magic.

Pow-Wow Tradition: found basically in Pennsylvania, and based on old German magic, the followers do not call themselves Witches. It comes from four hundred years of German magic in that state.

Roman Witchcraft: a branch of Witchcraft using ancient Roman deities and ideas.

Satanic Witch: like Christian Witch, this term is an oxymoron, meaning two conflicting words have been joined, thus canceling out each other. In other words, this is an impossibility. True Witches do not believe in or call upon the Christian Satan.

Seax-Wicca: a form of Witchcraft founded by Raymond Buckland in 1973, this is based on ancient Saxon beliefs and deities, with elements of the Gardnerian Tradition.

Solitary Witch: sometimes called a Natural Witch. The practitioners work alone, following whatever tradition or mixture of traditions they desire. In some ways, this branch is similar to the Eclectic Witch.

Strega Witchcraft: an Italian branch of Witchcraft said to have been founded by the woman Aradia about 1353.

Teutonic Witchcraft: a branch of Witchcraft based on ancient German and Scandinavian ideas and deities. It is also called the Nordic Tradition or Nordic Witchcraft.

Wiccan Shamanism: a blend of Witchcraft and shamanic ideas.

Wiccan Witch: a solitary Witch or group of Witches who rarely call the Goddess or the God by a name. This simple classification, however, is rare, as most Witches blend their religion with some aspects of ancient traditions.

As you can see by the number and variety of branches of Wicca, there really is no end of "traditions" that can arise in the religion of Witchcraft, and there is also no end to the disagreements over the definition of any named branch. Wicca is what any Witch makes it, as long as the branch is based upon Pagan ideas and deities.

Endnotes

1   Margaret Murray and Mircea Eliade both agree that Witchcraft has existed for thousands of years in Europe and the Mediterranean area. Margot Adler, *Drawing Down the Moon.*

2   Starhawk, *The Spiral Dance.*

3   Aidan Kelly, *Crafting the Art of Magic*, contains such research.

4   This gathering was sponsored by Carl Weschcke of Llewellyn Publications, who no longer practices Wicca.

Part II
A Course in Wicca

CHAPTER 4

Words and Terms Used in Wicca

In order to truly become a Witch, you must make a commitment to study and practice. You need to know all you can about this religion, if you hope to gain spiritually. You must learn and understand what you learn. If you dabble, you aren't really a Witch, but a "wannabee" who is too lazy or indecisive for commitment. Wicca is first and foremost a spiritual path, so consider carefully before you begin. As for magic, if you dabble in magic without a proper foundation, you are apt to get your fingers burned, and not know why. Just don't go around calling yourself a Witch because you think you can do spells. Wicca isn't magic, but a religion.

Study the chapters in this section of the book and do the exercises as you go. You can skim over the last two parts of the book to satisfy your curiosity, but I strongly recommend you leave them until last to practice. It may help you to have a special notebook in which you record the lessons and your thoughts. Writing things down not only helps clarify your thinking, but helps you discover, and uncover, your innermost feelings. Reading your comments later will reveal the strides you are making in your search for spiritual growth.

It is best for beginners or apprentices in Wicca to make themselves familiar with the following words. You may never hear some of these words in groups or among Wiccan friends, but sooner or later you will come across them in books. These are words that are known and used in the Wiccan, Pagan, and magical communities.

adept: a person who is very skilled in some form of magic.

Airts, Four: Scottish words for the four directions or, as the name implies, the four winds or airs.

Akashic Records: records of everyone's past lives and of ancient knowledge; these records are found only on the astral planes. These records cannot be accessed without a journey to those planes and without the training to find, read, and interpret what one sees. In India, it is believed that these records also record any future lives as well.

alphabets, magical: special alphabets used in the writing of some magical spells; they also are used to write secret words and names on tools. Originally, all alphabets were sacred and used for magic.

altar: a flat surface used only for performing rituals or making magic. An altar may be something as simple as a large, flat stone or a table.

amulets: a human-made object that is charmed for the protection of the wearer.

ankh: the ancient Egyptian cross, *crux ansata*, with a loop at the top; in ancient times it symbolized life and reincarnation.

apprentice: a beginner in Wicca. The words neophyte, novice, and postulant are also used, although these are more reminiscent of orthodox religious orders.

Aradia: according to Charles Godfrey Leland, this was an Italian woman who taught Witchcraft around 1353. She is traditionally recognized as the daughter of the goddess Diana and called Queen of the Witches.

Arcana: a name applied to the two parts of a tarot deck. There are twenty-two Major Arcana cards and fifty-six Minor Arcana cards. The Minor Arcana is further divided into four suits of Pentacles, Wands, Swords, and Cups, which represent the four Elements.

astral planes: other planes of reality that interpenetrate and co-exist with the physical plane on which humans live. These can be reached through directed astral travel or meditation. There are several levels or areas on the astral planes, all different and all containing different types of beings.

astral travel: the separation of the astral body from the physical body. The person retains consciousness and can use this astral form to explore the astral plane or journey across time and space.

astrology: the ancient science that uses the position of the stars at the time of a person's birth to predict a possible future. Astrology is also used to calculate the time of "birth" of a city, nation, or business to predict the future.

athame: the traditional black-hilted, double-edged knife used by Witches during rituals and in magic. It is not used to kill or cut anything.

Autumn Equinox: one of the Wiccan eight holy days; celebrated about September 21.

balefire: an old word for bonfire. The original word was Bel's fire, referring to the sun god Bel.

bane: a source of harm or destruction; a curse.

banish: to cast something out by magic, usually negative spirits, entities, or energies. The word is also used when referring to cutting the astral ritual circle. Some Wiccan groups use the word banish in reference to expelling a member.

Baphomet: a half-human, half-goat image of a deity. Originally, used by the Knights Templar, later by Satanists.

Beltane: one of the Wiccan eight holy days; celebrated on May 1. In Irish Gaelic it is *Bealtaine*; in Scottish Gaelic it is *Bealtuinn*.

besom: an old word for a broom. This special broom is used to symbolically sweep the circle clean before ritual.

bi-location: a phrase used to describe seeing a physical person in one place, while others see the astral body (which appears physical) of that person in another place.

bind: the use of magic to restrict the power and movement of people, entities, and energies. This is primarily used by Witches when they are attacked.

blasting: placing a curse on someone.

Blood of the Moon: a phrase used by some female Witches to describe the menstrual cycle.

bolline: a white-handled knife with a curved blade; primarily used to cut herbs, usually resembles a small hand sickle.

bonfires: fires lighted outdoors by ancient cultures to celebrate certain holy days. The name probably came from the words "bone-fire," "boon-fire," or "Bel's fire." The Celtic word *teinne* means fire, such as in the word Beltane. Surviving Scottish place-names, such as Craig-an-teine (rock of the fire) and Auch-an-teine (field of the fire), reveal their origins. The ashes from these fires were thought to be very lucky. People carried some home to attract luck and protect against evil and ill-wishing.

Book of Shadows: the traditional name for the book in which a Witch keeps her rituals, spells, and any other information she has learned. Although some Witches believe this can only be a black, bound book, others choose notebooks in colorful designs.

bune wand: an old Scottish term for anything a Witch used to fly upon. In Scottish folklore, bune wands are usually described as a forked stick or a staff. The forked stick, like antlers, symbolizes the Horned God.

Burning Times: the period during the Middle Ages when the Christian Church hunted down, tortured, and murdered anyone they suspected of being a Pagan or a Witch.

cakes and wine/cakes and ale: a phrase used by Gerald Gardner to describe the wine/ale/juice and cakes/cookies/bread used by some Wiccan groups during ritual.

call: a series of words or sounds that are used to invoke, or call, deities.

Candlemas: another name for the festival of Imbolc. (Any time you find the name of a Pagan holy day containing the suffix "mas," you know this name has been Christianized.)

cauldron: the cast iron kettle used by Witches for burning request papers, holding lighted candles, brewing up herbal potions for healing or magic, or as a symbol of the womb of the Great Goddess.

ceremonial magic: a magical system different from Wicca, in which no Goddess is mentioned. Begun in the Middle Ages, it was a magical system practiced by learned men and priests with ties to Christianity and Judaism. It uses a mixture of Hebrew and Greek words and calls upon the names of God, angels, and demons.

Cernunnos: the Horned God of the Celtic cultures; also called Lord of the Forests and Lord of the Animals.

chakras: the Hindu concept that describes seven major astral light centers or energy vortices in the physical/astral body of humans.

channeling: contacting and communicating with disembodied entities while in a trance state, or altered state of consciousness and allowing such entities to use the physical body and voice to communicate with other humans. It is also known as mediumship.

chanting: verbally repeating words or verses to build up power within a magic circle. This accumulated power is released as part of spellworking.

Charge of the Goddess, The: a message from the Goddess to Her followers, this appears in *Aradia: Gospel of Witches*. Gerald Gardner wrote a version, including much material by Aleister Crowley. Doreen Valiente wrote a later version, deleting the Crowley material. The Valiente version has since been adopted by most Wiccan groups and is frequently rewritten. It is also known simply as The Charge.

charms: chanted or sung magical spells. Also, amulets and talismans that have been chanted over to imbue them with power.

circle: a symbol of eternity. See magic circle.

clairvoyance, clairaudience, clairsentience: these terms refer to various ways of being aware of psychic happenings. Clairaudience means to hear music or voices. Clairsentience means to feel something, such as a touch. The word clairvoyance, although it means "clear-seeing," is frequently used to mean all three words.

cleansing: removing all negative energies or entities from an object, person, or place.

Cone of Power: the magical, psychic energy that is raised and contained within a consecrated circle. Psychically seen, the power emanates from the edge of the circle and rises to a peak high above. At its height, this power is released to manifest a desired result.

consecration: the purification and blessing of an object, person, or place.

coven: a group of Witches who work together regularly. Some believe a coven must have thirteen members or less, but never less than three. The word coven was first used in sixteenth-century Scotland.

covenstead: the place where Witches regularly meet.

cowan: a person who is not a Witch; a non-believer.

Craft, The: another name for Wicca or Witchcraft.

Craft name: the new, magical name taken by a Witch at initiation. This name is kept secret from all except those with whom the Witch works.

crossroads: the meeting places for those who followed the goddesses Hecate and Diana of the Three Ways.

curses: deliberate ill-wishing or blasting of a person.

dancing: a practice of some Wiccan groups to raise power and create a state of semi-hypnosis. Spiral dances symbolize entering the Inner Mysteries, while the circle or round dance represents the circling stars in the heavens.

Days of Power: generally speaking, these can be the holy days or New or Full Moon. Other days can be powerful for Witches because of eclipses, astrological alignments, or personal days of significance.

dedication: the oath made by Wiccan initiates that promise their life and self to the Wiccan religion.

degrees: in traditional Wiccan groups, there are three degrees of initiation, earned by study and practice. The last, called the Third Degree, makes one a High Priestess or High Priest.

deosil: to move in a clockwise or sunwise direction. Old spellings are *deiseal* and *deasail*.

Dianic: a segment of Wicca that has all-female groups who worship only the Goddess.

divination: to uncover the possible future or information by the use of certain tools, such as tarot cards, the I Ching, or rune stones. Divination is also used to find hidden things.

dowsing: to use a pendulum, forked stick, or L-rods to locate underground water, oil, or minerals. The pendulum can also be used as a divination tool.

Drawing Down the Moon: a Full Moon ritual, usually performed by a priestess or female Witch, to bring the essence of the Goddess within the woman.

earth magic: magic performed with natural objects found in or on the earth. Also, magic that uses power drawn from the earth.

Eclectic: a segment of Wicca that does not adhere to a particular magical system, but includes a variety of teachings in the magic and ritual.

elder: the title bestowed upon an older, knowledgeable member of some Wiccan groups. In traditional Wiccan groups, an elder is generally a Third Degree Witch.

Elementals: non-corporeal beings and creatures who inhabit the astral plane and are connected with the Elements. The most commonly known traditional Elementals are gnomes, undines, sylphs, and salamanders.

Elements: psychic energies connected with Earth, Air, Fire, Water, and Spirit.

enchantment: to use magic to influence the actions of a person or the outcome of an event.

Esbat: the Full and New Moon rituals of Witches.

evil eye: a malevolent power supposedly transmitted by a mere glance by certain persons.

evocation: the calling of a lower order of spirits into a triangle made outside the consecrated circle.

Fairies: a race of Otherworld beings who have long been connected with Witches.

familiar: a physical or astral creature that has a psychic bond with a Witch.

fascination: a magical power used to control another person.

fetch: an old word used to denote the projected astral body of a person; a form that is deliberately sent on a mission, usually to collect information.

Five-fold Kiss: a ritual practice used by Gardnerian and Alexandrian Witches, and practiced between a man and a woman.

Four Powers, The: also called the Four Powers of the Magus. These are "to know (Air), to dare (Water), to will (Fire), and to be silent (Earth)."

Gaea/Gaia: the Earth Mother; an aspect of the Goddess and representative of the planet Earth.

garter: a piece of fabric or leather that is laced, tied, or buckled around the thigh of the High Priestess of a coven.

genetic mind: the theory of Carl Jung that describes the superconscious mind, a mind that connects all cultures and people. It is also called the Collective Unconscious and the superconscious.

God, The: the consort of and co-creator with the Goddess; the masculine aspect of Divine Power.

Goddess, The: the creatrix of the universe and everything in it; the feminine aspect of Divine Power.

Great Rite: a symbolic sexual ritual of the Great Marriage between the Goddess and the God, High Priestess and High Priest. This is rarely physically enacted.

Green Man: an aspect of the God, this deity represented the Lord of the Forests. He is portrayed peering out from a mass of foliage.

grimoire: although some Wiccans use this term to refer to the Book of Shadows, it is more correctly a name linked with ceremonial magic.

Guardians: the psychic and astral entities who are called to guard the four quarters of a consecrated circle. It may also be used when referring to the spiritual guardians of a person.

handfasting: the Wiccan ritual for Pagan marriage.

Hermes Trismegistus: a combination of the Egyptian god Thoth and the Greek god Hermes, he is regarded as the author of the book called the *Kybalion*. This book should not be confused with the Jewish Qabala.

Hermetica: forty-two sacred books containing ancient wisdom; this collection of knowledge is attributed to the Egyptian Hermes Trismegistus.

hexagram: this six-pointed star has origins far older than Judaism. It is sometimes used to represent the Hermetic teaching "as above, so below." It is a symbol of the blending of female and male energies, a necessary ingredient in successful magic. The word is also used to denote the lined glyphs used in I Ching.

High Priest: the principal male leader of a coven. Second and Third Degree male Witches may also be priests, although they do not lead the coven.

High Priestess: the principal female leader of a coven. Second and Third Degree female Witches may also be priestesses, although they do not lead the coven.

hive off, to: when two or more members leave a group to start their own.

hocus pocus: a magical phrase found in ancient grimoires.

holey stones: stones that have a natural hole through them.

holy days: Pagan holidays. These eight days are Imbolc (February), Spring Equinox (March), Beltane (May), Summer Solstice (June), Lughnasadh (August), Autumn Equinox (September), Samhain (October), and Winter Solstice (December).

Horned God, The: another name for Cernunnos and the supreme Forest God.

I Ching: a Chinese divination system that uses randomly chosen glyphs of broken and unbroken lines.

Imbolc: one of the eight Wiccan holy days; celebrated on February 1. Also spelled as Imbolg and Oimelc.

incarnation: the present physical life.

incense: fragrant resins, gums, herbs, flowers, and woods burned during rituals and spellworking.

initiation: the formal ceremony performed when someone joins a Wiccan group. Self-initiations can be performed by solitary Witches, as an inner sign of total dedication to the Wiccan religion.

Inner Planes: other levels of consciousness and existence.

invocation: the part of a ritual in which higher powers and/or deities are invited into a consecrated circle.

karma: the law of cause and effect.

knots: part of binding and releasing spells.

labyrinth: a construction consisting of a path that spirals inward to a center; there is only one path that reaches the center, as opposed to a maze that may have many paths to the center. Walking the Labyrinth is a term used to describe the inner path each person must travel to reach the Divine Center within.

Lady, The: the Goddess.

Land of Faery: an old term used to denote the section of the Otherworld where the spirits of deceased people go.

left-hand path: the psychic road traveled by those who use negative magic. Sometimes this term is applied to Satanists.

Lord, The: the God.

Lords of Karma: powerful astral counselors who see that the laws of karma are carried out, and that, eventually, all karma is paid, whether a human believes in karma or not.

Lughnasadh: one of the Wiccan eight holy days; celebrated on August 1. Also spelled Lunasa. The name Lammas came at a later date from the Anglo-Saxons and means "loaf mass." Lammas is a Christianized version of the Pagan name.

macrocosm: the great outer world; the universe around us.

magic: the drawing down of energy from another realm and using that energy to create and shape a desired result. The Witch must create the result on the Inner Planes in order for it to follow universal laws and manifest on the physical plane. The results are rarely instantaneous.

magic circle: a circular space consecrated by a Witch or magical group, in which rituals and magic are performed.

magical systems: a variety of cultural traditions that call upon specific deities and powers when performing magic.

Magus: a title sometimes applied to Witches of the Second or Third Degree. It is more frequently used to denote an adept of ceremonial magic.

Malleus Maleficarum: also called the Witch Hammer or Hammer for Witches. A book written in the Middle Ages as a guideline for persecuting, torturing, and murdering people who did not agree with the Christian Church.

maze: an intricate network of passageways that has many dead ends and more than one way to the center.

measure: some covens measure an initiate with a thread and then keep the thread, a piece of hair, and a drop of blood in the coven's books. The objects can be used in magical ways to punish an initiate who leaves the group or divulges its secrets.

microcosm: the little inner world within us or our immediate personal surroundings.

mirrors: a common household item that can be used in magic. Mirrors are useful in reflecting back negative energies and spells and can also be used in scrying.

Moon, Full: the phase of the Moon in which all of its light is revealed. The period leading up to it is called the Waxing Moon. Witches frequently meet on a Full Moon for rituals and to use this power for magic.

Moon, New: the phase of the Moon when all of its light is obscured. The period leading up to it is called the Waning Moon. Some Witches hold rituals during this time and do magic to eliminate illnesses or life problems.

New Age: a term used to describe people who are not Wiccan/Pagan and frequently still adhere to orthodox religions, but use psychic practices.

Old Ways: a reference to the practices of Witchcraft and Paganism.

Otherworld: a term used to describe the astral planes. The Otherworld has many levels or areas. Lower levels house negative entities and souls, while higher levels house deities and progressed souls.

Pagan/Neo-Pagan: the name used to describe various non-Christian groups who base their religion on ancient traditions and pantheons of deities. A Witch is a Pagan (non-Christian believer), but a Pagan is not necessarily a Witch.

pantheon: traditional groups of deities. Each pantheon is connected with an ancient culture and tradition.

pentacle: a disk or plate of metal, ceramic, or wood on which is engraved or painted a five-pointed star; this is placed on a Witch's altar. It is representative of the Earth Element.

pentagram: a five-pointed star with one point upright. A symbol long used in connection with the Goddess. It is rarely used inverted by Pagans or Witches, and then only as a sign of Second Degree Witch initiation.

polytheism: the belief in more than one deity.

poppet: a cloth doll made to resemble a person. An old name for poppet was "mommet." This can be used in healing or to bind another person's actions.

precognition: to be aware of events before they happen.

Priest: a man dedicated to a certain deity or deities, who officiates at Wiccan and/or Pagan rituals.

Priestess: a woman dedicated to a certain deity or deities, who officiates at Wiccan and/or Pagan rituals.

psychometry: to read the vibrations from a physical object.

Qabala: the Jewish magical system. It can be spelled a number of ways, such as Cabala, Kabala, Kabbalah, and Qabalah.

reincarnation: the belief that everyone has lived many lives in the past and will live many more in the future.

rites of passage: rituals and celebrations done for birth, death, marriage, divorce, puberty, and entering elderhood.

ritual: any routinely repeated action. In spiritual areas, ritual means to enact a certain set of actions in order to achieve a transformation of consciousness.

runes: sacred symbols carved or painted on small stones by the Vikings and frequently used for divination of the future.

Sabbat: the eight holy days sacred to Wiccans. Witches call Imbolc, Beltane, Lughnasadh, and Samhain the Greater Sabbats, and the Solstices and Equinoxes the Lesser Sabbats.

Samhain: one of the Wiccan eight holy days; celebrated on October 31. We now know it as Halloween.

scourging: ritualized whipping, to purify the soul. This was an invention of Gerald Gardner, who seemed to enjoy this. This ritual action is more common among groups following the Gardnerian and Alexandrian traditions.

scrying: an old word that means to look into a mirror, crystal ball, or shiny piece of stone for visions of the future.

Sephira (pl. Sephiroth): the name for the ten spheres on the Qabalistic Tree of Life.

shaman: a person who uses certain techniques to communicate with and travel to the Otherworld.

sigil: a magical glyph or drawing used in magic.

silver: the metal favored by Witches; symbolically connected with the Moon.

skyclad: nude or naked during ritual. A practice most often found in groups that follow the Gardnerian and Alexandrian traditions.

Skyfather: the male god companion of the Earth Mother.

solitary: Witches who practice by themselves and do not belong to a group.

sorcery: usually associated with ceremonial magic. Several learned scholars and popes were connected with sorcery, black magic, necromancy, and pacts with the devil. These popes were: Leo I, Leo III, Sylvester II, Gregory VII, Honorius III, Boniface VIII, Benedict XIII, John XXIII, and Sixtus V.

soul mates: people who have shared many incarnations together. Sometimes the term twin souls is used.

spell: certain actions and words that make magic.

spiral: an inward-turning path that leads to a center and out again. A spiral dance is sometimes used as part of a ceremony, to symbolize death and rebirth through the Goddess.

Spring Equinox: one of the Wiccan eight holy days; celebrated about March 21.

Summerland: a Spiritualist term for life after death, or the place where souls of the dead go. This term arose during Victorian times.

Summer Solstice: one of the Wiccan eight holy days; celebrated about June 20.

talisman: often a natural object that is used to draw good luck or positive energies. Sometimes a talisman is constructed for a specific purpose and individual.

tarot cards: a special deck of seventy-eight cards used for divination.

telekinesis: the ability to physically move objects by the power of the mind.

temple: a specific building or room used for religious or magical working. This word is primarily connected with ceremonial magic.

Tree of Life: the central Qabalistic diagram on which are placed the ten Sephiroth. When it is called the World Tree, it represents the psychic axis between this world and the Otherworld, the bridge used by shamans and astral travelers to enter the Otherworld.

Threefold Law: an ethic more than a law, this is connected with karma. It is said that whatever you send out by deed or directed thought will return to you in triple strength. However ethically appropriate this "law" is, it was likely a creation of Gardner.

vampire: a physical person who psychically draws life energy from other people.

vision quest: a Native American shamanic practice that has been adopted by some Wiccan groups.

Warlock: the Scottish medieval term for a male sorcerer or Witch. Some writers believe that the word originally came from the Anglo-Saxon *waerloga*, which means "a traitor, deceiver, or liar." The word belongs more to ceremonial magic than Wicca, as it refers to a person who gains power through a pact with demons.

watchtowers: a term sometimes used to describe the four directions in a magical circle.

Wheel of the Year: a Celtic phrase to denote the Eight-Spoke Wheel of holy days and seasons that make up a year.

Wiccan Rede, The: the oft-quoted phrase "Do what you will if it harm none." This phrase doesn't appear until Gardner's time and may have been invented by him.

wiccaning: similar to a christening, but is a ritual for Wiccan children when they are formally presented to the Lord and the Lady.

widdershins: counterclockwise, or against the sun, movement. It is derived from the High German word *Widersinnes*. The Gaelic version is *Tuathal*.

Winter Solstice: one of the Wiccan eight holy days; celebrated about December 21.

Witch balls: the name applied to reflecting glass balls that are hung in windows to send back negative vibrations. The Victorians used such reflecting spheres in gardens.

Witch Queen: in the more traditional covens, this describes a High Priestess who has had at least two new covens hive off of hers.

Witch's hat: the traditional black hat has a tall, cone-shaped crown with a wide brim. This image of the Witch arose during the Burning Times, along with the black dress and cape, warts, and ugly features.

Witch's ladder: a string of forty beads or a cord with forty knots. This is used by a Witch to keep track of repetitive chants.

Witchcraft: also called Wicca and the Craft. The Old English word meant "wise-craft." A nature religion that honors the Great Goddess and Her consort.

Witching hour: traditionally, this is midnight.

Yule: the Anglo-Saxon word for the Winter Solstice.

CHAPTER 5

What Makes a Witch?

So you think you want to be a Witch. You are fascinated by black medieval-looking clothes, strange jewelry, multiple body piercings, and scads of tattoos. You've seen all the movies about the Craft and want to wave your fingers dramatically and get your desires fulfilled instantly. You think there are "secret" words that Witches know, words that will transform your life when you say them. You know someone you would like to make love you, or some "enemy" you would like to zap. You think Witchcraft might be a clever way to rebel and annoy your parents and family, to be outstandingly different. You think that dancing around nude would be cool. You believe that Witches have wild, uninhibited sex with the whole group, and that drugs and alcohol are rampant in covens. Or you already call yourself a Witch but haven't had any training whatsoever, and are only into Witchcraft for the attention it brings you.

Stop right here! If you fit this description, this book is not for you. In fact, no book on Wicca is. Further more, Wicca and Paganism do not need you. We have enough bad press as it is.

True Witches are those who are not satisfied with orthodox religions and feel there must be a better way. Witches are drawn to ancient pantheons of deities and honoring all nature. They feel the power in stones and are drawn to divination tools, such as tarot cards, pendulums, and rune stones. There is an inner response to the Full Moon and the changing of the seasons, a response that is deeper than usual. So far this description can fit either Paganism or Wicca.

True Witches, however, go a step further. They are particularly drawn to the Goddess in all Her aspects. When you think of honoring the Goddess, your heart leaps with joy. You understand that there must be female and male, Goddess and God, for universal balance, but the Goddess is the Great Mother of all, and the God is Her co-creator. You may have psychic abilities, such as telepathy, or you may have pre-cognitive dreams. You have thought long and hard about the principles of Wicca and have decided to dedicate yourself to this spiritual path. This is what makes a Witch.

True Witches make a total commitment to Wicca. They break all ties with orthodox religions, not out of hatred, but because those religions have nothing to offer them. True Witches feel no need to drag orthodox deity names into their rituals. Also, they feel no need to join in the centuries-long battle cry of "We have the most followers, so we are right and you are wrong!" In fact, Witches have no need to tell anyone what they believe or do. If you met true Witches in any social situation, you probably would not know they were Witches. They look and act very much like everyone else.

Witches do not believe in or worship the Christian devil or Satan. They do, however, believe there are evil spirits, some of them quite powerful and able on occasion to negatively influence human lives. You have to belong to an orthodox religion or believe in Christian teachings to be a Satanist, as satanic ceremonies are a negative parody of Christian ceremonies, and the devil a parody of their god.

Whatever you do, don't fall into the pattern of thinking you have to justify your existence in Wicca by inventing a fictitious family history of Witchcraft. Most of the tales you read about people learning everything about Wicca from their old grandmothers is wishful thinking.

Magic is a sideline of Wicca, not the heart of this path. Some Witches never go into the magical work, preferring instead to focus their attention on the spiritual side. This is a personal choice for each Witch.

Healing is an important part of Wicca and there are many ways to heal. You may choose to use herbs, reflexology, massage, or laying on of hands. You may prefer to widen your knowledge and skill of this subject by using stones, aromatherapy, poppets, or magic spells. All require study and practice. Witches feel that they are following the path of the Goddess by helping other people, animals, and even the earth itself to heal.

Some Witches feel that divination is a healing method, a tool that helps others to heal their emotions, minds, and souls. Witches have long been connected with divinatory powers. To them, glimpsing the future in order to make the right decisions or be prepared is a method of keeping in balance. A balanced person is happier and healthier.

Witches can be happy and satisfied in their choice of spiritual path whether they work alone or with a small group. It is the striving toward the Goddess that brings joy. A solitary Witch may, on occasion, join with other Witches for larger Sabbat gatherings or other celebrations.

There may be problems with others when you choose the Wiccan path, if you have a spouse, lover, or family that does not understand the true nature of Wicca and is not open to learning. Problems may become serious if you are dealing with strong believers in the Christian devil, or if you have a dominating, controlling spouse or lover, who recognizes that Wicca encourages every person to be independent and responsible, and sees that as threatening.

If you are a woman, your troubles may be even harder for you to handle. The freedom of a Witch is in opposition to the orthodox idea that a woman should be subservient and obedient to men. Wicca encourages women to be independent and strong, and to believe they are of as much value as men. Any woman can be a priestess and communicate directly with her Goddess and other deities, and Wiccan priestesses are honored.

Family problems can test a Witch's commitment to Wicca because no true Witch will put up with any manipulative or irrational challenge to their beliefs.

Being a Witch often is not an easy path to embrace. You will have to change some of your ingrained thinking, which can be a huge step for some people. Only you are responsible for what you do; you can blame no one else. And the laws of karma will be fulfilled, whether you like it or not. Your goal should be to bring yourself into a state of balance so that you do not accrue any more karma than necessary from daily living. You learn that everything in the universe, without exception, is connected. You become sensitized to your environment, especially to the vibrations coming from other people. You learn to dance around the ordinary, everyday negative vibrations that pollute your surroundings, and ward off those deliberately sent your way. And when necessary, you learn to fight back in powerful, subtle ways.

If you can meet these requirements, you are Witch material, but not yet fully and truly a Witch. Calling yourself a Witch does not make you one. Set aside a daily time for study and practice, for both study and practice are necessary. Traditional Witchcraft has always advocated that an apprentice study for a year and a day before being considered for initiation. The path of Wicca is well worth the effort.

Study Work

On a sheet of paper, write out exactly why you want to be a Witch. Under this, write what you will have to change in your life to reach this goal. Keep this, and refer back to it later in your studies. At a later date, write under this any changes in thought you may have.

CHAPTER 6

The Wiccan Rede

"Eight words the Wiccan Rede fulfill. And you harm none, do what you will." This is what is known as the Wiccan Rede. The word rede means "to give counsel or advice." Some Wiccan groups believe the Rede has been passed from generation to generation for hundreds of years. However, the Rede does not appear in any of the old literature or teachings before the 1940s or 1950s, and is very likely an invention of Gerald Gardner. This is a fine-sounding ethic, one of great spiritual value, and one that Witches live by most of the time. Witches firmly believe in "live and let live" and the sacredness of all life. Interpretation of the Rede includes not harming oneself or animals, as well as other people.

The well-known Witch Sybil Leek advised that a codicil should be added to the Rede: "Evil allowed to exist harms everyone," with which I agree. It is a Witch's duty to fight against evil, not to pretend it doesn't exist or will go away if you ignore it. This concept can confuse some apprentices who believe that to confront evil is "black" magic.

Apprentices in the Craft frequently proclaim that they will do only "white" magic. Many will change their minds later—not change their minds and do "black" magic, but move into the narrow realm between these two extremes, the realm of "gray" magic. A gray Witch is the most powerful of all Witches. Nothing in life is cut and dried, but always a mixture of things. To meet daily needs, the Witch must do what needs to be done in the least offensive manner, but certainly never turn away from evil as if it does not exist. Never compromise with evil.

To only believe in either white and black magic limits the exploration of truth and knowledge, because by their very natures white and black magic are extremes. There is little, if any, room in any extreme to see truth as the multiplicity it is. Gray magic gives the Witch the opportunity to look at all sides of any given situation and take necessary action with the least harm to all involved, particularly the Witch doing the spellwork, who works for the good of all, whether for Witches or not.

White magic is similar to a simple form of poetry and prayer to the Goddess and the God. Many Wiccans who fear to go beyond white magic also refuse to believe they should do anything to stop evil people, energies, or entities. The Goddess demands responsibility and action. Therefore, a Witch who only does white magic is living with blinders on.

Black magic deals entirely with evil negative energies or demons, and unethical actions to gain results, usually personal power over others. Black magic is predicated primarily on greed: greed for control, power, for possessions, or for any kind of self-aggrandizement. Black magicians rarely allow the ethical voice of conscience to interfere with their desires.

The word "demons" is not used in the Christian sense or interpretation. Demons are best described as negative non-physical spirits or energies, not related in any manner to the Christian devil. These negative entities can be controlled and coerced into helping the black magician, but there is a price to pay if the magician lets down their guard. And no magician, black or otherwise, can keep up their protective guard at all times. It is best to avoid demons, unless they are occupying your living space. In this instance, you must use whatever means necessary to evict them. The study of demons—demonology—has been around for a very long time. The Babylonians, Egyptians, and many other cultures wrote detailed accounts of these spirits.

Gray magic does everything white magic does. It works for healing, beneficial outcomes to problems and goals, expansion of consciousness, and greater spiritual growth, plus it adds the elimination of evils to the list. Stopping human criminals, abusers, rapists, and murderers has as high a priority as removing disease from the physical body. Gray magicians do not cast curses on people for infractions of courtesy. However, they are not doormats and will protect themselves and their families from danger, persecution, and evil in whatever manner is necessary.

All magicians learn that sooner or later they will confront evil entities in noncorporeal bodies. These beings, which you can't see, but which can affect your life, sanity, and safety, can be extremely frightening. White Witches may wring their hands, but gray Witches get to work and drive these beings back into the lower dimensions of the astral planes where they belong. The gray Witch believes that the non-corporeal and the dead should not be annoying or threatening the living.

Gray magic also demands more of the Witch. Every planned spell must be thought through carefully, choosing the method least likely to accrue a huge karmic load. It does not matter whether the spell is for healing or getting rid of the neighborhood drunk. Witches must ask themselves a series of questions and be very careful that the answers are not what they *want* to hear, but what *is* the truth.

Do sick people really want you to heal them? Some people subconsciously don't want a healing although they may say they do. Perhaps you need to do spellwork for relief of their family instead. If the diseased person is using the illness as a means of control over others, you may want to cast a spell to remove the control over others.

On rare occasions, Witches may find themselves the target of a magical curse, although curses do not occur as frequently as some believe. Most of life's sudden and unmerited problems come from one's own negative thoughts or the ill-wishing thoughts of jealous people. Ill-wishing is an old term that means someone is sending a flood of negative thoughts in your direction, probably without knowing precisely what they are doing, but rejoicing inside at the troubles you suddenly have. Ill-wishing can be remedied by putting up psychic protection around yourself, your family and pets, and the property.

Actual curses are another matter. These spells are performed deliberately and with forethought. Some curses are very specific, naming the person cursed, while others are more general. I ran across this problem when we purchased a Victorian home and restored it. In one corner of the living room was a huge, ugly hearth that was not original to the house since there was no fireplace. It weighed so much it was putting a strain on the floor and had to be removed. When we dismantled the hearth, we found a small plastic bag containing a detailed curse on whoever removed the hearth. It was one nasty curse, believe me. I didn't personally know the two men who built the hearth, but I was aware of their drug lifestyle. I took the curse to my altar and returned the energy to the senders without specifying any penalty. When the curse rebounded, the men had their hands full.

The point is, you don't have to be terrified of a curse. There is always something you can do about it. Just don't become so paranoid that you see a curse in everything. Or so dithering that you do nothing for fear that fighting back will build negative karma. You have to take action when threatened. Evil allowed to exist harms everyone.

The Wiccan Rede is a good ethic to follow, provided it includes Sybil Leek's codicil against evil. Wiccan apprentices should follow the Rede closely until they learn the questions to ask about true evil. In this manner, an apprentice will avoid much trouble.

Study Work

Draw a line down the middle of a sheet of paper. On one side, list the names of people toward whom you have negative thoughts and what the negatives are. On the other side, list all the positive things you have done with your life. Study each name on the negative side, and decide if they really are harming you or if the problem can be solved in a constructive way. Take the name that has the worst negatives attached to it, write it on a small piece of paper, and burn that paper in an ashtray or cauldron. Flush the ashes down the toilet, symbolically ridding yourself of the problem. After a week, choose another name and repeat the action. Only burn one name a week. By releasing the names through burning, you are breaking the tie between you and the person with whom you have problems.

CHAPTER 7

Dedication and Initiation

The words dedication and initiation have different meanings. When you dedicate an object, you set it aside for a sacred or special use. When you dedicate yourself, you promise yourself to a specific deity or religious path. An initiate is one who studies in a particular field, such as Wicca and/or magic, in order to be initiated, or formally admitted to the group teaching the field of knowledge.

Some Wiccan groups perform dedication ceremonies for everyone who begins study with them, while others do not. Apprentices usually don't participate in group rituals after a dedication. Apprentices are not admitted to circle work until after they have completed their studies to the satisfaction of the teacher and are initiated before the entire group. All groups have formal initiations for the admittance of accepted apprentices to their inner group work. Initiation is a very serious step in Wiccan development. It is a very moving, internal process. On rare occasions, someone may experience an initiation in a dream or vision.

A dedication, whether done by the self or by a group, is only a promise by the apprentice to study the Wiccan path and follow the Ancient Ones. Usually a year and a day is spent studying all phases of Wiccan beliefs, ethics, and ritual practices before undergoing any initiation. If the student desires to become more deeply involved during this time, they should focus on positive candle spells as a way of gaining magical experience and confidence. Also, learning a divination skill can be beneficial. All these studies, combined with the basics of Witchcraft, will prepare the student for solitary or group ritual work.

Some Wiccan groups and solitary Witches believe that it takes a Witch to make, or initiate, another Witch. This is not necessary. It assumes that certain Witches and Wiccan groups have greater power than what resides within each individual. Also, most people who want to become Witches have no access to group help and must study on their own. This situation does not invalidate their commitment, nor should it hinder them from self-initiation. On the other hand, some apprentices who study under a Witch and are initiated formally into a group should never have been initiated in the first place.

Anyone who wants to study with a Wiccan group should be very cautious and ask penetrating questions before becoming involved with the group to determine the moral and ethical qualities of the group.

If you are very certain that Wicca is the spiritual path for you, it is time to perform a dedication. This short rite is an important step, as it formally announces to the Goddess and the God that you promise to learn all you can about their ancient worship in preparation for the more serious rite of initiation or self-initiation. It is also a very serious step to take, so think long and hard before you commit yourself. The dedication is a vow and a vow is something that you do not make or break lightly.

You don't need to choose a Craft name at this point in your journey. That privilege only comes with the formal initiation later. Right now, you are promising the gods and yourself that you will study hard so that you become more knowledgeable about Wicca and can stand before the Goddess and the God with confidence and dignity.

You also do not need ritual tools now. The items you will use for this rite can all be found among the ordinary implements of any household. You will gather, or make, and consecrate your ritual tools later in your studies.

If you are ready to dedicate yourself to Wicca, you will need the following items: a small bowl of water; a pinch of salt in a small saucer; a white candle; an incense burner and a cone or stick of frankincense or lotus incense; a flat space to use as an altar.

Plan the ceremony to take place at night, on a Full Moon if possible, and make certain you will not be disturbed. Turn off or disconnect the telephone. Hang a "do not disturb" sign on the door. If the neighborhood is noisy enough to interfere with your concentration, play a non-vocal tape of soft music to help muffle background noises.

Clean your temporary altar thoroughly before you place your needed items on it. Place the altar so that you face the east when standing before it. Put the white candle in a holder in the center of the altar with the incense to one side. The water and salt should be placed within easy reach on the altar, but not directly in front of you. This will keep you from accidentally spilling the salt or water. During the time you are setting up the altar, think about what you are doing and why you are doing it.

Place your copy of the dedication ceremony, either written or typed, before the candle. You can use the one in this book, if you wish, however, it is more difficult to handle a book than a sheet of paper.

When you are ready to begin, light the candle and incense. Remove all your clothing. This symbolizes your intent to come before the ancient deities as your true self, shorn of material trappings and open for examination of your heart and conscience. Turn off the lights, leaving only the candle for illumination.

Kneel before the altar while you relax and prepare yourself for the dedication. Take several deep breaths to help with the relaxation. When you feel ready, stand facing the altar and the east. Raise your arms, and say:

> *This is a time that is not a time, in a place that is not a place, on a day that is not a day. I stand at the threshold between the worlds, before the Veil of the Mysteries. I ask that the Lord and the Lady be with me as I take my first steps on the ancient path.*

Hold your hands above the bowl of water, saying:

> *Bless this symbol of the great womb of the Goddess. May it be my source of inspiration and continuous blessings.*

Hold your hands above the salt, saying:

> *Bless this symbol of earth that it may be my strength and protection.*

Tip the salt into the water and then gently swirl the bowl. Hold up the bowl over the altar, saying:

> *As this salt and water mingle and bless each other, may my inner and outer bodies be mingled and blessed.*

Sprinkle the salt and water mixture lightly in a circle around your altar, beginning and ending in the east, and moving in a clockwise direction. Put the bowl back on the table. Kneel before the altar, and say:

> *As I have dedicated this sacred circle to the Goddess and the God, so do I dedicate my life to the spiritual path of Wicca. I come here tonight to make my pledge to the Ancient Ones. I promise to dedicate myself to the study of the Wiccan Way for a year and a day, that in time I may be worthy of stepping within the greater sacred circle of worship. I promise to*

hold the Goddess in reverence as the Great Mother who created every-
thing in the universe. I promise to hold the God in reverence as Her co-
creator and consort. Hear my words, for they are true and from my heart.

Sit quietly for a time as you contemplate the step you have taken into your new spiritual life. When ready, stand up and raise your arms, saying:

May I be blessed with peace, protection, and prosperity in my life, both
physically and spiritually. May I gain understanding of all that I study.
And may I be found worthy to call myself a Witch.

Symbolically cut the circle by waving your hand over it, saying:

The circle is open, but unbroken.

Turn on the lights, extinguish the candle, and clear away all that you used on the altar.
You are now a dedicated apprentice on the Wiccan path. (The rite of initiation, to be
done later, is explained and given in Chapter 35.)

Study Work

Write your thoughts on why you want to dedicate your life to the Goddess and the
Wiccan Way. Also, make a list of personal habits you need to change in order to
become a more positive person. Keep this list, and refer to it at a later time. Revise
the list as necessary.

Do not do a self-initiation at this time. Wiccan study traditionally lasted for a year
and a day—the old Celtic calendar—before the apprentice was initiated. This allowed
time for the student to learn all of the basics and make a correct decision about their
future in the Craft. If, however, you have a burning desire to be Wiccan, and you
know deep inside that your desire isn't a fad, you can dedicate yourself to Wicca, or
to a particular Goddess aspect at this time.

After the dedication, take time to write how you felt before, during, and after the
ceremony.

CHAPTER 8

The Threefold Law

The threefold law, simply explained, expresses the concept that whatever you send out in thought, word, deed, or magic comes back to you with three times the strength or three times the quantity. This law applies equally to your positive and negative behavior, whether deliberate or not.

After years of experience, I've added my own codicil to this law: There is a threefold return if the action is not justified. I do not mean that you are okay if you feel justified in doing what you do, but that your desire for a particular conclusion is justified by spiritual laws. Many Wiccans will disagree with me on this, believing that justification does not enter into it. However, over the years, I have thought much about the threefold law and I believe that the Goddess and the God have not established rigid laws that have no mercy or understanding in them.

For those interested in historical evidence of the existence of this law, there is none. It is not mentioned until Gerald Gardner released his books on Witchcraft, and is likely his invention.

On the positive side, this means that you are rewarded for the good things you do in life. Also, you can collect that reward in this lifetime, instead of having to die to claim it. Most of this positive reward will come through deeds of kindness that you did without an ulterior motive behind them, indeed, without realizing you did something good. It isn't the large deeds that bring the most rewards, but the small ones we rarely consider, such as a kind word and a smile to a tired checker at the supermarket or picking up the mail and groceries for an elderly person.

The most hazardous reaction to this law generally comes from deliberate negative deeds or magical spells. Some people want to enter Wicca only to learn magic. Perhaps, they want to make someone they know love them or give them money, or there is someone they hate and want to hurt. If these selfish motives are a the primary reason for wanting to study Wicca or magic, people should not be taught. Once they learn a little magic, these people create a constant chaos around themselves from rebounding spells, for which they blame Wicca and magic instead of their own selfishness and unethical behavior.

The threefold law also works with conditions other than magic spells. Concentrated thoughts can, and often do, become things in their own right. For any magic spell to work, before the result can appear in the physical, the Witch's visualization and concentration must build a manifestation in the astral realms first. Positive magic includes spells for healing, protection, guidance, and prosperity, for others as well as yourself.

This same principle of creating a mental result or "being" applies to thoughts. However, you don't have to be a Witch to create such a "being." Strong and repeated thoughts can take on a reality of their own, without a person knowing the first thing about magic. On the positive side, people create balls of energy for healing, protection, and guidance all the time. You may pray for protection when a loved one leaves on a trip, or send loving and healing thoughts to a friend in the hospital. These intense thoughts form into a ball of energy that hovers near that person until the need is gone.

If these strong, repeated thoughts are negative in nature, you will create a ball or "being" of negative energy that has the power to harm. Through such a mental creation, you could well reap the threefold return of your concentration. It all depends upon the intent of the creator-thinker and their ability to concentrate. When such negative creations do not find their target, or are repelled by someone knowing magical self-defense, they fly right back to their creator. Fortunately, casual negative thinking is not concentrated enough to build a long-lasting form.

Since it is difficult for any Witch to know exactly what will happen in every instance, most Witches are very careful about cursing anyone. The apprentice should stay clear of building karma through this law by adhering to it as much as possible.

Study Work

For the next two weeks, closely observe everything that goes on in your life. Keep a record of everything that happens, both positive and negative. Can you find any correlation to the past where you did something or thought strongly about something? This is not an exercise to place blame, but to make you aware of the interaction of all words, deeds, and strong thoughts.

CHAPTER 9

The Triple Goddess and the God

People have practiced Goddess worship since they first started seeking their spiritual path. Goddess worship dates back 20,000 to 30,000 years to Paleolithic times according to wall paintings and sculptures. The God, or male companion of the Goddess, was also portrayed, but in a lesser role, as shown by the smaller size and incomplete figures. The very earliest creation myths bear this out. They speak of a Goddess creating the universe and everything that inhabits the universe.

After the Goddess was relegated to a minor role in religions, many of Her traits were transferred to male deities, particularly Her Triple aspects. For example, this trinity can be found in the Hindu triad of Brahma, Vishnu, and Shiva, and in the Holy Trinity of Christianity.

The Goddess has been worshipped as a Triple Deity—Maiden, Mother, and Crone (Dark Mother, Wise Woman, the Hag)—from the beginning of religion. The number three, and multiples of three, are sacred in many ancient cultures. The priests of Babylon taught that three was a lucky number as well. In the writings of Pythagoras, we find that the philosopher called three a "triple Word," meaning that using the number three in particular circumstances, such as repeating spells and rituals three times, can create whatever is held in the mind of the user. Later in history, the alchemist Paracelsus associated the number three with gold; to alchemists, gold was not so much a physical metal as a symbol for spiritual enlightenment. The ancient Chinese philosopher Lao-Tsu said that three is the perfect number, for it engenders all things. In numerology, the number three represents creativity, activity, and knowledge.

Ancient Mystery Schools always had three main steps or degrees through which the student must pass. Today, we still find this idea of three degrees of knowledge used to designate a Witch's progress in a coven.

We can understand this trinity better if we compare it to the three stages of human life: youth and puberty, adulthood, and old age. Since the Goddess's power is all encompassing, She will present aspects that speak to all humans, regardless of their age. These esoteric ideas cover and comfort from birth to death and beyond.

The first Goddess aspect is the Maiden. This phase holds the matrix of creation, which will produce and create when the time is ripe. She is matter and energy held in suspension until the right time arrives. The Maiden, sometimes called the Virgin or the Huntress, represents the Spring of the year, the dawn, fresh beginnings of all life, the repeating cycle of birth and rebirth, the waxing moon and the crescent moon, enchantment, and seduction. Her traditional color is white. She is the Way-Shower, the Guide through the inner labyrinth to the Divine Center where the greatest of spiritual Mysteries lie.

The second Goddess aspect is the Mother. This is the matrix in motion, the archetype involved in active creation. In humans, the physical desire, the mental will and concentration, and the spiritual balance and understanding are all necessary to produce a desired result. It is easy for humans to identify with the Mother aspect, for they see the Mother around them in all human and animal mothers. The Mother aspect of the Goddess represents the Summer, blazing noon, reproduction and fertility, the ripeness of life, the Full Moon, and the high point in all cycles. Her traditional color is red, the color of blood and life itself. She is the Great Teacher of the Mysteries.

The last aspect is the Crone, also called the Dark Mother, the Old Wise One, or the Hag. Since this aspect symbolizes death and dissolution, it is frightening to many people. Everything in the universe has a life cycle, at the end of which they malfunction, decay, and transform into a different set of materials, elements that are recycled and reformed into something new. In humans, the soul is recycled by the Crone and her cauldron into a new incarnation. The Crone represents Winter, the night, the universal abyss where life rests before rebirth, the gateway to death and reincarnation, the waning moon and the New Moon, and the deepest of Mysteries and prophecies. Her traditional color is black, and sometimes the deepest of purples or dark blue. She is the Initiator into the Mysteries.

Understanding the archetypal image of the Goddess can take a lifetime of contemplation and study. However, the fact that She is a single archetype plus a trinity of aspects makes Her very complex. It is impossible to reduce the Goddess's spiritual form and meaning to words on paper. She is the beginning, the ending, and everything in between.

The Horned God has been recognized and worshipped as far back as the Stone Age, where we find paintings of horned, ithyphallic men. The Horned God is not the Christian devil. We find the image of the Pagan God in the Egyptian god Amun-Ra, with his ram's horns and in the Greek Great God Pan, with his goat horns and hooves. Among the Celts, the Horned God was called Cernunnos. This deity was sometimes linked with the Otherworld, particularly the Underworld section, and reincarnation. As Justine Glass, in *Witchcraft: The Sixth Sense*, points out, the Horned God is definitely related to Pan and other nature deities, and not to the Christian devil, who was taken from the Persian god Ahriman.

In the original myths concerning the God, one finds Him as the co-creator, vital companion, and mystical priest of the Goddess. His prime purpose is to join with Her to create order out of chaos, substance out of spiritual matter, life from universal energies swirling in the dark abyss. His next purpose is to carry out Her will and see that Her laws are obeyed.

The God is also frequently seen in trinity form, although, like the Goddess, He is more complex than this simple definition. The three major aspects are the Divine Child, the Son/Lover, and the Sacrificed Savior/Lord of Death. Even though these three aspects are the most important, the God has many others: Sky-Father and Ruler of the Heavens, Lord of the Forest and Animals, the Supreme Healer, the Trickster, God of Judgment, the Great Magus or Magician, God of the Waters, and the Hero-Warrior.

As the Divine Child, the God represents beginnings and the start of new cycles. This includes new hope and new opportunities, physical as well as mental, emotional, and spiritual. His traditional color is the dark green of plant life. The Divine Child is the signpost of the inner spiritual journey we each must take, the sign that says "begin here." We begin as a child, taking the first tentative steps along an unknown and unfamiliar path that leads to a mystical destination that is difficult to understand until we reach the end.

The Son/Lover aspect symbolizes maturity and responsibility, the desire to take into account the needs of others more than oneself. The God in this aspect balances sexual desire and need with companionship and tenderness. His traditional color is red, the color of the life force and the birth fluids. Combined with the powers of the Goddess, He shows us that there must be a blending of different energies to create.

This creation includes ideas, inventions, and the arts. He is the Companion on our spiritual journey, the one who points out the path if we start to go astray.

The Great Rite of Wicca is connected with the Mother aspect of the Goddess and the Son/Lover aspect of the God. This Rite can be misunderstood by those outside the Wiccan religion. The Great Rite has its roots in the ancient Sacred Marriage between priestess and King, which dates back to the Neolithic era. Originally, a king or tribal ruler could not hold the office unless he wed the Goddess. He had to be a Chosen One, either appointed by the High Priestess of the tribe's religion, or have passed certain stringent tests. This esoteric, spiritual marriage was symbolized by actual nuptials between the would-be king and the High Priestess of the Goddess of the land, which included sexual rites.

Today, Wiccan groups usually practice this Rite in symbolic form, rather than in actuality. The symbolic act is the dipping of the athame into a cup of wine or juice during a ritual (the cup symbolizes the womb of the Goddess and the athame the phallus of the God). Some Witches believe that the priestess should dip the athame into a cup of wine or juice held by the priest. In my personal rites, however, I reverse this, with the priestess holding the cup and the priest using the athame. If the Great Rite is physically performed, it is in private and with full consent of both the High Priestess and High Priest. Most Wiccan covens do not use sexual rituals. They feel that doing this can create an explosive atmosphere that can destroy all they work for.

The Sacrificed Savior/Lord of Death aspect of the God can be as difficult to understand as the dark aspect of the Crone. Mystery Religions frequently were connected with the Sacrificed Savior, who gave his life that spiritual knowledge and enlightenment could come into the world. This aspect of the God always resurrected and lived again, reminding us that everything is recycled and that human life reincarnates. The Greeks used the word *soter* for Savior; *soter* means "one who sows the seed." In mythology, the Sacrificed Savior was reborn of the Earth Mother aspect of the Goddess.

The Lord of Death was originally the Lord of Comfort for the souls who rest in the abyss before rebirth. At the will of the Goddess, He gathers souls at the proper time and guides them to the afterlife, while comforting those who fear or are in pain. Under His Celtic guise of Lord of the Wild Hunt, the God sees that karmic debts are paid and that destiny is fulfilled. In this, He is the equivalent of the Greek goddesses, the Erinyes. However, unlike the Erinyes, who relentlessly and mercilessly hunted down those guilty of the breaking of blood laws, the Lord of the Hunt makes certain that the souls He seeks are ready for the transition, that they are in the right place at the right time to meet their destiny.

Although His appearance and actions are fearsome, this aspect of the God is actually one of great compassion. His traditional color is the black of the abyss in the Underworld, the temporary black of death that absorbs and erases pain and suffering. He is the Gate-Keeper, who tests our worth before we are allowed to enter the deepest Mysteries.

Wicca acknowledges and honors the Goddess and the God, either by these titles or by specific names from pantheons. For example, the White Moon Goddess and her consort the Horned God are the oldest known deities in the Western world and are revered by Witches who use Celtic themes. Among modern Witches, the two deities are commonly known as the Lady and the Lord, with the Goddess having primary importance. This is a basic Wiccan idea, regardless of the deity names used or aspects called upon.

Study Work

Write out your personal understanding of the three aspects of the Goddess and the God. Relate each aspect to areas of your own life. Are you reluctant to acknowledge, or uncomfortable with, certain aspects? Write out why this is so. Keep working with this area of mental and inner restriction until you can accept this aspect.

CHAPTER 10

Pantheons of Goddesses and Gods

Basic Witchcraft is not monotheistic in nature, but polytheistic, in that Witches, like all Pagans, believe in the existence of more than one deity or energy pool. Even Dianic Witches who worship only the Goddess worship Her in the Triple Goddess, or Her three forms. Simplistically speaking, Witches believe in both a Goddess and a God, as well as other archetypal energies that are aspects or representations of the two main ones.

Webster's Dictionary defines archetype as "the original pattern from which all things of the same type are copies." In other words, regardless of the cultural pantheon, all goddesses are traceable to the original Goddess and all gods to the original God. Archetypes are psychic forces that influence our lives, particularly our spiritual lives. They form an unbreakable and invisible connection between all humans regardless of racial background, and link all humans with the Divine Source, however we view it.

Although Witches may have statues of various goddesses and gods in their sacred space, they do not worship idols. The statues are an inspirational concentration point, used as a psychic window into the Otherworld. They fully recognize that the statues have no power within them, that the actual archetypal power is not contained in any object. Jung recognized that all deity images, including statues of deities, whether thought to be actual or astral, merely represent the basic archetypes of universal power. With the Goddess and the God, this could be reduced to the titles of Universal Mother and Universal Father.

Having a diversity of deity forms actually allows for both unity and diversity in a spiritual sense. Witches fully understand that there is a human need for a great variety of spiritual paths, which is why there is no one way to practice Witchcraft or Paganism. They also recognize that deities can be worshipped without mentioning a particular name, although many Witches do use known names, as it is easier to relate to a deity this way.

Wiccan/Pagan spirituality is very different from orthodox religions in one sharply defined aspect. As Robert Graves wrote in *The White Goddess*, true Pagan spirituality forces one to think on two levels, the mythical and the rational, and to never confuse the two. This means that Witches realize that mythology contains vital clues to spiritual growth and understanding, and that the mythical, whether deity or creatures, has existence in the astral planes. At the same time, however, Witches live in the real physical world. They must move and act toward the physical in physical ways, and toward the mythical in psychic ways, and not let the two realms overlap so they do not function properly.

When we work our thoughts beyond the deity name in any pantheon, we come to the basic archetypal energies of the Goddess and the God. These energies are primal, full of universal void energy for creating. These energies generally are recognizable to all peoples and cultures, but not really understandable by anyone. They represent the positive/negative, male/female balance found within everything. There must be both types of energy for universal and spiritual balance, as well as the creation of something new. What we call extremes, or opposites, actually are not in opposition, which would make them destructive. They are necessary ingredients for compromise, centering, and neutrality, all necessary for the continuation of the universe and the constant creation of matter. Nothing in the universe is inactive or lacking of motion. Everything moves and changes constantly.

People who find their way to Wicca are retracing their ancestral roots back to the original deity, which is the Goddess. Western religions have effectively removed the Goddess from their worship, except for the watered-down version found in the Virgin Mary. To many Wiccans, it is a delightful discovery to find that you have a Great Mother. As you progress along the Wiccan path, you will discover the true identity and power of the Goddess in particular. When you reach this point in your growth, you get a true inkling of what spiritual reality actually is.

For those new to Wicca and who feel a desire to relate to the Goddess and the God by a name, pantheons of deities are listed below by cultures. These include Egypt, the Middle East, Greece and Rome, the Celtic realms, the Norse/Viking, and India. These pantheons are most frequently used by Pagans. If you desire to use other pantheons, research the deities in several books on the subject. Your racial background may have nothing to do with your desire to use a particular pantheon. Instead, a past life may influence your choice. Solitary Witches may choose whatever pantheon they desire, while covens have a particular pantheon they use exclusively in group work.

However, do not mix pantheon names during ritual as you may get a confusing blend of energies other than what you wanted. For example, if you call the Goddess by the name Isis, you should not call the God by the names Zeus or Odin. It is permissible, however, to call upon the Goddess and the God by several names at one time in a ritual, when you are recalling the vast number of aspects that have been known through time. An example would be: "Great Goddess, who is known as Isis, Demeter, Hera, Freyja, Mórrígan, and Kali" and "Great God, who is known as Pan, Jupiter, Osiris, Cernunnos, and Odin."

When Witches become more advanced and comfortable with magical workings, they can use one deity name in one ritual and another name in a different ritual, as necessary. Some deity aspects are more attuned to a particular energy than others for certain types of spells.

Each deity aspect in the following pantheons may be slightly different in universal meaning to those similar in other pantheons, so read carefully before you call upon a specific aspect for help, particularly in spells. If you already are attracted to a particular cultural pantheon, search out the appropriate deities in the following lists. However, you will benefit by reading through all the deities and broadening your knowledge.

Not all deities of each pantheon are listed here. I have not tried to adhere to the precise cultural names of some deities, or to the precise spelling of some names, but include instead the names with which the reader would be most familiar.

EGYPT

Amun/Amon/Amen: Although he is similar to Jupiter and called the "Great Father," Amun is not the Great God of Egypt. Sometimes, his name is connected with the sun god Ra, thus Amun-Ra. He forms a trinity with the goddess Mut and the god Khensu. Each ruling pharaoh was considered to be this god incarnated. A phallic and fertility deity, Amun rules over agriculture, reproduction, and prophecy.

Amenti/Ament: Known as the goddess of the West or the Underworld, Amenti is the consort of the god Amun. Tradition says that souls of the dead are welcomed by this goddess.

Anubis: A messenger from the gods to humans, the cult of this god is very ancient, and perhaps even older than that of Osiris. Portrayed with the dark-colored head of a jackal, Anubis rules over funerals and embalming. Along with the goddess Maat, he weighs the souls of the dead for truth. Anubis is a powerful guardian against lower astral entities.

Apep/Apophis: Envisioned as a huge snake of the Underworld, this deity is believed to be responsible for solar eclipses.

Bast/Bastet: A cat-headed goddess and wife of Ptah, this deity is connected with cats, healing, fertility, and pleasures.

Bes: This god is pictured as a dwarf with a large head, protruding tongue, and prominent eyes, quite unlike other Egyptian deities. He is called upon for childbirth, protection from night demons, and to protect the dead as they make their journey to the Underworld.

Buto/Uatchet: This goddess of protection is portrayed as a winged cobra.

Hathor/Hat-Hor: Sometimes pictured as a cow-headed woman, Hathor is the mother of all Egyptian deities. The seven Hathors were connected with the seven planets known to humans at that time. The sistrum and tambourine were used in her worship ceremonies. A protectress of women, Hathor also rules over motherhood, marriage, love, and good times.

Horus: Most often painted as a falcon-headed sun god, Horus is the son of Osiris and Isis, born after his father's death. His two eyes are the sun and the moon. He has power over prophecy, justice, success, and revenge.

Imhotep: This deity began as a deified human hero who was later transformed into a god. A son of Ptah, he is similar to the Greek Aesculapius and rules over healing, medicine, knowledge, and physicians.

Isis/Aset: The Great Goddess of the Egyptian pantheon, she is the sister-wife of the god Osiris. A patroness of priestesses, Isis helps with marriage, motherhood, domestic arts, fertility, magic, divination, protection, and success.

Khensu/Khons: Known as the Navigator, this deity is god of the moon, particularly the crescent moon. He can be called upon for exorcisms and healing.

Khepera: Shown as a scarab beetle, this god is a creator deity. His realm of expertise is in exorcism, healing, reincarnation, new beginnings, and miracles.

Khnemu/Khnum: Called the Molder and the Divine Potter, this god with a ram's head and wavy horns was said to create human bodies on a potter's wheel. He is a god of building and architecture, arts and crafts.

Maat: A daughter of Ra and the wife of Thoth, this goddess rules with laws that govern the three worlds, even the gods themselves. She weighs souls of the dead against a feather in the Hall of Double Justice, seeking for truth in a soul. She has power over justice, law, divine order, and reincarnation.

Mut: Called the Eye of Ra, the Mother, and the Great Sorceress, Mut is the wife of Amun-Ra and wears a vulture headdress. One of her symbols is three cauldrons. She primarily has power over marriage and creation. According to Egyptologists, her name is pronounced Moot.

Neith/Nit: Her name is pronounced Night. Called the Huntress and Opener of the Ways, Neith is said to be self-begotten. Part of her sanctuary was called the House of Life, where healing and mystical knowledge were available. A protectress of women, Neith rules over such diverse aspects as domestic arts, hunting, medicine, and war.

Nephthys: Sister of Isis, wife of the god Set, and mother of Anubis, Nephthys rules over hidden and mystical knowledge, death, protection, and dreams.

Nut: This Egyptian sky goddess is known as Mother of the Gods. Her name is pronounced Noot. An aspect of the Great Mother, Nut rules over reincarnation and creation.

Osiris: This deity has over two hundred different names in the Book of the Dead. He is the brother-husband of Isis and father of Horus; he also fathered Anubis with Nephthys. The ultimate Egyptian Great God and a patron of priests, Osiris rules over reincarnation, fertility and harvests, initiation, justice, agriculture, and religious ceremonies and laws.

Ptah: Another creator god, this deity is a symbol of the creative power behind the gods. One of his names is the Master Builder. He also is associated with the symbols of the Four Elements or Primary Forces. Pictured in mummy wrappings, he is the protector and patron of arts and artisans, as well as ruling over creative arts, architects, all manual skills, and regeneration.

Ra/Re: This deity is one of the Egyptian sun gods and called Father of the Gods. He was worshipped at Heliopolis in the form of an obelisk. He is the destroyer of all evil and a deity of magic, prosperity, spells, and destiny.

Sebek: A crocodile god, this deity was honored in the forms of his sacred crocodiles at Crocodilopolis, or Arsinoe. He is a god of cursing and dark magic.

Sekhmet: The dark opposite sister of Bast, Sekhmet has the head of a lioness, crowned with a disk and a cobra. Although she is the goddess of destructive action, she is also a deity of physicians, particularly those who set broken bones.

Set/Seth: The jealous brother of Osiris, this god is also the eternal enemy of Horus. He can change from one extreme mood to another swiftly and is unreliable. He deals primarily with chaos, destruction, revenge, suffering, and darkness.

Ta-Urt/Tauret: The Egyptian hieroglyph for this goddess was the *sa*, which is defined as the uterine blood of the Goddess. Portrayed as a female hippopotamus with pendulous breasts, Ta-Urt rules over pregnancy and childbirth.

Thoth: A god with the head of an ibis, Thoth invented the Four Laws of Magic, numbers, and hieroglyphs. He knows the secret of creating with the voice through the use of certain sounds. The *Kybalion* of Hermes Trismegistus was said to have been written by him. As the Supreme Magus, Thoth rules over prophecy and divination, writing, magic, inventions, the arts, healing, initiation, the sciences, the Akashic Records, and fate.

THE MIDDLE EAST

It is very difficult to separate many of the goddesses and gods into separate Middle East cultures as they frequently overlapped. Knowledge of these pantheons is fragmentary at best.

Adad/Haddad: Known in Babylon, Assyria, Syria, and Mesopotamia, this god rules over weather, storms, earthquakes, natural disasters, and divination.

Adonis: A god of ancient Semitic origin, Adonis is connected with Aphrodite and Persephone, whose death and resurrection were celebrated at Spring Equinox. He rules over rebirth, love, and the seasons.

Ahriman: This deity was known in Persia for his association with evil and death. He may be the source of the Christian devil. His powers rule over revenge, evil, and dark magic.

Ahura Mazdah: Also a Persian deity, this god is the opposite of Ahriman. He has power over prophetic revelation, purification, and universal law.

An(i)t/Qadesh/Anahita: A warrior goddess of Phoenicia and Ur, she is called the Mother of All Nations and Holy One. She is associated with the ankh, the moon disk, and lions. Her power is so great all other gods fear her. Her powers include revenge, fearlessness, and overcoming obstacles.

Anu: Known to Mesopotamia, Babylon, Assyria, and Sumeria, this god is called the Supreme God. His symbols are the star, scepter, crown, and staff. He has authority over justice, judgment, and fate.

Asherat-of-the-Sea: This goddess is deity of the sea in Phoenicia. She rules over motherhood, children, religion, and the arts.

Ashtart: This goddess was known as the Queen of Heaven in Phoenicia. The temple of Ashtart near a lake in Byblos held a sacred meteorite and great libraries. She rules over healing and prophecy. The word "bible" comes from the name Byblos.

Asshur: The national god of Assyria, this warrior deity is represented by a winged disk atop a bull. He has authority over weapon skills, protection, victory, and bravery.

Astarte: Another aspect of the goddess Ashtart, she was known in Babylon and Assyria as the Lady of Byblos and Mistress of Horses and Chariots.

Ba'al/Baal: An aspect of the god Addad, this deity was worshipped in Canaan and Phoenicia. He rules over storms, fertility, death, and resurrection.

Belit-Ili: This Mesopotamian goddess rules over the fate of each person, rather like the Norse goddesses, the Norns.

Dumuzi/Tammuz: Called the Only Begotten Son and Son of the Blood in Mesopotamia and Sumeria, this vegetation and fertility god is the consort of Ishtar. He rules over crops, new beginnings, and the spring.

Ea/Enki: This god is considered to be the source of all secret magical knowledge in Mesopotamia, Babylon, and Sumeria. He rules over manual skills, wisdom, the arts, oracles, incantations, divination, and justice.

El: A god of Canaan, Phoenicia, and Babylon, this deity may be the source of the Jewish god, who is sometimes called El. He rules over wars, victory, and fertility of the earth.

Enlil: Lord of the World in Sumeria, Babylon, and Assyria, this god rules over weather, natural disasters, the laws, and prosperity.

Ereshkigal: The opposite of the goddess Ishtar, this goddess was called Queen of the Underworld in Mesopotamia, Babylon, and Assyria. She rules over the land of the dead, dark magic, retribution, death, and regeneration.

Gibil: Another god of Assyria and Babylon, this deity's prime function is to judge all human judges found guilty of unscrupulousness. He has power over purification, initiation, justice, and intercession.

Inanna: Called the Queen of Heaven and Lady of the Land, Inanna was the most important goddess in Sumeria and Uruk. She is pictured as having wings and standing on the back of a sacred lion. Although she rules over war, victory, and destiny, she also has power over love, fertility, prosperity, justice, and civil and universal laws.

Ishtar: This goddess of Mesopotamia, Babylon, Assyria, Sumeria, Arabia, and Phoenicia was known in various aspects and by other names throughout the region. She was said to possess the Tables of Life's Records, or the Akashic Records. She carries weapons, rides on lions, and is associated with dragons. Her symbols are the eight-point star, the pentagram, doves, and the double-axe, or labrys. She also has a rainbow necklace, very similar to that of Freyja of the Vikings. Her powers extend beyond love, fertility, revenge, marriage, death, purification, initiation, and overcoming obstacles, to the positive and negative sides of all things.

Kamrusepas: This Hittite goddess rules over magic, spells, and healing.

Kusor: A god of Phoenicia, he rules over magical formulae, incantation, divination, and navigation.

Lilith: Known in Canaan among the Jews, Babylon, and Sumeria, this goddess was called the Patroness of Witches. The owl is her sacred bird. She gives protection to pregnant women and children, and rules over regeneration, feminine allure, powers of the moon, and enticing sorcery.

Marduk/Marduc: This deity was the national god of Babylon, and also was known in Mesopotamia, Canaan, Sumeria, and Assyria. Called the Great God, he killed the goddess Tiamat and took her Tablets of Destiny. He governs the four quarters of the earth, or the Four Elements or directions. A patron of priests, Marduk rules over fate, healing, magic, incantations, agriculture, storms, rebirth, purification, and initiation.

Mari/Mariham/Meri: This is a basic name for the Great Goddess in the Middle East. Her symbols are a blue robe and pearls, both connected with the sea. She rules over the moon, the sea, and childbirth.

Mithra/Mithras: Although this god originated in Persia, he was known throughout the area and eventually even into Rome, where his worship became a vital part of the Legions. Only men were allowed to worship him; his special day is December 25. He is a god of wrath, death, contracts, moral purity, predictions, war, sacred oaths, and spiritual illumination.

Nabu: In Mesopotamia and Sumeria, this god was known as the Patron of Scribes, and ruled over writing and destiny. He is associated with wisdom, accounting, speech, and intercession.

Nanna/Nina: This Great Mother of Sumeria is said to judge humans on the last day of every year and determine their futures. Her name is very ancient, and she is portrayed with a serpent tail or fishtail. She rules over the moon, healing, magic, interpretation of dreams, and herbs.

Nergal: This god of the Underworld and Judge of the Dead is pictured as a blackened disk that represents the Underworld Sun. He has power over desert winds, war, evil, diseases, dark magic, and revenge.

Ninurta: As a god of Sumeria, Assyria, Babylon, and Mesopotamia, he was known as the messenger from the gods to humans. Amethyst and lapis lazuli are sacred to him. He rules over water, destruction of evil and enemies, and fertility.

Shamash: This god was known in Mesopotamia, Sumeria, Babylon, and Assyria as protector of the poor and sublime judge. He is associated with divination, retribution, lawgiving, justice, and the future.

Sin: He was a god of the moon and the calendar in Mesopotamia, Ur, Assyria, Babylon, and Sumeria. He is the chief deity in a triad with the god Shamash and the goddess Ishtar. Sin rules over destiny, predictions, wisdom, and secrets.

Tiamat: Known as the she-dragon in Mesopotamia, Babylon, and Sumeria, she was the Great Mother of the primal abyss and at one time kept the Tablets of Destiny. When the god Marduk destroyed her, he built the universe with her body. She has power over revenge, karmic discipline, any salt water, despair, dark magic, rituals, and regeneration.

GREECE AND ROME

Most people are more familiar with the gods and goddesses of Greece and Rome than with those of other pantheons. The Greek and Roman pantheons are basically identical, with different names for the deities, but each pantheon has a few different deities. The first name listed for a deity is Greek, and the second name is Roman.

Aesculapius/Asklepios: The son of Apollo and a god of healing, this deity had two daughters, Hygeia (good health) and Panacea (helper); these women founded the college of medicine with vast libraries in his name. Much of his healing was based on the dreams of his patients. He rules over severe illnesses and all healing.

Aphrodite/Venus: A goddess of sexuality more than love, she rules over beauty, the joy of physical love, passion, all kinds of partnerships and relationships, fertility, and renewal. The Charities or Graces are her constant companions. This triad of moon goddesses is called Aglaia, Thalia, and Euphrosyne.

Apollo: Known by this name to both Greeks and Romans, this god is the lord of solar light, not the actual sun. The twin brother of Artemis, Apollo is second only to Zeus. He is a Patron of Priests, and skilled in music. His arrows can bring either healing or sickness. His sacred temple and oracle site are at Delphi. Apollo rules over prophecy, music, poetry, medicine, reason, inspiration, magic, the arts, and spiritual goals.

Ares/Mars: The Greeks weren't fond of this god and thought him a liar and blood-thirsty, while the Roman version was basically a god of war, who was insensitive and primarily concerned with his male image. He has power over raw energy, brute strength, and untamed passions.

Artemis/Diana: Known as the Virgin Huntress, the Bear Goddess, and Hunter of Souls, this goddess is also a shapeshifter who drives a chariot pulled by silver stags. The Amazons were loyal to her. Although her priestesses kept away from men, she was a deity of childbirth. She helps women who are harassed or threatened by men, and rules over animals, singing, enchantment, psychic power, fertility, purification, magic, sports, mental healing, dance, forests, and healing.

Athena/Minerva: Another Virgin Goddess, known as the Mother of Athens, this goddess is a warrior deity although she dislikes senseless violence. The owl, oak, and twined snakes are sacred to her. Her two main holidays fall in March and on December 25. She is the goddess of women's rights, the patroness of craftsmen and career women, and the protectress of cities. She has power over writing, music, the sciences, the arts, wisdom, renewal, true justice, peace, and battle strategy.

Circe: Known as the She-Falcon and Moon Goddess, Circe's name is taken from the death-bird or falcon (*kirkos*). She also is called the Fate-Spinner and Weaver of Destinies, and is an expert in knot magic. She rules over physical love, enchantments, vengeance, dark magic, and cauldrons.

Cronus (also spelled Kronos): This Father of the Gods has many other titles, such as Father Time, the Old King, the Great Lesson-Giver, and Ruler of the Golden Age. He is the Titan son of Gaea and Uranus. His powers extend over abundance, agriculture, riches from the earth, prosperity, the arts, and magic.

Cybele (also spelled Kybele): A Phrygian goddess of the earth and caverns, this Great Mother goddess is associated with the god Attis. The greatest and oldest center of her worship was in a cave at Pessinus in Phrygia, under the shadow of Mount Dindymon. She rules over wild animals, the natural world, dark magic, and initiations.

Demeter/Ceres: Called the Grain Mother, the Eternal Mother, and the Sorrowing Mother, this goddess is the mother of Persephone, who wed the lord of the

Underworld. She instituted the Eleusinian Mysteries. Her power extends over protection of women, crops, initiation, renewal, fertility, civilization, law, motherhood, marriage, and higher magic.

Dionysus: This god of wine and unbridled sexual pleasures is also called the Horned God, Savior, and the Twice-Born. His women followers are the Maenads, who frolic with centaurs and satyrs. At the Eleusinian Mysteries, Dionysus was represented as the Holy Child Iacchus in the winnowing basket. He rules over pleasure, total abandonment, the woodlands and nature, wine, initiations, rituals, and regeneration. The Roman deity Bacchus is very similar; his female followers are called the Bacchantes.

Erinyes/Eumenides: Known as the Avengers and Children of Eternal Night, these three virgin goddesses (Allecto, Tisiphone, and Megaera) defend mothers and the law of blood relationship, as well as bringing justice to those who break taboos, social, and bloodline laws.

Eros/Cupid: The Greek version of this god deals with erotic love of any kind, while the Roman version rules the gentler passions of love. As god of desire and physical attraction, this god is a dangerous force that can cause humans to perform acts of self-sacrifice.

Gaea/Gaia: Called Mother Earth, Great Mother, Supreme Goddess, and Primeval Prophetess, Gaea is the greatest of oracles whose temple was at Delphi before Apollo's. She rules over marriage, motherhood, agriculture, dreams, trance, divination, and healing.

The Graiae/Graeae: Although this triad of goddesses (Enyo, Pemphredo, and Deino) were called the Mothers of Greece, they are terrible deities of retribution and divination.

Hades: This brother of Zeus rules the Underworld and wealth in Greek mythology. He is the mysterious and terrifying god of death, as well as the god of prosperity. He rules over minerals and gems, material gain, and astral projection.

Hecate: This moon goddess came from Thrace to become Queen of the world of spirits, Patron of Priestesses, and the Goddess of Witchcraft. The Amazons knew and honored her. Her symbols are keys and cauldrons. All secret powers of nature are at her command. She has power over enchantments, averting evil, dark magic, riches, wisdom, transformation, purification, limits, incantations, and renewal.

Helios: This is the god of the physical sun who drove a golden chariot pulled by nine winged white horses. He rules over riches, enlightenment, and victory.

Hephaestus/Vulcan: An Underworld deity in Greece, he is a master of metal and gems, crafting all Olympian armor. He rules over thunder and lightning, subterranean fire, volcanoes, artisans, and all workers with metal. The Roman Vulcan was very similar.

Hera/Juno: As the wife of Zeus/Jupiter, this goddess is the Mother of the Gods and Queen of Heaven. She is the goddess of protection of the home, marriage, children, fertility, purification, the moon, and punishment.

Hermes/Mercury: This god is the messenger between the gods and humans, and leads the dead to the Underworld. He wears winged sandals and carries a caduceus (staff with twined snakes). He rules over music, astrology, commerce, profit, journeys, magic, gambling, thievery, alchemy, intelligence, and the Four Elements.

Hestia: One of the oldest Olympian deities, this goddess of the hearth and fire is a Virgin Goddess. She has power over discipline, duty, modesty, and service to others.

Janus: A very ancient Roman god, he existed before Jupiter and was honored the first day of every month. Portrayed with two heads looking in an opposite direction, this deity rules over beginnings and endings, departures and returns, doorways, journeys, harbors, and success.

Pan: Called the Horned God, the Goat-Foot God, and the Life Force of the World, Pan is one of the oldest Greek deities of the woodlands and animals. He is a deity of both positive and negative energy, of sexuality and fertility or unreasoning panic and fear. He has power over nature spirits, animals, gardening, healing, medicine, music, dance, and fishing. The Roman god Faunus is similar; he is also called Lupercus.

Persephone/Prosperina: This daughter of Demeter, whose original name was Kore, became Queen of the Underworld by marrying Hades. She is best invoked with her mother Demeter. She rules over the seasons, crops, the survivor, and overcoming obstacles.

Poseidon/Neptune: The god of the seas and earthquakes, this deity is associated with bulls and horses. He has power over human emotions, intuition, storms, ships, and weather.

Saturn: Similar to Cronus, this Roman god rules over karmic lessons, learning, prosperity, and vines.

Vesta: Like the Greek Hestia, the priestesses of this Roman goddess were virginal and kept an eternal sacred flame. She rules over hearth and home.

Uranus/Ouranos: The original Great God and husband of the goddess Gaea, he fathered all twelve of the divine Olympians. He rules over the sky.

Zeus/Jupiter: This deity is the Supreme God of the Greek and Roman pantheons, the Lord of the Heavens, and ruler of Olympia. His bird is the eagle. He rules over laws, justice, weather, mountains, wisdom, honor, riches, friendships, health, and good luck.

THE CELTS

The Celtic deities in this section cover those from Ireland, Scotland, and Wales.

Angus Mac Og: This Irish deity is also called the Young Son. He rules over love, youth, music, and beauty.

Anu: In Ireland, this Great Goddess is the deity of plenty and fertility. She also has power over prosperity and comfort.

Arawn: This god is the Welsh King of Annwn, or the Underworld. His power extends over revenge, terror, and war.

Arianrhod: Known to the Welsh as Silver Wheel and the goddess of reincarnation, this goddess rules over the Full Moon, beauty, fertility, and karma.

Badb/Badb Catha: This goddess is also known as Battle Raven and Scald-Crow, for she haunts battlefields with the Morrigan. She has power over life, wisdom, inspiration, enlightenment, and fate through violence.

Banba: This goddess is one of an Irish triad of Fotia and Eriu, protectresses of Ireland.

Bel/Belinus/Beli Mawr: This god is Bel or Belinus in Ireland and Beli Mawr in Wales. He is the primary male deity on the Holy Day of Beltane. His power extends over fire, science, healing, purification, fertility, cattle, success, prosperity, and crops.

Blodeuwedd: In Wales she is called Flower Face, White Flower, and Lily Maid. She is created by Math and Gwydion as a wife for Lleu. The owl and the moon are her symbols. She rules over wisdom, lunar mysteries, and initiations.

Boann: This Irish goddess of the River Boyne is the mother of Angus Mac Og by the Dagda. She rules over healing.

Bran the Blessed: This Welsh god's name means "blessed raven." He has power over prophecy, the arts, music, writing, the sun, and leadership.

Branwen: This Welsh goddess is the sister of Bran and rules over love and beauty.

Cailleach: This Great Goddess in her Destroyer aspect is known in Ireland, Scotland, and Wales. She has power over disease, cursing, and dark magic.

Cernunnos: Known to all Celtic areas, this god's name is spelled in various ways. He is the Horned One, whom the Druids knew as Hu Gadarn and Lord of the Animals. His power extends over animals, fertility, the woodlands, physical love, reincarnation, commerce, wealth, and crossroads.

Cerridwen: The symbols of this Welsh Moon Goddess are the white sow and the cauldron. All Welsh bards called themselves Cerddorion (sons of Cerridwen) because their initiation came from her. She rules over death, rebirth, fertility, inspiration, magic, astrology, science, spells, and knowledge.

The Dagda: In Ireland this god is known as the All-Father, the Good God, Lord of Life and Death, and Father of Gods and Men. He is the High King of the Tuatha De Danann. He has power over protection, magic, prophecy, reincarnation, the arts, initiation, healing, prosperity, music, and warriors.

Danu: This goddess is the ancestress of the Tuatha De Danann. She is the Patroness of wizards, and rules over water, prosperity, magic, plenty, and wisdom.

Dian Cecht/Diancecht: The Irish physician of the Tuatha, he rules over healing, medicine, herbs, regeneration, and magic.

Don/Donn: In Ireland this is Don, the god of the Land of the Dead. In Wales this is Donn, a goddess of the sea. Both rule over the Elements and eloquence.

Goibniu: In Ireland, he is one of a triad of craftsmen and works as a blacksmith. In Wales, he is called Govannon or Gofannon, and is also a blacksmith. He rules over the metal arts, brewing, and fire.

Gwydion: The brother of the Welsh goddess Arianrhod, he rules over enchantment, illusion, changes, magic, and healing.

Lugh: Connected with the celebration of Lughnasadh, this Irish god rules over craftsmen and the manual skills, reincarnation, the arts, healing, journeys, initiation, prophecy, and revenge.

Macha: Called Battle Crow, this Irish goddess is also honored at Lughnasadh. She has power over protection, war, death, cunning, sexuality, and dominance over males.

Manannán mac Lir: This shapeshifting Irish god ruled the sea and the Otherworld palace called Emain of the Apple Trees. His power extends over magic, navigators, storms, wealth, fertility, weather, the arts, and commerce. In Wales he is called Manawyddan.

The Morrigan: This goddess is known in Ireland, Wales, and Britain. Called Supreme War Goddess, Specter Queen, and a shapeshifter, she is a Patroness of Priestesses and Witches. She rules over water, revenge, magic, and prophecy.

Nuada: In Ireland, this god is known as Silver Hand. In Wales he is called Lludd. He rules over healing, the ocean, weapons, smiths and manual skills, magic, writing, and incantations.

Ogma: Similar to Hercules, this Irish god invented the ogham alphabet. His power extends over eloquence, poetry and writing, inspiration, language, physical strength, magic, the arts, and reincarnation.

Rhiannon: A Welsh goddess also known as the Great Queen, this deity rules over horses, enchantment, and the Underworld.

Scáthach: This goddess is known in both Ireland and Scotland as a destroyer aspect of the Goddess. She is called the Shadowy One and She Who Strikes Fear. She is the patroness of blacksmiths and warriors, as well as ruling over healing, magic, prophecy, and the martial arts.

Nordic-Germanic

Aegir: This Vanir god of the sea can be both positive and negative in his actions. He rules over prosperity, sailing, brewing, and control of wind and waves.

Balder/Baldur: Known as the Bright One, this Aesir god is a sun deity. He rules over advice, reconciliation, beauty, gentleness, reincarnation, wisdom, and happiness.

Freyja/Freya: The Great Goddess of the Norse pantheon, she is called the Goddess of Cats and leader of the Valkyries. Her number is thirteen and her day Friday. She has power over wealth, Witchcraft, magic, trance, love, sexuality, enchantment, poetry and writing, and protection.

Freyr/Frey: The brother of Freyja, this god rules over fertility, abundance, wealth, happiness, and weather, as well as being a guarantor of oaths.

Frigg/Frigga: The wife of Odin, this goddess is a shapeshifter and knows all things. She rules over childbirth, cleverness, love, wisdom, marriage, magic, and destiny.

Heimdall: This god is the guardian of Bifrost Bridge that led into Asgard. His power extends over beginnings and endings and defense against evil.

Hel: This goddess is called Queen of the Dead and Ruler of Niflheim. She rules over dark magic and revenge.

Holda: This goddess is the Germanic version of the Norse goddess Hel. She rules over fate, karma, the arts, dark magic, and revenge.

Loki: Blood brother of Odin and the Father of Lies, Loki is a trickster deity who is dangerous to invoke. He has power over natural disasters, deceit, cunning, thieves, revenge, destruction, lies, and dark magic.

The Norns: The Norse equivalents of the Greek Fate goddesses, the Norns are usually found near the World Tree. They rule over fate and karma.

Odin/Odhinn: Called King of the Gods, All-Father, and Lord of the Wild Hunt, this god is a shapeshifter who produced battle madness in warriors. Although he is connected with creativity and the arts, he is an untrustworthy god who frequently demanded payment in return for helping. He rules over runes, poetry, magic, divination, storms, death, knowledge, justice, reincarnation, initiation, the arts, and inspiration.

Thor/Thorr: Known to the northern Germans as Thunor or Donar, this Norse god is called the High Thunderer and Protector of the Common Man. His magic hammer Mjollnir is both a weapon and a ritual tool for blessing. He has power over law and order, defense, storms, trading voyages, trust, and protection.

Tyr: Called the bravest of all the gods, this deity is connected with law, legal contracts, bravery, judicial matters, victory, athletics, order, and solemn oaths.

INDIA

Agni: Called the Thrice-Born and Demon-Slayer, this god is the mediator between the gods and humans. He rules over weather, storms, protection of the home, wealth, power, new beginnings, justice, and rebirth.

Brahma: Among this god's titles are the Father of the Gods and Men, Creator of the Universe, and Guardian of the World. He is part of a triad with Vishnu and Shiva. The sacred *Vedas* sprang from his heads. His power extends over magic and wisdom.

Chandra/Soma: This moon god's name of Soma is derived from the hallucinogenic drink made by the gods. He rules over psychic dreams and visions.

Devi/Mahadevi: Known as the Shakti, or female energy, she is the consort of Shiva.

Durga: This goddess is one of a triad with Uma and Parvati. She rules over destruction, futility, comfort, aid, power, protection, and nurturing.

Ganesha/Ganesa: This god's name of Elephant-Face comes from his elephant-head. He is best known as Lord of Obstacles, since he can remove obstacles for his devotees. His power extends over wisdom, good luck, writing, success, prosperity, beginnings, overcoming obstacles, and combining force with cunning.

Indra: Known as King of the Gods, Lord of Storm, and Great God, this deity carries the thunderbolt Vajra in his right hand. He has power over weather, fertility, storms, warriors, reincarnation, bravery, love, the law, magic, and creativity.

Kali/Kali Ma: This goddess is called the Black Mother, Dark Goddess, Mother of Karma, the Crone, and the Terrible. She has a dual personality of gentleness and terrible death. She is one of the wives of Shiva and the Patroness of Witches. She is the representation of the trinity, Maiden, Mother, and Crone. She has power over regeneration, revenge, dark magic, and sexual activities.

Krishna: Called the Dark One, Stealer of Hearts, and the Savior God, this deity is one of the incarnations of Vishnu. The Hindus also call him Redeemer, Firstborn, Sin Bearer, and the Universal Word. His powers extend over erotic delights, sexual pleasures, and music.

Lakshmi: This goddess of love and beauty was born during the churning of the milk ocean. She rules over good fortune, prosperity, success, and love.

Parvati: Called Mother Goddess, she is one of Shiva's wives. She has power over the union of god and goddess, man and woman. She represents desire and ecstasy.

Rama: This god is an incarnation of Vishnu.

Rudra: This god of the dead and prince of demons is also called the Howler, the Dark God, and the Lord of Beasts. He is said to shoot arrows of death and illness. However, he has power over evil workers, healing herbs, death, wild animals, the woodlands, creation, prosperity, and storms.

Sarasvati: Myth says this goddess discovered the drink soma in the Himalayas. She is the consort of Brahma and rules over creative arts, science, and learning.

Shiva: One of a triad with Brahma and Vishnu, this god is called Lord of the Cosmic Dance, Lord of Yoga, He Who Gives and Takes Away, the Great Ascetic, and Cosmic Musician. Although he is a fertility deity, he is also recognized as an ascetic. His power extends over fertility, physical love, destruction, strength, medicine, storms, warriors, healing, magic, meditation, and judgment.

Uma: This deity is called the Corn Goddess, and is part of a trinity of Great Goddesses, along with Parvati and Kali. She rules over beauty, fertility, crops, the earth, and yogic asceticism.

Varuna: As creator of the cosmos, judge of human deeds, and god of Cosmic Law and Order, this deity has power over wind, truth, justice, law, magic, the creative will, the seasons, death, and prophecy.

Vishnu: Known as the Preserver, this god is the lord of the principle of Light that permeates the universe. This light is the inexplicable spiritual light that allows everything in the universe to exist. He is also an intermediary between the gods and humans. He is often shown riding the sunbird Garuda. He rules over judgment, peace, power, compassion, love, abundance, and success.

Yama: This Hindu deity is judge and god of the dead. He has power over judgment, destiny, death, and punishment.

Study Work

Spend at least two weeks deciding which pantheon appeals most to you. If no pantheon listed here feels right, research other pantheons until you find one with which you resonate and feel comfortable.

CHAPTER 11

The Eight Holy Days

Most ancient cultures celebrated the two Solstices and two Equinoxes of each year. They also used the powers of the New and Full Moons. Other cultural holidays were interspersed with these seasonal celebrations. Among the Celts, four other special year-points were recognized and observed. The Celtic names for these holy days are Imbolc, Beltane, Lughnasadh, and Samhain. In Celtic Wicca, these interspersed holy days are called the Greater Sabbats, while the Equinoxes and Solstices are called the Lesser Sabbats.

Religious rituals are important in the psychic, spiritual, and emotional growth of humans. Through properly done rituals, the worshippers are able to reach an altered state of consciousness that allows them to get closer to the energy of the deity they worship. In this exalted state it also is possible to create desired magical or spiritual results. This altered state of consciousness, which involves the collective unconscious or superconscious mind, is also important for balance and good health.

Wiccan rituals can align the worshippers to the flow of Earth's seasons, which are part of the universal flow of timing and rhythm. Since conversion to orthodox religions and the dawn of the industrial age, humans have lost their intimate contact with the inner subconscious connections to universal timing and rhythm. This has created a state that has led to spiritual imbalance, mental uneasiness, and ultimately a variety of serious physical and mental illnesses. As humans, we need this universal connection for our own inner peace, physical and mental health, and spiritual growth.

The practice of Witchcraft, or the oneness with all creation, allows humans access to their original spiritual nature. It symbolizes and encourages a psychic relationship—a connectedness—between humans, all creatures, Earth, and the entire universe.

The Celts celebrated their seasonal rituals on the eve of a day, since their days began at sunset and ended at the next sunset. However, you do not need to be so rigid that you do not celebrate before or after the date if it is necessary. The date is of far lesser importance than the process of connecting with the Goddess and the God and using the seasonal flows of energy. At the same time, you don't want to become so lax and lazy that you do not make an effort to do ritual on the proper day. With time and dedication, you will find that you will set aside these dates and free yourself from other obligations.

Since Solstice and Equinox dates may change a day or two from year to year, check a good astrological calendar for the exact dates. Such a calendar is also invaluable for the correct dates for the Full and New Moons in your time zone. When using a calendar, be certain to take into account changes due to daylight savings time.

The Celts were one of the few cultures that based their year on both the lunar and solar calendars. There were thirteen lunar—or moon—months in a year. Because twelve of these months did not correctly measure the solar year, their thirteenth month was only two to three days long. To keep the lunar and solar calendars balanced, the Druids added an extra day to the thirteenth month approximately every three years. This is the origin of the Celtic and Wiccan phrase "a year and a day." The Celts also began their year at the feast of Samhain at the end of October, while many other cultures began the year at Winter Solstice, with the rebirth of the sun.

The solar energies, reflected in the seasons, change only four times a year, and these changes occur on the Solstices and Equinoxes. They have much longer lasting effects than the four lunar changes each month.

The following descriptions of the eight holy days are given to prepare the apprentice for the actual celebration rituals for each, given in Chapters 40 through 47. Before you do the ritual itself, you should understand thoroughly the esoteric and spiritual symbolism underlying it.

Samhain: Among the Irish and Scottish Celts, this festival was celebrated from the eve of October 30 to the eve of November 1. It marked the end of one Celtic year and the beginning of a new one. Samhain is a Celtic name and is pronounced *SOW-en*. The *ow* in the word rhymes with *how*. Samhain was also known as Calan Gaeaf in Wales and Ancestor Night or Feast of the Dead in Britain and the Viking settlements. It has its counterparts in cultures around the world. The veil between the worlds of the living and the dead is very thin on this night, making it possible for communications between the two. This also makes it an excellent time for divinations. Wearing costumes at Samhain—or Halloween—symbolizes the souls of the dead, who are abroad and visiting their family and descendants on this night. The Celts also believed that if any person was murdered, badly wronged, or due justice that had not come in life, those souls could exact their revenge on Samhain. Bobbing for apples symbolized the apples of eternal life found on Manannán mac Lir's sacred isle.

Winter Solstice: This holy day occurs around December 21. Some Pagan cultures celebrated Winter Solstice as the turning point of a year instead of the Celtic Samhain. On this day, the sun is at its lowest point, producing the shortest day of the year as reckoned by daylight hours. In myth, this is the time of the death of the old Sun King and the birth of the new one in the form of the Divine Child. In Wales, this holy day was called Alban Arthuan. The decorated evergreen tree symbolizes the offerings made on the Tree of Life, while the holly represents the Holly King, or one aspect of the God, who rules this season. Candles and lights on the evergreen tree represent the growing light in the darkness.

Imbolc (or Imbolg): This holy day is celebrated on February 1. It is pronounced *IM-bolhk*. This holy day was known as Bwyl Mair Dechrau'r Gwanwyn in Wales. The Irish name may be derived from the Celtic words *imb-fholc* (washing oneself), or *i mbolg* (in the belly), a reference to the pregnant ewes at this season. Another name is Brigit's Day. It is a time for celebrating the awakened Maiden aspect of the Goddess and for preparing for renewal and new beginnings in your life. Special breads with candied fruit are baked in a round shape to represent the growing solar disk, with the fruit symbolizing the bounty of the goddess Brigit.

Spring Equinox: This holy day occurs about March 21, and was called Alban Eiler in Wales. A Christianized name is Lady Day. Light and dark are equal at this time, but the light is steadily growing stronger. The colored eggs of this seasonal ritual were connected in ancient times with the Goddess and rebirth. Giving red-colored eggs to friends and family has its roots as far back as the Mesopotamian culture. The hare or rabbit was a Goddess animal. The goddess Eostre, frequently mentioned in connection with Spring Equinox, was an Old English goddess, not a Celtic one.

Beltane: This celebration is also known by the later Christianized name of May Day. Known as Calan Mai in Wales, it was originally a fertility festival, but not considered to be a fortuitous time for marriage. The Scots knew this festival as Céitein. The Old Irish name was Belo-tenia, which means "bonfires of Belos the Bright." Bel, or Belos, was a sun god who ruled over healing and cattle. This holy day is pronounced *BELL-tayn*. Connected with the Lord of the Forest, the May Queen, and growing fairy magic, this day is excellent for celebrating the Sacred Marriage between the God as the Lord of the Greenwood and the Goddess as the Earth Mother. Nature beings are becoming more active at this time, in preparation for the Summer Solstice. The may-pole and the accompanying dances are remnants of ancient Pagan fertility festivals.

Summer Solstice: This occurs around June 21, when the hours of daylight are longest. The sun stands at its zenith and will soon begin its slide into darkness. The Welsh called this festival Alban Heruin. Tradition says that Fairies and Elves are abroad in great numbers on this night. Herbs gathered on Summer Solstice are believed to be the most powerful of any time in the year. Bonfires and lighted solar wheels were symbols used in ancient festivals on this day.

Lughnasadh: This holy day is on August 1. Another Pagan spelling for this day is Lunasa. Sometimes, the name Lammas is used. However, Lammas is an Anglo-Saxon term meaning "loaf mass," which refers to Christian ritual. Called Calan Awst in Wales, this holy day is one of two harvest festivals, the other occurs at the Autumn Equinox. The pronunciation is *loo-NAH-sah* or *LOO-nah-sah*. Originally, Lughnasadh was a celebration of the Celtic god Lugh's marriage to the Earth Mother. This is a good time to gather the last of the herbs, leaving what ripens later as seed for the next year. In ancient Ireland, this festival marked a time of feasting and games, such as physical sports.

Autumn Equinox: This celebration occurs about September 21, and was called Alban Elved in Wales. In ancient times it marked the end of the harvest and rest after labor. The hours of the day and night are again in balance, but the darkness is increasing. Preparations are made for the dark time of the year. Corn dollies were made from the last of the sheaves and kept for luck and prosperity until the next harvest.

The Celtic holy days or festivals are defined each year by the agricultural activities of the people. Although most Witches no longer live on farms nor do they respond daily to the agricultural cycles, all people, and especially Witches, are still linked to the ancient earthly rhythms of life through their psychic centers and the superconscious mind.

Study Work

For each of the eight holy days, write out a brief description of how you perceive them. Then, add a few lines that describe what important events in your personal life occurred around the time of each festival.

CHAPTER 12

Powers of the Moon

Knowledge of the Moon's powers dates back to the very beginnings of religious history and has always been closely associated with the Goddess. The carving of the Great Goddess of Laussel, one of the most ancient Goddess statues dating back to about 20,000 B.C.E., shows the full-bodied Goddess holding a bison horn with thirteen marks on it. These marks represent the thirteen moon months in a year. The first lunar calendars were based on the menstruation cycles of women, cycles that follow the moon phases. Although ancient cultures used the sun's yearly cycle of the rise and fall of light for agricultural and long-term projects, they all depended upon the monthly phases of the moon to set more accurate dates for religious holidays or meetings.

We know that the ocean tides of this planet are affected by the moon. So too are creatures such as herrings and grunions. Since the human body is predominantly water, it follows that we would also be affected by the moon. Knowing the influences of the moon upon humans, we can avoid or take advantage of situations. For example, you should avoid surgery at or near a Full Moon if possible, because you will bleed more.

By being aware of the moon and its phases, particularly the New and Full Moon, we can harness certain tides of energy in magic and ritual. Ancient teachings say that the New Moon, and the waning period after the Full Moon up to the New Moon, is best for doing spellwork for such things as binding, decreasing, and banishing. The Full Moon, and the waxing period after the New Moon up to the Full Moon, is best for building, increasing, and creating. A waxing moon is getting bigger, which culminates in the Full Moon, and a waning moon is getting smaller, culminating in the New Moon, or when the moon's light is hidden.

Esbats are Wiccan celebrations performed on the Full Moon, and sometimes on the New Moon as well. Full Moons have always been traditional monthly meeting times for Witches. More and more Witches now celebrate the New Moon as well. Margaret Murray may have coined the term Esbat, as it is not mentioned in any older texts on Witchcraft.

There is other ancient moon knowledge that is not frequently taught to Witches or anyone else. There are two periods of the moon that are more powerful in many ways than either the New or Full Moon. These are the two midway points, or quarters, which are about seven days after both the New and Full Moons. Since the moon cycle is approximately 29 1/2 days from one Full Moon to the next, you will need to consult an accurate astrological calendar in order to determine where these points are in each month. The Druids knew of these power points and used them for centuries.

Halfway between the New and Full Moons, when the moon is between the worlds of light and dark, when the moon lives on the edge of time-space and stands at the threshold between the worlds, this is a very powerful time, more powerful than any other time of a month. Gray Witches can use these midway points for some of their most potent magical spells.

The first midway point, the one that falls between the New and Full Moons, is an almost equal blend of light and dark energies, with the light energy holding a slight edge. This time can be useful for working Full Moon magic that has not produced satisfactory results when performed at the usual time. This is a time for positive magic that may need a dose of dark energy to blast away resistance, such as in healing or spelling for prosperity.

The second midway point, the one that falls between the Full and New Moons, is again a balance of light and dark energies. However, the dark energy is slightly stronger at this point. A Witch can use this energy flow to cut through barriers to success, remove psychic attacks that proved resistant to ordinary magic, or push ahead projects that have stalled.

Both of these midway points are extremely powerful when used for serious divination or for trance work. Rituals performed at these times, as well as at the New and Full Moons, generate a tremendous amount of energy that can be used for magic or contacting those who are deceased. During Wiccan ceremonies, it is considered possible for the souls of departed Witches to attend and offer advice and predictions. These midway points seem to make it easier for all spirits to make clear contact.

The moon also works its way through the zodiacal signs, residing in each sign for approximately two days. Any good astrological calendar should list the day that the moon slips into another zodiacal sign. Since the moon primarily affects the emotions and emotional reactions to events, a Witch can use these emotional energies when working magic.

Moon in Aries: This sign gives boldness, energy, and unfortunately a tendency toward impetuousness. People tend to be argumentative and aggressive. However, when the moon is in Aries it is a good time to start projects and channel energy for change.

Moon in Taurus: This energy is solid and well grounded, with little push to hurry or change anything. People usually are mellower, less likely to become stressed. It is a good time to work for consolidation of projects already started.

Moon in Gemini: The moon in this sign can be frenetic with the surge of wild energy compelling one to move and do. People are more inclined to become involved in social activities, although their thoughts may be scattered and their lives far less orderly than when the moon is in Taurus. This is a good time for magic that involves the search for answers, as the magician will be more inclined to look at a variety of possibilities.

Moon in Cancer: When the moon travels through this sign, emotions are closer to the surface than usual. Thoughts and activities center around the home and close family. People can become overly sensitive, which may cause misunderstandings and hasty words. This is a time for magical projects affecting the welfare of the family and home.

Moon in Leo: This sign projects energy that makes for drama and melodrama, a love of attention and the spotlight. People can blow the smallest scene out of proportion if they are not careful. This energy can be used to boost your self-esteem or to tackle an over-inflated ego.

Moon in Virgo: A discriminating zodiacal sign, the moon in Virgo is a good time for detailed work and tackling whatever needs to be done, no matter how mundane it is. People usually are more helpful and productive now. Use this moon sign for working on magical projects that require a close eye on all details and are tuned to ordinary, everyday solutions to make life better.

Moon in Libra: This sign affects the balance with which we view life, relationships, and partnerships. However, it can cause balance in the extreme so that people dither instead of making decisions. Use this energy when searching for the balance point needed in spells.

Moon in Scorpio: This is the most intense sign of the moon's journey through the zodiac. Extremes in mood are quite common. People tend to brood more over a slight offense than usual. This is an excellent time for magical spells and meditations that will enhance the understanding of the Mysteries and spirituality in general.

Moon in Sagittarius: The moon in Sagittarius brings out an inner need to search for knowledge and greater understanding. People can overdo or waste energy now in their haste to enjoy life. This is a time to study and/or practice with magic and divination.

Moon in Capricorn: The moon in this sign sometimes makes people pessimistic and cautious in all their dealings with others, particularly concerning their career. This energy often can be scattered or disruptive. It is a good time to work spells for your career or major life goals.

Moon in Aquarius: This zodiacal sign is one of rebellion. Not open rebellion as with the Moon in Aries, but a quiet, subtle rebellion that is primarily stubbornness to not listen to others. Sometimes people will do complete reversals in decisions at the last minute. This energy is good for spells to help you break out of the norm and create something new in your life.

Moon in Pisces: The moon in this sign can cast a veil of illusion over everything, blocking out reality and causing fuzzy thinking. However, what makes for an impressionable, unreal everyday life can be used in a positive manner during meditation. This energy can aid in becoming more spiritual and compassionate.

Study Work

Chart your emotional tides through three Full Moons. Do you see a correlation between emotional changes and certain moon phases? What astrological sign was the moon in when these changes took place? During this same period, pay attention to your local police records of violent crimes. See if you can chart the rise and fall of the crime rate.

CHAPTER 13

The Elements and Quarters

The Elements and quarters have been known for centuries to many cultures around the world. They are mentioned in many medieval texts on ceremonial magic. Whether or not Wicca used these definitions before the Middle Ages is not known with any accuracy. We do know that many ancient cultures used the Elements in religious ceremonies and magical spells, and that groups with shamanic beliefs knew of and used the four directions or four quarters of the heavens in their rituals. Today, it is quite common for Wiccans, solitary or in groups, to use the astral powers of the Elements and quarters in their work, religious or magical. Element is capitalized to differentiate it in the apprentice's mind from the scientific use of the word.

The four Elements or quarters used by Witches when they cast a circle are based on the four directions of the terrestrial plane. These Elements are called Earth, Air, Fire, and Water. The fifth element, Spirit, defines the center of the sacred circle. In ritual and magic, these Elements are associated with the four directions of a consecrated circle, the four directions of the zodiac, and the four directions of the universe.

These Elements are not the same as the elements that scientists speak about. It is impossible to prove by scientific means that magical Elements exist, as they are astral and spiritual in nature. However, this does not invalidate their existence. The scientific community cannot produce a photo of an atom or an electron, yet they know these exist by the behavior of other substances around them. The same applies to the magical Elements. We know of their existence by the results we get when working with them.

When Witches cast a circle, they define and seal the circumference of the circle first with a wand or athame and consecrated water. Then, they call up the guardians of the four directions, beginning in the east and ending in the north. Depending upon the preference of the solitary Witch or a group, these quarters may be called watchtowers, the Rulers, Lords and Ladies, or Gods and Goddesses. Some use the titles and beings listed in old grimoires of ceremonial magicians. These astral beings are called Elementals, meaning they are connected with the Elements. They have their existence in the Elements and work with the powers of the Elements.

The Elements should be thought of as states of being. They have force and form that exists on an astral level rather than being physical. Each Element possesses particular characteristics, qualities, and magical purposes that set it apart from each of the other Elements. Sometimes, the Elements are referred to as kingdoms and have kings or rulers. There are both positive and negative energies associated with these Elements and their Elementals.

Elementals can appear to the Witch in any form or shape that they wish. However, they usually will align themselves with the cultural description expected by the human calling upon them. Every country has its tales of elemental spirits. Although the names and descriptions may vary from country to country, the behavior and powers remain basically the same. Elementals take on the physical characteristics and appearance of the country or racial group with which they work. Therefore, someone who is Oriental in background will not usually see an Elemental with African or Native American features. All Elementals have some human resemblance, with the Earth and Water creatures having the most human-like physical characteristics.

Elementals exist on the astral levels and are as real in their plane as humans are on the physical plane. They are seen primarily through the "inner eyes" or their presence is perceived by intuitive feelings, rather than seen by the physical eyes. Elementals are alive and able to see, hear, feel, touch, and talk, although they do not act in the same manner as humans. They evolve and progress in their own special way, but never become human. Although they do not experience sickness as we know it, they can be injured or killed by violence.

Each Elemental exists and operates within its own Element, never venturing into the realms of other Elements. As living astral beings, Elementals can control their particular Element. They also are capable of molding that Element into a physical desire when properly approached by a magician and asked to cooperate. They can cooperate with the Elementals of the other Elements, but cannot use the powers of Elements other than their own.

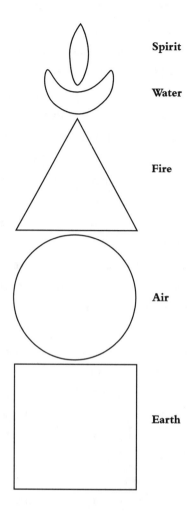

Spirit

Water

Fire

Air

Earth

Hindu Element Symbols

Elementals will respond to harmonious and friendly thoughts, although they do not ordinarily involve themselves with humans. Some can be very small in size, while others are large. All Elementals are capable of changing size at will. If provoked, they can be very mischievous, causing all kinds of problems and troubles.

Sometimes an Elemental will take up residence in a piece of jewelry, amulet, talisman, or statue. If the item is treated with love and respect, the Elemental will stay and bring good luck. We find this mentioned in old stories about the genie of the lamp or ring.

The following definitions and correspondences of the Elements are based primarily on texts of European ceremonial magic.

Earth: The Elementals of Earth are the Gnomes, Dwarves, Trolls, and certain kinds of Fairies (usually without wings). Although Gnomes and Dwarves are smaller than humans, they look very much like us. Trolls, however, look as if they are made of stone. The Fairies of this Element are the size of humans. These beings are attracted by powders, stones, and salt.

In ceremonial magic, the king or ruler of this Element is called Ghom, Ghob, or Gob, which may come from the words Goblin and Hobgoblin. Earth is associated with the physical plane and the sense of touch. It is represented by the Hindu symbol Prithivi, a yellow square. In Wicca, Earth is associated with the North and the color dark green or black. Among ritual tools, Earth is symbolized by the pentacle, images and statues, gems and stones, the salt, and cord magic. Symbolic images of Earth are the rocks and gems, mountains, soil, caves, and mines. I connect the Pentacles suit in tarot with the Earth Element. Ritual work with Earth can include surrendering self-will, prosperity, employment, stability, fertility, success, and partnerships. Earth is also connected with the astrological signs of Taurus, Virgo, and Capricorn.

Air: The Elementals of Air are the Sylphs, Zephyrs, and certain winged Fairies that inhabit the breezes and high mountains. Air Elementals are powerful beings that constantly change form. Their basic image is mysterious and wispy. These beings are attracted by oils and incenses.

In ceremonial magic, the king or ruler of this Element is called Paralda. Air is associated with the mental plane and processes, and the sense of smell. In the Hindu system, it is represented by Vayu, a blue circle. In Wicca, Air is associated with the East and the color yellow. Among ritual tools, Air is symbolized by the wand and incense. Symbolic images of Air are the sky, winds and breezes, clouds, the breath, and all vibrations. I connect the Wands suit in tarot with the Air Element, although others believe it should be Swords, and the ritual tool should be the sword. Wands describe the mental action of Air more appropriately than Swords, which represent physical action. Ritual work with Air can include creative visualization, the seeking of knowledge and inspiration, psychic hearing, harmony, herbal wisdom, plant growth, ideas, revealing the truth, finding lost objects or people, and the training of any psychic abilities. Air is also connected with the astrological signs of Gemini, Libra, and Aquarius.

Fire: The Elementals of Fire are the Salamanders and Firedrakes, or small Fire drag-ons, that inhabit the consciousness of all flames, large or small. Fire Elementals are usually quite small, but can become enormous when a fire gets out of control or enlarges. They are the most mischievous and unpredictable of all Elementals. These beings are attracted by candles, lamps, and fire in general.

The king or ruler is called Djin or Jinn, which may be a reference to the Arabian Elementals known as genies. Fire is associated with spiritual and physical sight. It is represented by the Hindu symbol Tijas, a red triangle. In Wicca, Fire is associated with the South and the color red. Among Wiccan ritual tools, Fire is symbolized by the sword, athame, candles, the incense burner, and burned herbs or papers. Some Wiccan groups believe the wand should be its ritual tool. Symbolic images of Fire are the sun, lightning, volcanoes, the rainbow, stars, and blood. I connect the Swords suit in tarot with the Element of Fire, as Fire is logically associated with physical energy rather than with Wands and mental energy. Ritual work with Fire can include changes, per-ception, illumination, love and passion, will power, destruction of barriers or prob-lems, healing, and purification. Fire also is connected with the astrological signs of Aries, Leo, and Sagittarius.

The Fire Element must be used with great care by the Witch and magician because it is the most difficult to control and manipulate. Apprentices should never work with the Fire Element alone.

Water: The Elementals of Water are Nymphs, Undines, Mer-folk, and certain tiny Fairies of the water plants. These beings can assume a very human-like image, even though they stay in or around water at all times. Folklore is full of tales of the Mer-folk and their interaction with humans. They are attracted by water, herbal solutions, and magical elixirs.

In ceremonial magic, Niksa or Necksa is the ruler of Water. The Element of Water is associated with the astral plane and the sense of taste. In the Hindu system it is represented by Apas, a silver crescent. In Wicca, Water is associated with the West and the color blue. Among ritual tools, Water is symbolized by the chalice, cauldron, mirrors, and all water or liquid. Symbolic images of Water are the ocean, lakes, rivers, wells, pools, rain, mist, and fog. I connect the Cups suit in tarot with the Water Element. Ritual work with Water can include healing, emotions, communicating with spirit, purification, the subconscious mind, love and friendships, fertility, marriage, sleep and dreams, and the psychic. Water is also connected with the astrological signs of Cancer, Scorpio, and Pisces.

Spirit: Although Spirit is the fifth Element it is seldom used, if at all, in magic. It is represented by the center of the circle and the color brilliant white. It has no rulers or beings other than the Goddess and the God. Ritual work with the Element of Spirit can include enlightenment, seeking the life's path, understanding karma, and the unveiling of the ancient spiritual Mysteries.

The Celtic cultures were well aware of the Elements and the Elementals. Ancient Pagan priests and priestesses of the Celts always included the four Elements in some way in all rituals.

The Old Scottish Gaelic term for the four directions was the Four Airts, or airs. This encompasses the four Elements and the four winds as well. The Scottish Gaelic colors for these differed from the colors adopted by Witches from ceremonial magic. The Scottish ones were crimson for the East and dawn; white for the South and noon; gray for the West and twilight; and black for the North and midnight. The specific Scottish Gaelic words for the four directions were *aiet* for the East; *deas* for the South; *iar* for the West; and *tuath* for the North.

Other cultures used different colors to represent the four Elements. The Hindus used a yellow square for Earth, a silver crescent for Water, a blue circle for Air, a red triangle for Fire, and a black or indigo ovoid for Spirit. In Enochian (or Qabalistic) magic, the Elements are referred to as castles: red is for East, white for South, green for West, and black for North.

China's representations of the Elements is slightly different, since they have more than one designation for each Element. One set of Elements lists Black Warrior, White Tiger, Vermillion Bird, and Azure Dragon, while another set lists North, black, Water, Winter; West, white, Metal, Autumn; South, red, Fire, Summer; East, green, Wood, Spring; and Center, yellow, Earth.

Native North American tribes also know of and use the Elements in their ceremonies. The directional descriptions depend upon the tribe and its cultural teachings. One list gives East, yellow, eagle; South, red, mouse; West, black, bear; and North, white, buffalo. Among the Navajo the list is East, white; South, blue; West, yellow; and North, black, while the Cheyenne use red, yellow, white, and black instead. However, the Zuni list Air, yellow; Water, blue; Fire, red; Earth, white; and the center as all colors.

In ancient Mexico we find still other descriptions of the Elements. The Mayan designation was East, red; South, yellow; West, black; and North, white. The other cultures of Mexico used North, red, Fire; West, yellow, Earth; South, blue, Air; East, green, Water; and again a center of all colors.

It is important to include symbols of all four Elements in every ritual so that the astral and spiritual energies will be balanced. An over-predominance of one Element will have an adverse effect on the ritual and the participants. Each Element will balance its opposite in the circle. Earth will balance Fire, keeping this volatile energy from causing chaos, just as Air balances Water.

All magic recognizes that the four Elements must be used to produce a satisfactory outcome from spellwork. This means that without the use of the Elements, Witches or magicians cannot create their desire on the astral plane and have that desire manifest in this physical world. These Elements correspond to four distinctive types of astral energy that can be molded by magical techniques into a desired form. Ancient occult philosophers taught that all life is composed of these Elements, and, without them, could not exist. Therefore, no magical spell has the power to create unless you use all four Elements.

Events in human lives also should contain the equivalent of the four Elements, or chaos will reign. Earth represents the physical body and common sense. Air symbolizes the mental level and study, thought, and constant learning. Fire is the physical activity, while Water represents the emotions. If a person studies, takes care of physical responsibilities, and is empathetic with others, but does no physical activities to bring about a desired result, that desire will never materialize. Also, if one expends all the necessary physical activity needed, is empathetic toward others, and studies, but doesn't use common sense, the desired manifestation will be off center and not what one wanted.

You can also look at the Elements in terms of personal responsibilities. Earth is taking care of the physical body; Air is responsibility to a job; Fire is spiritual seeking; and Water is responsibility to family. If a person shirks responsibility to family and self, while totally centering on spiritual seeking, that person is out of balance.

Study Work

For two weeks, connect all your activities and desires to the four Elements. See which, if any, are missing and creating problems for you. Change the ones possible to change, so that they more closely reflect a balance of Elements.

CHAPTER 14

Nature Spirits and
Other Invisible Helpers

Nearly all ancient cultures taught that humans have invisible helpers who exist on another plane of existence, but are capable of influencing and helping people on the earth plane. A variety of names have been used to designate these beings. For example, the great Greek philosopher Socrates wrote that he frequently communicated with his *daemon*, which is not the same word as demon, although it is considered so in Webster's definition. *Daemon*, according to the works of Socrates, is more closely connected with what we call guardians or spiritual teachers. The descriptions Witches give of their teachers and helpers are almost identical to what the orthodox churches teach are angels. It all comes down to a matter of semantics.

Most of the astral companions, by whatever name you call them, are basically human in form and thought. They can see farther into the future or into the past than we can, but still are not infallible or all knowing. These beings can work more easily and quickly with astral energies than humans can. They can be instructive, helping us to open to ancient knowledge and new experiences, such as astral travel. They can be healers, or know whom to contact on their level for healing. They are comforting in times of fear or sorrow, strict when we keep breaking universal rules, and protective when we find ourselves in danger.

There are three basic classes of guides and teachers. Most guides and teachers have been incarnated in human form at some time in history. Sometimes these guides are deceased ancestors, from your present incarnation or farther back in time. A smaller number of teachers are completely ethereal in nature and have not experienced earthly incarnations. These latter beings of shining light are sometimes called angels. However, the original term Shining Ones was applied to deities, guardians, and ethereal beings who had no earthly incarnations. You may or may not have teachers from each astral classification.

The Shining Ones are mentioned in nearly all the sacred books of the world religions. The Egyptians, Romans, Greeks, Persians, Muslims, Japanese Shintoists, Jewish Qabalists, Hindus, and the Maoris knew of these ethereal beings. Even the Arabic Koran speaks of angels. These celestial beings are composed of pure radiant energy, hence the name Shining Ones. Their activities appear to be confined to carrying out the Divine Will, whether that be through protection or messages. These beings never were, and never will be, in a physical human body, for they evolved separately from humans.

Generally, when one speaks of astral or spiritual teachers, the reference is not to angels, but to astral beings who once lived upon this earth and are now in a discarnate state. They have accepted the spiritual task of helping humans to grow spiritually.

Too many people get caught up in assigning some lofty title to their teachers, in an attempt to make them sound more important. When I became aware many years ago of the little Tibetan monk with me, I made the mistake of asking him if he was a Master or had some other title. He frowned and said, "What is a title? A name is a title, for it defines who you are. No one has need for more than that. Too many people attach pompous sounding titles to themselves or to their teachers and do not warrant such a title or description. They collect titles and initiations like other people collect stones or coins. When you die, the Judges do not ask what title or initiation you have. They only look at the name on your soul." The true movers and shakers of any era have all been the common people who did what was necessary for day-to-day living. So do not expect to have someone with a lofty title among your teachers. You will get more practical advice and aid from a teacher who worked their way through life, just as you are doing.

Eventually, you will discover that you have a number of different teachers working with you. They choose you; you do not choose them. Oftentimes, teachers will choose to be with you because of a past lifetime together. These teacher-guides stay around you at all times, instructing and protecting you, even though you may not be aware of their presence. They have access to much spiritual material. However, there must be a willingness on your part to learn.

One or two of these teachers will be what in New Age terms is called a "master teacher," although this is not a title not favored by these beings. I prefer to call them "chief administrators." It seems to be the job of these special ones to make certain that the other teachers offer the proper help. These administrators will remain with you throughout this lifetime, unless you reject them by your repeated negative habits and behavior or by refusing to accept their help at any time.

The other teachers may change from time to time as you grow and develop in spiritual consciousness. When your spiritual awareness takes a step upward, some of the teachers will leave to train others. This always happens when a new psychic gift is developing.

You may find it difficult to identify many of your regular teachers at first for they ordinarily do not appear unusual or different, as a new teacher will. These beings have been around you since childhood, and you will be subconsciously comfortable with their presences.

On rare occasions, the messages these teachers give you will be audible, or appear to be heard by the physical ears. However, most of the time their words will flow through your mind like a rush of thoughts that you will know are not your own. As you study and grow, you will learn to separate all the different teachers by their inflections, choices of words, and phrasing. Don't be discouraged if you are not given a name immediately. Your teachers will reveal names when they feel you are ready and if the name will not be a hindrance to you.

As you advance in understanding and acceptance, you will be able to see your teachers in your mind, or with your inner eye. You can exchange thoughts more swiftly than you could in words. Be critical, however, of any messages you receive, no matter the means or astral being giving them. Every message should be scrutinized carefully with common sense. No ethical teacher will demand that you do anything, especially anything against your moral values or against spiritual, universal laws, nor will they advise action that will throw your life into chaos and cause you trouble. If you receive messages of this kind, think hard about your own inner desires in case you might be hearing what you want to hear, not what is truth. Then, if the thought did not come from your own subconscious mind, decide how you feel about the astral sender of the message. You may need to request that the particular teacher be removed from your presence if she/he continues to demand certain actions from you or is consistent in offering bad advice.

It is not unusual for deceased ancestors, relatives, or friends to visit you from time to time. Naturally, they are interested in your progress and growth. However, if one of them proves to be troublesome, you have the right to ask your other teachers to remove that entity. You may have to demand that they not be allowed to return if they are really annoying. One of my deceased relatives was manipulative, complaining, and critical in life; she did not change when she died. After a temper tantrum that included throwing books off shelves in a fit of astral pique, she is permanently barred from my surroundings.

Some of a Witch's invisible companions do not call themselves guides or teachers. They are the Fairies, Gnomes, and similar beings who coexist with us, but are not always human in form or thought. However, they, too, can help us if approached in the proper manner. Although they prefer to keep out of human sight because of past negative experiences, often they can be coaxed to share their knowledge and help. The Witch cannot expect to order these beings to do anything, as this will most frequently produce the opposite effect, no help at all. The best way to work with them is first to cultivate a sense of friendship. Then, they often can be enticed to help with magic. These beings primarily exist in the astral realms, but can roam the physical realm whenever they please. The Witch must take care not to think of these Otherworld creatures as having human thoughts, feelings, or reactions, as they will not.

There are many types of Fairies and similar entities. The apprentice and even the experienced Witch need to clearly understand each kind so they don't offend or alienate them. The beings mentioned below are only those well-known in the European cultures and the list does not contain every such being known. If you are choosing a different racial pantheon in which to work, research that culture's folklore for the beings you may wish to work with.

In traditional Wiccan lore, there are four primary groups of elemental spirits or nature entities that are directly connected with the four Elements. These are the Gnomes, Sylphs, Undines, and Salamanders. However, each Element actually has many more elemental beings than just these four.

Gnomes, Dwarves, Trolls, and the large Fairies work with the Earth Element; Sylphs, Zephyrs, tiny winged Fairies, and Elves with the Air Element East; Salamanders, Firedrakes, and Dragons with the Fire Element; and Undines, Mer-folk, and certain other Fairies with the Water Element. Since Salamanders, Firedrakes, and other Dragons more closely fit descriptions of animal allies, they are discussed in Chapter 15.

Do not assume that you already know about the Elementals and other similar beings, as much of what we have been taught is negatively colored by prejudicial opinions. The following list will help you get to the truth, an essential part of your Wiccan training.

Bogies: These mischievous beings are known by many names: Bogeymen, Bogles, Bog-a-boos, Boggies, and Bogey-beasts. Residents of the Isle of Man know them as Boggans. The Irish branch of these creatures is called Ballybogs and are not as intelligent as those found elsewhere.

Bogies prefer to keep out of human sight. Their form is vague, appearing more as a puff of dust or a wispy wavering in the air. However, their hollow, gleaming eyes reveal their true character. Since Bogies like to create an atmosphere of chaos and disruption, they tend to live where they have ample opportunities to do this, such as cluttered closets, basements, caves, hollow trees, and sometimes even under the sink.

They usually come out only at night, but may appear when everything is very quiet during the day. One of their favorite activities is to hover behind humans and pets and make them uneasy.

Under ordinary circumstances, Bogies are not a threat to humans. However, it is best to never invite them into your home or ritual circle. Once given an invitation, Bogies can be extremely difficult to evict. Their annoying antics, although not malicious, can be very troublesome.

Brownies: Brownies seem to have originated in Scotland, then spread around the world as the Scottish people emigrated to other countries. They are never more than three feet tall with flat faces and lots of body hair. Documented sightings all report that Brownies are male. It may be that the females are shyer and do not let humans see them.

Similar beings are known as Yumboes in North Africa and Choa Phum Phi in China. In Wales, their name is Bwbachod (pronounced *boobachod*); this family of Brownies definitely does not like ministers or teetotalers. The Manx Brownie is much larger and hairier than others and quite ugly; he is known as a Fenoderee (pronounced *fin-ord-er-ree*).

Brownies prefer to be active at night, although a few can be seen during daylight hours. These cheerful, helpful creatures usually attach themselves to a household, staying with a family for generations, although on occasion more solitary Brownies can be found in hollow trees or old ruins. They like the company of humans, but will leave if offended. However, there are certain human characteristics that they will not tolerate. Among these are cheating, lying, messy living, or ministers.

If you are fortunate to have Brownies residing in your house, you need not fear an invasion of Goblins or other troublesome beings. Brownies will not tolerate the presence of such creatures. Brownies are connected to the Element of Earth.

Dryads: These woodland sprites live in trees and groves, particularly oaks. They are slightly smaller than humans, with greenish-tinted skin and hair. They are very strong, like the roots of the trees they cultivate and protect. When their trees and groves are threatened by humans, they can create a strange terror or cause accidents to happen to the humans involved. Very cautious around humans of any kind, Dryads sometimes can be coaxed to give inspiration. Dryads can work in both the Elements of Water and Earth.

Dwarves: This race of Otherworld beings originated in Scandinavia and Germany. As with the Brownies, Dwarves seem to have emigrated to other countries with the people of those areas. Dwarves are larger than most of the Otherworld creatures. They have large heads, rugged faces, and their skin, hair, and eye coloring are varying shades of earth tones.

They are seldom seen by humans, have a king, and are known for their expertise in metallurgy and gemstones. Scandinavian tradition calls their underground cities the Land of the Nibelungen, or Niebelungen. Like the Celts, certain Dwarves are trained to remember the oral histories and knowledge of their particular clan. Their written language is primarily used for engraving on jewelry, swords, and charms. On rare occasions, they will write out a message.

Although Dwarves do not fear humans, they prefer to stay out of sight and avoid human company whenever possible. On rare occasions they may enter a home to escape bad weather. If you should find yourself hosting Dwarves, be careful that you do not insult them by rudeness. When subjected to this type of behavior, Dwarves have a tendency to see that misfortune comes your way.

The physical descriptions of Dwarves vary slightly from country to country. People of the Baltic Sea island called Rugen say that Dwarves have three classifications, each one of a different physical appearance. Icelandic and Zealand Dwarves also differ in looks. Even Hindu tradition speaks of a being, named Kubera, who fits the description of a Dwarf. Kubera lives in the Himalayas, is a small, ugly being, and is an expert in metals and gems.

Dwarves are directly connected to the Element of Earth and the Northern direction or quarter of a circle. They can help with prosperity, career success, and material gain of any kind.

Elves: This class of Otherworld being originated in the Scandinavian and North Germanic areas of Europe. The traditional word for a male Elf is *aelf* or *ylf*, while the word for female is *aelfen* or *elfen*. The English erroneously call Elves the Trooping Fairies.

Generally speaking, Elves are friendly toward humans, although German tradition says they can have a nasty temperament if offended. There are also instances in Scottish and English lore that tell of Elves causing illness and disability by their arrows. In Danish tradition, Elves are called the Elle-people, and are said to raise blue cattle. Similar beings in Japan are called Chin-Chin Kobakama; they appear as elderly beings who are very concerned about the cleanliness of a house. In northern Italy, wood Elves are called Gianes (pronounced *gee-ahwn-ayes*); they carry a little spinning wheel with which they divine the future. Similar creatures in Hindu stories are called the Rubhus; the sons of the god Indra, these beings are expert artisans and concerned with herbs and creativity.

Elves are not the nonsensical creatures usually portrayed in modern stories. Elves are as tall, or taller, than humans, but can change their size at will. They are quite beautiful, with slightly pointed ears and tipped green or brown eyes. Their eyes are not slanted, but tipped, like you find on some cats. Their skin is fair, but the hair ranges from white-blonde to black.

Socrates, Plato, and Paracelsus all wrote of Elves having beautiful palaces and sacred places, many of them built in the center of ancient groves or in the trees themselves. Elves are ruled by a king and a queen. They may live up to a thousand years, and are the guardians of vast libraries of ancient knowledge. They also are quite adept at foretelling.

There appears to be two broad classifications of Elves: light Elves and dark Elves. Light Elves are more likely to interact with humans, while dark Elves, although not directly harmful, do not care for human company. Light Elves prefer light, airy spaces for their colonies. Dark Elves prefer dark, gloomy places.

The name Elphame is a Scottish version of the Norse word *Alfheim*, or country of the Elves. Some people erroneously apply this word to the Land of Faery, or the Celtic Land of the Dead.

Elves are connected with the Element of Air, and the Eastern direction and quarter of a circle.

Fairies: There are many different names for Fairies in the European Celtic areas. On the Isle of Man, they are known as the Ferrishyn (pronounced *ferrishin*), the Little People (*Mooinjer veggey*), or Little Boys (*Guillyn veggey*). To avoid insulting Fairies, the people of Ireland and Wales call them the Gentry, the Good Folk, the Wee Folk, the Good Neighbors, or other such polite names. One of the earliest names for European Fairies was *Fays*.

Modern writers on mythology also frequently use the term Fairies to include other beings such as Anglo-Saxon Elves, the Irish gods called the Tuatha Dé Danann, and others. This is a misconception, as the remaining Celtic tales are quite clear in separating the two. Fairies are a separate Otherworld species with their own culture and history.

Dr. Katherine Briggs, in her many books on Fairy lore, states that the lore of Witches and Fairies are frequently interwoven, especially in the Celtic countries of Ireland, Scotland, and the areas settled by the Vikings. This is reasonable, as Witches frequently see and communicate with Fairies.

In Ireland and Scotland, the names Sidhe, Sidh, Sith, and Si, all pronounced *shee*, are applied to both the Fairies themselves and the barrows, mounds, or subterranean places where they live. Tradition says all of these palaces have doors connecting them with the mortal world; these doors open automatically on ancient Celtic holy days, or can be opened by a human walking counterclockwise around the entrance at the Full Moon.

Under the name Fairy, there are several species that differ in looks, habitat, behavior, and temperament, but are all part of the broad family called Fairies. Witches must know the difference to avoid offending the Fairies with whom they come in contact. Some species of Fairy are amiable toward humans, while others, particularly the solitary ones, appear wild and alien. Most Fairies live in clans or groups, but a few live by themselves.

All Celtic Fairies who wear human-like clothing are fond of the color green, with red as the next favorite. However, Manx Fairies are said to prefer blue or white. Other bright colors such as yellow, blue, and red are prominent.

All Fairies require food and sleep. They can be killed, injured, or fall ill with diseases. They are fond of dancing, singing, and music. Fairy women may spin and weave.

Fairy clans have fairs, hunts, markets, games, feasts, dances, musical contests, and processional rides. The shaggy, gray speckled horses of the Fairies are their favorite domesticated animals.

All Fairies detest humans spying on their activities and will take offense at this. If you wish to befriend Fairies, you should do five things: do not watch them without permission, be neat in your person and house, know how to keep a secret, be generous, and do not disturb their homes or dancing circles. Fairies are very cautious about humans learning their true names, and will usually give false names when asked. They are experts at creating *glamour* spells. Many of them also can shapeshift into small animals or birds when needing to escape from humans.

Solitary Fairies are the least friendly toward humans and the most likely to be offended. You never see them with other Fairies. They are cautious little entities, scarcely as large as your hand, with dark eyes and skin and tangled leaf-brown hair. They may dress in such things as old moleskins, leaves, green moss, flowers, fox skins, or cobwebs.

A diminutive species of winged Fairy, smaller than the solitaries, likes to live in gardens or around potted flowers and plants. Some of them will reside within a human house if there are well cared for plants there. These Fairies dress in leaves and flower petals held together with cobwebs. They are shy, but friendlier to humans than the wild, outdoor solitary Fairies and can teach humans how to communicate with the plant kingdom.

Very tiny, winged Water Fairies are found only around water plants. These entities make their clothing out of tiny fish scales held together by cobwebs. Their skin has an iridescent sheen like their clothing, while their almost-white hair is usually very short.

Wind Fairies are the most elusive and difficult to see, as they are almost transparent. They are little interested in communicating with humans, and prefer to spend their time flying through the air on dandelion seed, thistle bloom, and tiny leaves. They weave their clothing out of thistle down. They help to distribute wind-carried seeds of various plants to new locations.

The Seelie (Blessed) Court of Scotland are human-sized Fairies and have no wings. They are trooping Fairies, meaning that they move from one location to another at certain times of year; these moves correspond to four of the Celtic holy days: Imbolc, Beltane, Lughnasadh, and Samhain. When they ride across the country, they follow old Fairy paths, which appear to follow energy lines in the earth. Although generally friendly toward humans, they are quick to exact revenge for any insult or injury.

The Unseelie (Unblessed or evil) Court of Scotland are similar to the Seelie Court. However, these Fairies are never friendly to humans. The name Unseelie is frequently applied to solitary unpredictable Fairies, while the term Sluagh (*slooah*), or the Host, is applied to bands of these malicious Fairies. The Sluagh are the most formidable of Highland Fairies and should be avoided, unless the Witch is a staunch believer in the Old Ways. During the Wild Hunt at night, the Sluagh, accompanied by their terrifying hounds, are believed to kidnap any humans who happen to be abroad in the dark.

Members of both the Seelie and Unseelie Courts of Scotland wear plaids and bonnets, and carry swords at their sides. They always have bagpipers and musicians with them.

Fairies work in all Elements except Fire. Some of them are more proficient in one Element than in others.

Fauns: The tradition of Fauns arose in the Mediterranean area and then spread to other parts of Europe. Fauns are a milder form of the lecherous Satyr. Fauns are described as being smaller than humans, with twisted ram-horns, pointed ears, and a small goat's tail. They are half-human form and half-goat. Some species of Fauns have the legs, tail, and ears of a deer with the body and face of a young human male. They live in forests and care for the wild animals. Their hauntingly beautiful music can entice humans to dance in the moonlight.

The leader of the Fauns was known as Faunus or Lupercus to the Romans and Silvanus in Roman Britain. This leader may be another version of the Celtic god Cernunnos.

Fauns provide valuable assistance when humans are working with agriculture, animals, music, dance, or woodlands. They work with the Element of Earth.

Gargoyles: Most people know Gargoyles only because they decorate church buildings, primarily in Europe. However, Gargoyles are a much older species of Otherworld beings; their history goes much farther into the past than Christianity. The word Gargoyle probably comes from the Greek *gargarizein* (gargle) and the Latin *Gargarizare* (gargle) or *gurgulio* (gullet). Instead of being connected with the expulsion of water as is commonly associated with Gargoyles, they should be associated with the intake of air. Air is filled with spiritual power, a fact known by ancient mystics and magicians. Gargoyles know how to tap into this power and use it. Their voices are rough sounding.

Gargoyles can help with draining away negative emotions, people, and events that are affecting our lives. They are experts in moving through time and space. You need much patience when working with Gargoyles, as they are slow and deliberate in their actions. They work with the Elements of Water, Earth, and Air.

Gnomes: Like Dwarves, Gnomes are closely connected with the Element of Earth. Their name is derived from the Greek word *genomus* (earth dweller) or *gnoma* (the knowing ones). The lowland Germans called these beings Edrmanleins, while in the German Alps they were known as Heinzemannchens. The Danish and Norwegian name for them was Nisse; the Swedish name, Nissen. The Balkan cultures had more than one name for the Gnomes: Gnom, Djude, and Mano. In Denmark and Sweden, people said that nothing would go right until a Gnome came to live in the house.

Gnomes can be from four to twelve inches tall, with rosy cheeks and little round faces. The males prefer to wear a red-pointed hat, multi-colored stockings, and a long tunic that reaches to just above the knees; older males frequently have beards. The females wear long skirts, blouses, aprons, and multi-colored stockings; married females wear headscarves.

Gnomes can live for several hundred years. They marry and have families, as well as work in their chosen occupations as healers, plant growers and protectors, the study of animals, woodworking, or weaving. They are very wise in the use of wild plants and herbs for good health. Gnomes can be found living in dim forests, under large trees, in thick shrubbery, or empty birdhouses.

Since Gnomes have a great understanding of universal energy and how it can be used, they are excellent healers and magicians.

Goblins and Hobgoblins: These creatures are extremely malicious beings and should not be encouraged to take up residence anywhere in or near your house and property. They are so cunning and nasty that most other Earth Elementals will not allow them to live anywhere near them. Old traditions say that Goblins entered Europe from the Pyrenees mountains and rapidly spread across the continent and into Britain. We don't know exactly where they originated.

The Germans call them Gobelins; the Scots, Brags. One British name for these beings is Robin Hobgoblin. In northern England they are known as Padfoot or Hobgoblin, while another Scottish name for them is Boggart. Originally, they were not as malicious as they are now, but learned their evil ways from associating with undesirable humans. Fortunately, Goblins are not interested in tinkering with machinery of any kind.

Most Goblins are small, but a few have learned to shift their shape to almost human-size. Their ears are stubby, their eyes glittering with malice. Their wide grins are evil. They frequently present themselves to humans as a dark blob that quickly disappears. They are very strong and prefer to be active at night.

Goblins do not make permanent homes, but move frequently. They like old ruins, basements, and dead trees, and often run in gangs. No Witch will allow them to stay around because they are such a nuisance.

Green Men: Green Men also are known as Jack in the Green. These fairy-like woodland spirits are green in color, rather human-shaped, and wear leaves as clothing. They care for the forests and all trees, and are rarely seen by humans. One form of Green Man was Arddhu (the Dark One), or Atho; this was a Welsh semi-deity who resembled Cernunnos.

In Scotland and Cornwall, areas with vast patches of moorlands, there are no Green Men, but Brown Men or Moor Men instead. These creatures have coppery-red hair and wear moorland foliage for clothes. Oak Men are found in Germany and parts of Scandinavia, where they guard ancient groves of oak trees.

Although not particularly friendly toward humans, Green Men, Oak, and Moor Men will not harm anyone. They work with the Elements of Earth and Water.

Knockers: Knockers originally lived only in Cornish mines. However, tradition says that they found their way into Britain with the Phoenician traders centuries ago. Now they have traveled as far away as Australia, where they are called Knackers. The people of Wales know them as Coblynaus. In southern France they are called Gommes and in Germany, Wichlein.

These creatures live entirely underground, preferring to build colonies in mines and tunnels. They are friendly toward humans, but shy about being seen. They communicate by a series of knocks, hence their name. They have been known to warn miners about coming disasters or lead them to new veins of whatever ore is being mined. On occasion, they have been known to lead search parties to trapped miners. In return, miners will not whistle, swear, or talk about religion while underground, as the Knockers will be offended by these actions. Like Dwarves, Knockers work with the Element of Earth.

Mer-folk: Tales of Mer-folk exist in nearly every country that has connections with the sea. The name may come from the Latin *mare* (sea), the German *meer* (sea), the English *mere* (lake or sea), or the French *mer* (sea). In the Mediterranean cultures, these creatures were called Nereids, while in Germany their names were the Lorelei, Meriminni, or Meerfrau. They were also known in other countries: in Iceland, the Marmenill; in Denmark, the Maremind; in France, the Morgans or Morgens; in Ireland, the Merrow. In Hispanic folklore they were known as the Water-Maidens, and had a star on their foreheads. African mythology mentions Yemaya, a sea goddess with hair of long green seaweed. In Polynesia, Vatea was a half-human, half-fish man who was father of the gods and humans. Images of these creatures can be found in the ancient art of Persia, Assyria, and Babylon as well.

European folklore says that Mer-folk are human-looking down to the hips, with large flukes on a fish's tail. They live beneath the sea, coming out to sit along the shores in the sunshine. Although they have a language of their own, they can speak the language of the humans who live nearby their homes. Their hair color can be silver blonde, a strawberry-blonde, or light brown, while their eyes are either blue-green or green. Their upper body skin has a pearl-like sheen from tiny scales. Although they are beautiful, it is a cold type of beauty, not understood by humans. On occasion, Mer-folk have the magical power to change their tails into legs, thus enabling them to go ashore and mingle with unsuspecting humans.

Tradition says that if you can cultivate a friendship with the Mer-folk, they can grant you wishes and give psychic powers. All Mer-folk work with the Element of Water.

Nixies: German water sprites are known as Nixies. Nixies are also found in Scandinavia, Estonia, and Latvia. Other names for them are Neckan, Necker, Nakki, Neck, or Nickers (Iceland). They have a humanoid body with greenish skin. Their eyes are silver or bluish-silver, while their hair can be green or silver-blonde. Although they have no fishtail, their fingers and toes are webbed. They inhabit rivers and lakes instead of the ocean.

Nixies project a dangerous allure to humans, who can be bewitched by their ethereal beauty and drowned in the water. Devoid of human emotions, Nixies can be a dangerous species of Otherworld creatures. They are masters of music and spells. Nixies work with the Element of Water.

Pixies: No one knows exactly in what country the Pixies originated. At some time in the distant past, they did settle in western areas of England, particularly Cornwall, where their name is usually rendered as Piskies. Because of their mischievous behavior, they have given the word *pesky* to our language.

Although Pixies can increase or decease their size, their normal form is never larger than a human hand. Prominent characteristics are bright red hair, freckles, turned-up noses, green eyes, and sharply pointed ears. They like hats made out of foxglove blossoms or toadstools. When they wear clothing, they prefer outfits in colors that will camouflage them in the fields and forests. They love to sing, dance, make music, and play annoying tricks on humans or Otherworld creatures who are unfortunate enough to catch their attention. Fairies and Pixies will not inhabit the same areas, as there is enmity between these two species, an animosity that frequently erupts into battles.

Although the Witch must be constantly on guard when dealing with Pixies, they can teach you to be more relaxed when doing magic. They work with the Elements of Earth and Air.

Pooka and Puck: In England, this being is called Pooka or Puca. He is a solitary, mischievous type of sprite and a shapeshifter. Puck is another English name. Puck has pointed ears and likes to wear a suit of forest-green clothing. Although he prefers wild animals, he will help with domesticated ones if asked.

In Wales, they have a version of Puck called the Pwca. The Welsh Pwca is ugly, bad tempered, and likes to quarrel. English Pookas will not enter a human house, but the Welsh Pwca will. In Scandinavia and Germany, Pookas are known as Kornbockes. In Iceland it is the Puki, an evil spirit. It is not wise to try to communicate with the Pooka. The Pooka works with the Element of Earth.

Selkies: This type of Otherworld creature lives only around the Faroe Islands, the Orkney Islands, and the Shetlands near Scotland. They are not members of the Merfolk, but are Seal-folk instead. They live in underwater cities surrounded by huge air bubbles, and wear their seal-form only to get from one place to another. They work with the Elements of Water and Earth.

Their usual shape and appearance is like that of humans, but with large, liquid eyes. Selkies are amorous beings and will woo human women into a relationship, although they will not stay with them. Several families in Scotland claim they descend from Selkies. Selkies often come out of the water at night and visit nearby taverns. Although they have an amiable relationship with most humans, Selkies do not like seal hunters. When they encounter such men, they will call up wild storms and try to sink the boats. A member of the Water Element, Selkies can teach you to control your emotions.

Sylphs: This Otherworld creature does not have a solid body at all. Rather, its shape and appearance are constantly changing and wispy as a breeze. There is little actual folklore about sylphs, who are so ethereal in nature and thought that they rarely communicate with humans. Their attention span is extremely short, their emotions fleeting, and their only goal is riding the breezes and winds. Members of the Air Element, Sylphs are helpful in teaching Witches to open their minds to a wide range of associations and ideas.

Zephyrs are larger than Sylphs and tend to ride storm winds and stronger breezes. They also are ethereal in appearance. Both Sylphs and Zephyrs work with the Element of Air.

Trolls: Trolls lived in the Scandinavian and North Germanic areas for thousands of years before they emigrated to other parts of the world. The Swedish people call them Trolds, while in Denmark they are Hill Men or Berg People. Trolls come in all sizes, from very small to enormous, are often indistinct in form, and can be invisible at will. Primarily, they resemble moss-covered rocks shaped vaguely like humans, but with little or no necks. Although they are very strong, they are not known for intelligence. However, a few Trolls have learned to work at the forge or do mechanics. They are most active at night, as they cannot tolerate the sun.

Trolls usually prefer to live in the mountains, deep forests, or underground, far away from human cities. Every hill, however small, has the possibility of being the home of Trolls and their family.

People in the Scandinavian countries believe that Trolls are very dangerous. So do the people of the Feroes Islands, who call them the Foddenskkmaend, Underground People, or Hollow Men.

If you are very cautious and respectful toward Trolls, they can teach you the magic of mountains and stones. Trolls work only with the Element of Earth.

Undines: The name Undine comes from the Latin word *unda*, which means wave. The name of their traditional leader is Nicksa or Necksa. They work only with the Element of Water.

Sometimes called the Water-folk, Undines, in one form or another, live in every source of non-oceanic water, such as springs, creeks, rivers, lakes, marshes, and waterfalls. A small species of Undine can be found near fountains, tiny slow-moving creeks, and little springs.

Undines, like the Mer-folk, have scales and webbed hands and feet. They have sharp, pointed teeth, tiny scales all over their bodies, and huge, round, fish-like eyes. There are webs between their fingers and toes, and their stringy hair resembles slimy dead grass. Undines come in a variety of sizes, speak the human language of their area, and can communicate if they wish. All Water-folk love music and singing. However, some species of these Undines are very unreliable and try to tempt humans into the water where they drown. They are unpredictable and not to be trusted.

The Water-folk who inhabit fountains, little springs, and tiny creeks are quite small. Tiny iridescent scales cover their human-like bodies and sparkle with beautiful rainbow colors in the sunlight. Their children have small tails like tadpoles and cannot leave the water until they mature. The adults, who resemble miniature humans, have the ability to propel themselves up waterfalls, dancing in the water as they go. They do not have wings or fins. They are very shy, only revealing themselves to humans who are patient enough to cultivate their friendship.

Undines of the larger waterfalls are human-sized and very much like their smaller relatives of the fountains. Their beautiful bodies twist, leap, and dance in the water and the spray. Their young also go through a tadpole-like stage. They are very knowledgeable about healing, but seldom work with humans.

Another species of Undine live in fast-moving streams and larger rivers. Some of these attractive creatures have fishtails, while others do not.

The Lake-folk is the most amiable species of Undines and very wise in the ancient arts of healing, magic, and divination. This species looks most like humans, with the webs of their fingers and toes being almost undetectable. Although they have a paler complexion than humans, they rarely have any scales. They are capable of leaving their lake homes and living with humans for long periods of times. Sometimes they will marry humans and have children. Frequently, these children are very psychic and skilled in medicine. In Wales, these Lake-folk are sometimes called the Gwragedd Annwn (pronounced *goorageth anoon*).

Not all astral companions are even remotely human in nature, but come from the animal kingdom. Native Americans speak of their totem animal helpers, while European shamans call them animal allies. These creatures are explained more fully in Chapter 15.

Study Work

Set up a small space dedicated to a particular type of Elemental or Otherworld creature. Do *not* try to contact any of the negative personality beings in the above list. Their descriptions are given only to warn you should you find them in your vicinity. Sit near this space for a short time each day and send thoughts of greeting and friendship. Note any unusual activity, such as movement seen in the corner of your eye, the feeling of fingers in your hair, a sense of warmth or coldness, or whispery sounds that you can't quite understand. When an incident occurs, close your eyes and reach out with your intuition. Don't think you know what or who it is. Let the impressions flow without interruption. Note your first impression, which is more likely to be true than impressions that you run through the analytical part of your mind.

After a week, change the items on the elemental shelf to match those of a different Otherworld entity. Again, observe and record your experiences. Repeat this action until you have tried to contact many of the Otherworld creatures listed here.

CHAPTER 15

Animal Allies and Familiars

The traditional Witch's familiar was, and still is, usually thought to be a physical entity such as a cat (particularly a black one), a toad, or a dog. However, it is more likely that Witches will have astral creatures as familiars—or animal allies—to help with magic. These helpers develop a psychic link with the Witch. Witches may also use these animal allies as guides during meditation or as models for strengthening their character in some manner.

Totem Animals is a term belonging to the Native American culture, not to Wicca. Wicca is a European religion with some ancient connections to European shamanism, which used the term Animal Allies instead. Celtic clan totems were known, such as the Epidii (Horse People), the Cattraighe (Cat Folk), Brannovices (Raven Folk), and the Caerini (People of the Sheep). The clans displayed the pelt of their totem animal on a pole or shield in their villages, and the head of the animal was sculpted on their helmets and the animal's symbol painted on shields or their bodies. Some of their legendary heroes were also connected with certain animals and they were forbidden to kill or eat them. We still find animal allies used as sports mascots.

The word Familiar means a creature, human or otherwise, from this physical world or the Otherworld, that one frequently sees, experiences, and communicates with. Witches use familiars, primarily Otherworld ones, to act as their eyes and ears for discovering information in this world or other worlds. The advantage of having an Otherworld familiar is that, since its body is not of physical vibration, it can cross time, space, and worlds to find information that the Witch needs or wants. Physical world familiars are limited only to what they see and hear in their immediate vicinity.

To find and befriend an Otherworld familiar, the Witch must go on a journey that crosses the boundaries between the worlds, into Otherworld planes of existence. This is usually done through a meditation directed toward this goal.

Another reason for studying physical animals and befriending the same creatures in the Otherworld is to tap into their Otherworld energy so that you can use the power of shapeshifting and invisibility. The art of shapeshifting and invisibility are mental powers only. The human body cannot change into an animal form, nor can it become invisible to the human eye.

In shapeshifting, Witches, in their mind, assume an animal's traits, characteristics, and behavior, thus creating that animal's image in the subconscious mind of anyone who sees them. If the observer is extremely alert and aware, Witches will not be able to impress that person's subconscious mind. However, the vast majority of people are not that aware of everything in their immediate surroundings at any given time, which makes it possible for the Witch to pass unnoticed most of the time. However, you must choose an animal that would normally be seen in the circumstances in which you find yourself. Otherwise, the very appearance of a strange animal not normally found in that area will draw attention to you. Reptiles are not good choices unless they are native to the environment, while aquatic creatures are useful only if you are in their natural habitat. However, you can use any animal ally as a guide or teacher, or as a model if you need certain traits strengthened in your personality and character.

It takes a tremendous amount of practice before you become proficient at shapeshifting. A very adept shapeshifter's illusion will hold up to close scrutiny, but there are few such adepts. Most Witches can learn to hold the illusion long enough to remove themselves from any situation, unless they are being watched by another astute Witch or a learned magician.

Shapeshifting has always been closely connected with certain deities and hero-deities. This may be the reason that some deities are portrayed in partial animal forms, are said to be able to assume animal shapes, or have specific animals as their symbols. The Egyptian pantheon is an excellent example of partial animal forms, while the Celtic deities, among others, are said to be adept at shapeshifting.

A Witch may feel drawn to an animal or animals immediately and be repelled by others. Begin your study of shapeshifting and animal allies by working with one animal that attracts you. Although it is advantageous to learn to communicate with all animals in this world or the Otherworld, Witches will discover that some creatures simply will not allow them to work with them. Take such action as a sign that these animals will not be amenable to helping you and are best avoided.

The best method for familiarizing yourself with your animal allies, indeed with all astral animals, is to meet them in meditation and on astral journeys. You can enhance your connections with such creatures by using little statues, pictures, or naturally gathered parts, such as feathers and tufts of fur.

Invisibility, which requires the same techniques as shapeshifting, does not mean the human body suddenly becomes transparent to the physical eyes of anyone in the area. It means that the Witch mentally assumes concealing traits or characteristics of specific animals, not the bodily image of these animals, as with shapeshifting. These traits enable Witches to use the wiliness of the chosen animal to remove themselves from dangerous or uncomfortable situations or to avoid notice by particular people.

Another use for assuming animal characteristics is if Witches need to instill in their own spirit and personality certain traits needed to accomplish specific tasks, such as having to face a person who verbally attacked or threatened you in the past. For example, you find that you must meet with someone once close to you who has the nasty habit of verbally attacking you and making you feel insecure. Witches might meditate upon, and call into themselves, the protective qualities of the wolf or the fox. The wolf is very intelligent, known to outwit the most intelligent of hunters, and protects itself by moving in a pack. The fox, on the other hand, is extremely wily in avoiding traps and escaping danger unharmed. Projecting the fearless wolf is helpful if you need to force another person to leave you alone physically, but the fox is better for outwitting stronger and larger enemies and getting you out of tight spots without a physical confrontation.

The following list of animals is by no means complete. If you are attracted to an animal not on this list, study the animal's characteristics carefully and then practice assuming its traits.

Badger: The badger is an animal that is not often seen, as it generally shuns areas of human habitation. It is extremely tenacious for its size. It will back into a hole where its attacker must come from one direction. From this position of power, the badger can easily face down adversaries that are much larger and stronger. This animal can help you learn to fight for your rights and spiritual ideas.

Bat: The bat is primarily a creature of the night, unless forced from its daylight roosting places. It can travel at high speed without colliding with anything because of its very efficient method of guidance by its cries, a type of radar.

Bear: The bear has been respected by every culture in which it is known. A creature of dreams, visions, and astral travel, the bear is useful in learning patience, transformation, balance, harmony, and defense.

Bee: Many cultures believed that bees were the souls of the dead. Sometimes this insect was considered to be a solar creature, sometimes a lunar one. Many deities were associated with bees. It is impossible to communicate one-on-one with a single bee, as this insect does not think independently of the swarm to which it belongs. Thus, working with bees goes best if one has a group project where one must have harmony and balance to succeed.

Blackbird: To the Irish and Welsh, the blackbird was associated with goddesses. The Welsh goddess Rhiannon had three blackbirds that sang humans into trances from their perch in the World Tree of the Otherworlds. This bird aids with deep meditations, the learning of trance, and shows how to discover mystic secrets.

Butterfly: To the Chinese, the butterfly symbolized immortality, beauty in old age, long life, and joy. The Greek, German, and Slavonic words for butterfly also mean nightmare, which connects this creature with Underworld goddesses. Several cultures believed that butterflies were the souls of the dead. Call upon the butterfly to study reincarnation, transform your life, and divine the future.

Cat, Domestic: Known as a creature that will fight fiercely when cornered or threatened, the domestic cat can be a strong protector. It is also wise in the ways of retreat when necessary. The cat can help on astral journeys when you are seeking hidden information, or teach you how to be more perceptive in seeing spirits.

Cattle: Cattle are known to many cultures throughout the world. The general classification is further broken down into the bull and the cow. The Bull is always connected with the Pagan God and fertility, while the Cow is the creature of many goddesses. Both will aid in learning how to be aware of all that happens around you, how to be content with your life, and when to retreat from danger.

Cheetah: This member of the cat family has many features that resemble those of a dog: hair texture, non-retractable claws, and the pads of its feet. Known for its swiftness and inscrutable gaze, the cheetah can help you develop self-esteem, fearlessness, and a more confident bearing.

Cock or Rooster: Cocks are associated with many deities, such as Athena, Demeter, Apollo, Hermes, Anubis, Osiris, and Nephthys. Scandinavian legend tells of two powerful roosters: Vidofnir who sits on top of the World Tree and Fjalar who lives in Valhalla and will warn of the end of the world by his crowing. Cocks can teach how to dispel evil and negativity by the use of the voice. They are excellent psychic guardians.

Crane: Another sacred bird said to be a messenger for the deities, the crane is also considered a weather prophet. In China it was said to carry souls of the dead into the afterlife, while in Ireland and Scotland it was associated with the goddess Cailleach and the god Manannán mac Lir. The crane aids in learning to enter a higher state of consciousness, in learning magic and astral travel, and in reaching the deeper mysteries.

Crow: This bird, although considered very wise, is most frequently associated with gods/goddesses of death and the Underworld. A bird of ambivalent qualities, the crow teaches prophesying and shapeshifting, as well as boldness, skill, cunning, and how to access past lives.

Deer: The *Stag* has long been a symbol of the Lord of the Underworld or the Otherworld, while the *Doe* was connected with shapeshifting and magic. Any white deer seen in a meditation or while on an astral journey will lead you to a person or place that will reveal messages to you. Such white deer in Celtic lore always had red ears and eyes. Deer aid in discovering alternate paths to a goal, in interpreting dreams, in understanding a necessary transformation, or in teaching how to accept others as they are.

Dog or Hound: The domesticated dog can be valuable for tracing information through a confusion of situations, thus finding the truth. It can also help with companionship, intuition, and protection.

Dolphin or Porpoise: A creature of the Element of Water, the dolphin has long captured the attention of humans. The Greeks associated these creatures with the ocean goddesses called Nereides, the goddess Thetis, and the god Apollo. Dolphins can aid in discovering the truth, learning elemental magic, releasing negatives, and learning eloquence, trust, and change.

Dragon: A variety of dragons have been known in nearly every world culture. It is one of the earliest symbols of the Great Goddess. Many cultures chose this creature to symbolize royalty or power. The dragon can help with any need of the Witch or magician, however, their strongest powers are in teaching spiritual subjects, the powers of change and transformation, and protection.

Dragonfly: This insect has much the same symbolism as the butterfly. However, it can teach you about the meaning of dreams, uncovering and identifying illusions, and receiving mystic messages from spirit.

Eagle: Some species of this bird is known around the world. As a solar creature, the eagle has long been associated with power, courage, and victory. Use the eagle to gain keen insight, take swift action, find hidden spiritual truths, and create a strong connection with Otherworld entities and guides.

Eel: The eel seldom attracts admiration. However, it is helpful in teaching how to get out of bad situations.

Elephant: As with the Hindu god Ganesha, elephants help with the removal of obstacles and barriers to success. Buddhists believe that the elephant represents wisdom, strength, prudence, and fertility.

Falcon: These swift birds are related to hawks and eagles. The Egyptian god Horus was associated with the falcon, as was the Greek goddess Circe. This bird is always connected with magic, shamans, and astral travel. Use the falcon's talents to send soul-healing energy to a dying person or in any healing.

Fox: Although a member of the dog family, the fox has elliptical eyes, not circular as do dogs. There are species of fox in many places around the world. The fox is traditionally known for its great cunning, endurance, and the ability to turn the tables on pursuers. This creature can help when dealing with difficult people, or when you want to be inconspicuous.

Frog: Since Neolithic times, the frog has been a symbol of the Goddess in Her Mother and rebirth phase. In China, the frog was associated with prosperity and healing, while in Greece and Rome it symbolized fertility and harmony with one's lover. Ask the frog for help in initiation, transformation, and clearing negatives from your life. Like frogs, *toads* help with long life, prosperity, new beginnings, and good luck.

Griffin: This creature was described as enormous in size, with the head and front parts of an eagle and the back parts of a lion. It frequently was associated with solar deities, especially in the Middle East and Mediterranean areas. If you need instruction on the relationship between psychic energy and spiritual enlightenment, call upon the griffin.

Hare or Rabbit: Rabbits and hares are not the same animals, though they look much the same. The Hindus connected the hare with the moon, as did the Chinese. The Germanic tribes associated the hare with the Spring goddess Eostre. These animals can aid with transformations, intuition, quick thinking, and hidden wisdom.

Hawk: The sharp-eyed hawk is related to the falcon. Its symbolism is nearly identical to that of the falcon and eagle. A solar bird, the hawk was associated with Horus and Ptah in ancient Egypt, Apollo and Artemis in Greece, and Mithra in Persia. In Celtic legend there is a story of the greatest and wisest animal, the Hawk of Achill. Use the hawk to develop clear-sightedness, recall past lives, to overcome problems, and to make the right decisions.

Hedgehog: This little spiny creature is only found in the Old World and the Orient. They are sacred in China. The hedgehog can protect itself without harming others.

Heron: The heron has always been a mystical bird that carries messages from the gods to humans. This bird can aid in gaining self-confidence, being patient, and succeeding by methodical work.

Horse: The horse has been a sacred, spiritual animal in many world cultures. It was known to the Babylonians as far back as 2,300 B.C.E. In such diverse cultures as Scandinavia, China, and the Celts, horses, particularly white ones, were connected with the gods and goddesses. Horses can aid as guardians on journeys (physical or astral), help overcome obstacles, and are a symbol of freedom.

Jaguar: This jungle inhabitant is the largest cat of the Western Hemisphere. Although sometimes black, the jaguar is usually a tawny color marked with black rosettes. Extremely cunning and fearless, this creature can help you to walk in the Otherworlds without fear.

Leopard: This cat, although similar in some appearances to the jaguar, is very different. It is very cunning, fierce, and intelligent. You can call upon the astral leopard for perseverance and cunning, particularly on astral journeys.

Lion: This tawny beast of Africa can help with family problems, particularly when desiring to strengthen family ties. It can also teach you to release stress and tension.

Lizard: This creature is related to both snakes and crocodiles, and lives all over the world, except in extremely cold climates. To the Greeks and Egyptians, the lizard symbolized good fortune and mystical wisdom, but the Persians viewed it as a creature of the god of Darkness. The lizard can aid you in understanding dreams and facing difficult decisions. The *chameleon*, a member of the lizard family, is most helpful in learning how to stay out of trouble and be inconspicuous when danger approaches.

Magpie: The magpie is a member of the crow family. In the East, this bird symbolized joy and good fortune, while in the West it represented trouble and bad omens. Use the magpie's talents to learn divination.

Mouse: Although the common mouse has been a troublesome creature all over the world, many cultures held it in high regard at one time. The mouse can teach cunning, the ability to remain inconspicuous, attention to small details, and harmony.

Otter: There are two species of otters; one that lives in fresh water, and one that prefers the sea. The Celts considered the otter a very magical creature that frequently accompanied the god Cernunnos. This animal is helpful in uncovering hidden talents and treasures, gaining wisdom, surviving a crisis, and making new friends.

Owl: Since the beginning of time, the owl has been associated with goddesses, wisdom, Underworld deities, and prophecy. In Scotland, the word *cailleach*, which means "owl," is the same as the name for the goddess of death. Learn from this bird how to interpret dreams, to prophesy, to unmask people who try to deceive you, to practice magic and shapeshifting, and to find hidden spiritual truths.

Pig: In many cultures in which the pig was known, the classification of pig, in a spiritual sense, was broken down into the categories of boar and sow. The wild *Boar* once ranged across Europe, North Africa, the West Coast of the United States, and into Asia and Siberia. It was a vicious, unpredictable animal. The boar aids with courage, concealment, and protection. The *Sow* can be even more unpredictable if she has young with her. She represents cunning, intelligence, the knowledge of past lives, and the ability to set up an effective ambush to take care of attackers.

Rat: Rats have an ambivalent history in most cultures, since they carry diseases and cause more crop damage than any other rodent. However, the Japanese use the rat as the first sign in their zodiac and a symbol of wealth. Their god Daikoku, deity of prosperity, has a white rat as his companion. Rats represent cunning, stealth, and tracking down something you seek.

Raven: Like the crow, the raven has long been connected to gods and goddesses of death, war, and the Underworld. However, it was used to represent one of the grades of initiation to the Persian god Mithra. In Wales and Ireland, the word *bran* means "raven"; it is particularly associated with Celtic deities such as Branwen, Bran the Blessed, Mórrígan, and Badb. The raven is of great help in learning divination and traveling through the Underworld during astral journeys.

Salmon: The salmon was considered sacred by the Celtic and Norse cultures. It is always associated with great wisdom, particularly spiritual wisdom. Call upon this fish to learn deep meditation and divination.

Scorpion: Technically a member of the spider family, this creature has had evil and/or negative connotations in many cultures. However, the Egyptian goddess Selket, who protected the dead, always had a scorpion on her head. Use scorpion power carefully. However, it is valuable in sending negative energy back to the senders.

Snake: Snakes in general have long been creatures of the Goddess. They can help with developing psychic talents and creative power, as well as transmuting your life to a level of higher goals. The *adder* is known in Britain, Scotland, and Wales. It provides knowledge about reincarnation, and how to shed one phase of life for another. The deadly *cobra* is native to Africa, India, Asia, and the Near East. It is useful in seeking spiritual Goddess wisdom.

Spiders: Although spiders have a long association with such deities as Athena, the Norns, Holda, and Spider Woman, most people are uncomfortable working with these creatures, even on the astral level. One must not have ambiguous goals in mind when working with spider energy. This insect can teach how to untangle yourself from a negative situation, as well as making new beginnings, finding wisdom, and starting a new life.

Squirrel: There are a wide variety of these tree-climbing animals in the world. In Scandinavian folklore, a squirrel was the messenger of the gods. This creature was an emblem of the Celtic queen Medb. Squirrels can teach how to prepare for the future and how to rest when you are not busy. They can help you become aware of subtle messages of coming change and potential dangers.

Swan: This bird is graceful, beautiful, and very aggressive. In ancient Greece, it was connected with Apollo, the Muses, and Aphrodite. The Hindus associated it with the goddesses Devi and Sarasvati and the god Brahma. In Norse tales a form of this bird was taken by the shapeshifting Valkyries. Swans aid in the interpretation of symbolic dream images, help you develop your intuition and psychic abilities, and help you make any type of transition in life.

Tiger: This huge member of the cat family is found from Siberia to India and the Malay Peninsula. Most tigers are yellow with black stripes, although those in Siberia may be white with black stripes. The tiger outdoes all members of the cat family in strength, savagery, and cunning. The tiger as an animal ally is useful in learning how to deal quickly with problems without overanalyzing them.

Turtle or Tortoise: Several Chinese deities were associated with this creature: P'an Ku (the world-architect), Wu Hsien, and Hsi Wang-Mu. To the Hindus, the tortoise is a lunar animal that supports the world and is a creature of the god Prajapati. In ancient Greece and Rome, the turtle was the animal of Aphrodite and Hermes. This creature is valuable to call upon for learning patience and how to protect yourself with psychic armor.

Unicorn: This animal is a favorite mythical beast with many people. The chariot of the goddess Artemis was pulled by eight unicorns. The unicorn was also associated with other lunar deities in many cultures. This animal can help you discover your unlimited individual power, wisdom, success, prosperity, gentleness, and purity of the soul.

Wolf: Like the dog, the wolf prefers companionship and will remain with a pack. Wolves are very intelligent and can lead you to an Otherworld teacher when you need help. The wolf is also valuable when you need to outwit those who want to harm you, when you are seeking the meaning of dreams, and when you desire protection and wisdom.

Vulture: Several Egyptian goddesses were portrayed as wearing vulture headdresses. This bird has always been connected with death and rebirth, the Underworld, and the Dark Goddess. Use the vulture's traits to understand the cycle of death and rebirth and communicate with dead loved ones.

Whale: This creature is the largest of the sea mammals. The connection with deities goes back to at least the Babylonian goddess Derceto, who swallowed and then rebirthed the god Ea-Oannes. The Slavic culture has a story of the world supported by four giant whales. The whale can teach you how to use music and sound to balance, heal, and do magic.

Wren: This tiny bird was particularly sacred to the Druids, who divined the future from its music. The wren aids in receiving messages from the gods and learning to live your life to the fullest.

Study Work

Carefully observe what you see each day for two weeks. You may see actual animals or pictures or statues of certain animals a number of times within that period. When you see the animal or a representation of that animal more than five times in a week, meditate upon the creature to see what it has to teach you.

CHAPTER 16

Sacred Space

Sacred space is the area that you use only for ritual and magic. It can be as simple or elaborate as the individual wishes. This space can be a large permanent place, small areas in more than one place, or a temporary spot set up while traveling. Broadly defined, any place is sacred when certain ritual items are set up and/or a consecrated circle is cast there. However, except for rituals by very experienced groups, a public place that may have cowan watchers is not a good idea. The more skeptics and hecklers you have watching, the more your concentration is eroded and the more the raised power is dissipated.

Ancient Witches either cast their sacred circles secretly in their homes or out in nature at natural power places, such as crossroads, stone circles, hilltops, or near ancient healing wells that were visited by others very rarely. They met at night because that was the ancient practice and because fewer non-Wiccan people would see them. To be reported as a Witch meant a death sentence.

If you have an extra room to turn into a ritual room, feel fortunate. Otherwise, you must devise some way to set aside a corner of a room in which you allow no intrusion of everyday items. If you have a room you can dedicate to rituals and magic, there are a few things you should consider. Try to locate the room away from central areas of household traffic so you can have privacy in your work. If necessary, install a lock on the door. The last thing you want is someone entering the room to ask what you are doing in the middle of a spell or ritual.

If you share the house with others, you may wish to make a sign that says, "Do not disturb. Work in progress," to hang on the door. Unless someone is bleeding profusely, someone is dying, the house is on fire, the police are battering down the door, or a crowd with pitchforks and torches is at the threshold, family members should be instructed not to interrupt when your door is closed and the sign out.

You may also wish to consider removing any carpet from the room and replacing it with tile. This is a safety precaution, as accidentally spilled burning incense and charcoal incense blocks can start fires, and candle wax is difficult to remove from carpet. Essential oils stain carpets and can be impossible to remove. If you do get candle wax in carpets, you can remove most of it with a warm iron and paper towels. Place two paper towels over the wax spill and move the warm iron gently over it. However, certain colors will leave a permanent stain whatever you do.

Windows can present another problem for the ritual worker. You obviously do not want your neighbors setting up their chairs complete with soft drinks and popcorn to watch what you are doing. A good set of heavy drapes or blinds can solve this problem.

Decorating a dedicated ritual room is the dream of all Witches. You may want to use restraint in decorating the rest of the house, but when doing a ritual room, all your creativity can come out. Although you may think you would like the walls painted black or the darkest blue you can find, the color white is the best choice. Dark colors can make you feel like you are standing in a very small, enclosed place, as they tend to visually diminish the room's size. The color white encompasses and reflects all other colors, and opens up the visual dimensions of a room. If you want a dark color in the room, consider painting black or dark blue on the ceiling, and then decorate that area with small, silvery stars, the moon, or clouds. If you are an artist, you can paint murals on the walls and ceiling, provided you are not renting the house. In lieu of murals, you can decorate the walls with pictures and posters that remind you of the Goddess and the God, or other Pagan symbols and scenes.

The main feature of your ritual room should always be the altar. This can be a small table or a dresser with rollers on the bottom. Whether your altar is permanently set, or must be put up and taken down each time, most Witches say that the altar should be positioned either in the center of the working area or on the eastern edge of the circle. In the beginning, the apprentice should follow this rule and stand at the altar, facing the eastern direction. Only when Witches become adept at working should they consider other positions. My altar stands in the center of the circle, thus making it easier to move completely around the circle. However, it is my personal choice to stand in the North when working with a partner, or to stand facing the

North when working alone. I still follow the traditional method of casting the circle by beginning and ending in the east.

There should be small sturdy stands at each of the four directions to hold candles for the quarter guardians. Place each candle in a metal or fireproof holder with a large edge to catch drips.

Fabric covers for altars are very nice, particularly if you have several different ones, perhaps to reflect the seasonal holy days. These are discussed in more detail in Chapter 17.

If you have the space, you may also wish to have within the ritual room a large cupboard or a dresser with drawers for storing supplies you use frequently and for exhibiting deity statues, extra tools, collections of stones, and perhaps your magical books. The closet can hold ritual garments and sets of shelves for extra supplies. If you like music with your rituals, be sure to save a space for a tape deck. Bookcases are also useful for exhibiting and storing collections of deity statues, extra ritual tools, stones, shells, and supplies you might want at hand during a ritual.

Many Witches prefer to do their rituals with the only light coming from altar candles. If you find, however, that this makes it too difficult to see your Book of Shadows, use the electric lights. This doesn't make you a nontraditional Witch. Some people see better than others in the near dark.

If you do not have a separate room for ritual, you can still be a faithful, practicing Witch. Choose an out-of-the-way place in your apartment or house where you can work undisturbed. In this space, have a dresser with rollers or a special small table that can be placed in the proper position when needed. Keep your ritual tools and supplies in a place that is separate from mundane articles. If you choose the dresser, you can use the drawers for storage of these items. You can set up and take down your altar each time you do ritual.

Besides your primary altar, you may wish to have several smaller altars or devotional spaces around your home. These can be shelves, ledges, or corner tables where you can arrange small statues, stones, shells, flowers, or other articles that remind you of a particular deity or deity aspect. These are nice as reminders throughout the day to remember your calling as a Witch and to remind yourself that the Goddess and the God are part of everyday life.

Wherever you plan to use candles, however, be very certain that the lighted candle is well away from the wall, draperies, or other flammable objects. The heat from a candle flame can start a fire up to two feet away. If you choose to use a shelf for an altar, I strongly recommend that you do not use lighted candles.

When you set up a devotional altar, or even your regular altar, you should think about the symbolism and significance of what you are doing. Each object should speak to you of a step along your spiritual path. Do not choose objects because you admired them on someone else's altar or in a book. It is best to not clutter your spiritual ritual space with items that have no meaning to you.

Above all, do not spend hundreds of dollars for an altar and/or devotional shelves. Begin with what you have at hand. You can always replace or refinish furniture later if you wish.

Study Work

Choose a place in your home or room and set it aside for spiritual and ritual purposes only. You may have both a shelf or space on a dresser for everyday workings, where you place your ritual items only when you need them. Choose a special dresser, cabinet, or at least a drawer that holds your basic ritual and magical supplies. Allow nothing mundane to encroach on this dedicated space.

CHAPTER 17

Ritual Tools

There are a few basic, traditional ritual tools that are used by all Witches. These are the dagger, wand, two goblets, the pentacle disk, a white pillar candle, an incense burner, a bottle for consecrated water, a container for salt, a candlesnuffer, non-flammable candle holders and candles for the four directions, a small metal cauldron, and your Book of Shadows. See Chapter 33 for more information on the Book of Shadows. These are the basic, minimum tools for ritual and spellworking.

In fact, when starting out with ritual, you can get by with a bare minimum of tools, which includes a wand, incense burner, white pillar candle, and cups for the water and juice. People under a certain age are forbidden by the laws of many states from having a dagger, which is considered a weapon. Whatever you acquire for ritual tools, do it slowly and with much thought before purchase.

Please remember that expensive, elaborate tools do not make a better Witch. All power comes from Witches themselves, not from a tool. A Witch must be responsible at all times, and when you spend vast sums of money for tools, you are not being responsible. The elaborate glass wands are a good example. They are too easily broken to be practical, and cost more than anyone should pay for a good, serviceable wand. Start with inexpensive items that meet your needs. You can always add new tools later. Some of the best rituals tools are those you make yourself.

Tradition says that a Witch should never haggle over the price paid for any ritual item or supply. To haggle and think ill of the cost fills the items with negative vibrations. If you purchase whatever you need without haggling, you will find that good fortune comes to you.

Every ritual tool should be blessed and consecrated before using it. The ritual method for doing this is given at the end of this chapter. Some Witches believe that every tool should be marked with the Witch's name or strange symbols, sigils, runes, and words from an ancient, magical, or nonsensical language; this practice comes from ceremonial magic, not ancient Witchcraft. No sensible Witch from ancient times would have put her name on anything that might have condemned her to the stocks or worse. The idea behind this is that Witches must make the tool theirs and impart to it their personal vibrations. You can do this without engraving or painting. You consecrate each tool, claim it as yours alone, use it during rituals, and don't let others handle it.

Witches, during early times, did not have special ritual tools. Common household items did the work of these tools, thus making it difficult for persecutors to put "tools" on display at trials. Most Witches were not wealthy enough to have a separate set of tools, and the possession of a sword by a commoner could bring instant punishment. It was common for Witches of later centuries to have a special container, sometimes referred to as a "trash box," for keeping their special ritual tools out of sight.

Every new Witch knows about the black-handled, double-bladed dagger, called the athame (pronounced *ah-THAY-mee*), and every new Witch dreams of having a dagger that is beautiful and different. The truth is, in a pinch, a common kitchen knife works just as well. I suspect that the definition of the "traditional athame" may have arisen in medieval ceremonial magic or with Gerald Gardner. Today, many Witches have athames that do not have black handles. If you want to make your own dagger, buy a blade from a knife supplier and glue on a wooden handle that you can shape to fit your hand and paint black. However, you can choose to purchase a suitable knife (black handle or not), and it will be appropriate. Daggers should not be too long. A nine- or ten-inch dagger, measured from end of hilt to end of blade, is quite sufficient. Daggers are not used to cut or kill anything. They are a means of summoning, controlling, or banishing spirits and Otherworldly powers. The ritual dagger is also used to trace out a magic circle. The dagger is of the Element of Fire.

It is nice to have a leather sheath for your dagger to prevent it from getting dirty or to keep people from cutting their fingers. The sheath is also handy to attach to a belt or cord girdle if you are taking part in a group ritual.

Among artifacts of ancient Egypt, archaeologists have discovered an ivory ceremonial knife used by magicians. It is a flat, thin, curved instrument that is carved with images of animals and mythical creatures. Ancient texts say this knife was used to draw an invisible line of magic around a person or place.

The wand is a symbol of the Element of Air and the magician or Witch's will power. Unlike the dagger that compels and controls, the wand directs energy, will power, and thought. Aleister Crowley considered this tool to be the means by which a magician or Witch could draw down spiritual fire, just as the god Prometheus brought fire from heaven. It is not a threatening, demanding tool, but one of persuasion. Wands need not be expensive and fragile to be powerful. A simple wand made from a small tree branch can be just as effective. However, like the dagger, a Witch soon seems to collect a number of different types of wands for various purposes. Pagan shops have quite a collection of unique, handmade wands at reasonable prices.

If you want to make your own wand, and have no access to discarded tree limbs, purchase a piece of small doweling no longer than eighteen inches. Since the wand is a tool used to direct magical energy, you can fasten or glue a crystal or another stone onto one end to aid in this. Handmade wands can be painted, decorated with cording or stones, or carved to suit a Witch's individual desires.

The two goblets or chalices can be made of metal, ceramic, glass, or pewter. If you choose pewter or ceramics, be certain to purchase a goblet made to U.S. safety standards. Foreign pewter and ceramics frequently will leach lead into the juice or wine. One goblet will hold the consecrated water, used to seal the circle. The other will hold the juice or wine, used during the ritual to symbolize the joining of the Goddess and the God. Goblets or chalices are of the Element of Water.

The pentacle is a wooden, metallic, or ceramic disk with a five-pointed star painted or engraved on it. The pentacle represents the Element of Earth on the altar. Aleister Crowley and others consider the pentacle an inert object. However, it symbolizes the grounding and manifestation point for the arrival of spiritual energy into the physical world. Small wooden circles can be purchased at hobby shops, and then covered entirely on the top surface and edges with silver or gold paint. When this paint is dry, paint the pentagram, or five-pointed star, in the center of this disk. If you wish, you can paint zodiacal signs or Wiccan/Pagan symbols at the edge around this star. Both goblets are set on the pentacle disk during certain parts of the ritual.

The four essential candles and their holders are mentioned in Chapter 16, Sacred Space. One candle is placed in each of the four directions or quarters. Since they are burning during most of the ritual, metal holders are safest. It is also a good idea to place each of these candles on a small table or stand of a convenient height. The traditional Western candle colors are in the East, yellow; in the South, red; in the West,

Pentacle Disk

blue; and in the North, dark green or black. Candles can be of both the Element of Fire and the Element of Air.

Some groups have elaborate tall, metal candelabras at each direction. However, the taller the holder, the more unstable it can be, and these candelabras are quite expensive. Also, do not place candles directly on the floor. It only takes a moment of carelessness to set someone's robe on fire.

The thick white pillar candle is placed on the altar so the Witch can read the ritual. Some writers recommend both a white and a black pillar candle on the altar to symbolize balance. However, since I use electric lights instead of trying to see my work with a candle flame, I use a single white pillar candle. I also use this main candle for lighting the small taper that is used to ignite quarter candles, lighting paper requests to be burned, and any other task that requires flame. I light this larger candle before any ceremony begins, and snuff it after the ritual is ended and the circle cut. When I light it, it is a visible sign to my subconscious mind that a shift in consciousness is required to do ritual and magic. Although the altar candle can be of the Element of Fire, it more appropriately represents the Element of Spirit because it is the center point of light on the altar.

Some Wiccans believe that you should pinch out a burning candle at the end of a ritual, and that blowing out a candle blows away the power you raised. I, however, use a candlesnuffer as it is less messy and I avoid burned fingers. It also has a certain elegance about it that I like.

The incense burner, also called a censer, can range from a can of sand to hold sticks and cones to the larger burners with a lid and chains to hold while it is carried around the circle. Choose one that appeals to you, fits your budget, and will do the job. The burner is of the Element of Fire.

Incense comes in a number of different forms. There are sticks, cones, and powdered or ground herbal incenses. The powders require special charcoal blocks for burning. Whatever you do, do not use barbecue charcoal, which is dangerous when burned in a closed room or anywhere inside a house. Charcoal blocks for incense burning can be purchased from any Pagan store or religious supply center. You will eventually acquire quite a variety of incense to use for different rituals and spells. Various types of incense for various uses are discussed in Chapter 65. If you burn cones or powdered incense, a layer of sand in the incense burner will make it easier to clean up the ashes later. The sticks, if not used in a stick holder, can be pushed upright in a can of sand, which will catch the ashes. Lighted incense in any form can be as dangerous as candles, so take care in using it. Incense is of the Element of Air.

Incense has a long religious history, far beyond ancient Egypt. The Babylonian magicians knew of the power of incense and used it in their ceremonies, as did all ancient priests and priestesses. During excavations of burial barrows on Salisbury Plain near Stonehenge, round pottery vessels with perforated sides were uncovered, obviously an early incense burner.

Water must always be purified magically before using it in ritual. The instructions for this are given at the end of the chapter. When a large amount of water is blessed, you can fill a smaller glass bottle for immediate use on the altar. This way you are not juggling a large bottle to pour a small amount into the goblet. There are inexpensive capped bottles with a cut-glass ornamentation that look quite nice. Water, of course, belongs to the Element of Water.

Ritual salt should be kept separate from regular salt used in everyday cooking, although when in need, use what is at hand. A small container with a lid keeps ritual salt from spilling on the altar. Some Witches believe that only sea salt can be used for authentic ritual, but, in my opinion, since all salt is made by the Goddess, all salt is perfectly fine to use for ritual. Salt is an Element of Earth.

The little cauldron can be of any type of metal or ceramic. However, the best kind, that gives the least trouble and lasts the longest, is one made of cast iron. These can be found in kitchen supply stores, marketed as "soup bowls," or in Pagan shops. They may or may not have three little legs on the bottom and a bail or handle on top. The cauldron is a symbol of the vast, unending womb of the Goddess and can represent both the Element of Earth and the Element of Spirit. Cauldrons are invaluable as a receptacle for burning request papers or holding candles for long-burning candle spells. If using candles for spellworking, coat the inside bottom of the cauldron with the appropriate essential oil. This will keep the candle wax from sticking.

Like the broom, the iron cauldron has a long history among various cultures. It was the primary cooking vessel that could be used over a fireplace or outdoor bonfire. To a Witch, the cauldron represents the creating womb of the Great Mother, as well as the Triple Goddess as Maiden, Mother, and Crone. Four Elements are necessary for a cauldron to produce a transformation of raw food into a meal: water to fill it; fire to boil it; earth herbs, vegetables, and sometimes meat to season it; and air or steam to rise into the air. The same combination of Elements is necessary when a Witch uses the cauldron to brew an herbal potion for healing, or an herbal brew for magic.

Some Wiccans recommend that you not use sulfur matches to light anything during a ritual. It adds the odor of sulfur to the air. The use of sulfur is questionable in all rituals, in my opinion, although some of the old grimoires call for it in certain types of spells. Many of the spell ingredients from ancient grimoires can be dangerous. Instead, use a lighter, particularly those long ones used to light fireplaces. This produces a more manageable, longer-lasting flame for lighting charcoal and candles.

Always clean up and dispose of any used candle wax when the ritual or spellworking is over. In fact, after a reasonable amount of time to relax after ritual or spells, clean up your entire ritual area. Wipe the dagger blade to remove any juice or wine that may stain or pit it. Clean the drips off the candles and do the same with the holders. Replace any candles that are burned too far down. Empty and wipe clean the goblets. Wipe down the altar, pentacle, and any other tool you used. Always show respect to the Higher Powers by being tidy. Think how embarrassed you would be if these Powers suddenly appeared in a physical form in your ritual area and it was a mess!

There are a number of useful minor ritual tools and items that you may want to add later. Certain types of rituals may call for special tools. Minor ritual tools and equipment are essential if you are a dedicated Witch. Some of these make ritual easier, while others are vital to certain spellworkings. Witches tend to be pack rats, knowing that sooner or later a use for the items will be found.

The sword is probably the most expensive item any Witch will buy. Actually, the sword duplicates the use of the dagger and is not absolutely necessary. A tool of the Element of Fire, the sword is a larger, commanding version of the dagger. However, be careful not to get carried away with dreams of magnificent, long swords. Besides being extremely expensive and beyond the pocketbooks of most Witches, these actually aren't very practical and can even be dangerous. Examples are the Scottish Claymore or others of similar weight and length. Maneuvering in a circle with a Claymore can be downright deadly to other people, besides knocking things off the altar. A sword length should be no longer than seventeen to nineteen inches for a woman and twenty-one to twenty-three inches for a man. Authentically reproduced swords can be extremely heavy and difficult to use. Like the dagger, the sword is not used to cut or kill anything. It is used for magical gestures during protection rituals, or used at times to call up the quarter guardians, or, like the dagger, to trace out the circle.

The bolline is a white-handled knife, usually sharp on one side only, although it can be shaped like a small hand sickle. This is traditionally used to cut herbs. If you choose a bolline with a straight blade, you will find it handy to carve symbols into candles, cut cords and thread, and generally do the little cutting tasks within a circle.

You may wish to consider a number of altar cloths with various designs depicting the seasonal holy days. You can make these yourself by buying various colors of fabric, cutting each to fit the altar with a slight overhang on the edge, hemming the edges, and then painting or embroidering the cloth with various designs and symbols.

If you go to all this trouble, or make cloths out of such fabrics as silk or velvet, you really should think about a glass cover for your altar. I had a piece of glass cut to fit the top of my round altar. The edges are beveled to prevent cuts. I spread the various altar cloths under this glass to keep dripped candle wax, spilled juice, and other accidents off the cloth itself. It is much easier to clean the glass top than to try to remove stains from a hand-painted cloth. If glass and different altar cloths do not appeal to you, consider having a piece of marble cut to fit your altar. Marble has the amazing ability to hold power for long periods of time. However, a marble top is much more expensive than glass.

If you want to use a smaller piece of marble, set it in the center of your altar to act as a power sink stone for collecting energy during rituals. Any flat stone with suitable vibrations can be used in this manner. The power sink stone acts as an energizer and cleanser for other ritual items.

The broom has been an ordinary household item for thousands of years. The original broomstick in Britain was made of the *Planta genista*, or Scotch broom, tied onto one end of a stick. As a ritual tool of the Witch, the broom symbolized several things, the most notorious of these being a sexual symbol. However, the broom also was thought to deflect the evil eye and bring luck. A Witch's broom is used to sweep the ritual area clean of all negative vibrations before setting up the altar. This broom can be a handmade hearth broom or one of the old types of corn straw kitchen brooms. Some brooms are elaborately decorated with Wiccan items. However, if you have cats, be prepared to have the decorations serve as toys and eventually be strewn about the house.

On the subject of cats, a cat is one of the few creatures I know that can cross the line of a cast circle and not disturb the power. If a person steps across a cast circle, the movement will immediately destroy all you worked to set up.

The bune wand is a Scottish phrase used to describe anything on which a Witch was said to fly, the same as the broom. Early texts describe the bune wand as a forked stick or staff, sometimes even a dead flower stalk. Any forked stick can represent the Horned God.

For storing herbals, incenses, powders, and herbal mixtures, plus a supply of various herbs, you will need a quantity of sterilized glass jars with lids, wooden boxes, ceramic containers, and cloth and leather bags. Essential oils should be stored in dark-colored bottles with tight lids. Eyedroppers are essential for measuring out oils. Large quantities of oils can be stored in the bottles in which you buy them. You will also need bowls and wooden spoons for mixing. If you measure out herbs for healing, you will benefit by having a small scale.

Witches used, and still use, a mortar and pestle to grind up herbal ingredients for a spell. By doing this, Witches impart personal power to the herbs. This magical connection only occurs if they concentrate upon their actions and verbally or mentally repeat the reason for making the spells while grinding the herbs.

The Witch's ladder is the name for a string of forty beads, or a cord with forty knots. When Witches want to chant a word, phrase, or verse for a certain number of times, the Witch's ladder helps them keep correct count.

The scourge is not a traditional Witch tool and probably was invented by Gerald Gardner, who seemed to like scourgings. In some Wiccan groups, the scourge is used during initiation ceremonies. It consists of a short wooden handle with several lightweight, knotted cords. I do not believe in using the scourge except in third-degree initiations.

You frequently find a bell on a Witch's altar for use in certain ceremonies. This is rung a prescribed number of times for emphasis or to attract the attention of Otherworld powers.

There are also a number of less important items that can be found in a Witch's supply cupboard. These items basically are used in spellworking, and are nice to have on hand to meet magical needs and emergencies. Every Witch keeps a supply of various colors and types of candles. There are times when a number of consecutive rituals are necessary to accomplish a goal. Small pieces of paper and a pen are needed for writing out requests, which may be burned in the cauldron, set under candles, or stuffed into talisman bags. A variety of small bags, feathers, felt, beads, rawhide strips, scissors, and thread are frequently needed when making up charms, amulets, and talismans. Pieces of material are necessary for making poppets for healing and other uses. Nearly every Witch I know has a collection of crystals and stones for use in spellworking. Colored cords are necessary if you do cord magic to bind up someone's actions. Cords and knots can also be used when storing power at the Full Moon to be released for use during the waning moon. If you like nonvocal music during your rituals, you may wish to have a supply of tapes on hand, each tape perhaps suited to a particular type of ritual.

Witches like to have a number of different divination tools on hand. What works with one type of question for a Witch may not work with another question. Crystal balls and magic mirrors are known as scrying devices. The pendulum works best with "yes" or "no" questions only. Tarot cards, the I Ching, and rune stones work well for getting in-depth answers on a question.

CONSECRATION OF TOOLS

Some books, especially those of ceremonial magic, have very elaborate individual spells for consecrating each ritual tool. Using these spells, it can take many hours to consecrate your tools. Fortunately, all this expenditure of time and energy isn't necessary.

Place on your altar the tools you want to consecrate. Have ready a goblet of water, the pentacle disk, a lighted white candle, and burning incense. Frankincense incense is the best for this. Also have a small piece of cloth for drying the tools when finished. Take one tool at a time and begin.

CONSECRATION

Hold the tool in both hands to your heart. Say:

> *I claim this (name of the tool) as mine. Through this (name of the tool)*
> *I shall direct Otherworld power to accomplish what needs to be done.*

Lightly sprinkle the tool with the water, saying:

> *With Water I bless you.*

Wave the tool three times in the heat over the candle flame, saying:

> *With Fire I cleanse you.*

Wave the tool three times in the incense smoke, saying:

> *With Air I connect you with the Otherworld and the deities.*

Lay it on the pentacle disk and say:

> *With Earth I give you purpose to follow my will.*

Hold the tool in both hands to your heart. Say:

> *Each time I hold this (name the tool), I will remember my dedication to*
> *the Old Ways.*

Carefully wipe the tool dry and clean. Then lay it on the altar while you consecrate any other tools you have at hand.

CONSECRATED WATER

There are many recipes or formulas for making your own blessed or consecrated water. You will need a glass jar or jug of spring or rain water. It is not necessary to use spring or rain water, as tap water will do, but if you feel that you must use the purest water available, use water that has been run through a water-filtering system.

Be sure that you store this water in a sterilized bottle with a tight-fitting lid. You don't want to go through the entire ritual of making blessed water just to have it become filled with mold because the bottle wasn't clean.

WATER CONSECRATION

Set the bottle of water out in the moonlight during a Full Moon. Hold your hands on the bottle and chant:

Moonlight, starlight, cleanse this water on this night. Fill it with power and purity. This is my wish, so mote it be.

Leave the bottle in the moonlight all night if possible.

You can add a teaspoonful of blessed salt and some rose water to this bottle if you wish. You can quickly bless the salt by holding it on the palm of your power hand (the hand you regularly use) and calling upon the Goddess to bless it.

PREPARATION OF ROSE WATER

You can also make your own rose water if you have access to fresh roses. In a pinch, dried rose petals will work, although the scent will not be as strong. Put a pint of water into a kettle. Add a cup of rose petals to the water, and simmer gently for at least thirty minutes. Strain out the petals and pour the water into a sterilized jar. You can make the mixture stronger by adding more petals, or increase the amount of rose water you make by doubling the amount of water and petals used. Add a quarter cup of rose water to a gallon of blessed water.

Study Work

Consecrate your basic ritual tools and store them properly in your supply cabinet or on your altar. Also, make up a bottle of consecrated water to be used later in ritual.

CHAPTER 18

Jewelry, Robes, and Other Paraphernalia

The old idea of the wrinkled and bent older woman in a serviceable black dress does not apply to modern Witches. They like to dress in a far more spectacular manner. What good is it to be a Witch inside a consecrated circle if you don't feel the part? As for the "old woman" part, some of today's grandmothers could cause anyone to stop and take a second look.

Next to the dagger, apprentices desire to possess a special ritual robe; a special kind of costume that will make them feel different when practicing ritual and magic. Since you should never work in a consecrated ritual circle wearing everyday garb, this is an excellent addition to the Witch's wardrobe. Most women prefer long dress-like gowns in a variety of types and colors. A few women are attracted to the Hindu sari. Some men do not mind wearing long gowns, while others draw the line at a "dress." For those men who are uncomfortable with a long gown, seek out a pair of exotic lounging pajamas. These come in all colors and styles. You can add embroidery, beading, or painted Pagan symbols if you wish.

Most Witches like to wear robes for ritual and magic, although some prefer to be nude, or to use Gardner's expression "skyclad." Donning a special robe helps turn the subconscious mind to the serious matters at hand, and helps set the stage for powerful connections to the Otherworld. Besides, I don't know any Witch who likes to be cold. Being cold is being uncomfortable, and being uncomfortable or self-conscious in any way detracts from the work you want to do.

If you are working solitary, you can wear a robe or practice skyclad if you want. If you work in a group, the group will decide which they prefer for rituals. Personally, I have reservations about group nudity. It can too easily become an explosive sexual and emotional issue unless the group works extremely well together. Even in the best groups, ritual nudity can cause problems.

Robes can run the gamut from the very simple to the very elaborate, depending upon the mood and preferences of the solitary Witch, or the decision by a group. Although I do not care for the hooded robes that make you look like an orthodox monk, some people like these.

In Celtic countries, a female coven member would dress in a green robe to represent the Goddess. Green was called "the Fairies' fatal color," because communication with Fairies was discouraged by the Christians, and set one apart as a Pagan or Witch. At one time, the English conquerors outlawed the wearing of the green in Ireland in an attempt to dissuade the local people from practicing the Old Ways and fertility rituals. It did not work, even when they started hanging people for these practices.

To keep your feet warm on a cold floor, add sandals or ballet slippers. Unless you are part of a group that does not allow wearing a cord belt or girdle until you have passed through a degree initiation, you may want to tie a silver or gold cord around your waist. From this cord you can hang the dagger sheath and a small bag to hold essentials. Remember, even if you should sneeze, you can't leave the cast circle for a tissue.

For some Sabbats, elaborate costumes are sometimes worn by certain group members to symbolize an aspect of a particular deity. Masks can also be worn by a few or all of the members. The wearing of masks is an ancient practice that helps the Witch shift into another level of consciousness and reach deeper into the psychic vibrations of the ritual. Originally, the masks now worn at Halloween represented Otherworld entities and the spirits of deceased loved ones. When wearing a mask, Witches can invoke, or call down, the power of a deity or being, so that they can, for a short time, use that energy in the ritual or spellworking.

Exotic feathered masks of many kinds are available around the Samhain or Halloween season. You can make your own elaborate mask by purchasing the basic black "Lone Ranger" mask and decorating it with beads, paint, and feathers.

The hooded, black cloak was once used for anonymity and secrecy when a Witch had to travel at night. It still can be used for anonymity, but also has the same psychological power as a mask to help a Witch shift levels of consciousness. This can be very helpful if you are meditating on or working with the Underworld deities and past lives.

Most Witches, both men and women, like certain kinds of jewelry. They wear some jewelry every day as amulets or talismans, while other pieces are reserved for ritual. Clear quartz crystals in pendants, bracelets, and earrings are popular. For an in-depth discussion on the meaning of some stones, read Chapter 30.

The fossil stones of amber and jet have long been associated with priestesses and Witches. Some Wiccans believe that only the High Priestess of a coven should wear a necklace of alternating beads of amber and jet. However, I believe that every Witch, female or male, has a right to wear these stones as a symbol of connection to ancient times and ancient ways.

If you decide to purchase any jet jewelry, be very careful to obtain it from a reputable dealer. Much of what is called jet on the market today is actually plastic. Since jet itself is lightweight and slick to the touch, it can be difficult to tell if it is the real thing. Most good jet jewelry comes from England, where certain areas have mined and cut jet for centuries.

Some High Priestesses, who have had groups hive off the original coven, wear a laced, tied, or buckled cloth garter around one thigh. This practice seems to be a recent innovation in Wiccan history. It's a nice way to brag without saying anything. Some writers say that the practice is much older, and that the British Order of the Garter originated from this Wiccan idea. There is no definitive historical evidence to refute or prove this.

Tiaras or circlets are frequently worn during ritual. Many of these circlets have an upturned crescent moon in the center on the forehead. The band itself may be made of solid metal or a light chain. Sometimes, the High Priest wears a crown with small antlers on it, to represent the God during ritual. Wearing of a circlet is an individual or group decision. Some women like to wear the Hindu *Bindi*, which is a small body jewel temporarily glued to the center of the forehead and surrounded by painted designs.

Wristbands or cuff bracelets are quite popular with men, as are such pendants as Thorr's hammer, the pentagram, or clear quartz crystal. Women usually prefer the more exotic bracelets or coiling snake armbands, along with their necklaces or pendants. Both sexes often wear earrings of Pagan design.

Wear whatever jewelry pleases you unless you begin to clank when you move. Excessive jewelry only exhibits what you own, it does not point out your preferences with taste.

Whatever robes or jewelry you decide to use should be reserved for ritual use and should not become everyday items or for public display. Your religion should be sacred and private to you.

Study Work

Purchase or make a simple robe for ritual, if you decide to wear robes. Write down exactly why you are choosing or not choosing to wear a robe. Are your reasons based on practicality or past programming? Choose one piece of simple jewelry that represents your commitment to Wicca. If you decide to wear this jewelry every day, be discreet and do not exhibit it to the world.

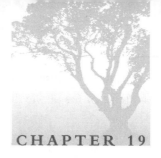

CHAPTER 19

The Magical or Craft Name

It is traditional for Witches to choose a different name to be used for ritual working and magic. They use this special name within the ritual circle as a psychic message to the deities that they are laying aside the mundane and taking up the mystical and spiritual. However, apprentices should not use this name until they are initiated, either solitary or by a group. The choice of such a name takes time if done properly; therefore, apprentices should give this choice much deep thought before making a decision.

Many Witches and Pagans choose magical names that are reminiscent of Native American names, such as Silver Moon or Black Wolf. If you are attracted to names like these, consider the full meaning of the animal and the color before deciding. You want to choose a name that reflects your inner self. Other Witches prefer to take a name that belongs to an aspect of the Goddess or the God. Here again, read carefully about a deity before assuming a name linked to that deity.

There is another, quite different method for making a magical name. This involves the practice of numerology. In numerology, each letter is assigned a number. Then, the numbers of the letters in a name are added up until the total is reduced to a single digit. The only exceptions to this single digit total are the numbers eleven, twenty-two, and thirty-three, which are considered prime numbers and are never reduced. With this method, the Witch should try to select a name that adds up to the same number as the birth number, which is the total of the month, the day, and the year the Witch was born.

To use the numerology method of name-choosing, decide your birth number. Make a list of names that appeal to you. Using the following numerical-alphabet letter list, add up the total of each name to see if one may match your birth number. Some Pagan numerologists suggest that the number should equal that of your actual everyday name. This may not be a good way to calculate a new Craft name, especially if you are trying to cut personal ties that resonate with your physical name.

A, J, S	1	D, M, V	4	G, P, Y	7
B, K, T	2	E, N, W	5	H, Q, Z	8
C, L, U	3	F, O, X	6	I, R	9

If the name you really like doesn't quite match your birth number, play with the addition or subtraction of a letter, or the changing of one letter for another, to see if the total will match. If this still doesn't work, or if you aren't quite certain about a name, play with combining letters to make a name until you find one that appeals to you and matches your birth number. You may find that you create the perfect name, and that the number total ceases to matter.

Sometimes Witches will choose a new name at some point in their life, usually because vast life, character, or goal changes have occurred. However, this is not done on a whim, as a Craft name is important to the magical character of the Witch.

Before actually accepting a name as the one you want, think about it seriously for several weeks before you make a decision. It is best to take your time instead of rushing and ending up with a name you soon do not like.

Whatever magical or Craft name you choose, take great care in revealing it to others. This is your personal, psychic link to the Otherworld. It can be used against you by unscrupulous magicians.

Study Work

Decide on several magical names that appeal to you. Write these down and study them for three weeks before making a final decision. Does the name describe your inner self? Your magical goals? Does it match your birth number? Think of yourself by this magical name while you are working on rituals or studying. However, do not use it aloud until you reach the point of self-initiation. This goal of waiting to use the name until you are actually an initiated Witch can make your spiritual journey much sweeter.

CHAPTER 20

Invoking, Evoking, and Banishing

Apprentices and non-Wiccans can become very confused about the meaning of the words invoking, evoking, and banishing. Invoke means "to call to" or "to call into," while evoke means "to call out" or "to call forth." In broad terms, you *invoke* a god into the circle. You *evoke* a spirit into the triangle outside the cast circle. In invocation, the macrocosm, or the larger universal world, which consists of this world and the Otherworld, floods the Witches' consciousness. In evocation, Witches, having aligned themselves with the macrocosm, create an astral microcosm, or small world, within the triangle outside the circle, which will allow a spirit to enter there.

At the end of this chapter are a practice invocation ritual and a practice banishing ritual for the apprentice to use. No examples of evocations are given, since, at this stage, no apprentice should practice such a ritual.

There are three main methods of invoking any deity or higher spirit. The first method consists of devotion, prayers, and calls to a particular deity or higher spirit. The second method is the straightforward ceremonial invocation, such as Calling Down the Moon, which is discussed in Chapter 37. The third method is use of the dramatic, in the form of costumes, masks, and reenactments of myths. In each case the magician identifies himself with the deity invoked.

Invoking is rather like an invitation; it is never used as a command. A Witch may invoke a deity presence into the circle, or, in the case of Calling Down the Moon, into the High Priestess. Invoking can be as simple as a heartfelt prayer that asks for the presence of the Goddess or the God for a ritual or meditation. Invoking can also be used to request the presence of the higher spirits, personal spiritual guardians, or astral teachers.

It is not unusual for Witches to deliberately invoke certain deity archetypes into the magic circle. It is a spiritually uplifting experience to feel the archetypal power accumulate during a ritual, to make your psychic insight clear and your spirit filled with power. When these archetypal powers are released at the end of the ceremony, there is a void, exhausting and fulfilling at the same time.

To invoke by means of the dramatic can be done deliberately, as with reenactments of myths during a ritual, or accidentally, as when someone dons the mask and costume of a trickster deity and begins to act like that spirit. This accidental invocation may be what happens to certain people during Halloween gatherings.

Evoking, however, is a command for certain lower entities to appear in a designated area near the Witch. Nothing is ever evoked into the consecrated circle, but instead is ordered into a specially formed triangle outside the circle. Entities should always be evoked into a specially designated spot, as one does not want them wandering around wherever they please. Entities and beings that are evoked are not always entirely friendly to humans or they are helpful but too mischievous to trust. Evoking is actually a ceremonial magic practice that is used by some Witches. To help the invisible entity form a body that can be seen, the magician will burn Dittany of Crete (*Origanum dictamnus*) within the triangle. This entity will use the smoke to form a temporary visible body. No one, apprentice or Witch, should play with evoking until they have gained much experience in handling troublesome Otherworld entities at a distance or in meditation.

Banishing simply means, "to order something to be gone." This may mean gone from your environment or vicinity, or gone back to the energy's source. This is a command given by the Witch to whatever needs to be banished. This may take the form of banishing ghosts, possessing entities, or troublemaking nature spirits. This action is also used to return created negative thought forms to their senders.

There are various degrees of banishing, the use of which will depend upon the strength, earthly connection, and personality of the spirit being banished. Sometimes all that is needed is for someone to give a sharp command for the spirit to be gone. You may need to sprinkle the person or house with blessed water and salt to prevent a return. Other times, the ghost or spirit is so attached to its earthly abode, whether by its own strength or, in the case of personal possession, by the subconscious weaknesses or strengths of the person involved, that a full banishing ritual or exorcism must be performed. It is unusual to find a spirit that is stronger than the determination of a Witch to remove it.

In all cases in which a spirit has attached itself to a residence or person, you must determine what symbols have meaning to that particular spirit. If it is sensitive to the symbols of orthodox religions, you may find it helpful to use a cross and holy water from a church. If the spirit is not impressed with these, the use of power from the hands or the sprinkling consecrated water along with burning incense and ringing a bell may send it away. However, in the case of powerful nonorthodox-oriented spirits the Witch will be wise to work with other Witches or Pagans in a full Wiccan or Pagan exorcism.

Many spirits or ghosts that take up residence in a house or building are attached by a strong emotional tie to that place from their physical life. With some forethought and determination these beings can usually be evicted without a long process. However, personal possession of the body of a living human can pose many problems. In the first place, the possessed person probably has some affinity with the spirit or something within their personality that allowed the spirit to enter and stay. This may range from the use of alcohol and drugs, to playing with trance and divination boards without training, to an emotional connection with a deceased person. The possessed person absolutely must desire freedom from the spirit for any exorcism to truly be successful.

A Practice Invocation

Light frankincense or lotus incense and a white candle. Sit in a comfortable position for your meditation. If you do not know how to meditate, instructions are given in Chapter 24. Close your eyes and visualize white light surrounding you. You are completely protected and have nothing to fear. Nothing can harm you.

Take three slow, deep breaths. Begin to silently chant the word Goddess or God in your mind. Let whatever mental pictures appear float up into your mind. Look at each of them with your inner sight for a brief time, and then allow another picture to take its place. Reach out with your psychic feelings to the Goddess or the God. Do not try to force anything. Merely float on the sound of your inner chant. If you feel impelled to offer up a prayer, do so.

When the images fade away, take a deep breath and think of your body. Move your hands and feet until you feel your physical body again. Open your eyes. The invocation is finished.

A PRACTICE BANISHMENT

Everyone has negative thought forms bouncing around their personal environment, but fortunately most of these are not very powerful. We can create these ourselves by obsessing on problems, or sometimes they are sent subconsciously by others who want us to fail in something. If a number of small irritating problems are plaguing you, this is a good indication that your apartment, room, or house needs a psychic housecleaning or banishing. Banishings seem to work best if done at night.

Although a banishing can be done by one person, it is easier if two people are involved. Gather on a small tray the following items: burning frankincense incense, a small bell, a goblet of consecrated water with a little salt in it, and a burning white candle.

A banishing is done room by room, starting at the left side of the door and working around the room clockwise until you are back at the door. If you have several rooms in your apartment or house, plan your route so that you end up at a door that exits your home.

Take the goblet of water and salt. With your power hand (the hand you use regularly), lightly sprinkle around the room in the direction noted above. This includes sprinkling into every closet. When you come to a window, door, or mirror, lightly touch your damp finger to all the sides.

Then carry the tray with the incense and candle around the room in the same direction, ringing the bell as you go. If two people are performing this ritual, one can follow the other. When you finish a room, move to the next one.

When the entire house, including any basements or accessible attic spaces, has been psychically cleaned, you should be standing at the main exit door. Open the door and firmly command all negative energies and spirits to leave at once. Do not be surprised if you feel a draft of cold air pushing out of your house into the night. Shut the door and sprinkle it with the water.

To end the banishing, call upon the Goddess and the God to fill your home with positive energy.

Study Work

Practice invoking the Goddess or the God in meditation without calling the deity by a specific name. Keep practicing this lesson until you "feel" a presence around you. Thank and dismiss the deity when you are finished. Write down your feelings about this presence. Did it make you feel uncomfortable, or was the discomfort your own fears of this practice? Did you feel energized and at peace? Did practicing this invocation technique strengthen your psychic abilities? How long did the effect last?

When you performed your banishing, what mental images or feelings did you have? What was the feeling inside your home before and after the banishing?

CHAPTER 21

Protection and Self-Defense

Witches are very sensitive to the vibrations of any place, and particularly to their house and environment. Negative, hateful, and/or jealous visitors, as well as illness, a streak of bad luck, or family quarrels, can pollute the atmosphere to the point that little, if any, positive energy can exist. Most of this is ordinary, non-magical pollution that happens to everyone. Usually an ordinary water and bell banishing will clear the area.

However, there is also the category of deliberate ill-wishing. This may be done by a person who subconsciously or consciously wishes you to have bad luck but who has no magical training. This type of thinking creates negative thought forms that find their way into your life and cause problems. Or, you may be the target of someone who deliberately is doing candle-burning or some other small ritual to harm or control you. If you find yourself the victim of a sudden run of bad luck, clumsiness, or ill health, you need to consider other methods of defending yourself.

Some Witches are afraid that using protection and defense spells will create "bad" karma. Remember the codicil to the Rede that evil allowed to exist harms everyone. You have every right to defend yourself, your loved ones, pets, and property from negative influences. In fact, it is your duty to take care of your own.

Apprentices may think of protection and defense spells as curses, but rarely do true modern Witches curse someone. They are too aware of the laws of karma to take such an action. Some people associated the word curse with hex, which comes from the German word for Witch. However, among the Pennsylvania Dutch (or Germans in Pennsylvania), hex means magic used for both positive and negative results. The word blasting is also frequently connected with cursing. However, blasting with magic is very concentrated and needs much experience, as it is cast to make humans or animals impotent or infertile.

Someone with the evil eye is said to be able to cause illness in the spirit or soul of another person, as well as cause them bad luck, merely by looking at them. Near Eastern cultures still use bright blue beads to deflect the evil eye. These beads are worn on cords around the neck, hung on horses' bridles, or attached to baby carriers. In ancient Egypt, the Eye of Horus was used to repel evil. Natural stones with an eye formation are also thought to be powerful protectors against all evil and ill-wishing. Modern replicas of the Eye of Horus and natural eye stones can be worn as personal protection jewelry or hung in a car for the same purpose. The subject of amulets and talismans is covered in Chapter 68.

One way to rid your house of negative vibrations is to place onions in each room. Cut each onion into quarters and put one quarter on a saucer in each corner of every room overnight. The next day, wear gloves to gather up the onions. Place them on a chopping board that you can wash thoroughly after use. Chop the onions into fairly small pieces and bury them in the ground. Do this for three, five, or seven days. By the end of that time, the vibrations should have changed drastically.

Another method of protection from negativity is to twine or interlace a cord or thread into a tangle of knots. Do this with a number of threads. As you interlace and tie the knots, chant: "Tie and bind, tie and bind. No harm comes to me or mine." Bury the threads on each side of the porch or steps into your home.

Europeans of the Middle Ages frequently hung shiny glass balls, called Witch balls, in windows for the same purpose as the blue bead. In the practice of Feng Shui, crystals in windows and other areas of the house are hung to break up negative energy flows and bring in positive energy.

An old variation of the Witch ball is the Witch's bottle filled with bent nails and pins, and knotted threads. Some old descriptions require the person to fill the bottle with these, then with the person's urine. The bottle is sealed and buried near the threshold. If you live in an apartment, you obviously cannot be digging near your threshold. In this case, make a small packet of the threads and tape them above the main entry door.

Another protection and banishing spell calls for a small kitchen knife, a saucer, a small cup of water, the pentacle disk, a lemon, a half cup of salt, four white candles, and patchouli incense. Put the pentacle disk in front of you on your altar, place the salt in the North, the cup of water in the West, the burning incense in the East, and the burning candle in the South. You now have physical representations of the four Elements with which you always work magic.

Hold the lemon in your power hand and chant:

Sour lemon, hear my call. You must bind and gather all wrong vibrations and negativity. This is my will, so mote it be.

Put the lemon on the saucer. With a small kitchen knife, slice the lemon into four round slices; do not quarter the lemon. Sprinkle the salt heavily over the slices of lemon, while chanting:

Salt defends and salt will bind all evil sent to me and mine.

Leave the lemon on your altar until it has completely dried out. If it molds instead of drying, you are dealing with heavy negative vibrations. Repeat the spell until you get a lemon that dries.

When the lemon is completely dried, dispose of it. Some writers recommend that you bury all lemons, candle wax, or other disposable remains after a spell as a way to safely dispose of remains that might have power left in them. However, dumping them into the garbage is just fine, as is a quick flush of the commode for ashes. If you have performed the spell properly, there will be no power remaining in the used material. If Witches buried the remains of all their spellwork, they would soon have the entire yard dug up.

Most protection and defense spells are best done on the New Moon or during the waxing moon.

You will find a full protection ritual in Chapter 55 and more spells in Chapter 71.

Study Work

Make a packet of tangled threads to protect your home. Either bury it near the threshold or place the packet above the entry door. If you want this inside packet concealed, consider placing some decoration on top of it.

CHAPTER 22

The Traditional Salutes and Gestures

Although some people believe that Witches wave their arms and hands in esoteric gestures, not all Witches use salutes or gestures in their rituals. This seems to be a matter of personal or group choice. Except for the salutes, arm movements, and hand gestures that are seen in ancient wall paintings and statues, most of the gestures used today have been taken from much later medieval ceremonial magic. Some of the following gestures are not standard in modern Wicca, but come from ancient sculptures, drawings, and descriptions from surviving texts far older than ceremonial magic. In Europe, some gestures have survived in folklore, usually with a modern sexual or magical, protective meaning attached to them. A few hand movements, especially in the Mediterranean area, are used specifically to avert the evil eye, or dark magic.

The ritual gesture for the Horned God is very old. It consists of holding the middle and ring fingers down with the thumb and extending the forefinger and little finger. This is called the *Mano Cornuta*. This produces a symbol of the horns with which the God is associated. Unfortunately, in the United States, this gesture has been corrupted into a sexual vulgarity in modern times. In some European countries the sign is made to avert evil. However, in India this gesture is still used as a sacred *mudra* of Jagadamba, Mother of the World.

The *Mano in Fica*, or the sign of the fig, is an Italian gesture to symbolize a woman's genitals. This gesture goes back to Goddess times. It is made by clenching the fingers into a fist, with the thumb protruding between the middle and ring fingers. Both the *Mano Cornuta* and the *Mano in Fica* were possibly used by Witches to secretly identify themselves to other Witches during the Middle Ages.

When Witches hold up the wand or dagger to each of the quarters of the circle while calling up the guardians, they are saluting the powers of the Elements. Saluting

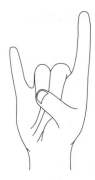

Horned God Gesture

with the dagger is also done at other appropriate times. This salute can be performed with the wand as well. This gesture is rather like a knight saluting a respected person or a worthy opponent with his sword.

The invoking and banishing pentagrams, mentioned earlier, are also used as salutes and gestures. When using the invoking pentagram to call the guardians of the quarters, the Witch makes the movements in the air before her at the quarter direction, using her dagger. To make the invoking pentagram, she starts at the top point, goes down the left side angle to the left "foot," then up to the right crosspiece, across to the left crosspiece, down to the right "foot," and back up to the top point. Some Witches continue the movement from the top point back down to the left "foot" again.

If a Witch uses an invoking pentagram to call the guardians, she must use the banishing pentagram to dismiss them. Again, she stands before each quarter direction and

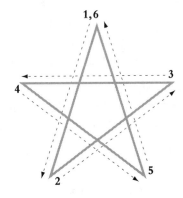

Invoking Pentagram

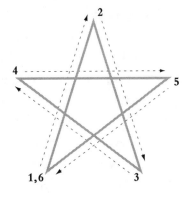

Banishing Pentagram

marks the pentagram in the air with her dagger. To make the banishing pentagram, she starts at the left "foot," goes up to the top point, down to the right "foot," up to the left crosspiece, across to the right crosspiece, and back down to the left "foot" again. Some Witches continue the movement from the left "foot" back up to the top point again.

The invoking and banishing pentagrams can be used for other than calling up the guardians. If a Witch wanted to invoke a deity presence for personal protection or help, they could draw the invoking pentagram in the air before them. The same applies to the banishing pentagram if a Witch feels the need to push away dark magic or entities.

The purpose of ringing the bell or the Witch rapping her knuckles or wand on the altar is usually to draw attention to what comes next in the ritual. Other times the bell or the knock emphasizes what has just been done. The bell can also be used in exorcisms and cleansing rituals. The sound of the bell in this case forewarns all negative entities to leave at once or be evicted. This custom may have originated in the Oriental traditions, where children wore small bells to avert the evil eye and repel negative spirits.

The Isis and Osiris poses are common in groups following the Gardnerian or Alexandra branches of Wicca. These poses come at specific parts of a ritual and involve only the High Priestess and the High Priest.

To assume the Isis pose, the priestess, and sometimes the priest, stands with her feet apart and her arms outstretched to each side. She may hold a dagger or wand in one hand. Although called the Isis pose, after the Egyptian Great Goddess, this pose is also seen in paintings of the Goddess in other ancient cultures. This is also known as the Blessing Position.

To assume the Osiris pose, the priest, and sometimes the priestess, stands with his feet together, his elbows at his sides, and his forearms crossed at the wrists on his chest. He holds the wand in his left hand and the scourge in his right hand. The shafts of the tools are crossed above the wrists. This pose is reminiscent of paintings of Osiris in tombs and texts. If you or your group do not use the scourge, you can substitute the dagger or sword. Or, you may wish for the priest/priestess to hold nothing in the hands, but simply just to cross the wrists.

Both the Isis and Osiris poses are used by many modern Wiccan groups and individuals, although there is no historical evidence that they were part of authentic Wicca,

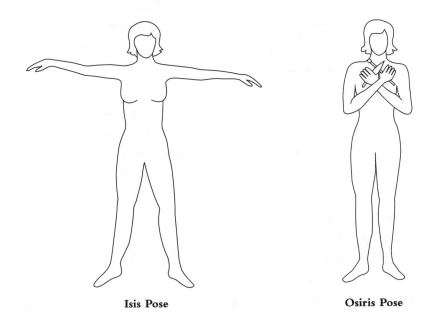

Isis Pose

Osiris Pose

but may have surfaced after the term "Witchcraft" came to be used. However, the ritual poses may go far beyond ancient Egypt into the matriarchal cultures of the Goddess.

Many people have heard of the five-fold kiss in Wicca. In the Gardnerian and Alexandrian traditions, this salute to the High Priestess as the Goddess incarnate is performed by the High Priest. It is part of the Drawing Down the Moon ceremony, which in itself is part of the greater ritual. Drawing Down the Moon is discussed in more detail in Chapter 37. The High Priestess stands before the altar and assumes the Osiris pose. The High Priest kneels at her feet. As he kisses each part on her body mentioned in the rite, he recites an appropriate text. He begins by kissing her right foot. Then, he kisses the left foot, right knee, left knee, the lower belly, right breast, left breast, and lips. When the High Priest kisses on the lower belly (called the womb in most texts), the High Priestess opens her arms and stands in the Blessing Position. When they kiss on the lips, they embrace with their feet touching. Although the five-fold kiss is connected with the Drawing Down the Moon part of a ritual, it can be performed by the High Priestess on the High Priest in a Drawing Down the Sun ritual.

Traditionally, the five-fold kiss, as with the gestures used at initiation, are always performed by a man to a woman, or a woman to a man, never by the same sexes. However, this can be altered to fit groups consisting of only men or women. Some individuals and groups may wish to dispense with this part of the ritual and substitute kneeling at the feet of the High Priestess/Priest and simply kissing her/his feet as a sign of respect. However, I am not fond of using the foot-kissing part either, as I feel that this encourages a feeling of class or degree importance that is not appropriate in Wicca. I prefer to simply give the kiss of greeting on the lips.

There are also certain gestures used during formal initiation rites in Wicca. In the First Degree initiation rites of the Gardnerian branch, the initiating Witch puts blessed oil on the tip of their forefinger. Then they touch the initiate on the lower belly, the right breast, the left breast, and again on the lower belly. This represents the inverted triangle of the First Degree.

In Second Degree initiations, the initiating Witch touches blessed oil on the initiate's lower belly, right breast, left hip, right hip, left breast, and again on the lower belly. This represents the inverted pentagram of the Second Degree.

During the Third Degree initiation, the gestures are more elaborate. The High Priest (or High Priestess) kisses the female (male) initiate on the lower belly, right foot, left knee, right knee, left foot, and on the lower belly again. Then he continues by kissing the lips, the left breast, right breast, and the lips again. These gestures form an upright pentagram on the lower body and an upright triangle on the upper body.

Those new to Wicca should understand that the initiation gestures listed above, as well as the Isis and Osiris poses, were invented or adopted by Gerald Gardner. Therefore, if any Wiccan group wishes to substitute something else, there is no reason they cannot. In my opinion, Gardner seems to have been obsessed with nudity, sex, and scourging, traits that may not have appeal to other Witches.

In Doreen Valiente's book *Witchcraft for Tomorrow*, she has a different approach to initiation gestures, one that is more appealing to me. At a certain point in the initiation ceremony, the initiating Witch puts anointing oil on the tip of her forefinger. An X is marked on the initiate's forehead, then on the center of the breast, and finally on the lower belly. This is followed by a standard kiss of greeting on the lips.

The Welcoming of the Moon posture comes from very ancient wall paintings. An early Nile sculpture, with no facial features, was discovered in this pose. In this posture, the priestess stands tall with her feet together and her arms gently curved over her head. This is a very elegant, expressive pose that a Witch can use to greet the moon or to invoke the Goddess.

A similar gesture is the one sometimes used when calling to the quarter guardians, but only if you are on good working terms with the Kings of the Elements

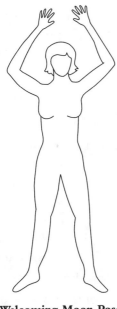

Welcoming Moon Pose

Gesture of Blessing

and do not salute them with a dagger or sword. In this pose the Witch stands tall, feet together, and both arms raised over the head in greeting.

A very ancient gesture of blessing is to hold the hand upright with the thumb extended to the side, the fore and middle fingers extended upward together, and the remaining fingers bent down to the palm of the hand. The fingers used represent the Mother Goddess, the Father God, and the Divine Child, in other words, the sacred Triple Deity of the joining of positive and negative energies to create a manifestation. This hand gesture is rarely used, unless the priest or priestess has successfully invoked the God or the Goddess within their body and is giving the blessing directly from the deity.

If you decide to incorporate some of these gestures into your rituals, be certain that you fully understand their meaning and the proper places in the rite to use them.

Study Work

Practice the invoking and banishing pentagrams until you can form the pentagrams in one unbroken, smooth movement. Do the invoking pentagram at your altar to draw in positive energy and entities. Follow this with the banishing pentagrams at every door and window of your home to expel any negative energy or entities.

CHAPTER 23

Sacred Symbols

Witches, as well as magicians, use a number of signs and symbols in their practices. Although most of these were taken from medieval ceremonial magic, even the ceremonial symbols were copied from much earlier, pre-Christian religions. Some of these, such as the swastika, are no longer in favor because of their misuse and abuse. During medieval times, Witches probably used certain symbols and a mysterious alphabet not known to cowans as a means of passing messages without being detected if their messages were intercepted.

Horns have been a symbol of the Horned God, the consort of the Goddess, for thousands of years. Two horns with a disk between them were used in ancient Egypt, while a horned head with a torch between the horns can be traced to India. In matriarchal cultures, the bull and its horns were a lunar and fertility symbol of the Great Mother. We find evidence of this in the carving of the Great Goddess of Laussel, who is shown holding a horn with thirteen marks on it. These thirteen marks represent the yearly lunar months, the opportunities for female pregnancy. When a deity wore the horns alone, it sometimes represented a god/goddess of war, such as with certain aspects of Astarte. Under the patriarchal influences, the bull with its crescent horns came to represent sun gods, such as Attis and Mithra.

The *crescent moon* sign was basically a symbol of the feminine principle of creation. Therefore, most moon deities were goddesses. However, there were some moon gods, such as Sin in Babylon and Khensu in Egypt. Sometimes, modern Witches use a circle with an outward-pointing crescent moon on each side to symbolize the Goddess. To the Amazons, this symbol represented the Virgin Goddess, whom they worshipped. In the Celtic cultures, the goddess Arianrhod was connected with the moon and death. The Celtic name Emania means "Moon-land," or land of death.

The Great Goddess of Laussel

The *labrys*, or double-axe, was a prominent symbol in matriarchal cultures. This weapon was used as a scepter in such places as the Amazon territories, Crete, and Delphi. The *labrys* is formed by two crescent moons back to back, with the horns pointing outward. It was a Goddess and lunar symbol that represented the renewing of life. The Amazons used the *labrys* as both an ordinary tool and a weapon in war. The Greek Hera was associated with the double-axe, a clue that at one time she was not the submissive deity of marriage that she later became. Other goddesses of the double-axe were Gaea, Demeter, Rhea, and Artemis. Later, the symbolic form of this axe was reflected in the stylized Celtic butterfly, which represented the souls of the dead. The word labyrinth comes from the ancient word *labrys*.

The *pentagram* is a five-point star with a long history in relationship to the Goddess and spirituality. Its spiritual use can be traced back to Ur of Chaldea. Later, in Greece, the followers of Pythagoras adopted the pentagram as their symbol because of its "golden section" mathematics. When the figure of a man is interposed onto the drawing of a pentagram, it represents the idea that the microcosm, or the little universe, resides within humans.

To Witches, the pentagram represents the four Elements plus Spirit; the necessary ingredients in magic to create a physical manifestation of desires and goals. Some covens use the reversed pentagram as a sign of an upper degree initiation. Unfortunately, the

Satanists have adopted the reversed pentagram, with one point downward, thus making it into a negative symbol.

A *pentacle* is a disk or plate of metal, ceramic, or wood that has a pentagram carved or painted on it. A Witch puts a pentacle on her/his altar to represent the Element of Earth, and to use to empower objects.

The *apple* is a symbol connected with many goddesses, particularly those associated with death and rebirth, such as the Norse Idunn and the Greek Hera. The Greek goddess Nemesis is always shown with an apple in her hand, representing destiny. In some Wiccan rituals, the apple and its hidden symbolism play an important part. The apple is solemnly cut in half crosswise to reveal the hidden pentagram marked out by the fruit's seeds.

The *hexagram* is a six-point star made of two interlaced triangles, one pointing up, and the other pointing down. Another name for this symbol is the Seal of Solomon, although the history behind this star goes much farther back in history than Solomon. The two triangles of this symbol represent the God/Goddess, male/female, positive/negative, yin/yang of magical energy and all creation. Since these are equilateral triangles, their total sum is three hundred sixty degrees, or a circle.

The *seven-point star* is known as the mystic star. It was used in ceremonial magic to invoke the seven planetary spirits, who represented the seven known planets. This idea can be traced back to the culture of Akkadia where these spirits were known as the *maskim* ("creative spirits"). This design, which is drawn with one continuous line, is said to be very effective against evil influences and spells. In magic, the number three is the most powerful number, with the number seven next.

The *eight-point star* was a symbol of the goddess Ashtart of Phoenicia. In ancient astrology, this star, usually pictured as black, represented all the stars.

The *nine-point star* represents the Ninefold Goddess (three times three, the most sacred of all numbers), the Nine Worlds of Norse myth, the nine Morgans of the later Celtic paradise, and the Greek Nine Muses. It consists of three interlocking triangles. Nine is a number of completion, the end of one cycle and the beginning of another.

The *circle* is a symbol of infinity, of cycles of action and existence without beginning or end. The Hindus say that the Great God is "an unbroken circle with no circumference, for it is nowhere and everywhere." This is reminiscent of the Wicca saying "this is a time that is not a time, in a place that is not a place." Casting a sacred circle creates a space that dwells on the threshold between this world and the

Otherworld. When a circle encloses a pentagram or hexagram, it is the ultimate symbol of eternity and infinity. Before the circle became attached to the physical sun and sun gods, it symbolized the birth canal , the opening of the Great Goddess.

The *black circle*, referred to as the Black Sun in many religions, represented the opposing force of darkness against the light, and was used in petitioning some of the Underworld gods. The Babylonian god Nergal personified the Black Sun. The Underworld deities were not all evil; some of them were extremely wise.

The astrological symbol for the Sun is a circle with a dot in the middle of it. Modern Witches sometimes use a circle with a semicircle, ends upward, on top of it to represent the God. If one added a small cross below this symbol, you would have the astrological sign for the planet Mercury. The planets Mars and Uranus also incorporate circles into their signs. The astrological symbol for Earth is a circle surrounding an equal-armed cross. In China, the disk or circle represented the heavens. In ancient cultures, when a disk was shown with wings on each side, it was a sign of spiritual fire. To alchemists, this sign symbolized physical matter that was in a state of transformation.

The *trefoil*, or three small circles linked together in a pyramid-like shape, has always been a symbol of the Triple Goddess, long before orthodox religions borrowed the concept for their male gods. The Celtic shamrock represented the Three Mothers, a concept based on the Goddess aspects of Maiden, Mother, and Crone. The Triple Goddess was known by these ideas as far back as the Neolithic era. However, the mysterious Celtic god Trefuilngid Tre-Eochair was also connected with the trefoil and bore the title of the Triple Bearer of the Triple Key.

The *spiral* is a very ancient symbol of rebirth (whether through initiation or reincarnation) and spirituality. Another name for the spiral could be the labyrinth, as both describe a singular twisting path that leads to a center. The maze, however, does not have a single path, and frequently has many dead-end passages. When Witches walk along a spiral laid out on the ground, or trace a spiral path drawn on paper, they are subconsciously, and inwardly, treading the ancient mystical path to the Sacred Center. In ancient religions, the initiate had to walk a spiral route; this symbolized death in the entering, regeneration when at the center, and rebirth on the route back out. The spiral dance done to raise power within a ritual circle is a replica of the cycle of death and rebirth. When two spirals, going two different directions, are placed side by side, they become an ancient eye symbol.

The *pointed oval* is another yonic or sexual sign used in ancient cultures. Called the *vesica piscis* (the Vessel of the Fish), it was a symbol of the feminine genitals.

The *lemniscate*, or a figure eight lying on its side, is an ancient Hindu symbol for eternity. Like the Chinese yin-yang, the *lemniscate* also represents a balance of masculine and feminine energies.

The figure of the round, *staring eye,* as a Goddess symbol has been in use for thousands of years in the Mediterranean areas and Europe. Archaeologists discovered thousands of little female figurines dominated by wide staring eyes on the face. Most of these are connected with the Sumerian culture from 3500 B.C.E. to 3000 B.C.E. These all-seeing eyes represented that truth and breaking of the law could not be hidden from the Goddess. In later Egypt the eye became associated with certain goddesses, but was then appropriated by the god Horus where it represented both the sun and the moon. The stylized eye, known as the *utchat* to the Egyptians, is still a popular amulet. The eye can represent wisdom, spiritual light, or judgment by the Goddess.

The circular *eight-spoked wheel* was very important to the ancient Celts, who saw in this design their yearly round of eight holy days. However, the wheel in general was associated with many other world deities. The Hindu goddess Kali's wheel is the Wheel of Time (the *Kalacakra*), for she rules over destiny and karma. The Celtic Welsh goddess Arianrhod was connected with the Silver Wheel (the stars that turn in the heavens). The hub of the Silver Wheel was her spirit-castle, Caer Sidi, where the dead came.

The *ankh* is a cross with a looped top that was used by the ancient Egyptians. It symbolized eternal life, and is used by many Witches today. The astrological symbol for the planet Venus is very similar: a cross mounted by a circle. If you look closely, the shape of the ankh is reminiscent of the Isis Pose mentioned in the last chapter: the circle being the head, the stem the body and feet, and the crossbar the outstretched arms. Therefore, the original meaning may have been the Goddess Herself, who is eternal life. The ankh also has similar meanings to the cross and the World Tree; that of the sacrifice connected with the savior aspect of the God. Cultures as diverse as the Norse, the Hindu, and the Mayans all have myths of the sacrificed savior God.

The *mirror* has a long history as a symbol of the Goddess, the moon, and foretelling. Some cultures had a moon god, but the majority of lunar deities are goddesses. The Egyptian god Thoth had the lunar disk as one of his symbols. The mirror of the Egyptian goddess Hathor was said to make very powerful magic. The sign of Venus, which is likely connected with the Egyptian ankh, is called the "mirror of

Venus." Traditions say that if one does the proper magic with a mirror, another's soul can be captured within it. This may be the idea behind the old superstition of covering all the mirrors in a house when someone dies. Witches sometimes make black mirrors for scrying.

The goddesses Freyja and Ishtar both wore what were called *"rainbow" necklaces*. All necklaces, like the circle symbol, can represent the vaginal opening for creation. As a circle, the necklace also represents a cosmic bond with the Otherworld and universal power. Rings have the same meaning. When three rings were linked together, it was said they could be used to contact the Fates.

The *cauldron* has a very ancient history of association with the Great Mother. It was referred to as the belly-vessel of rebirth of the Goddess. Many old myths tell stories of the dead when placed in the cauldron being reborn. The Celtic Bards of Wales believed that only by initiation in the cauldron of the goddess Cerridwen could they become true, powerful Bards. The chalice or goblet is simply a smaller version of the cauldron. In Egypt, a symbol of the goddess Mut (pronounced moot) was three cauldrons set together, sometimes in a pyramid-like shape. Earth goddesses, such as the Greek Gaea and the Thracian Hecate, were frequently associated with cauldrons, as a sign of their regenerative powers.

The halo seen surrounding the heads of people in Christian art originated in the Hindu culture where it represented the successful rising of the Kundalini force through the chakra at the top of the head. It symbolizes a person who has made much spiritual progress.

Drawings of *snakes* or symbols representing them are found in such ancient matriarchal culture remains as Crete, where Goddess or priestess statues show snakes twined about the arms. An ancient statue of the Greek goddess Athena shows her with snakes on her arms and decorating her robes. The cobra (or uraeus) was connected with Egyptian goddesses, such as Buto. Egyptian deities are frequently pictured with a raised cobra on the forehead, or symbolized by a disk capped with a cobra. The symbol of snakes twined about a staff or wand is found in ancient Babylonian art, where the creatures represent the dual aspects of healing and spirituality. Later, this twined snake symbol, or caduceus, was transferred to the Greek Hermes, messenger of the gods to humans. Today, it is a symbol of the healing professions.

There seems to be a connection between snakes and the Neolithic *meander* sign. The meander is a set of three sharply waving lines, one above the other, like three crawling serpents. This represented the spiritual power of the Element of Water, and was associated with both healing and spiritual wisdom.

The *crossroads*, like the equal-armed cross, is another Goddess symbol, and is sometimes connected with such Underworld deities as Hecate. Hermes and Diana were also associated with crossroads. This type of cross represents a balance of positive and negative energies.

The *cube* or *square* can symbolize the four Elements, which give stability to the physical world. The square is also a symbol representing the four elemental kings or powers who are said to "hold up the sky" or "hold up the world," a mystical explanation of universe's reliance on the balance of the four Elements. The Babylonians called these kings the four corner-gods.

The Elements have their own set of symbols, circular or triangular drawings that are recognizable by Witches and magicians. Earth is a downward-pointing triangle with a crossbar. Fire is an upright triangle without any other markings, while Air is an upward-pointing triangle with a crossbar. Water is a downward pointing-triangle with no other markings. The circular set for the Elements consists of a plain circle for Fire, a circle with a central dot for Air, a circle with a crossbar for Water, and a circle containing an equal-armed cross for Earth.

The *cat* has been associated with the Goddess in many of Her aspects (Isis, Bast, Artemis, Diana, and Freyja) for as long as cats have lived among humans. They were very sacred in Egypt, and protected by stringent laws. It was not until the Middle Ages that cats become associated with Witchcraft and evil. The symbol of a cat can represent a Witch who uses magic and journeys to the Otherworld, or, if the cat is black, a healer. The black cat sign for healing originated in ancient Egypt.

Although the *fish* symbolizes the subconscious mind and its connection to all aspects of time whether past or future, at one time it represented sexuality and fertility. Many ancient cultures used the fish symbol as a sign that the Great Mother and the life-giving sea (Her womb) were connected.

The *horseshoe* remains a popular European good luck symbol. Like the cauldron and the circle, the horseshoe originally was a yonic symbol. Some wooden Celtic temples were built in a horseshoe shape, as are some of the ancient stone circles. The Greek Omega symbol is a horseshoe design.

Lightning has long been a symbol of certain deities, such as thunder and storm gods like the Norse Thorr and the Greek Zeus. In some cases, bulls and lightning are found together, as with the Babylonian god Addad. The saw-toothed dagger carried by the Mesopotamian god Marduk represents a lightning bolt. Arrows frequently represent lightning bolts, since both symbols can represent a sudden, shocking transformation or awakening.

In many of the very ancient cave paintings, one will see a number of *handprints* and *footprints*, usually in red paint, on the walls. Priestesses of the ancient Goddess were known to have reddened their feet with henna as a sign of their devotion to the Great Mother. Red is a color of life and birth. Bodies were colored with red ocher at burial as a symbol of reincarnation or rebirth. In India, these red prints are still called the Footprints of the Buddha or the Feet of Vishnu. The symbol of the foot represents human contact with the power and the body of the Earth Mother, an aspect of the Great Goddess. Priestesses and priests frequently went barefoot during rituals so that they could draw upon the energy arising from the earth.

The *handprint* symbolizes strength and manifestational power that issues forth from the power center, or minor chakra, in the palms of the hands. The symbol of the open hand is still used by Moslems for protection and guidance. In China and Japan, the open hand with an eye in the center was a symbol of mystical revelation and the dispelling of fear. Today, the same symbolic drawing is a symbol for clairvoyant power.

Certain *fingers* also have symbolic meanings. The forefinger, called the Mother finger, held before the lips represented the secrecy demanded of all initiates of the Mystery Religions. When this finger was shaken, people thought that the person was laying a curse. The middle finger was known as the Father finger. When it was extended while the other fingers were held down, it was a phallic and sexual symbol. When the first and middle fingers were crossed, it produced a charm to ward off any punishment for lying. In Egypt, this gesture was the amulet of the Two Fingers.

The ancient Greeks stamped on the ground or the floor with one foot when they wanted to attract the attention of an Underworld deity during their rituals. Their Underworld deities included such gods as Hades, Hephaestus, and Poseidon, and such goddesses as Hecate, Persephone, and Cybele. To the ancient cultures the Underworld was not a terrible place of punishment, such as the Christian hell. It was a place of Crone wisdom and the deepest mysteries.

Keys have long been associated with the Mystery Religions of Egypt, Greece, and the older Mediterranean cultures. Keys symbolize the binding and loosening in magical rites, as well as the spiritual keys, or wisdom, needed to unlock the inner doors that lead to the Otherworld. They were particularly associated with such goddesses as Hecate, Artemis, and Persephone. At one time, the Egyptian ankh was considered to be a key. The Egyptians also taught that certain magical, verbal words and spells were keys to the inner Sacred Circle. In fact, their word *hekau* meant "words of power." The European word *hag*, which originally meant a wise elder person, may have come from this Egyptian word.

A *pillar* or a column frequently is a symbol of the mythical World Tree or Tree of Life, the invisible, divine connection between the Otherworld and this world. The Canaanite goddess Asherah had a special pole or sacred tree at her temples. This pole commemorated her son/lover, whose death joined the two worlds. However, the obelisk and pillar also represent phallic gods, such as the Hindu Shiva and the Japanese god Nu-boko.

The meaning of a *pyramid* depends upon the number of sides it has. Those with three sides are Goddess symbols with the same meaning as the trefoil, that of creation and regeneration. Those with four sides are God symbols, representative of physical matter.

The *triangle*, the trefoil, the tripod, and the number three are all emblems of the Triple Goddess, the three-in-one unity. The downward-pointing triangle represents the feminine principle of creation, while the upward-pointing triangle represents the masculine. The downward-pointing triangle is known to the Hindus as the *yoni yantra*, and visually represents the feminine triangle of sexual organs.

When three triangles sit together or are interlaced, the symbol represents the Fate goddesses. A patch of interwoven lines, or weaving, also symbolizes the Fates, magical creating, and the web of human lives.

The *balance scales* are linked with Fate and Underworld deities, such as the Egyptian Maat and Anubis, and the Greek Themis. Such scales also symbolize the balance of cause and effect and divine retribution.

Seashells have always been important to the Goddess and Her followers. Ancient China called them one of their eight emblems. Spiral shells have the same meaning as the spiral path and the labyrinth, while the little cowry shells are emblems of the creative vaginal opening. Cockleshells in particular were associated with the Greek goddess Aphrodite, deity of love and sex.

The *hand sickle* is a symbol of harvest, whether it be physical crops or human souls. The god Saturn, a lord of karma, was portrayed with a sickle, as was Artemis in her aspect as the Virgin Huntress of retribution. Grain goddesses, such as Demeter and Ceres, were portrayed with a sickle. One of the symbols of the Phrygian earth goddess Cybele was the sickle, in this case a reminder of her connection with her son/lover who sacrificed himself for her.

Study Work

Choose the symbols you think best describe yourself at this point in your studies. Write them in your notebook. At the end of six months, look at these symbols again, and see which ones you would not choose.

CHAPTER 24

Meditation and Visualization

The art of meditation is very ancient. It has different names in different cultures, but the method and general purpose is the same. For example, among the Celts, meditation was known as the *dercad*. The *dercad* was taught only to those who did advanced studies in the ancient Celtic schools of knowledge. Today, most people associate meditation with Hindu gurus, not realizing that the art was much wider-spread than India.

Meditation and visualization are vital components of a Witch's studies and life. Without them, a Witch cannot expect to have success in magical manifestation or healing. For some Witches it is easier to visualize results while in a meditation. In all cases, both meditation and visualization are entwined, for both are part of the other.

Meditation is the act of sitting in silence, turning off the world around you, and entering a state of consciousness that enables you to reach into the Otherworld for power, knowledge, aid, and guidance. Sometimes, meditation, when deep enough, triggers an astral journey into the Otherworld.

Visualization is the act of seeing a specified result or scene within your mind. Visualization is used frequently by those who are not in Wicca or magic. For example, when people see and know exactly how they will execute a project or reach a goal, they are visualizing. Those people who can see most clearly the perfect end result are those who get exactly what they want. If Witches cannot see within their mind the completed goal for which they do ritual or magic, there is little chance they will manifest the desire. Lack of concentration and visualization, or the ability to see only part, produces only a partial result of what we worked for. That is the reason we sometimes do not attain the exact manifestation we had in mind.

If Witches do not take the time to learn visualization, they cannot expect to get successful results from magic. When doing magic, Witches must be able to see with their inner eyes the complete end result of their desires in exact detail. All manifestations must form within the Otherworld before they can become reality in this world. This follows from the principle: "As above, so below."

If you have difficulty visualizing things within your mind, there are exercises that will help you. It is simply a matter of training your right brain and the subconscious mind. Patience, persistence, and practice are vital in visualization and meditation. Results rarely come quickly, but require that you persist until you get the results you want.

To help with visualization, the first step is to learn to do the red dot exercise. Either cut out a one-inch circle from red paper, or purchase red dots with the adhesive backing in office supply stores. If you have a white wall, place the dot at eye level on the wall: eye level for you when sitting in a comfortable chair. If you do not have a white wall, place the red dot on a sheet of white paper or piece of poster board. Then attach the white paper to the wall so the red dot is at eye level. Sit in your chair and look intently at the red dot for about one minute. Now, close your eyes and see the red dot in your mind. At first, the dot may disappear within a few seconds. Continue to practice this exercise until you can hold the dot image within your mind for a long period of time.

Another good exercise is to sit and look at a candle flame for a time. Then, close your eyes and see the flame within your mind. As with the red dot, continue this exercise until you can hold the flame image for longer and longer periods of time.

The next exercise is more complicated. Place three small items on a tray, or arrange them on your desk or table. Look at the items for about ten seconds. Close your eyes and try to see each item in every detail. When you accomplish this, change the items and repeat the process. You can add more items as you become more proficient.

This last exercise not only teaches you to visualize, but it also teaches you to be aware of small details. Specifying details in some spells can make the difference between manifesting a general desire and getting your desire exactly as you wanted it.

Visualization is also an important part of a good meditation. The longer you practice meditation and the better you get at visualization, the more extremely detailed meditations you will have.

Many people are so afraid of meditation that they will not even try. Some fear that they will lose their "souls" or have some negative entity take over their bodies. This is a fallacy. Neither of these things will happen in meditation. However, people with certain mental illnesses, those taking medications that affect their mental processes, or those with addictions should not meditate, nor should they even consider deliberate astral travel. If people use the excuse that they just can't sit still and concentrate for meditation, then they need desperately to learn the art. The silence and serenity gained in meditation is valuable for keeping you calm and centered in everyday life.

Meditation requires few props or materials. Sit in a comfortable chair and make certain you are not disturbed. I do not recommend lying down, as this too easily leads to falling asleep. However, a few things will make meditating easier, especially when you begin the practice. You can read the following guided meditations into a tape recorder and then play them back when you meditate. In this manner, you can relax and follow the instructions without having to think about them.

Adding a background of soft, nonvocal music also helps, as it masks small environmental noises. If you want to burn a candle, be certain that it is in a safe place where it will not be knocked over. If you use incense, make sure that it will not be so strong that it hampers your concentration or breathing. Turn off or silence the telephone. Hang a "do not disturb" sign on the door. Nothing is more nerve-jarring than to have the phone or doorbell ring while you are in meditation.

Exclude any pets or children from the room when you meditate. Anyone moving around the room, rattling papers, or asking questions will keep you from meditating.

When you sit down for meditation, sit in a relaxed position with your hands in your lap and your feet flat on the floor. Breathe slowly and deeply, willing your muscles to relax. Do not dwell on whether or not your muscles are relaxing, for this will consume your attention when you should have it on the meditation. Simply tell your muscles to relax while you visualize them doing so.

Since deep meditation places you either in the astral world or on the edges of it, you should surround yourself with a brilliant white light. This light has a twofold purpose: one, it signals to your subconscious mind that you are perfectly and totally protected from any negativity while in meditation, and second, it advises your spiritual guides that you are on your way into another realm of consciousness where they can meet with you.

You also should avoid carrying negative emotions into a meditation. Since it is difficult to simply tell yourself to get rid of these negatives, the image of a well is helpful. Visualize yourself standing by a well. Drop all the negative emotions, events, and people in your life into the well. Then, walk away and leave them behind. This is a signal to your subconscious mind that you no longer want these things in your life. If the image of a well does not appeal to you, substitute a small stream or a garbage can.

You may leave a meditation any time you wish. You are *never* trapped in a meditation. All you have to do to return is to think of your physical body and open your eyes. When you first return, you may feel a bit disoriented, depending upon the depth of the meditation. In this case, wiggle your fingers and toes and take several deep breaths, until you feel grounded and centered once more.

When you tape the following meditations, do so in a slow, even voice. You may want to tape your voice several times until you discover the right pace for you.

There are several reasons for learning to meditate. First, the practice is relaxing and calming, something all people need in this fast-paced society. Second, you will strengthen your ability to visualize and your contact with spiritual guides. Proficient Witches cultivate both of these, so they can be successful in magical work. Third, deep meditation is an excellent way to do astral travel. When you reach this stage, your meditational experiences will change and become clearer, incorporating bright colors, sharp sounds, smells, and senses of taste and touch. Fourth, meditation can either create or strengthen the psychic conduit between you and the Otherworld. This is necessary in order to receive clear messages from your teacher guides and develop psychic abilities. Of course, you must open yourself to the truth only, or all you will hear will be what you want to hear. It is better to be a little skeptical than too gullible.

Do not judge your skill at meditating by the successes of others. People proceed at their own pace. It is best for beginners to practice meditation two times a week. It may not be wise even for those skilled in meditation to practice every day. This can become an escape from the ordinary world. Although meditation is valuable in many ways, it is best not to do it more than three times a week. Some people can lose themselves in too much meditation and become somewhat detached from reality.

You will go through certain stages of emotions when meditating. When you first learn to meditate, you will experience relaxation and pleasure. This state of mind may continue for some time. However, be prepared for a period to come that is not so pleasant. This will not be the fault of the meditation, but rather arises from a conflict between your conscious and subconscious minds. You may experience dissatisfaction, poor connections with the Otherworld, a skepticism about what you see in meditation, or a general lassitude of spirit, almost a depression. Do not give up at this point, for this will pass in a short time. Then, you will find that your meditations take on a whole new meaning and depth. Everything in the universe runs in cycles, and meditation is no exception.

Before you begin to use the following meditations, read through them several times. This will ease your mind about meditation, and prepare you for the meditation itself. Tape them for use. Be certain to leave blank spaces at the appropriate places, so you can have time to explore and experience things. When you meditate using the tape, do not try to think what comes next. Instead, relax and follow along as events are suggested. Remember, if a meditation starts to take you some place other than that described on the tape, flow with it. Some of the most pleasant, eventful, and interesting meditations occur this way.

THE QUIET FOREST MEDITATION

Sit comfortably in a relaxed position with your hands in your lap. Breathe slowly and deeply while telling your muscles to relax. Surround yourself with the brilliant white light; breathe it in and wrap it around you.

Now see a small well before you. Drop all the negatives in your life into the well. Watch them fall down into the darkness, away from you. Walk away and leave them there.

You find yourself walking along a path across a small meadow. Not far ahead of you is a grove of trees. The sun is warm on your skin. You smell the flowers blooming in the meadow grass and hear the songs of birds from the grove of trees. You follow the path until you reach the trees.

As you walk under the shade of the trees, you smell the sharp scent of pine needles and fir. You reach out one hand to touch the bark on a tree. Little patches of sunlight fall through the trees onto the path before you. You continue to follow the path, aware of birds and flowers along your way. You may even see squirrels and deer.

Soon you arrive at a tiny waterfall in the midst of the grove. Around the waterfall are large flat rocks that border the little stream that carries the water away. There are patches of brilliantly colored flowers, beds of tall ferns, and smaller trees by the waterfall. Dragonflies hover over the water, and butterflies dance in the air above it. Small harmless lizards bask on one of the rocks.

You sit down on one of the flat rocks. This is a place at the edge between the worlds, a place where you can meet Elves, Fairies, and other nature spirits. If any animal approaches you, try to communicate with it, for it may be an Otherworld familiar come to make you aware of its friendship. If nature spirits approach you, you may talk with them also.

As you sit and relax in the warm sun, you see a figure coming toward you through the trees. You feel a wave of love and friendship come to you from the person moving toward you. In a short time, the figure steps out into the open near the waterfall. You can see the person clearly now. This is one of your spiritual teachers. Be aware of whether this person is a man or a woman, tall or short, dark or fair. How are they dressed? What color are their eyes? Take in every detail you can.

Your teacher greets you as they sit beside you on the rock. The two of you sit and talk beside the waterfall. You may ask your teacher any question you wish. If the teacher cannot answer at this time, they will tell you so. Do not try to force an answer you wish, or the result will not be reliable. Take all the time you need to become acquainted with this teacher.

Soon, the teacher bids you farewell and goes back into the forest. You again follow the path back through the trees until you come to the meadow. In the air before you is the bright outline of a door. You step through the door and find yourself back in your physical body. You open your eyes, and the meditation is ended.

THE SACRED GARDEN MEDITATION

Sit comfortably in a relaxed position with your hands in your lap. Breathe slowly and deeply while telling your muscles to relax. Surround yourself with the brilliant white light; breathe it in and wrap it around you.

Now see a small well before you. Drop all the negatives in your life into the well. Watch them fall down into the darkness, away from you. Walk away and leave them there.

You find yourself walking along a path across a small meadow. Not far ahead of you is a high, stone wall. The sun is warm on your skin. You smell the flowers blooming along the path. Birds sing as they dart in the breezes over the meadow. You may see animals in the tall grass, but none of them will harm you.

You follow the path until you reach the wall. There is a gate in the wall at the end of the path. You press against it with one hand, and it opens easily. As you step inside, the gate closes behind you.

Before you is a huge garden. There are gravel paths leading off among trees, beds of flowers, and shrubbery. In the distance you see beautiful buildings. Along the paths are marble statues, fountains, and benches. The teacher you met at the waterfall is waiting for you, smiling and happy to see you again.

The two of you talk as the teacher guides you deeper into the garden. You may sit on one of the benches to talk further, or you may go to any of the buildings. Some of these buildings are temples. Others are vast libraries, holding all the knowledge learned by humans over thousands of years. Still others are centers of healing.

As you and your teacher walk along the paths, you may see groups of other people gathered around teachers who are lecturing on various psychic subjects. You may stop and listen if you wish.

There are many things to learn and see in this sacred garden. You and your teacher can go anywhere you desire. Take all the time you want to explore this special place.

At last, the teacher takes you back to the gate and bids you farewell. You push against the gate until it swings open. In the air before you is the bright outline of a door. You step through the door and find yourself back in your physical body. You open your eyes, and the meditation is ended.

As you can now see, meditation is not a complicated exercise. The discipline and techniques you learn in meditation will be valuable when you begin your exercises on astral travel.

Study Work

Begin a regular schedule of meditation. In your notebook, date and record your experiences in each meditation. This will help you to see your progress.

CHAPTER 25

Astral Projection

The idea of and belief in the astral planes is far older than ancient Egypt and Greece. In fact, we have no way to determine how ancient the belief in the astral is. We recognize the principle by descriptions and teachings in fragments of very old records.

The word *astral* comes from the Latin word *astrum*, which means "a star." Webster's definition is: "consisting of a super-sensible substance held in theosophy to be next above the tangible world in refinement." The ancients realized that it is impossible to give a description of the astral to anyone who does not believe in it. Therefore, they sensibly called it the Otherworld, to distinguish it from this world, and let it go at that. Those people who were members of the Mystery Religions and studied more than mundane subjects learned about the astral, and how to connect with it or go there. So did shamans in various cultures around the world.

The Otherworld is not a special place "out there" in the universe, as if it were a sun or a planet. It occupies the same space that this physical world does, but remains distinct from it. The physical world as we know it is surrounded and interpenetrated by the astral realms, or the Otherworld. The Otherworld consists of a different type of energy that vibrates at a higher rate than anything in the physical world around us. Since we know that everything physical vibrates at different frequencies, even inanimate objects, this is a logical conclusion.

This astral plane is very responsive to human thoughts and emotions. Since the physical body cannot go into the astral plane, or into the Otherworld, because of the differences in vibrational frequency, logically we must reach it by another part of our being. This leaves only the mind. Please notice, I did not say the brain, which is a separate body organ, whose primary function is to regulate activities within the physical body. Scientists realize that there is a difference between the functions of the brain and the mind, although they do not know where the mind resides.

The word *mind* comes from the Greek word *menos*, which means "spirit." Therefore, the mind may reside in the spirit. The Hindus and other ancient cultures understood that each human has more bodies than the physical one. And that there is a difference between the soul spirit (the essence that leaves the body upon death) and the astral body, whose vibrations closely match those of the Otherworld. The astral body is the part of each human spirit that can travel to the Otherworld and return at will.

Before you can understand the Otherworld and the human ability to go there, you must understand a few things about the brain and the mind. The physical brain has two parts: the right brain and the left brain. The left brain is usually dominant, for it controls the body and is logical. It is the seat of the conscious mind, that part which enables us to function in this world. Activity in the left brain can be measured by its fast, low-voltage waves of 14 to 28 cycles per second; these are called Beta waves. Under stress, these waves can reach over fifty cycles.

The subconscious mind is connected with the right brain, that part of the mind that is creative, intuitive, visualizing, and associated with what we term imagination. The waves of the right brain are called Alpha waves and usually measure 8 to 13 cycles per second.

Theta waves vibrate at 4 to 7 cycles per second. When you reach the Theta state, you have truly reached the subconscious mind, which has ten times the power of the conscious mind. When you realize that the average human only uses ten percent of the conscious mind, the possibilities are staggering. When Alpha and Theta waves begin to occur at the same time, or in close cycles, the individual is prepared to have a deep meditation or travel into the Otherworld. This is the desired state to reach when you want a deep and meaningful meditation, or when you want to visit the Otherworld. You can clearly remember your experiences during a Theta state. In this state you reach an altered state of consciousness.

Brain waves during sleep are called Delta waves, and vibrate at 0.5 to 3 cycles per second. Since this state appears only when the body is totally relaxed and unaware of the surroundings, it is of little use during meditation or deliberate astral travels. However, the astral body can and does spontaneously travel during sleep, although we seldom clearly remember the experiences and tend to call them "dreams" when we do.

It is not necessary to purchase a machine to measure brain waves to know when you are in an altered state of consciousness. You will learn from your meditative experiences. Whenever you have a meditation in which you experience brilliant colors, complete with sounds, smells, tastes, and the sense of touch, you have reached an altered state.

This altered state of consciousness also has a physical impact upon the body. It aids the nerve endings in the brain to come closer together. When these dendrites and axons of the nerves link up, our nervous system works more smoothly, without strain. In people with senility, this linkage has been shown to decrease the symptoms of that disease.

All cultural traditions say that the Otherworld consists of many levels, from lower to higher. Most state that there are seven levels, which may indicate that these levels in some manner are connected with the seven chakras of the human astral body. Each level is inhabited by spirits or souls that resonate to its particular rate of vibrations. These levels have nothing to do with social class, outward earthly appearance, or the amount of time spent in worship. The levels are based on spiritual consciousness and growth. In other words, these multiple levels of the Otherworld are each inhabited by the souls that resonate to its frequency, whether these souls are evolved, higher souls, the middle range of souls, or devolved, criminal-like souls.

The Otherworld is also inhabited by elemental spirits, a belief that is shared by all shamanic cultures. Nature spirits, the souls of animals, and entities created by strongly projected thoughts of humans also reside there. These spirits come and go as they wish between worlds. An astral traveler may also meet other astral travelers on the astral plane.

Some people aver that when in the astral body there are no emotions left. However, I have not found this to be the case. If anything, the emotions and the five senses are heightened. Emotions are not physical body traits, although they are connected with physical experiences. If it were true that there are no emotions in the astral realm, the spirits of deceased loved ones would not care to return to comfort and help those left behind on the earth plane. We have thousands of years of testimony to the return of spirits seeking to comfort or warn those left behind or to demand justice for wrongs done to them.

The highest level of the Otherworld cannot be accessed by astral travelers. Only the guardian spirits and spiritual teachers can travel to this realm, and they only go to a limited area there to receive instructions. It is the residence of the Supreme Creating Power. This Power consists of both the Male and Female Principles of the universe, or the Goddess and the God, who are the ultimate archetypes. These great deities may make themselves known to us, but we do not have the privilege of entering their realm.

Just below this level is the area in which a traveler may meet the pantheons of gods and goddesses, which are aspects of the Goddess and the God. Each pantheon has a special area where the temples and buildings are in the architectural style associated with the culture that believed in them.

The greatest part of the Otherworld is like a middle level. This is the resting place of ordinary souls between incarnations. The average soul may reside here for hundreds of years before reincarnation. Before returning, these souls have long discussions with the Great Council about a life plan, what goals it wants to accomplish, and what other souls it wishes to be with and why. Each soul also tries to improve itself spiritually and learn as much as possible.

Any souls that arrive confused or still experiencing pain in this beautiful realm of the Otherworld are taken immediately to a sleeping temple. There, they are placed in a deep, healing sleep for as long as is needed to erase the fear, pain, and confusion they experienced at their death. This sleep may last from a few weeks to several months. When a soul is healed of these impressions, it is awakened and allowed to mingle with the other souls in this area.

The souls in this "middle" area of the astral plane have access to many temples and schools of learning on every subject imaginable. Great and wise teachers hold classes for anyone interested. Here, they will find crystal gardens, beautiful flower gardens, and areas for peaceful meditations. Magnificent art and music are everywhere to be enjoyed. These souls are allowed to visit friends, family, and loved ones on the physical plane whenever they wish. Souls with which one experienced past incarnations are also here. This is the area most visited by humans who astral travel in their sleep.

Teachers, guides, and the guardian spirits that some people call "angels" inhabit the middle area also. So do the astral familiars and the souls of earthly animals. This is the area to which astral travelers go when they want to talk to their teachers and guides, visited with deceased friends and loved ones, discover their personal astral familiars, undergo astral initiations, or find ancient knowledge.

There are vast libraries to be explored here, including the temple that holds the repository of all records—the Akashic Records. It takes experience to use the Akashic

Records to discover one's past lives. However, teachers and guides will frequently aid astral travelers in this task.

The immensely powerful and important Great Council has a special temple in this area. It is one of the Council's duties to advise each soul before it returns to the earth plane, as well as work on the karmic plan for this planet and all nations on it. Certain Council members also work in retrieving souls from mass disasters and wars.

The next to the lowest realm is the place where souls go that are not really evil, but have separated themselves from the Divine Creating Spirit for some reason. Among these are people who committed suicide because of despair or great pain. Although they did not end their lives to spite or harm another, but did it because of great pain, stress, or fear, they have little input into their next incarnation. All suicides must return to live out however long they would have lived before, even if it is one hour. Souls from this area must wait for the Council to determine when and where they should reincarnate. The Council arranges a life that they think is best for the soul's spiritual growth.

The very lowest realm of the Otherworld contains the criminal-like souls, the spiritual essences of truly evil, cruel, unethical, and unrepentant humans. Examples of human souls in this area are people who committed suicide in an attempt to harm or demoralize another, serial killers, personalities such as Hitler and other evil people, cruel and manipulative people who have no respect for other lives, those who willfully break physical and spiritual laws, and malicious people who abuse and/or torture other humans and animals. Entities that we term demons also occupy this area. This is an area where you definitely do not want to go. Souls here make an immediate fast return into another body, in fact, the first body available.

This is a general map of the Otherworld regions. If we want to go there, obviously we cannot travel in a physical body. This leaves only the astral body as a vehicle for travel. Many people do not believe they can astral travel because they believe that they must go through the "looking back at yourself from the ceiling" phenomena. In fact, the simplest and safest method for astral travel is to go into a deep meditation, which will gently allow one's astral body to slip out and go where it wishes. This is also the best method when it comes to remembering astral travels in all their vividness. You direct the astral body in travel.

You cannot force astral travel. You must learn to relax into the meditation until you are completely unaware of your surroundings. You will feel no discomfort when your astral body separates. In fact, you may not notice the transition until you realize that your meditation has taken on a life of its own, complete with an amplification of the senses, and vivid experiences. When your experiences no longer match the meditation tape you use, but take on a life of their own; when you cannot change a part of a meditational experience, such as colors, then you are in the astral.

You never need to worry about being possessed by an evil spirit while astral traveling. Your teachers will not allow this. Also, the white light you use at the beginning of every meditation will reinforce your natural defense against such entities. For a possession to truly take place, you either must invite such an entity to be with you, or have a severe character flaw, such as alcoholism or drug addiction, that will form a weak spot. Other problems that form an opening are habitual lying, cruelty, manipulation of others, and similar unsavory characteristics.

The best and safest way to learn astral travel is to be persistent in your meditations. When your teachers believe you are ready for a higher experience, they will aid you in slipping smoothly from a regular meditation to astral travel.

Study Work

Keep records of all your meditations. Begin to note any different experiences and how they may relate to beginning astral travels.

CHAPTER 26

The Akashic Records, Death, Reincarnation, and Karma

Almost all Witches believe in reincarnation. So do a great many other religions and cultures around the world. Actually, those who believe in reincarnation far outnumber those who do not. Scientists know that nothing in the universe can actually be totally destroyed. When one substance appears to be destroyed, it is simply transmuted into something else. Burning wood, for example, becomes heat, ashes, and smoke. In other words, any destroyed physical object changes form. Therefore, it is reasonable to assume that the human soul and individuality are not extinguished at death. The soul and individuality are not of a physical nature, and therefore do not transmute according to physical laws as we know them. This is in line with the law "As above, so below." Spiritual forms on the higher realms or levels are not destroyed, but continue to exist in one form or another. Therefore, the spiritual part of everything that dies on the earthly realm will do the same.

Each of us has lived many lives before our present one. All of these lives make up and influence our present likes, dislikes, phobias, character traits, and predilections to certain actions and reactions. Too many people delude themselves into believing that they were very famous, important people in other lives. The fact is, very few of us were. In every era it is the common, hard-working, everyday person who has the most impact on society, and whose life experiences make the biggest impression both on the spiritual soul and the development of physical cultures. We all experience being male and female and incarnate into different civilizations for the uplifting experiences such lives bring to our total soul development.

Humans come with a built-in protection against seeking death or taking serious risks that might kill them. Sometimes, because of karmic circumstances, environmental problems, or unusual events, humans will choose to place themselves in death's path. Ordinarily, however, humans are afraid of death. This is partly because we no longer have the spiritual instruction that teaches us the truth about death. We have been taught that death is painful and terrible, that when we die all we can expect is total boredom of perfected nothingness or eternal punishment for being human. The cause of death may be painful, but not the actual process of dying. There is nothing terrible about being "reborn" into a new life. Hypnotized people remember their birth as being a far more painful, frightening process than the final act of leaving the physical body.

At one time, certain cultures, such as the Celts, had special priestesses who helped the dying make the transition through the use of music and song. They guided the sick on meditational journeys that taught them how to die painlessly and joyfully. These guided tours showed the sick how to safely cross the barrier between the worlds and what and who they would find there.

Between incarnations, souls rest in a part of the astral planes known as the Land of Faery or other Pagan names. The ancient Celts knew it as the Blesséd Isles. Summerland is a much later term that arose with the founding of the Spiritualist churches during the 1800s. Since this Pagan paradise is part of the astral realms, it can also be reached through dreams, meditation, and astral travel to communicate with the dead.

We are given choices before we take the step of being reincarnated. Unless a soul is relegated to the lower astral levels, each soul can formulate its own life plan, with the help and advice of teachers and the Great Council. Our choices are frequently influenced by our belief that we can help change the lives of others or right great wrongs.

After entering the new body, the subconscious mind becomes very aware of all the challenges and obstacles the new family raises against these altruistic desires. Although the conscious mind is not aware of this, the subconscious mind knows the goals cannot be met fully, or sometimes only partially. What we learn out in our new life will not be what we expected. However, all life experiences have value. As on the physical, ordinary level of life, not all choices are wise ones. Most choices will be made out of necessity. Nevertheless, the necessary choices frequently turn out to be the wisest ones and of the most value to spiritual growth.

Karma is very much involved with reincarnation. Karma is the law of cause and effect. Every action causes a reaction that equalizes and balances. Contrary to the beliefs of the uninformed karma is not all negative. You can build up the astral equivalent of a positive balance from past lives, or even the present one. It is like having a spiritual bank account. We can add to it by positive experiences and morals, or we can be forced to pay for negative experiences and morals.

The best way to know what your karmic debits or credits might be is to practice visiting the Hall of Akashic Records. There, with the help of our teachers, we can look through our past lives and get glimpses of what we should or should not be doing in this life to correct any flaws. That is why all Witches should do magic with the aim of doing the least karmic damage to themselves and others.

Be careful not to fall into the trap of labeling every event in your life as karmic or the hand of destiny. Often this is a way for people to deny responsibility for their decision for fear that they might be wrong or will create an unpleasant scene. This attitude is passing the buck, just as the orthodox believers might say, "The Devil made me do it," or "It's God's will and I can't change it." Unfortunately, the word destiny has become an excuse for not making a choice or decision, a reason for the tyrant or criminal to excuse their crimes, and for the fool to avoid standing up to the tyrant or criminal. It is rare that people do not have choices in the overall path of their lives. Some life experiences may be more difficult than others, and we may have less impact on what happens, but there are always little choices we can make to effect changes.

Some people get caught up in trying to find their "life's purpose," or "goal." Every person's purpose in life is to improve spiritually, see the truth, live it daily, and be the best person they can be.

A good life does not always follow a wretched, miserable life. Each life depends entirely upon the life plan we agree to before we incarnate. We may have several difficult lives, one after another, or we may see a varied pattern of lives through the space of many lifetimes.

Some groups believe that you can live two lives at the same time. This idea does not follow any spiritual or physical laws that I know. Unless the soul leaves a body, and the physical body is kept alive by mechanical means, it is impossible for the same soul to have been in two separate and different bodies during the same incarnation. This phenomenon has been found in certain causes of insanity and may possibly explain multiple personalities.

The only logical and meaningful reason to find out about our past lives is so we can improve the one we are living now. By truthfully remembering past lives, we can better understand ourselves, what may have influenced us, what hidden talents we may have to develop, what our past relationships with present people were, and what we need to do to grow spiritually.

The Hall of Akashic Records in the Otherworld is a beautiful, white, marble building, set in a serene landscape of ornamental pools, statues, fountains, trees, and flowers. It contains the record of every single life any person has ever lived. The Hall reminds one of a great library. Although there may be soft music playing in the background, there are no loud voices from the other figures you see. Until you are very familiar with this Hall and know how to correctly use the records, you should be accompanied by one of your teachers. This teacher will help you to find your personal records and teach you how to use the various devices that show you these records in visual and audio form.

One of the best devices to use is a large table with a flat, or nearly flat, surface. At times, this table will appear with a slightly domed top. By activating the proper buttons (or what appear as buttons) on the edge, you can access your past lives in visual pictures complete with sound. For the first few times you visit the Hall, you may have trouble hearing any sound from these records. This seems to be normal, and the problem will disappear with practice. There also are books containing the same lives. Sometimes these will show moving pictures when opened. Other times there is a text, frequently in ancient alphabets. Your teacher-guide may need to interpret these for you. All people have many volumes, which together make up the entire sequence of their lives.

The guided meditation that follows will help you learn to find and use the Hall of Akashic Records. Each time you use this meditation to go there, the experience may be different, and the lives you see will be the ones of most value to you at the time. So be certain to consider carefully what you learned when you return. You may not see the relevance of a past life at first. With a little thought, though, the truth will reveal itself.

Take care that you see what is the truth, and not something you want to see. If you close yourself to the truth, it will not benefit you to visit the Hall of Akashic Records.

The Hall of Akashic Records

Sit comfortably in a relaxed position with your hands in your lap. Breathe slowly and deeply while telling your muscles to relax. Surround yourself with brilliant white light; breathe it in and wrap it around you.

Now see a small well before you. Drop all the negatives in your life into the well. Watch them fall down into the darkness, away from you. Walk away and leave them there.

You find yourself walking along a path across a small meadow. Not far ahead of you is a high, stone wall. The sun is warm on your skin. You smell the flowers blooming along the path. Birds sing as they dart in the breezes over the meadow. You may see animals in the tall grass, but none of them will harm you.

You follow the path until you reach the wall. There is a gate in the wall at the end of the path. You press against it with one hand, and it opens easily. As you step inside, the gate closes behind you.

Before you is the huge garden you visited before. You glance quickly around and see gravel paths leading off among trees, beds of flowers, and shrubbery. In the distance are the shimmering forms of beautiful buildings. One of your teachers comes toward you, smiling and happy to see you again.

The two of you talk as the teacher guides you deeper into the garden. Through the trees you see a white, marble building with fluted, tall columns across the front. Soon you are climbing the seven steps to the doors that are opened wide to the pleasant garden outside. Over this entrance are carved the words "Hall of Akashic Records." Inside the building you see tier after tier of shelves, with stairs to each level. The shelves are all full of books. The main floor before you has rows of tables with comfortable chairs arranged around them. Along both sides of the room are larger tables with strange, glass-like tops. There are many other people here, all intent upon reading the books or gazing into the viewing tables. Sitting at four desks on raised platforms, and spaced about the room, are several people whose job it is to help.

Your teacher takes you to the section that holds the volumes of your past lives. You are allowed to choose one volume. You take it back with you to one of the tables. You and your teacher look through the book. The teacher helps you to understand many things about the life you are viewing. Then the teacher takes you to one of the viewing tables, where the two of you watch this life in moving form. Take all the time you need to absorb important facts from this life and see how it applies to your present incarnation. Ask your teacher any questions you wish.

At last, the teacher takes you back to the gate and bids you farewell. You push against the gate until it swings open. In the air before you is the bright outline of a door. You step through the door and find yourself back in your physical body. You open your eyes, and the meditation is ended.

It may take you time to fully understand the effects of this past life on your present life. However, with introspection, you will see the connection. You can use this meditation to return to the Hall innumerable times, looking into a different past life at each visit.

Study Work
Make a journey to the Hall of Akashic Records. When you return, write down your experience in detail in your notebook. Below it, write what importance you think it has for you. After a month or two, again write down what you think the experience taught you.

CHAPTER 27

Dreams and Dream Journals

Every Witch should have both a personal journal and a dream journal. Make a daily practice of writing in both journals. The activity of writing will help you to understand and clarify many problems, as well as charting your path through life.

Dreams are a gateway to the subconscious and superconscious minds. The dreams we have each night are strictly controlled by the entity known as the Guardian of the Threshold. These dreams rarely show us more than we are capable of comprehending and handling. However, the subconscious mind only speaks to us in symbols. This is why the largest percentage of dreams is in symbolic form, a miscellany of images that frequently do not make sense without a lot of thought.

Some people try to force dreams, particularly if they are intent on getting answers about the future or past lives. This action puts one in conflict with the Guardian of the Threshold, who allows dreams of this kind when the person is emotionally, mentally, and spiritually prepared. If people deliberately force their way through this gateway, the outcome may range from unpleasant dreams to disastrous repercussions on mental and emotional levels. Until they are prepared to face all they are now, have been in past lives, and will be in the future, the total truth of everything pleasant and unpleasant, it is best to leave this gateway under the control of the Guardian.

The Guardian of the Threshold is an Otherworld entity that guards the gateway into the subconscious, and thus the superconscious, mind. This Guardian does more than regulate the type of dreams you have. It also has jurisdiction over whether you enter certain areas of the Otherworld or are turned back. There will come a time in your spiritual growth when the Guardian will challenge you. If you cannot successfully pass the challenge, which is different for every person, you are not allowed to continue at that time into the deeper Mysteries.

There are four basic types of dreams. The dreams in which your subconscious mind sorts out the day's events are the most common and frequent. There are also dreams that are actually astral projection and travel. These are frequently filled with symbolic images along with scenes and people you know. The third category consists of dreams that are reliving a past life. These often are more difficult to decipher, depending upon whether the dream shows you only a few scenes or goes into great detail. The fourth category of dreams consists of the ones that convey prophetic messages and portray future events.

The only way you can gain control over understanding your dreams, and which type of dream you have, is to keep a dream journal. By making the effort to understand the symbolic images you see each night, the Guardian presents you with more and more detailed, explicit information.

When your subconscious mind is sorting out daily problems and presenting you with symbolic imagery, it can be difficult to understand what is actually being said and what it all means. Some symbols have a universal meaning that seems to come from deep within the superconscious, or genetic, mind. In other words, these symbols have the same meaning that they did hundreds of years ago, and mean the same to several cultures. Other symbols can only be interpreted according to what they personally mean to each person. This is why most dream dictionaries are of little use, unless the user knows to translate some symbols into different meanings.

Astral travel dreams frequently involve people with whom you are familiar or places you know. What you see and hear you can later substantiate. These travels may be of a casual nature or they may present you with information that is vital. If you should find yourself viewing an embarrassing situation, however, it is better if you do not share with others the fact that you saw what you did.

Past-life dreams most commonly present the dreamer with a deeply emotional scene from a past life. This scene has great meaning in the present life. Sometimes, it represents a problem with which you are again dealing. Other times, the scene may show you why you have a certain phobia or are experiencing a particular illness or injury. Infrequently, these dreams will reveal entire large sections of a life, or all of a life. These can be extremely unsettling, as there is no way you can avoid seeing the truth of what you once were. You know who you are in the dream, even though you may recognize that you are different than you are now.

Prophetic dreams are the most frustrating type of dream. Usually, they will present you with an event or circumstance, whether mundane or disastrous, but will not reveal a date or even an exact place. You will know what will happen by what you see, and perhaps even get a sense of the place by the scenery. You may hear the voice of someone you cannot see, telling you what is happening. If you are fortunate, the voice may reveal where the scene is taking place. Most dreams in this category take the form of disasters. You will not be able to stop the future disaster, but I guarantee you will worry about it. By the time a future event becomes so solid in its outcome as to appear in prophetic dreams, it is beyond anyone's control to force changes. The positive outcome of such a dream is that it shows you that your psychic abilities are increasing.

Since all dreams arise from the subconscious and superconscious minds, you should make an effort to understand them as best you can. The following dream dictionary will help you, especially in interpreting the images that have universal meaning. Nevertheless, you will have to interpret many of the symbols according to your personal feelings. For example, cats in dreams can mean bad luck to someone who dislikes cats. For a cat lover, the meaning would be good luck, depending upon how the cat was behaving in the dream.

Both Carl Jung and Sigmund Freud associated most dream symbols with sexuality in one form or another. From my experience, dream symbols go far beyond this limited definition, and most frequently have little to do with sex.

DREAM DICTIONARY

Airplane: This may symbolize an approaching period of excitement and relaxation for the dreamer. It can also mean coming success.

Animals: The symbolism depends upon whether the animal is friendly or threatening, and what the dreamer feels about the animal. Usually, animals represent people and the dreamer's relationship with them.

Automobile: Riding in a car that is out of control indicates a loss of direction in life, or that the dreamer feels they have no control over what is happening in life. Driving a car and keeping control represents the dreamer being on the right life track.

Birds: Birds are messengers or bringers of omens, good or bad. If the bird is aggressive, it can represent jealousy. If it is a thief, such as a magpie or crow, it can represent a possible threat to a relationship, or the dreamer feels part of their life has been stolen by another person.

Bones: Broken bones represent a weakness of which the dreamer needs to be aware. Bare bones symbolize the end of a relationship or cycle of life.

Bottles: Describing the meaning of this symbol depends on what the bottle holds. If it holds gas or other dangerous ingredients, the dreamer may be repressing deep anger and frustration. If the bottle contains nothing, or something innocuous, the symbol can mean that the dreamer feels "bottled up" or stifled.

Bridge: This signifies a change either in the present or coming very soon. The smoothness of the transition depends upon the condition of the bridge and the difficulty or ease with which you crossed it.

Cards, playing: If the dreamer is involved in a game of cards, this may represent the dreamer's feelings that fate is in control of life.

Cemetery: This symbol may represent the end of something in the dreamer's life, or the need to end a relationship or job.

Chase: Being chased by a frightening, unseen presence can mean either that you are afraid of aspects of yourself that you don't want to acknowledge, or that you feel deeply threatened by circumstances in your life. If you can turn and confront what chases you, you can move beyond the fear.

Clothing: If you dream of yourself in strange or tight clothing, you are anxious about accepting a proposed change.

Communication: If you can't make yourself heard to others in your dream, you feel inadequate in dealing with people. If they hear you but can't understand you, there is a weakness in your ideas.

Crossroads: This dream image represents a need for the dreamer to make a decision.

Cup: A full cup symbolizes prosperity, but an empty cup predicts hard times ahead.

Door: Ringing a bell or knocking on a door that does not open indicates that you think of yourself as a failure. The same meaning applies to purchasing something and having no money to pay.

Drowning, struggle in water: You feel as if you are going under in your life, perhaps because of daily problems or illness.

Elevator: If the elevator is going up, there will be a period of positive change. If going down, the change will be negative.

Eyes: Closed eyes in a dream indicate that you, or the person you see, are not willing to face reality. Eyes that refuse to look at the dreamer represent someone who is telling a lie.

Falling: Usually in these dreams a person is falling from a great height, and is symbolic of fear of failure. The dreamer lacks confidence in what they are doing or considering doing in life.

Feathers: This is frequently a symbol of a gift of some kind.

Feces, manure: This widely known symbol indicates success and money.

Fence: This symbol represents an obstacle in your life. If you manage to jump over it, or get around it in some manner, you will be successful in meeting the challenge of the obstacle.

Fire: Threatening fire may symbolize loss of a relationship, job, or way of life. It can also mean disruptive emotional confrontations. Non-threatening fire represents a cleansing or a new beginning.

Fog, mist: When you are lost in a fog or mist, you feel you have lost direction in your life.

Funeral: This gloomy dream symbol represents the need for an end to some part of the dreamer's life.

Gifts: If the dreamer feels pressured to take the gift, it indicates unwanted attention or control from another person. If the gift is acceptable, it means the dreamer will gain recognition and be self-sufficient.

Hat: Wearing or being given a hat, especially a hat with a tall crown, represents being given a position of authority or being recognized for something. If the hat is knocked off, or blows off in a wind, the dreamer is anxious about losing this recognition.

Hospital: Being in a hospital can have two meanings. First, the dreamer fears losing control over their life. Second, the person in the hospital may have a hidden health problem that needs attention.

Hotel: This symbol represents something of a transitory nature in the dreamer's life.

House: Sometimes a house represents the body of the dreamer. Other times it symbolizes the dreamer's life. Whether it is positive or negative depends upon the dreamer's feelings about and toward the house. If a house is dark and empty, the dreamer is depressed about the future.

Isolation: This image has two meanings. First, if the dreamer is comfortable with the secluded area, as with an island, desert, or deep forest, they feel a strong need to avoid anything new for a time, such as troublesome people. If the dream is uncomfortable, the dreamer needs to work at changing their life.

Knife: If another person holds a knife, the dreamer feels threatened by someone. If the dreamer holds the knife, it represents control. If the dreamer threatens another with a knife, it may mean deep anger that could become destructive.

Letters: Seeing or receiving a letter in a dream symbolizes a message. The content of the message depends upon whether the dreamer felt positive or negative about the letter.

Light: Seeing a brilliant light represents either an approaching religious experience, or the dreamer being enlightened about a problem.

Mail: Whether positive or negative, this image symbolizes messages.

Map, chart: Finding or being given a map represents that you are being guided through this portion of your life to events and people that will help you.

Mask: Masked people in a dream signify that something secret is being kept from you. The actions of the masked people indicate whether the secret is positive or negative. If you wear a mask, you are hiding something or feel you need to hide your true self from others.

Maze: Finding yourself in a maze can represent a deep internal search for a connection with the subconscious mind. It also can mean that you feel trapped and panicked by the tangle of your life.

Mirror: If you see your reflection in a mirror, you are satisfied with yourself at the moment. If you see a strange reflection, you are not happy with your identity.

Money: If the dreamer has or finds money, this image represents self-confidence and security. If the dreamer is without money, it means lack of self-confidence and that personal security feels threatened.

Mud: This is a symbol known in many cultures as an indication of success and prosperity.

Nudity: If the nude person or people in a dream are not embarrassed, this symbolizes love and friendship with nothing to hide. If the nude dreamer is embarrassed, it represents lack of self-confidence.

Paper: Stacks of paper represent the dreamer's anxiety about handling a demanding task. Single sheets of paper may indicate a message.

Purse: This represents the financial security in life. A full purse symbolizes a comfortable future, while an empty one shows the dreamer's anxiety about finances.

Race: Races in dreams always indicate goals you want to achieve.

Rose: The red rose is a traditional symbol of love and affection. The white rose is a symbol of spiritual accomplishment.

Running, movement: When you try to run but are stuck in some manner, this indicates a sense of entrapment in life. Slowly making your way through mud, snow, or similar substances shows that you will progress at a very slow pace for a time.

School: Finding oneself in school represents that the dreamer feels insecure in knowing how to handle a life or career situation.

Seasons: When one season follows another in logical sequence in a dream, it is an indication of personal transformation taking place. If the seasons go backward, it means you will either experience a period where your progress appears to reverse, or that forward movement stops and life becomes static.

Seeking, hunting: When you frantically seek for the right room, street, or road in a dream, you fear losing something important to your personal identity.

Shoes: Traditionally, well-worn shoes represent success, while new shoes mean over-confidence that is not warranted.

Spiders: Few people have good feelings about spiders. When seen in a dream, a spider can represent someone who is using guilt and deceit to control the dreamer. Or it may symbolize a feeling that the dreamer is being trapped and threatened in some way by a negative person. Frequently, this negative person is a parent, spouse, one in authority, and so forth.

Surroundings, unfamiliar: If you feel lost or confused, you are trying to force changes for which you are not ready. If you feel excited and pleased, you are ready for change.

Toilet: Having to go to the bathroom in a dream represents the dreamer's need to release anxiety.

Train: This symbol represents help coming to the dreamer. If the dreamer is on the wrong train, it means missed opportunities.

War: The dreamer is having difficulty reconciling what they feel is right with what others demand they do.

Water: If the water is clear and calm, an approaching period in life will be positive. If the water is muddy and/or turbulent, life will be filled with problems.

Weddings: Frequently, this image represents the dreamer's need for a lasting relationship. However, it also can mean that the dreamer is successfully balancing all parts of life.

Weight: A loss of weight in a dream means that demanding people are draining off the dreamer's energy.

Study Work

Keep a regular journal of your dreams. Write down your immediate impression of each dream. Later, return and write what you think of the dream at the later date.

CHAPTER 28

Developing Psychic Abilities

Witches believe that humans have access to more than the five physical senses, that the five physical senses have their counterparts in the astral. Since this physical world is only part of total reality, the senses of the astral, spiritual body can be trained to pick up messages, impressions, and other information from the astral planes.

There are all kinds of explanations for why people are psychic, or why science believes no one is, but these really do not matter. The fact is, most people have one or more psychic abilities of varying degrees of strength. Almost all Witches work with at least one psychic ability in their spiritual work and magic. According to the laws of science, the bumblebee shouldn't be able to fly. However, the bumblebee doesn't know this and flies anyway. It doesn't matter if other people know of your abilities, what matters is that you know what you can do.

The words clairvoyance, clairaudience, and clairsentience all refer to various ways of referring to the psychic senses and being aware of psychic happenings. Clairaudience means to hear music or voices that are not audible to the physical ears. Clairsentience, which is "clear-knowing," means to receive information that the receiver has no way of perceiving in the physical. People often say, "I just know," when they are using this sense. The word clairvoyance, or "clear-seeing," refers to non-physical insight and perception, and is connected with inner vision.

Nearly everyone is familiar with the term "gut instincts." These are the intuitive feelings that arise from deep within to let you know if you are making a positive or negative decision about something. Most people rely on their intuition when deciding if they like or dislike a new acquaintance or when dealing with such decisions as signing a contract or purchasing something. If you go against these "first impressions," you usually wish you had followed them.

Empathic people pick up on the emotions of others, often when they would rather not do so. They can sense the underlying mood of a group simply by walking into a room. Unfortunately, until these psychics learn to shield themselves, they also are open to others drawing off their physical energy. People who rob the energy of another are known as psychic vampires.

Both the United States and the Soviet Union have used the psychic abilities of certain people for years to spy on rival countries or people they deemed questionable. People with psychic ability called "remote viewing" were used for this work. Remote viewing is done by concentrating the mind on a remote destination, such as an office, person, or house, and letting your subconscious mind send you impressions about it. Many of the psychics involved in these experiments were greatly harassed if they chose to leave the program. For more information on this, read *Psychic Warrior: Inside the CIA's Stargate Program* by David Morehouse. This career military man paints an unvarnished, upsetting, but true picture of a government-controlled psychic. It should be a warning to all psychics to stay away from anyone who wants to control your abilities.

The best way to find out what your psychic abilities are, and then strengthen them, is through enjoyable exercises. Always be motivated enough to keep learning, but never so fixated that you are stressed and not having fun.

It can be difficult to enlist your psychic abilities if you were forced to shut them down early in life because they were against your religion, upset the family, or no one believed you. The best method for overcoming this barrier is patience, practice, and time.

If you think you would like to be a psychic with paying clients and fame, consider the downside of publicly revealing that you are a psychic reader. You may be laughed at, perhaps hounded by local orthodox ministers and the police, and your privacy and personal life will be forever gone. People may call you at 3 A.M. and demand a free reading over the phone. It is best if you only read for a select, small group of friends and recommended people.

Please realize that not everyone will be good at every form of psychic ability. Some people are very accurate with tarot card readings, but couldn't guess a Zenner card if they had to.

There are certain simple exercises one can use to strengthen psychic abilities. They do not require exotic or expensive materials, nor must you leave home to use them. One such exercise is the use of the Zenner cards. Zenner cards were employed by Dr. J. B. Rhine from Duke University to test psychic abilities. In these tests, one person looked at a card while another person tried to pick up the symbol on the card by mental powers. The card symbols consisted of a red equal-armed cross, a green five-pointed star, a black square, an orange circle, and three blue wavy lines, one above the other. The card deck had a total of twenty-five cards, five of each symbol. (Notice that the symbols he used are universally recognized sacred symbols: See Chapter 23.)

You can easily make your own Zenner deck by drawing the symbols on identical pieces of heavy paper or poster board. Or you can purchase a blank card deck and paint the symbols on these with felt markers. You can mix up the cards, turn them over on a table, and draw one. While holding the card with the symbol away from you, try to get an impression of what the symbol is. At first, you may only get flashes of color that will help you. If you have a working partner, one person can hold a card while the other relates the impressions they get.

Another method is to cut out three- or four-inch square pieces of different colors of construction paper. Place one of each colored square in a plain mailing envelope, tucking in the flap, but not sealing it. Then hold an envelope and see if you can get an impression of the color inside.

Psychometry is defined as the ability to read vibrations of an object belonging to another person by touching it. The word comes from the Greek *psyche*, which means soul. Frequently, this does not work well if you are handling leather or paper, but it can be done. By holding the object in your hands, you can get mental images or symbols relating to the history of the object and the people who owned or handled it. This is best done with objects of which you know nothing. When a group of budding psychics get together, it is entertaining to have everyone put an object into a basket. The basket is passed around, and each person takes an object that is not theirs. Then, each tells the impressions and symbols they receive from the object in their hands. If you have difficulty getting impressions from an object by holding it in your hands, press it lightly to the center of your forehead, where your third eye for inner sight is found.

To work on telepathy, which is the exchange of information from one person's mind to another person's mind, you need to work with someone else. One person should act as sender, while the other is the receiver. Sit facing each other, both with the eyes closed. The sender thinks of the image they want the receiver to get. In the beginning, choose simple things, such as single numbers, colors, or images from the Zenner cards.

If you have a pet, you can work on sending the pet messages, and see if you get a response. Mentally call the pet's name, and see if it will come to you, or at least look at you. As with humans, both you and your pet should be open to the psychic, or this will not work. You may find your pet sending you messages, such as an empty food dish.

Automatic writing is the process of a spirit sending messages through the hand of a psychic who is holding a pen on paper. The greatest difficulties for the psychic are leaving the hand free to move without physical intervention, not worrying about grammar or punctuation, and not being concerned if it is your conscious mind picking up the message. In the beginning of working with this gift, the psychic often gets only scrawls or doodles. Automatic writing takes a great deal of patience and practice to learn.

Operating the Ouija™ Board is much the same as the process used in automatic writing. In both cases, psychics should be certain to insist that only higher level spirits work with them. There is no evil in the Ouija™ Board unless one of the sitters brings negative vibrations in with them, or doesn't care what kind of entity speaks through the board. Both automatic writing and the Ouija™ Board should not be used for frivolous purposes. The pendulum, tarot cards, and rune stones work on the same basic principle.

Scrying is an old word for gazing into a crystal ball, black mirror, cup of water, or puddle of ink. Although the generalized image of a scryer is one who actually sees images within the crystal ball, this is not always the way this psychic ability works. Many users get mental images and impressions instead. The crystal balls one usually sees for sale, or in the possession of one who gazes, are totally clear. However, clarity is not the best for everyone. Crystal balls with veils and inclusions work better for some psychics than the clear ones. There is also the debate that only real, clear quartz crystals will work for scrying. This is not true. The power does not rest in the crystal, but in the psychic. Therefore, a good manmade crystal ball will work just as well. Neither does the size of the ball have anything to do with the messages received. The larger crystal balls are heavy, very expensive, and difficult to handle when cleaning them.

Black mirrors, a dark cup filled with water, or a pool of ink work on the same principle as the crystal ball. There are books available that detail how to make a black mirror according to ceremonial magic's specifications. However, the ancient black mirror was not a piece of glass coated with black paint. It was a slab of polished black onyx or obsidian.

Psychics often see mental symbols as messages, whether they are scrying or simply asking for mental answers. A red broken heart will reveal that the person for whom the psychic is reading has relationship problems or great emotional anguish. A fence between a person and the rest of their family represents a separation that may be caused by distance or disagreements. A boat or plane may symbolize a journey. Each psychic must learn what their personal symbols mean so these messages can be correctly interpreted.

Coming up with a date or time in a reading is very difficult. The idea of time is an earthly human concept to measure our lives. Our concept of time has nothing to do with how time and timing work on the astral plane. Some psychics have more success than others with pinpointing dates and times.

Beyond the irritating concept of receiving a time in an answer, frequently there can be the uncertainty of an exact outcome. If the answer to a question involves only one person, the outcome is clearer and more likely to be set. Even then, though, the person involved has free will to change the outcome. Perhaps not the entire outcome, but at least small parts of it, which will in turn affect the outcome itself. However, the more people involved in the outcome of a question, the more likely will free will allow for changes in the outcome to occur, making it very uncertain.

Every psychic must face the prospect of the conscious mind interfering with messages from the astral plane. In that case the answer may be what you or the people for whom you are reading want, and not what is the truth. You may try to rationalize the first impression you receive, until you convince yourself that the answer is actually something else. Also, if you try to force yourself to get an answer, instead of patiently waiting, you will narrow the connection to the astral and only receive false answers supplied by the conscious mind. You must realize that not every answer will be to your liking, and that you may not receive an answer every time you ask. A good psychic knows when to say, "I get nothing."

If you should receive a very negative message for someone, don't blurt it out. Think about whether it would harm or help the person asking. Even then, you should carefully phrase the answer to avoid as much unnecessary stress as possible. Even though most people will reassure you that they want only the truth, no matter how distressing, they really do not. For example, if you receive a message that a sick loved one will not recover, it might be best to respond by saying "I see more problems ahead. I would suggest that you do all you can to help your loved one get through this trying time." Some people may view this as a devious method of getting around an unpleasant answer. In a way, it is. However, you don't want to gain a reputation as a doom and gloom seer, or cause anyone deep emotional distress. Psychics should help people, not hurt them.

Choose a single psychic ability to try at one time. Work at it until you are comfortable with the process. Getting messages through these techniques will help the Witch in other areas, such as healing.

Some people have more success using psychic abilities near or at a New or Full Moon. If you notice that you have a run of successes followed by difficulty getting psychic messages or impressions, chart your positive and negative days. See if they correspond to certain phases of the moon.

Study Work

Chart your progress with one psychic ability until you have gone as far as you can at the time. Work on a second ability, and chart it also. Do not try more than three abilities within a six-month period.

CHAPTER 29

Healing

There are many forms of healing, and a good Witch will try to learn something about all healing methods. A technique that works well on one person may not have satisfactory results with another. Many of the old surviving remedies and practices still have value today. Although society has "progressed," people still have aches, pains, and diseases that frequently are not helped by modern medicine.

Witches must take care that they do not advise anyone to dispense with a physician, diagnose diseases for patients who don't go to a doctor, or tell any patient to stop orthodox treatment. Any and all of these actions can cause a Witch great trouble with the A.M.A. and the police. Such behavior is called practicing medicine without a license, and is against the law.

A Witch also needs to learn that some people subconsciously do not want a healing, however much they say they do. These people get the sympathy and attention they want from their illness, besides using the disease to control those around them. No healing will take if a person is determined not to be healed. A positive attitude and a desire to get well compose at least 85 percent of the healing process.

Among the most common healing methods are herbal remedies and laying on of stones. The use of herbs requires an intense study of such remedies. Witches should not assume they know how to dispense such remedies after a few months' study of the subject. Placing specific stones on the body in certain patterns for certain diseases is safer for the apprentice Witch, but still requires study.

Acupressure and massage have been used successfully in the Orient for hundreds of years. Correct, deep massage can only be learned through study with a professional. If done incorrectly, such massage may harm instead of heal. However, a healer can use a less intense massage to help a person relax.

Acupressure works on the same principle as acupuncture, but does not use needles inserted into the patient's skin. Instead, the healer presses hard on specific pressure points to break up constrictions and blockages. These pressure points, of which there are hundreds, are located along what are called meridian lines. Meridian lines flow all through the body in specific, charted areas. Acupressure, as with herbs, stones, and other noninvasive, non-chemical treatments, does not immediately produce results. Improvement is seen over a period of time. If you, or a patient, suffers from heart problems, circulatory disorders, or has a severe inflammation, neither acupressure nor massage is recommended. Also, take great care in treating pregnant women.

Sometimes a Witch will use an oil, such as almond, scented with certain essential oils while doing massage or acupressure. The oil prevents friction of the hands, which can cause discomfort in the patient. The essential oils, discussed further in Chapter 65, affect the body's aura (see below) through the skin and the sense of smell. Take care to test a little of the oil on the inside of a patient's elbow before using it more widely. Some people are allergic to certain types of oils.

To help alleviate anxiety, press gently under the heel bone of the hand where it joins the wrist. Hold about one minute. Follow this by pressing about two fingers' width above this on the inside, but outer edge of the lower arm.

For heartburn and belching, use the right leg. The area you press is below the knee to the outside, one finger's width to the side of the shinbone.

Headaches are a common malady. Immersing the arms up to the elbow in cold water for about thirty seconds may help. If not, press gently on the upper lip, in the small hollow in the center. Follow this by pressing three fingers' width behind the ear and at the base of the skull where it curves slightly upward. Migraine headaches, however, require a slightly different treatment. Measure four fingers' width above the navel and in the center of the abdomen, and press gently.

Motion sickness can be devastating to the person experiencing it. Press in the middle of the inside of the lower arm, three fingers above the wrist. Continued pressure should relieve the sickness. There are wristbands now available that target this area.

Modern medicine has little treatment that helps psoriasis. Although it is not contagious, the person experiencing psoriasis is uncomfortable and embarrassed by the red, scaling patches. The acupressure point for this disease is on the sole of the foot. Press in the upper center of the foot level with the ball of the foot, on the line where the skin makes a furrow.

Intense pain, such as is experienced during labor, can be made bearable by pressing firmly into the web area between the thumb and forefinger. The pressure point here lies deep in the muscles where the two digits meet. This point may also help some types of headaches.

Healing damaged portions of the aura can also stimulate a cure for diseases. The aura is the invisible, astral envelope that surrounds the physical body. It is composed of several layers of energy. However, it is not necessary to make a detailed study of the aura and its many layers to work at healing through it. The chakras are also located within this energy field.

To work with auras, you must first detect your own aura. The simplest method for doing this is to rub the hands briskly together. Then hold the hands about six inches apart, the palms facing. You will feel a slight tingling sensation emanating from your hands. This is your aura. Gradually move your hands apart until you reach the limit of the tingling feeling. You have created a ball of aural energy between your hands.

If you are working with friends, have someone sit in front of a white wall. If you do not have a white wall, pin a sheet up behind the chair. Place a soft light or candle between the person sitting in the chair and the wall. Turn out the lights. Stand back at least eight to ten feet and look just beyond the sitter. You may find it helpful to half-close your eyes. With practice, you will see a slightly wavering force surrounding the head and shoulders of the person in the chair. You may also see flashes of colors or receive mental symbols.

When working with the aura of another person, have the patient sit in a chair. After rubbing the patient's hands together to stimulate and sensitize the chakras in the palms of the hands, slowly move your hands around the patient's body in slow, long sweeps. Keep the hands about three to four inches from the body without touching the patient. The aura may feel tingling and/or warm. A healthy aura will be compact in all areas. Usually, damaged areas will feel cold, and the energy may dip inward sharply. Other times, such areas will feel intensely hot, with flares of energy shooting out beyond the rest of the aura. Move your hands repeatedly over the damaged area until it harmonizes with the rest of the patient's aura. At the end of such treatments, shake the hands of the patient to dispel the energy, or wash them. One treatment may not remedy the problem.

You can also send energy into a flare or aural depression to mend it. Be certain, however, that you are not sending your personal energy, but drawing upon unlimited universal energy instead. If you deplete yourself, you become open to illnesses.

If you do not have another person with whom to work, you can practice detecting the aura around pets.

Some people see the aura, while others only feel it. Every healer can learn to sense aura colors. Sensing aura colors can be valuable when a Witch seeks the root causes of an illness or wishes to know the patient's emotional state. Healthy aura colors are clear shades without being muddy or ugly. Fire-engine red to a dark vivid red suggests anger or a tendency to lose the temper easily. Yellow-green frequently hints at deception and lies. Dark muddy blues show depression. Ugly green points to jealousy and a gossipy nature. Murky yellows represent distrust, untrustworthiness, and manipulation. Dark purples point to a tendency to be controlling and have an unhealthy superior attitude. Although these are basics for the beginner, Witches must learn what certain colors mean to them.

There also are other methods of healing. One old magical remedy called for Witches to find and clean a round stone, no bigger than their fist. A spell was cast on the stone to prepare it for healing purposes. When needed, the stone was heated in the oven until just warm and then gently rolled over the painful portion of a patient's body. The heat and the gentle stone massage helped to relieve discomfort.

The Witch must be careful to choose a stone that will not burst when heated. If you are not certain about a stone found in nature, it is best to purchase a shaped stone. Good choices are jasper, agate, amethyst, fluorite, or rose quartz. The stone does not have to be large, nor must it be round like a ball. There are cheaper shapes available, such as the three- to four-inch long "wands" that are either rounded on the long sides, or cut with six sides. Whichever you choose, do not heat the stone quickly or too much. A stable stone, too quickly heated, may burst or break. And a stone too hot cannot be safely handled by the Witch nor tolerated by the patient. This treatment works well on sprains, muscle aches, broken bones, stomach ailments, and bursitis. For the traditional meanings of stones, refer to Chapter 30.

Using candle magic and poppets for healing are discussed in Part IV.

Study Work

Practice seeing your own aura. Then try to see the auras of other people and your pets. Are you best at seeing the aura or feeling it? Do you get mental flashes of colors? Do any symbols that arise have meaning for the person whom you are watching?

CHAPTER 30

Magical Stones

Since the beginning of human use of ritual and magic, stones have played an important part in religion. Archaeologists have found unpolished and uncut stones in many Neolithic graves. These were primarily worn as necklaces and pendants. Later, during periods of more sophisticated jewelry-making, stones were polished and faceted to wear in earrings, bracelets, rings, necklaces, and crowns or tiaras. People chose stones first for their magical and spiritual qualities, second for their look.

Witches still use many stones to surround candles during candle-burning spells, add to bags with herbs for protection and health, inset into poppets for health, prosperity, or binding, and wear in jewelry to attract all kinds of magical vibrations into their lives. Sometimes Witches have a bag of special stones without artificial markings that they use for divination. Certain stones are also placed in readily available places around the home and used as energy correctors and worry stones.

The following list of stones will help you to decide which to use during specific rituals and spells. I have included only those stones that are least expensive and easiest to obtain. Some stones, such as clear quartz crystals, are frequently set on the altar to help amplify any energy that is raised during a ritual.

Various fossils have been used by humans as charms for centuries. Fossils and raw amber were the first stones humans picked up in nature and learned to use.

Shepherd's crown, Sea urchin: The fossilized shepherd's crown, or sea urchin, is heart-shaped, with a five-pointed pattern on the top. It may have also been known as the *glane-stone* of the Druids. It was used to avert the evil eye and bad luck.

Sand dollar: The fossil sand dollar, or Witch-stone, was for protection and good luck. These have a natural hole in them, giving them much the same qualities as holey stones. They are helpful in all spells, as they represent the Elements.

Turitella: Black agate dotted with tiny gray and white fossils. You can use them in spells for making adjustments to changes or neutralizing fear.

Ammonites: The remains of spiral-shaped sea creatures. At one time they were known as snakestones or dragonstones. This fossil is most useful when treading the spiral path during past-life meditations.

Tigillite: Worm tunnels that were fossilized. They are used in spells to heal, calm, and rebalance after crises.

Belemnite, Cephalopod: Fossil known used for luck; another name for this fossil was the thunderstone.

Amber: Fossilized tree sap, approximately one hundred twenty million years old. It comes in several colors, ranging from orange and red to the rare colors of blue and green. Amber containing insects, leaves, and other foreign matter has the highest value, except for the rare colors. Magical uses for amber are prosperity, good luck, protection, helping to uncover past lives, communication with spiritual teachers, and healing.

Jet and amber were sometimes worn together to bring luck and give protection. Today, many Wiccan priestesses wear necklaces of jet and amber as a symbol of their position in a group, such as a High Priestess.

Jet: Jet is fossilized wood buried millions of years ago. It is usually a waxy black color. It is very difficult to tell true jet from plastic, so buy only from a reputable dealer. At one time it was called Black Amber, because, like amber, jet will have a small static electrical charge when rubbed with a cloth. Jet is useful in drawing negative energy out of a person's aura, understanding karmic issues, and bringing up psychic talents.

Holey stones: Stones found with natural holes through them. Also called the hag stone, it is said to prevent nightmares if hung above a bed. A Celtic tradition says to look through a holey stone if you want to see Fairies and ghosts. Holey stones are carried to attract luck and to repel evil.

Geodes: Hollow nodules filled with crystals and mineral deposits; they are usually cut in half to produce a small cave-like stone. They are useful for past-life meditations.

Amethyst: A very popular stone in jewelry with its attractive purple color. It is usually sold in single crystal points, much as clear quartz crystal is, although it can be purchased in clusters. This stone can enhance psychic abilities, heal, facilitate communications with the Otherworld, strengthen the power of divination tools, attract love, bring good fortune, and protect from black magic.

Aventurine: Usually sold in the green color, although it does come in dark red, peach, and brown. It has a calming and balancing vibration that makes it useful in personal healing of mental or emotional problems. As an amplifier of creative inspiration, it is useful to those in the fields of the arts. It also attracts love and prosperity.

Bloodstone: A dark green stone with red flecks. It is not popular for jewelry as it is not as flashy as crystal or gemstones. However, bloodstone has a long history in magic. It brings good things to the wearer, as well as protection. It can attract good fortune with finances and tear down walls to gain success.

Carnelian: An orange or reddish-orange stone of the chalcedony family. It was widely used in ancient magic and medicine. A powerful stone, it reflects any spells directed at you. It is one of the best fast-acting stones for career progress. Use it to protect from ill-wishing and evil, heal family problems, remember astral journeys, and strengthen concentration.

Chrsyocolla: A blue-green or turquoise-blue stone that is rarely found in jewelry. It is valuable when releasing old resentments, dealing with anger and fear, letting go of tension, and removing blocks to creativity.

Chrysoprase: An apple-green stone that can lead to the truth in personal problems, soothe the emotions, and attract prosperity.

Fluorite: Frequently found with more than one color to a stone. It is a powerful healer that can cleanse the aura, cut off astral emotional ties with other people, and help with rebalancing. It also is useful to establish communications with Otherworld beings, such as Fairies and nature spirits.

Garnet: A popular stone for jewelry because of its color range from bright ruby-red to the purple-red. The garnet is a powerful protector, as it deflects negativity and spells. It also can lift depression and open up your life for business success.

Hematite: A black or iron-gray stone with a metallic luster. It will repel and dissolve negativity, thus breaking up stress. Traditionally, it is used in spells for a favorable outcome to lawsuits and court cases. All modern marcasite is actually hematite.

Jade: Although we primarily think of jade as being green, it also comes in a wide variety of other colors. It deflects negative vibrations, attracts good fortune, calms, heals, and helps one to remember dreams.

Jasper: Usually marketed in the brick-red color. It is very powerful for adding energy to spells and repelling magical attacks.

Lapis lazuli: A stone used for many centuries by ancient cultures. Its vibrations are so high that it is best used by people who are on a dedicated spiritual path. It balances, releases tension, calms, increases psychic talents, and aids in communicating with deities and Otherworld beings.

Malachite: A two-tone green stone that will amplify any energy you are feeling at the moment. So if you are tense or overemotional, do not wear malachite. However, it also is good for strengthening intuition and the psychic, attracting love and money, and repelling evil.

Black obsidian: A stone with a long history of being used for scrying and divination. It will absorb and transmute negative energy. If placed near money, it will multiply it.

Onyx: Although most frequently marketed as a black stone, it also comes in brown and creamy white. It repels negative vibrations, calms, and helps to recall past lives.

Pyrite: A gold metallic stone that is also called fool's gold. Use it for calming tense relationships or business problems.

Clear quartz crystal: A very popular stone and familiar to everyone. Amethyst, rose quartz, and smoky quartz are part of the same family. This stone is an all-purpose healer, an enhancer of energy and the psychic, a divination aid as with a crystal ball, and a talisman for attracting good fortune. **Rose quartz** works best to attract love and good health, while **smoky quartz** breaks up subconscious blocks and negativity.

Tiger's eye: Ordinarily sold as a golden brown stone with cat's eye qualities. It is excellent for protection against evil spells and negativity. It also helps to attract good luck, reveal the truth in any situation, and bleed off excess energy.

Green tourmaline: An excellent healer and attractor of money, while **watermelon tourmaline** can remove conflicts and confusion.

Turquoise: Another stone revered and used by ancient cultures. Because of its high spiritual vibrations, turquoise can increase psychic powers and help one to communicate clearly with the Otherworld.

All stones should be cleansed by holding them under cool, running water when you get them home. Dry thoroughly. Those purchased in shops may take more than one cleansing to remove all the vibrations left on them by other people.

Study Work

Decide on two stones that you will use for the next month. Put each stone in a place where you can frequently pick up the stone, roll it in your hands, and feel its vibrations. Write down your first impressions upon handling the stone. In a week see if those impressions have changed. What are your impressions at the end of a month?

CHAPTER 31

Magical Herbs

There is a long history of the use of herbs in healing and magic. Herbal medicines were the only cures for diseases for thousands of years. For magical purposes, the herbs were burned in rituals or as incenses, put into little spell bags, and made into infusions and powders. The woods of certain trees were favored for making a variety of wands, boxes, and bowls, as well as being burned in rituals.

Store your thoroughly dried herbs in tight-capped containers out of the sunlight. Use herbs to stuff spell bags and poppets. Crush or grind them into powders to add to incense. Sprinkle them in bathwater for cleansing. Heat them in water to make infusions for cleaning rooms of negative vibrations. Carry them as a type of amulet.

Where ingesting an herb is dangerous, a warning is given. However, it is safer to not eat any herb, with the exception of those used in cooking, without consulting a trained herb healer.

The following list is not complete, as herbal magic is an entire study course in itself.

Angelica (*Angelica archangelica, A. officinalis*). Burn the dried leaves for exorcisms, protection, and to ward off enchantments.

Anise (*Pimpinella anisum*). These licorice-scented seeds can be stuffed into a small pillow to ward off nightmares. They also avert the evil eye.

Ash, Mountain (*Fraxinus excelsior* or *F. americana*). Scatter the leaves to the four quarters or directions around the outside of your home to repel negativity. The wood is sometimes made into healing wands.

Avens (*Geum urbanum*). This herb is also called Herb Bennet and Star of the Earth. Add its leaves to incense for exorcisms. The leaves may also be carried to attract the opposite sex. The leaves grow in groups of three, which can be used to represent the Triple Goddess.

Basil (*Ocimum basilicum*). If you do a ritual cleansing of your home, follow it by sprinkling a little basil in the corners of each room and into a bath for yourself. Burn the dried leaves to chase out negative vibrations.

Bay Laurel (*Laurus nobilis*). Burn the leaves for visions and aid in divination. Carry as an amulet to deflect negativity. Put a leaf under your pillow to help with prophetic dreams. Add to purification and healing incenses.

Bergamot (*Monarda didyma*). Also called Bee Balm, the leaves of this herb make a delightful tea. Use in powders, incenses, and spell bags for good health and friendship.

Betony (*Stachys officinalis, Betonica officinalis, Stachys betonica*). This herb, sacred to the Druids, is also called Bishopwort. It is a very protective, powerful herb that is used in spells to evict evil spirits and stop nightmares. Burn it in incenses, particularly at Summer Solstice, to purify and protect. If you sprinkle the dried herb near doors and windows, it will form a protective barrier.

Bistort (*Polygonum bistorta*). This plant is also known as Patience Dock and Snakeweed. Because of its ability to strengthen psychic powers, it is added to divination incenses. To attract money, sprinkle a little in your wallet or purse. Carry the dried root if you want to conceive a child.

Boneset (*Eupatorium perfoliatum*). Stuff dried leaves of this herb into poppets for binding spells.

Briar (*Rosa rubiginosa*). This Wild Rose can be used in place of regular roses in spells. Drink a tea of rose petals for divination. Burn the dried petals in love incenses. You can also use the petals to stuff spell bags.

Broom, Scotch (*Cytisus scoparius*). This was a Druid sacred "tree." Folklore says to burn the blossoms to calm the wind.

Burdock (*Arctium lappa*). Sprinkle around the house to cleanse the house of negativity. Use in incenses and bathwater for purification.

Cedar (*Cedrus libani, Cedar of Lebanon, the Old World species; Thuja occidentalis, Yellow Cedar or Arbor Vitae; Juniperus virginiana, Red Cedar*). Wood and needles from this tree

---

were used by many ancient cultures in religious and magical rituals. It is associated with the Summer Solstice. Burn the wood or needles to repel evil and attract good spirits. Use a bough as a broom to sweep a ritual area.

Celandine (*Chelidonium major, C. minus, Ranunculis ficaria*). Tradition says that you should carry this herb to court if you want a decision made in your favor. Carry a spell bag stuffed with this herb to avoid unlawful imprisonment.

Centaury (*Erythraea centaurium*). Folklore says that snakes will not go around this plant. It is added to incenses to repel negative entities.

Chamomile (*Anthemis noblis* or *Matricaria chamomilla*). Roman chamomile smells like fresh apples, while vulgar (or common) chamomile or dog fennel has a repulsive odor. Vulgar (or common) chamomile is frequently found growing wild. Grow this herb in your garden to reverse spells cast against you. Add it to incense and spell bags to attract prosperity.

Cinnamon (*Cinnamonum zeylanicum* or *C. lauraceae*). This ancient herb has a wide variety of magical uses. Burn it to attract the very highest spirits, heal, and stimulate clairvoyance. A mixture of cinnamon and myrrh makes a wonderful all-purpose incense. It also attracts prosperity.

Clove (*Eugenia caryophyllata, Caryophyllus aromaticus, Syzygium aromaticum*). The part of the clove used is the undeveloped blossoms. Grind and add to incenses and powders to stop gossip and repel negative forces. Add to spell bags to attract the opposite sex.

Comfrey (*Symphytum officinale*). Put a piece of root in your luggage to ensure its safe arrival at your destination.

Coriander (*Coriandrum sativum*). Use the seeds in love charms.

Dittany of Crete (*Origanum dictamnus*). Also called Hop Marjoram, this herb is powerful when used in incenses to help spirits manifest a visual form. It is also helpful when burned in divination incenses.

Dragon's Blood (*Daemonorops draco, Dracaena draco*). This "herb" is actually the resin of the fruit from a tree. Usually only a pinch is needed in incenses for its power to be felt. Add to incenses and bath salts for love, purification, and protection.

Elder (*Sambucus nigra*). This Druid sacred "tree" was once used to both bless and curse. It is sacred to the Goddess and an herb of the Summer Solstice. Stand under an elder tree on Summer Solstice to see Otherworld beings.

Feverfew (*Chrysanthemum parthenium* or *Pyrethrum parthenium*). This herb can be carried to protect against sickness and accidents.

Frankincense (*Boswellia carterii, B. thurifera*). Sometimes called olibanum, the part of this "herb" used is actually the resin or gum from a tree. It is burned to raise vibrations, purify, consecrate, protect, and exorcise. It also aids meditation.

Ginger (*Zingiber officinale*). The root can be placed on the altar as an offering to Fairies and other nature spirits.

Hawthorn (*Crataegus oxyacantha*). Make an infusion of the hawthorn blossoms that bloom near the first of May; it will purify anything it is sprinkled upon. Folklore says that the blossoms have a highly erotic scent that affects men.

Hazel (*Corylus spp.*). Another tree sacred to the Druids, forked wands from this tree can be used as dowsing rods. Hanging a string of hazelnuts will attract Fairies.

High John the Conqueror (*Impomoea purga, Convolvulus jalapa, Ipomea jalapa*). This is a popular root for attracting money and taking care of legal difficulties.

Holly (*Ilex aquifolium*). The variety commonly found in the United States is the *Ilex opaca*. Folklore connects this tree with the Druids and the Winter Solstice. Grown near a house, the holly will repel negative spells and protect. The custom of decorating with holly boughs at Winter Solstice is an ancient Pagan custom.

Hyssop (*Hyssopus officinalis*). Long used as a purification herb, hyssop can be added to consecrated water for cleansing sacred spots. Place at each window to ward off psychic attacks.

Iceland Moss. Add this to bags or poppets when working for prosperity or an increase in money.

Irish Moss (*Chondrus crispus*). Sprinkle into your wallet or purse for luck and a steady inflow of money.

Jasmine (*Jasminum officinale, J. odoratissimum*). Add the dried flowers to love and prosperity charms.

Juniper (*Juniperus communis*). Folklore says it was a holy tree in northern Europe. Mix it with thyme, and add to divination or trance incenses. A string of berries can be hung to attract love.

Lavender (*Lavendula officinale, L. vera*). The ancient Egyptians used the flowers of this plant in purification baths. Add it to incenses for healing and to see ghosts.

Lemon Balm (*Melissa officinalis*). The leaves of this lemon-scented herb can be brewed into tea to help with depression. Use the dried leaves in love charms.

Loosestrife, Purple (*Lythrum salicaria*). This herb can be used in incenses or simply sprinkled around the house for its powers of stopping arguments and restoring harmony.

Marigold (*Calendula officinalis*). This herb is also known as Calendula, Holigold, and Ruddes. If you want to see Fairies, Elves, and Otherworld beings, pick it on a Full Moon to use in incenses and washes. Carry a flower in your pocket to obtain a favorable court decision.

Marjoram (*Origanum majorana*). It is also called Sweet Marjoram and Pot Marjoram. Put it in spell bags to draw money and prosperity and happiness. Make an infusion of marjoram and peppermint to cleanse your ritual tools and room of negative vibrations, especially if a cowan touches your ritual belongings.

Meadowsweet (*Filipendula ulmaria, Spirea ulmaria*). This was one of the three most sacred Druid herbs, along with wild mint and vervain. Sprinkle around the house and ritual area to attract blessings from the gods.

Mint (*Mentha piperita, M. spicata, M. crispa*). Add to incenses to cleanse and purify. Use it in poppets for healing and love spells.

Mistletoe (*Viscum album*). Berries of this herb are poisonous if eaten by humans or pets. Tradition calls this an all-purpose herb that is hung to attract love, money, good health, and protection.

Mugwort (*Artemisia vulgaris*). This herb can be added to incenses for scrying with a crystal ball or magic mirror, divination, and strengthening psychic powers. Its powers are strongest when picked on the Full Moon. Gather it on the Summer Solstice for good luck.

Mullein (*Verbascum thapsus*). This herb is also known as Hag's Taper and Candlewick Plant. The oil from its flowers is a good remedy for children's earaches. If you are using a spell calling for "graveyard dust," this is an acceptable substitute.

Myrrh (*Commiphoria myrrha*). Another resin, burn myrrh to purify and protect, heal and exorcise.

Oakmoss (*Evernia pruastri*). This lichen from oak trees fixes the scent in incenses. Add it for money and protection.

Orris (*Iris florentina, I. germanica, I. pallida*). Use the powdered root in spell bags for love.

Patchouli (*Pogostemon cablin, P. patchouli*). Use this herb sparingly, as the odor can be quite strong. Use in incenses for clairvoyance and divination.

Peppermint (*Mentha piperita*). Make an infusion of peppermint leaves and sprinkle this around a ritual room to get rid of negative vibrations.

Pine (*Pinus spp.*). Burn the crushed needles to purify the home. A stronger blend for this purpose consists of pine, cedar, and juniper. Put the needles into dream pillows.

Red Sanders (*Pterocarpus santalinus*). Also known as red sandalwood, the ground wood of this tree is used in incenses for protection, purification, love, and healing.

Rosemary (*Rosemarinus officinalis*). The needles of this shrub were used in religious ceremonies of many ancient cultures. It is powerful against evil influences of any kind. Add to incenses and bathwater for purification, cleansing, exorcism, love, and clear thinking.

Rue (*Ruta graveolens*). The Celts used this herb to defend against curses and spells of dark magic. Use a fresh sprig to sprinkle consecrated water when doing blessings and healings. Burn it to get things moving in your life.

Sage (*Salvia officinalis varieties*). Although now associated with Native American practices, this herb has other connections also. Use it in healing and prosperity spell bags and incenses. Hang it over the door to repel ill fortune.

St. John's Wort (*Hypericum perforatum*). If picked on Summer Solstice and hung in a window, it will repel ghosts and unwanted spirits.

Sandalwood, White (*Santalum album*). Use the powdered wood alone or with other herbs in incenses for gaining occult knowledge, removing anxiety, protection, exorcism, and purification. The red sandalwood, or red sanders, has different purposes and is not as strong as white sandalwood.

Savory, Summer (*Satureia hortensis*). This herb has a slightly peppery taste. Use it in incenses and spell bags for love, dreams, and creativity.

Savory, Winter (*Satureia montana*). This has the same uses as summer savory.

Spearmint (*Menta spicata, Mentha viridis*). Although like peppermint, this herb is less powerful. It was highly esteemed by ancient cultures, which used its aromatic, cleansing properties when scouring tables. Add to healing incenses.

Thistle, Blessed (*Carbenia benedicta, Cnicus benedictus, Carduus benedictus*). Also known as Holy Thistle, this herb can be added to incenses to break hexes or curses. Folklore says to grow it to deter thieves.

Thyme, Garden (*Thymus vulgaris*) and **Wild Thyme** (*T. serpyllum*). Another name for wild thyme is Mother of Thyme. Use the smoke of the burning leaves to purify an area or object. Crush a fresh leaf against your third eye to strengthen psychic powers.

Tonka Bean (*Coumarouna odorata, Dipsteryx odorata*). Carry a bean to attract love.

Trefoil (*Trifolium spp.*). This three-leafed herb symbolizes all triple deities. Carry a sprig for protection and luck. Always leave a pinch of ginger as payment to the Fairies when you pick trefoil.

Valerian (*Valeriana officinalis*). Although this herb has a pungent odor, it can be used in spell bags for protection.

Vervain/Verbena (*Verbana officinalis; Blue Vervain, V. hastate*). Sometimes called Van-Van or Herb of Enchantment, use in spells for cleansing, purification, love, and protection. Make an infusion of the leaves, and sprinkle it around a house or area for exorcism. Grow plants in your garden for a steady flow of money. Burn it in incenses to defend against psychic attack.

Vetiver (*Vetiveria zizanioides*). Also known as khus-khus and Vetivert, this herb's root smells faintly like violets. Add it with rose petals to love incenses.

Woodruff (*Asperula odorata*). This Druid herb acquires its sweet scent after drying. Carry a piece to change the course of your life. Burn it to clear away barriers to success.

Wormwood (*Artemisia absinthium*). This is an addictive and *poisonous* herb if eaten or swallowed. It has a long history of being burned in incenses for prophecy, divination, and astral projection.

Yarrow (*Achillea millefolium*). Folklore calls this herb Soldier's Woundwort as it was used to stop bleeding. The dried stalks are used to make I Ching sticks for divination. Burn it in divination incenses.

Yellow Dock (*Rumex crispus*). The powder of this herb stains badly, so store and use it in items where a stain will not matter. Use this ground herb in magical powders for money.

Study Work

Check your kitchen supplies, and see how many herbs you use on a daily basis. Make a small, cloth spell bag with a specific purpose in mind. Stuff it with the appropriate herbs, then carry it with you or leave it under your pillow for two weeks. Write down all changes that occurred after you started carrying the bag.

Writing Your Own Rituals

There are certain requirements for all properly performed full Wiccan rituals, such as casting the circle, calling the Elements, calling of the Goddess and the God, the Charge, sharing of the wine/juice, dismissal of the Elements, and closing of the circle. Some Witches draw an invoking pentagram at each quarter when calling up the guardians and a banishing pentagram at the end when the guardians are dismissed. See the illustration in Chapter 22.

All the other parts of a ritual can be changed or rewritten to suit your personal needs and desires. Since all original rituals had to be written by someone, whatever the religion, there is no reason you cannot write your own rituals. However, when starting out in ritual, it is best for the beginner to follow a prepared procedure until you become more proficient and comfortable with what you are doing and why you are doing it. There are examples of full rituals in Part III, the Book of Rituals, in this book. You will also find prepared rituals in many other books on Wicca.

All Wiccan rituals are performed inside what is called a cast and consecrated circle. A full description of casting the circle is found in Chapter 34. To do this, the Witch blesses the water and the salt, the incense and the censer. The words used for this blessing may vary from Witch to Witch, but the essential idea remains the same. A little of the salt is added to the water, and incense is either lit or placed on burning charcoal. Some groups do not mix the salt and water, but sprinkle the salt as a separate movement.

Next, the Witch uses the dagger to trace a circle in the air around their ritual area. Movement begins at the eastern side of the circle and continues clockwise or to the right. The Witch should visualize in their mind a blue-white flame coming from the tip of the dagger or the end of the wand. When the Witch returns to the East, they make certain the invisible line overlaps from where they began. Some Witches use the dagger for all quarter salutes and tracing out the circle. However, I use the wand for such movements unless I am casting a widdershins (counter-clockwise) circle, for which I use the dagger or sword. The dagger and sword are commanding tools, in my opinion, not necessary for deosil (clockwise) circles for positive energy.

This action is followed by a light sprinkling of water, again beginning in the East and moving clockwise. The final step is to carry the burning incense around the circle in the same direction.

These three separate parts open a ritual and constitute the casting of a circle.

The next step in ritual is the calling of the Elements or the quarter guardians. This, also, begins in the East and ends after calling the guardians of the North. This usually consists of lighting the properly colored candle in a direction, saluting the guardians with an upraised dagger or wand, and chanting a greeting. For all apprentice purposes, this movement is done deosil, or in a clockwise direction.

The calling of the Goddess and the God is a chant next given while standing at the altar. Your altar will be facing the East, even though you may center it in your ritual area. This welcoming chant is actually an invocation for the deities to join you in the ritual and add their power and wisdom to your work.

The Charge (see examples in Chapter 35), which was not known until Charles Godfrey Leland published his *Aradia: Queen of the Witches*, is a hymn of praise to the Goddess and a reminder of Her powers and aspects. Since the Goddess in true Wicca is central to all worship, this is a vital part of the ritual. There are several versions of the Charge available in books on Wicca, but almost all of them are based on either the one given in Leland's book or the Charge written by Doreen Valiente. Witches frequently borrow versions of the Charge from each other, changing a few words to make the Charge more personal to them.

Midway through the ritual the blessing and sharing of the wine or juice occurs. In a group, this is performed by the High Priest and High Priestess, representing the God and the Goddess. If you work solitary, however, you can still perform this blessing by expressing both the Goddess and the God within yourself, since all humans have both male and female hormones and characteristics. The act of dipping the ritual dagger into the chalice or goblet of juice or wine is an ancient part of ritual, far earlier than the dawn of Christianity. This action represents the union of the God (the dagger) with the Goddess (the chalice) to bring forth fertility to all creatures, nature, and ideas in the world. This is a symbolic reenactment of the ancient ceremony called the Sacred Marriage.

When the blessing is finished, all participants within the circle share a drink from the chalice. I always leave a little in the cup so that the nature spirits can also enjoy it after the ritual is completed.

Some Witches insist that only wine can be used. However, some people do not like wine, nor should some be drinking anything with alcohol in it. It is perfectly acceptable to substitute juice for the wine.

Before you close, or "cut open," the circle, you should always dismiss the Elements. Beginning in the East, salute the quarter guardian, chant the dismissal, and extinguish the candle. Continue around the circle, ending with the North. Some Witches salute with the dagger or wand when doing this. However, I find it awkward to juggle a wand and a candlesnuffer at the same time. Therefore, I salute with the candlesnuffer, knowing that it is the respect in the heart that counts, not the outward show of symbolic action. Move around the circle in a clockwise direction until all the guardians are dismissed. As a final act, stand facing the altar and thank the Goddess, the God, and all other Otherworld beings who helped you.

When your ritual work is finished, you must close the circle before you cross the invisible boundary. This is accomplished by symbolically "cutting" a door in the area above the edge, or sweeping your dagger to your left across the area. Do this while saying a phrase, such as, "This circle is open, but unbroken."

You may change or alter the words for all your chants within the circle as long as you do not go too far astray from the original idea. However, the above-mentioned steps in a ritual should not be changed from their performed order. For the circle to be correctly cast, and therefore protective, you need to follow this outline.

There is ample room between the Charge and the blessing of the wine for you to add anything else. This may be certain celebratory acts to commemorate a seasonal holy day, a moon ritual, or a rite of passage. You may also include specific magical spellworking at this time.

Study Work

Practice visualizing the blue-white light coming from the tip of your dagger or the end of your wand until you feel confident that it exists in the astral plane. You can work with this protective light by drawing a circle around yourself. While inside this temporary circle, do you feel any change in the atmosphere around you? Always remember to cut the circle when finished.

Part III

THE BOOK OF RITUALS

CHAPTER 33

The Witch's Book of Shadows

As an apprentice you have presumably worked your way through the lessons and understand what you have studied. You are ready to create your own ritual book, the Book of Shadows, which can be done before you do your self-initiation ceremony, given in Chapter 35. Although you may write several rituals in your book now, you will add to it the rest of your life in Wicca.

Now is a vital time for you to learn the value of secrecy. Good reasons for this were mentioned in earlier chapters of this book. However, if you still doubt the necessity of this, go onto the Internet and visit the many sites of anti-Witchcraft groups that preach hatred and death to Witches.

There are also two other excellent reasons for practicing the art of secrecy. First, few Wiccan groups will take you in if you have a bad habit of talking about everything that you do and learn. Second, from a magical standpoint, you will have difficulty manifesting your desires and goals if you tell everyone, as this dissipates the energy of the spell. To understand this, study the Four Laws of the Magus. These Laws are discussed in Chapter 57.

The Book of Shadows is a fairly modern name for the book that contains Wiccan spells, rituals, teachings, and divination records. Until approximately the middle of the twentieth century, it was not considered wise to write down anything that could be used by the law and the Christian Church to persecute a Witch. In some parts of the country, you still should store your ritual book and tools in a hidden place, so they cannot be taken by the police for infringements of local laws, stolen by overzealous orthodox-oriented family members, or destroyed by local hate-mongers. Often, police will do little if anything to prosecute orthodox groups or members who steal from or persecute Witches. Even if you live in a safe place, you should not ever leave your materials, tools, or the Book of Shadows out where people can handle them.

The name of your ritual book, the Book of Shadows, is an appropriate one, as it describes a Witch's feelings about the relationship of this world to the Otherworld, of rituals done on the earth plane that are linked to great reservoirs of power on the astral plane. The rituals and magic of this world are only a shadow of the powerful reality of magic and ritual in the Otherworld; hence the name, Book of Shadows. The Witch's Book of Shadows, whether the Witch is solitary or part of a group, is important, as it should contain all the rituals and spells the Witch will perform. Each Book of Shadows will become a personal history of the Witch who uses it.

Some people call this book a grimoire. However, that name is more correctly applied to the book of a ceremonial magician and is not used by Witches. Both names, Book of Shadows and grimoire, were not used before medieval times.

Traditionalists say that the Book should be a black book with a bound cover. However, it is much easier to use a ringed notebook, so that the Witch can lay it flat on the altar or a stand. Nothing is more frustrating than for pages of the ritual book to start moving when you are in the middle of a ritual. Using a ringed notebook with punched pages actually gives you two ways to work with the book. The notebook itself will lie flat on the altar during ritual, and you can remove for use the exact pages you need for any ritual or spell, returning them to the notebook when you are finished.

Actually, a series of binders is better than one large, unwieldy book. This way the Witch can dedicate each binder to a specific purpose. You can have one binder for each of the following items, or for groups of items: regular rituals, miscellaneous spellcasting, herb magic, dreams, spiritual messages, symbols, astrological correspondences, ethics and beliefs, crystal magic, elemental magic and the Elements, alphabets, moon and sun magic, gems and stones, the chakras, color magic, healing, ritual tool instructions, the magic and pantheons of deities of other cultures (other than the one you plan to use), and the notes of the results of all the spellwork you do. Binders are also helpful for a variety of divination methods, such as the tarot cards, runes, and Goddess symbols. Although you may not envision yourself needing a supply of notebooks at the moment, you will see the practicality behind this method in the future when your collection of rituals and spells begins to grow.

Use index dividers to separate the various sections of your notebook Book of Shadows. This way you will not have to leaf through all the pages to find the section you want.

If you wish, you can write all your regular rituals and the spellwork most often used in a hardbound Book of Shadows. This works well, as you can write the rituals in their order of usage: New Moon, Full Moon, the eight holy days in the proper order, and the rites of passage. Then you can use the notebooks for the other subjects that you will use less often. However, remember that the pages of hardbound books tend to turn when you don't want them to.

Although your main rituals are written out in the order of their yearly appearance, such things as spells should be grouped together according to their usage; for example, protection, love, prosperity, and so forth. You will be adding to the groups of spells as you progress. It is much easier to enter new spells in the proper grouping if you are not working with a bound book.

Whatever kind of book or notebook you choose, be certain that it appeals to you. If you get a book simply to have one, and the style or color is not to your liking, the power you put into the book when you write the rituals will be weakened. Take your time in making your choice, just as you should when choosing ritual tools.

When you copy any ritual or spell into your binders, please remember to write down who the author is and which book contains the material you copied. You do not want to give the impression that this is your own ritual, especially if you share this ritual with another Witch.

Before you get carried away with the idea of writing everything in the Book of Shadows in a secret alphabet, stop and think about the difficulty you will have each time you try to read something out of the Book. It makes life much easier if you write out the contents of your Book in your everyday language, and then keep your Book safely out of sight of cowans and other troublemakers. Save the magical alphabets for certain types of spellworking.

Each Book of Shadows must first be cleansed and consecrated. The rite for this follows. Then the Book Blessing is written on the first page. Do not write anything in your Book of Shadows until it has been consecrated and the Book Blessing page written.

CLEANSING OF THE BOOK OF SHADOWS

This is best done on the night of a Full Moon. You will need a pentacle, wand, dagger, white candle, frankincense incense, a chalice of water, and a small container of salt.

Place your Book of Shadows on your altar next to the pentacle, which should be centered and in front of where you will stand. Set the white candle and incense to the rear of the altar and behind the pentacle. Light both the candle and the incense. Put the chalice of water on the pentacle, with the salt beside it.

Cast the circle according to the directions in Chapter 34. When you finish, return to stand facing the altar. Set the chalice to one side of the pentacle. Place the Book of Shadows on top of the pentacle. Take several deep breaths and mentally reach out to the Otherworld. Feel the flow of power that announces the arrival of the Goddess and the God into your ritual circle.

Raise your arms and say:

> *My words go out across the worlds. The Old Gods hear my fervent plea. Bring blessings strong into this book. So do I wish, so shall it be.*

Take the Book into your power hand and wave it over the burning incense. Say:

> *Element of Air, vitalize this Book of Shadows. Let its contents be an inspiration to my life.*

Wave the Book over the lighted candle, taking care not to get too close. Say:

> *Element of Fire, purify this Book of Shadows. May the purity of spiritual Fire also touch my life.*

Using the fingers of your power hand, lightly sprinkle a few drops of consecrated water onto the book. Say:

> *Element of Water, consecrate this Book of Shadows. As I have consecrated my life to the Old Ones, may all rituals and spells within this Book honor them.*

Place the Book back on the pentacle and place your power hand flat on top of the Book. Say:

> *Element of Earth, ground the power in this Book of Shadows by connecting it to the will of the Lady and the Lord. May the power I wield always be in balance.*

Lay your dagger on top of the Book, with the wand over it. Say:

> *Element of Spirit, may what is written within this Book of Shadows always be connected with the Otherworld. Air to vitalize it. Fire to purify it. Water to consecrate it. Earth to ground it. Spirit to blend all Elements together into an unbreakable link with the Goddess and the God. So mote it be.*

Place both hands palm down on the altar to ground any remaining power within you. Raise your arms and say:

My thanks to all who came this night, to help me in this sacred rite. The Lord and Lady, proud and old, the Elementals strong and bold. My blessings to you, all creatures free. As I will, so mote it be.

Break the circle, put away your tools, and clean up the altar. If you wish, and can do so without anyone interfering, leave the Book of Shadows on the altar overnight.

The next step is to enter the Book Blessing on the first page of your Book of Shadows. The Book Blessing page can be decorated with whatever artwork appeals to you. It is on this page that you will also write out your Craft name, but not your legal name, establishing your ownership of the book in both this world and the Otherworld. The covers of hardbound books usually are difficult to paint because of their cloth roughness or the slickness of plastic; however, you may also decorate the cover if you wish.

There is no one special way the Book Blessing should be written out. Following is a description of one example of this page that you may copy or change if you wish. The page is bordered with Celtic twining beasts in bold colors. In medieval writing script, done in black ink, are the words: "May the Old Ones place their blessings upon this Book. Air vitalizes it. Fire purifies it. Water consecrates it. Earth grounds it. Spirit connects it to the Otherworld. This write is by the hand of Moon Raven." (The name Moon Raven is the Craft name of the Witch making the Book.)

Your next step will be to write in this Book the rituals for the New and Full Moon, the eight holy days, and the rites of passage. Write in the best hand you can, and in large enough script to easily read when you stand at the altar. Black ink is best, as it is most visible on a white page.

Study Work

Purchase, without haggling, a bound book or a notebook for your Book of Shadows. Consecrate it. Write out the Book Blessing on the first page of the Book of Shadows, using your Craft name to claim it as your own. Then copy into this book the rituals given in Chapters 34 through 55.

CHAPTER 34

The Mechanics of Casting a Circle

The use of circles in ritual and magic is mentioned as far back as ancient Assyria. Certain clay tablets tell of its use and note that the circle then was called *usurtu*. In ancient India, and still in some areas of India today, the circle was marked out by placing red or black stones around its edge. At one time, secret cults in Morocco met at crossroads, raised power within a magic circle, and called their meetings *Zabbats*. The word *Zabbats* may be connected to the Witch word Sabbats. The circle is a worldwide symbol of eternity and infinity, with no beginning and no end. The alchemical symbol of this circle was a dragon with its tail in its mouth.

Almost all Witches, whether solitary or in a coven, cast a psychic, magical circle to work within when doing rituals or magic. A point of historical interest, mentioned in *The Witch in History*, which was edited by Venetia Newall, is that the word "coven" was first used in sixteenth-century Scotland.

The circle with its invisible boundary creates a place between the worlds, between this world and the Otherworld. The circle is a neutral working space that is capable of regenerating and amplifying the type of power raised by the Witch. This explains the opening statement in many rituals that says, "This is a time that is not a time, in a place that is not a place, on a day that is not a day. We stand at the threshold between the worlds, before the Veil of the Mysteries."

Standing within a consecrated, cast circle represents a return from multiplicity to a point of unity or oneness, from a place of time to timelessness, from a mind ruled by consciousness to one governed by the subconscious. It is the ultimate state of Oneness with the Goddess and the God.

When properly drawn, the magical circle becomes a mandala upon which the Witch stands. A mandala is any diagram, elaborate or simple, that is symmetrical in layout and based upon spiritual symbology. In India, these are drawn and meditated upon as mystical maps of the Otherworld. Carl Jung wrote that a circle is actually a mandala, or glyph, that can speak to the subconscious and superconscious minds of all humans.

A psychically marked and ritually consecrated magic circle has other purposes. It produces protection for the worshippers from evil and unbalanced forces, and both a meeting place for the gods and a reservoir for the power built up during the ritual. This power is deliberately directed toward a goal and released during a crucial point of the ritual. This power may be raised by dancing, chanting, or through a specific spell.

The power raised within a circle is frequently spoken of as a Cone of Power. Seen by outsiders with psychic sight, the cone may have been the original idea behind the pointed Witch's hat. To the psychic eyes, this cone looks like an upside-down ice cream cone, with its top edge matching the cast circle and its peaked bottom rising above the center point.

The traditional Witch's circle is first marked out by an athame or sword drawing the line in the air, then by sprinkling this circle with blessed water and salt. Almost all circles are cast with the Witch moving in a deosil, or clockwise, direction. Traditionalists say that the circle should have a nine-foot diameter, although this is far too small for large groups, and often far too large for the solitary Witch who may not have much room.

Crowley believed that when the circle was cast properly by beginning and ending in the East, the macrocosmic force within the circle was aroused. The macrocosm arises from and is controlled by the archetypal powers of the Supreme Creator in the aspect of the deities. Therefore, if Witches set up the proper conditions within a circle, they have access to unlimited, vast amounts of universal energy.

Most Wiccan circles are cast deosil, or sunwise (clockwise). However, some occasions may call for a circle made widdershins, or counterclockwise. The Irish Celtic word for widdershins was *tuathal*, while the Anglo-Saxon word *sith* meant, "to walk against." However, most Witches and apprentices should involve themselves only with a deosil circle.

Cleanliness is important to a good, positive ritual, so make certain that your ritual area, the altar, and your tools are clean. Laziness and dirt attract negative energies and beings, thus creating difficulty in making your circle absolutely impregnable to unbalanced forces.

The altar is either set in the center of the circle or close to the eastern edge, so that the participants face the East when working. However, not all Witches face the East when working in a circle. I prefer to stand in the North when working with anyone, or stand facing the North when working alone. To me, the North is a position of great power.

Four Element candles of the appropriate colors for each cardinal direction are placed near the circle's edge. The rulers of these Elements are called or invoked for assistance and protection at the proper place in the ritual.

To begin the actual circle casting, the circle is sealed by retracing the line in the air with the athame or a sword. Next, the circle is blessed and cleansed by sprinkling its circumference with a mixture of salt and water. Sometimes, this procedure is repeated by carrying lighted incense around the circle. This offers protection against potentially malevolent and dangerous forces or spirits. The circle line is begun in the East, drawn deosil, and finishes in the East by overlapping the ends.

Do not cross the circle boundary once it is cast. If you must leave, cut a symbolic door in the air with your dagger, go through, and then re-mark the line to seal it. Lay your dagger on the floor in front of this "door." When you return, cut the door again, go through, and reseal the boundary. However, it is best if you simply do not leave the circle until you are finished.

The cardinal directions of a circle are then oriented by the lighting of a candle at each cardinal direction and calling the spirits of that direction. Some Witches draw an invoking pentagram at each quarter when calling up the guardians and a banishing pentagram at the end of the ritual when the guardians are dismissed.

Even if you do not use the invoking and banishing pentagrams at each quarter direction, Witches or magicians should banish all attracted entities before they cut the circle. This can be done by formally thanking the gathered entities. You must also ground any remaining power from the Otherworld. If you are proficient in magic, you can do this by word alone. Since most apprentices and beginning Witches are not, you can do this by placing your power hand on the altar or the floor. This grounds whatever energy is left within the circle, and will not leave you with unwanted, troublesome pockets of energy. Pouring this energy into a power sink stone kept on the altar is also an excellent method of grounding the remaining energies. Finally, the circle should be ritually broken with the dagger or sword.

Sometimes, two people (a couple or friends) will do rituals together. In this case, divide the ritual parts so each has something to do and say. Read the Coven Initiation

(Chapter 35) to see how this can be done. In calling the quarter guardians, for example, one person could do the East and South, while the other person does the West and North.

CASTING THE CIRCLE

The wording of this partial ritual, and all those that follow, is given for a solitary Witch. For group work, simply change the wording from "I" to "we," "child" to "children," and so on.

All rituals in this book contain parts of rituals from other books and parts that are original to the author.

Actually casting the circle is the second step in preparing your ritual area for ceremony and magic. The first step is to put all the tools you will need on the altar, and anything less vital, but still to be used, at least within the area that will be enclosed by the circle. Once the circle is cast, you cannot cross it to get something you forgot. Using the broom, ritually sweep, in a clockwise movement, all negative energy and entities out of the ritual area, while saying: *All negative out, all positive in.*

General items needed on the altar are the pentacle, dagger, the white pillar candle, a small taper candle, a candlesnuffer, the four Element candles, a chalice of water, a container of salt, a small hand bell, incense and a censer, and the paper or book with this ritual. The small white taper candle is used to light the Element candles. You will also need a lighter for the charcoal and candles.

The pentacle is placed in the forward center of your altar, close to where you will stand. Set the chalice of water on it, with the container of salt nearby. Have the paper with the ritual near this. Place the white pillar candle to the right of this and light it. Lay the small taper candle near the pillar candle, with the snuffer beside it. Put the censer on the left side of the altar. If you use a charcoal tablet, light it well in advance of the ritual, so it can be properly heated. Place the container of incense or incense cones near the censer. Put the dagger near you on the right side of the altar so you will know where it is at all times. Near the dagger, place the hand bell.

If you do not have charcoal tablets and powdered incense, and are using incense sticks or cones, point the dagger at these while saying both parts of the ritual intended separately for the burning charcoal and the incense.

The Element candles are set, one at each quarter mark of the circle. The modern colors most often used are yellow in the East, red in the South, blue in the West, and dark green or black in the North. Before you begin a circle casting, you should decide what form you will use in addressing the Elements (Lords and Ladies; Watchtowers; or the names of the elemental rulers) and the colors of candles you will set out (East, yellow; South, red; West, blue; North, dark green; or in the Celtic manner of East, white; South, red; West, gray; and North, black).

Stand before the altar. Close your eyes, breathe deeply, and center your thoughts on the upcoming ritual and the reason behind it. Ring the bell once and say:

This ritual has begun.

Next, move to the eastern edge of the ritual area, holding your dagger in your power hand. Visualize a blue-white flame issuing from the tip of the dagger. Point it at the floor in the East. Walk clockwise or deosil around the circle, drawing the circle mark in the air as you go. Be sure to overlap the ends in the East as you finish.

As you walk, say:

I consecrate this circle to the Goddess and the God. Here may they manifest and bless their child.

Return to the altar and stand facing it. Raise your arms with the dagger in your power hand, and say:

This is a time that is not a time, in a place that is not a place, on a day that is not a day. I stand at the threshold between the worlds, before the Veil of the Mysteries. May the Old Ones protect me that I may walk the true path forever. By the bright circle of the golden sun, by the bright courses of the glorious moon, by the dread potency of every star in the mysterious zodiac's burning girth, by each and all of these supernal signs, I do call and command you with this sacred blade. Guard me in this time and place from all evil and unbalanced forces.

Lay the dagger on the altar, raise your arms in greeting, and say:

Come, all those who would help me here this night. I give you welcome within this sacred circle. Join your powers with my desires that I may create and accomplish.

Take up the dagger and hold it point down over the chalice of water. (Some Witches believe the dagger should touch the water, salt, and incense.) Say:

The blessings of the Goddess be upon this water, symbol of Water. May it ever remind me of the endless cauldron waters of rebirth.

Hold the dagger with the point down over the container of salt. Say:

The blessings of the Goddess be upon this salt, symbol of Earth. May I ever honor the blesséd earth that is Her body in the physical world.

With the tip of your dagger, scoop up a little of the salt and tip it into the chalice of water. Put the dagger aside and take up the chalice in your power hand. Swirl it gently three times in a clockwise movement.

Hold the chalice high over the altar and say:

Water and Earth, Elements of birth. By touch, purify. By power, sanctify. Great Goddess, be you adored!

Using the fingers of your power hand, lightly sprinkle the water around the edge of the circle, beginning and ending in the East.

Replace the chalice on the altar, and take the dagger in your power hand. Hold it point down over the burning charcoal and say:

May the blessings of the God be upon this charcoal, symbol of Fire. May I ever honor the sacred Fire that dances within me.

Hold the dagger point down over the incense and say:

May the blessings of the God be upon this incense, symbol of Air. May I always listen to the spiritual inspiration that whispers to my soul.

Lay the dagger aside. Put a small amount of the incense on the burning charcoal. Hold the burner high over the altar and say:

Fire and Air, Elements so fair. By touch, purify. By power, sanctify. Great God, be you adored!

Carry the burning incense around the circle, beginning and ending in the East. Return the censer to the altar.

Stand facing the altar and say:

Round and round, the power has bound, this circle tonight in Otherworld light. No evil may enter, no harm befall me. For this is my will, and so shall it be.

Take the small taper candle and light it from the white pillar candle. With your dagger in your power hand and the taper in the other, go to the East. Light the yellow candle. Trace the invoking pentagram in the air over the candle, while saying:

> *Lords and Ladies of the East, all those ruled by the Element of Air, I do summon you to witness this ritual and to guard this circle.*

Go to the South; light the red candle. Trace the invoking pentagram in the air over the candle, while saying:

> *Lords and Ladies of the South, all those ruled by the Element of Fire, I do summon you to witness this ritual and to guard this circle.*

Go to the West; light the blue candle. Trace the invoking pentagram in the air over the candle, while saying:

> *Lords and Ladies of the West, all those ruled by the Element of Water, I do summon you to witness this ritual and to guard this circle.*

Go to the North; light the green candle. Trace the invoking pentagram in the air over the candle, while saying:

> *Lords and Ladies of the North, all those ruled by the Element of Earth, I do summon you to witness this ritual and to guard this circle.*

Return to the altar, snuff out the taper candle, and lay it and the dagger aside.

(This concludes the casting the circle part of a ritual. This is usually followed by the Charge of the Goddess, the blessing of the wine/juice, and a suitable celebration. These celebrations can be of the New or Full Moon, a rite of passage, or one of the eight holy days. Spellwork also can be performed at this time.)

CLOSING THE CIRCLE

When the complete ritual is finished, take your dagger in your power hand and the candlesnuffer in the other.

Go to the East. Extinguish the candle flame and trace the banishing pentagram in the air over the candle. Say:

> *Lords and Ladies of the East, all those ruled by the Element of Air, I bid you peacefully depart. My thanks, and farewell.*

Go to the South. Extinguish the candle flame and trace the banishing pentagram in the air over the candle. Say:

> *Lords and Ladies of the South, all those ruled by the Element of Fire, I bid you peacefully depart. My thanks, and farewell.*

Go to the West. Extinguish the candle flame and trace the banishing pentagram in the air over the candle. Say:

> *Lords and Ladies of the West, all those ruled by the Element of Water, I bid you peacefully depart. My thanks, and farewell.*

Go to the North. Extinguish the candle flame and trace the banishing pentagram in the air over the candle. Say:

> *Lords and Ladies of the North, all those ruled by the Element of Earth, I bid you peacefully depart. My thanks, and farewell.*

Return to the altar. Lay aside the candlesnuffer. Lay both hands, palms down, on the altar to ground any remaining power.

Raise your arms in greetings as you say:

> *Fairies, Spirits, Elementals, and all in the invisible, I give my thanks and my blessings. May we always work in harmony together. Blessèd be.*

Take your dagger and go to the eastern edge of the circle. Sweep the dagger across the invisible circle from right to left. Say:

> *The circle is cut, but the blessings long remain. Merry meet and merry part and merry meet again. Blessèd be!*

You have just successfully cast and cut your circle.

Study Work

Cast a complete ritual circle, complete with calling up of the quarter guardians and the cutting of the circle at the end. What were your feelings while doing this? Were there any unusual sounds or odors, or any unexplainable flashes of movement?

Initiation into Wicca

Initiation is the solemn, formal oath taken upon entering a coven, or for practice as a solitary Witch. People being initiated swear that they will be loyal to Wicca and keep Craft secrets, particularly from any who are not members of the coven or Craft. This secrecy remains important, although we have moved away from the eras of the terrible Inquisition and persecution by the anti-Witch laws. Witches may no longer be burned at the stake in the middle of town, but they can be harassed in court, on the job, and in their private lives. The last thing you want is an orthodox group or church praying for your death or that you will go to "hell" because you talked about your private spiritual methods. Powerful, concentrated, and repeated thoughts are a form of spell, and can be just as powerful as a Witch's spell.

In preparation for initiation, the apprentice decides upon a Craft name to be used only within the magic circle and only known to other friendly Witches. I say friendly Witches because you certainly do not want to share this name with unfriendly ones, who might decide you need to be under a binding spell or something similar.

This Craft name allows the initiate, or Witch, to lay aside the physical persona and adopt a magical one whenever they cast a circle and stand within it to do a ritual or spell. George may be an ordinary person every day of his life, worrying about bills and the traffic. But when George steps into the circle, he sees himself as Raven Moon, a Witch who can tap into powers that can turn the ordinary into the extraordinary. As Raven Moon, he changes his mind-set and opens his subconscious mind to the Lady and the Lord. By doing this, he leaves the magical circle a more balanced person than when he entered.

I only give the First Degree initiation in this book because I believe that is all it really takes to make a person a full-fledged Witch. If you, or any coven, wish to use the Second and Third degree initiations, you will find examples in several available books.

Plan your initiation for the night of a Full Moon. In preparation for your self-initiation, you should fast for one day, provided you do not have health problems that prevent this. You may drink water or unsweetened juice, but do not eat food or indulge in coffee or sodas. Take any medications that you ordinarily take.

Be certain that you have the necessary ritual items on hand well before you plan to do your initiation. Extra materials you will need are a bottle of anointing oil or lotus oil, the Charge written on a piece of paper (not too large), and a flexible small white cord. Always choose a thin, tough, but very flexible and soft cord. Tradition says the cord should be nine feet long. It is best to knot the cord ends to keep them from unraveling.

Many covens use colored cords to symbolize what degree each member holds within their group. White is used by all those having a First Degree initiation. Red can be used to signify Second Degree, and black the Third and highest degree. Frequently, Third Degree Witches braid the three colors together into one cord and wear this cord during all rituals. White, red, and black have been Goddess colors for thousands of years.

Just before you plan to do this ceremony, take a ritual bath. You should take your time bathing, so run a tub full of warm water, and sprinkle a little consecrated salt into it. You can also use appropriate Wiccan bath salts available at Pagan shops. While you bathe and soak, think of the solemnity of the upcoming ritual. Prepare yourself mentally, emotionally, and spiritually for this important step in your spiritual path. Burn a white candle while bathing; then take the candle with you when you enter the circle for initiation. This candle is placed on the altar beside the Charge you will sign.

If you are to be alone while performing the initiation, you should go to the altar without clothing. If you have others joining you, and particularly if both sexes will be present, you can wear a light robe that opens in the front. This will allow the sacred oil to be placed on the appropriate spots without embarrassment.

If you have others present, they can set up the altar while you are bathing. You will stand outside the circle until the person who will initiate you comes for you. If you are alone, set up the altar yourself after your cleansing bath. Think about each tool you place on the altar and each movement you make within the ritual area. When you are ready, use the appropriate ceremony given later in this chapter.

Remember, when you copy the rituals into your Book of Shadows, always write the procedure for the circle casting and cutting in the proper places in each ritual. Then you will have every ritual step available when you do the ritual.

Initiations, whether self-initiation or in a coven, should include a document signed by the initiate. This solemn paper is a promise to obey certain principles and rules. In covens, this is known as the Coven Charge and sometimes is written in red ink. For a coven initiation, this Coven Charge outlines what the initiate must promise as a good member, such as secrecy and certain rules of behavior.

In both cases, initiates must *thoroughly* understand what they are signing well before the initiation ceremony takes place. An example of each Charge follows. Covens may wish to add to the Charge, listing more specific rules.

Some covens use blindfolding, binding with a cord, and scourging as part of the initiation ceremony. Some even measure initiates with a string, keeping the string, a drop of the initiates' blood, and a lock of hair in case they decide to leave the coven. These were Gardner's inventions. No coven needs to use these practices in order to perform a true initiation.

The biggest problem for covens is the responsibility of sorting out those who are not sincere about Wicca, but want to be in a group for selfish and unprincipled reasons. If initiates are not screened closely, their admission to the coven will eventually shatter it.

SELF-INITIATE CHARGE

I solemnly promise never to reveal to anyone the secrets of the Craft, unless that person has qualified to become a Witch in thought, word, deed, and true desire. I will never divulge the names of other Witches, where they live and work, or where they meet, unless they agree. I will not teach the Wiccan religion or magical secrets to anyone under the legal age of adulthood. I will not actively recruit any to the religion of Wicca, although I will attempt to find a worthy pupil to whom I will pass on my knowledge.

I promise to honor and follow the Goddess and the God to the best of my ability, never leaving the sacred path or repenting of my decision. I will work and study to master the art of magic, using that art for good and for protection, not for evil or self-aggrandizement.

If I break this vow, I understand that I will suffer the fate I have made for myself, according to the laws of karma.

(Initiate's signature)

COVEN CHARGE

I solemnly promise to hold inviolate the secrets of this coven, and never reveal to anyone the secrets of the coven or the Craft, unless the coven agrees that person has qualified to become a Witch in thought, word, deed, and true desire. I will never divulge the names of other Witches, where they live and work, or where they meet, unless they agree. I will not teach the Wiccan religion or magical secrets to anyone under the legal age of adulthood. I will not actively recruit any to the religion of Wicca, although I will attempt to find a worthy pupil to whom I will pass on my knowledge.

I promise to honor and follow the Goddess and the God to the best of my ability, never leaving the sacred path or repenting of my decision. I will work and study to master the art of magic, using that art for good and for protection, not for evil or self-aggrandizement.

If I break this vow, I understand that I will suffer the fate I have made for myself, according to the laws of karma.

(Initiate's signature)

This is read to the initiate during the coven initiation ceremony. Actually, it makes more sense to read this to the initiate the day before the initiation. Then, if the person rejects any of the Charge, the initiate is never admitted into the presence of the full coven. Once within the circle, the initiate must agree to the Charge and sign it, or the initiation is immediately stopped. If this happens, the circle is opened, and the initiate is removed from the coven's presence at once without any further discussion. If an initiate refuses to sign, that person will never be readmitted, for they have proved untrustworthy and unreliable.

In covens, various members are appointed to call and dismiss each of the quarter guardians, using the coven's name preference for the quarters. The High Priestess and High Priest usually consecrate the water, salt, and incense, and then cast the circle. They also bless the wine/juice and any bread that is on the altar. The other coven members can take part in various functions, as well as respond in certain sections of the ritual. The Initiator need not be the High Priestess or High Priest, but is usually the teacher of the initiate.

In the following coven initiation ritual, the parts of the High Priestess will be marked as HPS, while the High Priest's parts are marked as HP. Most of the rituals in this book are for the solitary Witch and will not have these abbreviations, unless deemed necessary.

SELF-INITIATION FIRST DEGREE CEREMONY

TIME: Night of the Full Moon.

ITEMS NEEDED: The pentacle, dagger, the white pillar candle, candlesnuffer, the four Element candles, a chalice of water, a container of salt, a small hand bell, incense and a censer, a small cauldron, a small bottle of anointing oil or lotus oil, chalice of wine or juice, the white cord, and the paper or book with this ritual. Have a small white taper candle to use in lighting the Element candles. You will also need a lighter for the charcoal and the altar candle. Have a copy of the Charge ready to sign, with a pen available.

The altar candle and the charcoal block are lit before the ceremony begins. Check to see that everything needed is on the altar, or at least within the ritual area where it can be reached without breaking the boundary once the circle is cast.

Create the circle as described in Chapter 34.

After the circle is cast, say:

> *All creatures are born of the Goddess and the God, and are Their children. The Goddess breathes within us the breath of life and a soul of shining light. She is the great and loving Mother of all. Therefore, as Her child, I thank Her for what I have, yet may I also ask Her for what I need.*

(Observe silence while you give thanks to the Goddess and the God and ask for what you need.)

Raise your arms and say:

> *Great Goddess, I call upon You by all Your names, known and unknown. Be here within this sacred circle that I might feel Your power and love. Hear my words, all you creatures of this world. The Goddess is the Great Mother of all! I am never alone or abandoned. She hears every secret longing of my heart, sees every step I take along my life's path. She is everywhere, in everything. Nothing and no one exists without Her.*
>
> *The Goddess is the beauty of this earth and everything upon it. She reflects Herself in the glowing moon, the brilliant sun, and every star in the heavens. Nothing is born without Her plan and power, and all things return to Her at the end of their life cycle. Although the Goddess is the*

gatherer Crone, She is also the Maiden of desire. All acts of love and joy and pleasure are rituals in Her eyes.

I cast my circle at each Full Moon in accordance with Her ancient worship that I may honor Her and ask for what I need. I follow Her words that say I must value my freedom and strive for the highest of ideals, without being hindered or turned aside. For if I do not learn to value myself, others may lead me into slavery.

The Goddess is the gateway to the ancient Inner Mysteries. Her secret teachings lead me through the spiritual labyrinth to the Sacred Center. All who seek Her must understand Her ancient words. All your seeking and yearning will avail you nothing, unless you know the Mystery: For if what you seek you find not within, you will never find without. For behold, the Goddess has been with us from the beginning, and She will gather us to Her breast at the end of all things.

Stand before the altar for a few moments of silence. Say:

I come before this altar that I might worship the Lady and the Lord. I have the courage to stand at the threshold between this world and the Otherworld. I vow to hold true to the Old Ways.

Loop the white cord loosely around your hands. Say:

This binding symbolizes my state within the presence of the Goddess. I am neither bound nor free. My heart is bound to Her tighter than any knot, yet I am free of absolute control. I give perfect love and perfect trust to the Goddess and the God.

Unwind the cord and place it on the altar. Take up the paper with the Charge written on it and read it aloud.

I solemnly promise never to reveal to anyone the secrets of the Craft, unless that person has qualified to become a Witch in thought, word, deed, and true desire. I will never divulge the names of other Witches, where they live and work, or where they meet, unless they agree. I will not teach the Wiccan religion or magical secrets to anyone under the legal age of adulthood. I will not actively recruit any to the religion of Wicca. I promise to honor and follow the Goddess and the God to the best of my ability, never leaving the sacred path or repenting of my decision. I will work and study to master the art of magic, using that art for good and for protection, not for evil or self-aggrandizement.

If I break this vow, I understand that I will suffer the fate I have made for myself, according to the laws of karma.

The initiate kneels and places one hand on the pentacle that is on the altar.

Initiate: *I understand the Charge and swear that I will uphold it at all times. May the Goddess and the God hear my words.*

The initiate signs the Charge pledge, lights the paper with the altar candle, and then burns it in the cauldron, saying:

As this smoke rises above this sacred circle, it carries my promise to the Goddess and the God. These words can never be revoked or erased. By the power of earth and sea, this is my will. So mote it be.

Take the bottle of anointing oil. Put a drop on the index finger of your power hand. Mark an X in the center of your forehead and say:

Let my mind be free.

Mark an X in the center of your chest over the heart and say:

Let my heart be free.

Mark an X on the lower belly and say:

Let my body be free.

Stand before the altar and say:

I take the name of _____ (your Craft name). I am a standing stone in the ancient circle of the Goddess. I am firm upon the earth, yet open to the winds of heaven and enduring through all time. I give my oath, keep troth!

Take the white cord from the altar and wrap it around your waist, but do not tie it in a knot.

Set the chalice of wine on the pentacle. Take the dagger and gently touch the tip to the wine/juice, saying:

As this athame is the male, so this cup is the female, and joined they bring blessings.

Raise the chalice high over the altar and say:

To the Old Ones! Merry meet and merry part and merry meet again! Blessed be!

Drink from the cup, leaving a little for the nature spirits.

Close the circle as described in Chapter 34.

The ritual is ended.

CEREMONY FOR A COVEN FIRST DEGREE INITIATION

TIME: Night of the Full Moon.

ITEMS NEEDED: The pentacle, dagger, the white pillar candle, candlesnuffer, the four Element candles, a chalice of water, a container of salt, a small hand bell, incense and a censer, a small cauldron, a small bottle of anointing oil or lotus oil, chalice of wine or juice, and the paper or book with this ritual. Have a small white taper candle to use in lighting the Element candles. You will also need a lighter for the charcoal and the altar candle. Have a copy of the Coven Charge ready to be signed, with a pen at hand. The initiate must bring a white cord.

Before the ritual begins, four of the coven members should be appointed to light and extinguish the quarter candles.

The altar candle and the charcoal block are lit before the ceremony begins. Check to see that everything needed is on the altar, or at least within the ritual area where it can be reached without breaking the boundary once the circle is cast.

All coven members, except the initiate, stand within the ritual area. The initiate waits well away from the circle or in another room. The HP and HPS stand before the altar, facing each other, the HPS in the East, and the HP in the West.

HP rings the bell once and says:

This ritual has begun.

The HP casts the circle with his dagger, beginning and ending in the East, and moving in a deosil direction. HP says:

I consecrate this circle to the Goddess and the God. Here may they manifest and bless their children.

He returns to the altar and stands facing the HPS.

The HPS raises her arms with the dagger or wand in her power hand, and says:
This is a time that is not a time, in a place that is not a place, on a day that is not a day. We stand at the threshold between the worlds, before the Veil of the Mysteries. May the Old Ones protect us that we may walk the true path forever. By the bright circle of the golden sun, by the bright courses of the glorious moon, by the dread potency of every star in the mysterious zodiac's burning girth, by each and all of these supernal signs I do call and command you with this sacred blade. Guard us in this time and place from all evil and unbalanced forces.

HP and HPS lay their daggers on the altar. HP raises his arms in greeting, and says:
Come, all those who would help us here this night. We give you welcome within this sacred circle. Join your powers with our desires that we may create and accomplish.

HPS takes up the dagger and holds it point down over the chalice of water. Says:
The blessings of the Goddess be upon this water, symbol of Water. May it ever remind us of the endless cauldron waters of rebirth.

HPS holds the dagger with the point down over the container of salt. Says:
The blessings of the Goddess be upon this salt, symbol of Earth. May we ever honor the blesséd earth that is Her body in the physical world.

She scoops up a little of the salt and tips it into the chalice of water. Then she puts the dagger aside. She takes up the chalice in her power hand and swirls it gently three times in a clockwise movement.

HPS holds the chalice high over the altar and says:
Water and Earth, Elements of birth. By touch, purify. By power, sanctify. Great Goddess, be you adored!

She lightly sprinkles the water around the edge of the circle, beginning and ending in the East. When finished, she replaces the chalice on the altar.

HP takes the dagger and holds it point down over the burning charcoal. He says:

> *May the blessings of the God be upon this charcoal, symbol of Fire. May we ever honor the sacred Fire that dances within us.*

HP holds the dagger the incense and says:

> *May the blessings of the God be upon this incense, symbol of Air. May we always listen to the spiritual inspiration that whispers to our souls.*

He lays the dagger aside, puts a small amount of the incense on the burning charcoal, and then holds the burner high over the altar, saying:

> *Fire and Air, Elements so fair. By touch, purify. By power, sanctify. Great God, be you adored!*

He carries the burning incense around the circle, beginning and ending in the East. He returns the censer to the altar.

HPS: *Round and round, the power has bound this circle tonight in Otherworld light. No evil may enter; no harm shall befall. For this is our will, and so shall be it all.*

Entire coven: *Blessed be!*

HPS takes the small taper candle and lights it from the altar candle. She hands it to the Witch responsible for lighting the East candle.

The Witch lights the yellow candle, then traces the invoking pentagram in the air over the candle, while saying:

> *Lords and Ladies of the East, all those ruled by Air, I do summon you to witness this ritual and to guard this circle.*

The Witch passes the taper to the Witch in the South who lights the red candle, then traces the invoking pentagram in the air over the candle, while saying:

> *Lords and Ladies of the South, all those ruled by the Element of Fire, I do summon you to witness this ritual and to guard this circle.*

This witch passes the taper to the Witch in the West who lights the blue candle, then traces the invoking pentagram in the air over the candle, while saying:

> *Lords and Ladies of the West, all those ruled by the Element of Water, I do summon you to witness this ritual and to guard this circle.*

This witch passes the taper to the Witch in the North who lights the green candle, then traces the invoking pentagram in the air over the candle, while saying:

> *Lords and Ladies of the North, all those ruled by the Element of Earth, I do summon you to witness this ritual and to guard this circle.*

The last Witch returns the taper to the HPS, who snuffs it out and lays it aside.

HPS raises her arms and says:

> *All creatures are born of the Goddess and the God, and are Their children. The Goddess breathes within us the breath of life and a soul of shining light. She is the great and loving Mother of all. Therefore, as Her children, we thank Her for what we have, yet may we also ask Her for what we need.*

(Silence is observed while all give thanks to the Goddess and the God and ask for what they need.)

HPS: *Great Goddess, I call upon You by all Your names, known and unknown. Be here within this sacred circle that we might feel Your power and love. Hear my words, all you creatures of this world. The Goddess is the Great Mother of all! We are never alone or abandoned. She hears every secret longing of our hearts, sees every step we take along our life's paths. She is everywhere, in everything. Nothing and no one exists without Her.*

> *The Goddess is the beauty of this earth and everything upon it. She reflects Herself in the glowing moon, the brilliant sun, and every star in the heavens. Nothing is born without Her plan and power, and all things return to Her at the end of their life cycle. Although the Goddess is the gatherer Crone, She is also the Maiden of desire. All acts of love and joy and pleasure are rituals in Her eyes.*

> *We cast our circle at each Full Moon in accordance with Her ancient worship that we may honor Her and ask for what we need. We follow Her words that say we must value our freedom and strive for the highest of ideals, without being hindered or turned aside. For if we do not learn to value ourselves, others may lead us into slavery.*

> *The Goddess is the gateway to the ancient Inner Mysteries. Her secret teachings lead us through the spiritual labyrinth to the Sacred*

Center. All who seek Her must understand Her ancient words. All your seeking and yearning will avail you nothing, unless you know the Mystery: For if what you seek you find not within, you will never find without. For behold, the Goddess has been with us from the beginning, and She will gather us to Her breast at the end of all things.

The HPS uses her dagger to cut a symbolic door in the circle for the Initiator, who leaves to get the initiate. The door is sealed behind the Initiator.

When the Initiator returns with the initiate, the HPS challenges them at the circle's edge.

HPS: *Who comes to this sacred place?*

Initiator: *It is I,* _____(magical name). *I bring one who would join with us in the Old Ways.*

HPS opens the circle and allows the Initiator and initiate to enter. She seals the circle behind the two. She returns to the altar. The Initiator leads the initiate to the altar near the HPS.

Initiator: *I bring this initiate before this altar that she/he might worship the Lady and the Lord.*

HPS takes up her dagger or sword and touches the tip against the initiate's chest, saying: *You stand at the threshold between this world and the Otherworld. Do you have the courage to stand with us?*

Initiate: *I do.*

HPS: *It is better that you perish than give false witness, for the Goddess has no need of those who waver in their faith. There are two passwords required to enter the presence of the Lady and Her Lord: perfect love and perfect trust.*

Initiate: *I vow to hold true to the Old Ways. I offer perfect love and perfect trust.*

The HPS returns the dagger to the altar. The Initiator takes the initiate's white cord and loosely loops it around both of the initiate's hands.

Initiator: *This binding symbolizes your state within the presence of the Goddess. You are neither bound nor free. For your heart must be bound to Her tighter than any knot, yet are you free of absolute control.*

Initiate: *I give my love and trust to the Goddess and the God.*

The Initiator unwinds the white cord and gives it to the HPS, who places it on the altar until the end of the ritual.

The Initiator reads the Coven Charge to the initiate, as follows:

I solemnly promise to hold inviolate the secrets of this coven, and never reveal to anyone the secrets of the coven or the Craft, unless the coven agrees that person has qualified to become a Witch in thought, word, deed, and true desire. I will never divulge the names of other Witches, where they live and work, or where they meet, unless they agree. I will not teach the Wiccan religion or magical secrets to anyone under the legal age of adulthood. I will not actively recruit any to the religion of Wicca.

I promise to honor and follow the Goddess and the God to the best of my ability, never leaving the sacred path or repenting of my decision. I will work and study to master the art of magic, using that art for good and for protection, not for evil or self-aggrandizement.

If I break this vow, I understand that I will suffer the fate I have made for myself, according to the laws of karma.

Initiator: *Will you promise to obey this Charge and keep it in your heart forever?*

The initiate must say: *I will.* Then the initiate signs the paper.

Initiator: *Kneel before this altar. With your hand on the pentacle, repeat after me the following words.*

The initiate kneels and places one hand on the pentacle.

Initiator: *I understand the Charge and swear that I will uphold it at all times. May the Goddess and the God hear my words.*

The initiate repeats the words.

The Initiator lights the signed paper with the altar candles and burns it in the cauldron, saying:

> *As this smoke rises above this sacred circle, it carries your promise to the Goddess and the God. These words can never be revoked or erased. By the power of earth and sea, this is our will. So mote it be.*

Entire coven: *So mote it be!*

The initiate stands. The Initiator takes the bottle of anointing oil and puts a drop on the index finger of the power hand.

The Initiator marks an X in the center of the initiate's forehead and says:

> *Let your mind be free.*

The Initiator marks an X in the center of the initiate's chest over the heart and says:

> *Let your heart be free.*

The Initiator marks an X on the lower belly of the initiate and says:

> *Let your body be free.*

The Initiator turns to the altar and says:

> *I give this woman (man) the name of* _____ (the chosen Craft name). *She/he is a standing stone in the ancient circle of the Goddess. She/he is firm upon the earth, yet open to the winds of heaven and enduring through all time.*

Entire coven: *Coven oath, keep troth!*

The kiss of greeting is given the initiate by the HPS, if initiate is a man, or the HP, if the initiate is a woman.

The Initiator and initiate join the circle of members around the altar.

The HPS holds the chalice of wine, while the HP takes his dagger and gently touches the tip to the wine/juice. HP says:

> *As this athame is the male, so this cup is the female, and joined they bring blessings.*

HPS raises the chalice high over the altar and says:

To the Old Ones! Merry meet and merry part and merry meet again!
Blessed be!

Entire coven: *Blesséd be!*

HPS drinks from the cup, and then passes it to the HP who drinks. HP gives the cup to a Witch, who drinks and passes it deosil around the circle. A little of wine/juice is saved to leave for the nature spirits.

When the complete ritual is finished, the HPS gives the candlesnuffer to the Witch in the East. This Witch extinguishes the candle flame and traces the banishing pentagram in the air over the candle, while saying:

> *Lords and Ladies of the East, all those ruled by the Element of Air, I bid*
> *you peacefully depart. My thanks, and farewell.*

This Witch passes the snuffer to the Witch in the South who extinguishes the candle flame and traces the banishing pentagram in the air over the candle, while saying:

> *Lords and Ladies of the South, all those ruled by the Element of Fire, I*
> *bid you peacefully depart. My thanks, and farewell.*

This Witch passes the snuffer to the Witch in the West who extinguishes the candle flame and traces the banishing pentagram in the air over the candle, while saying:

> *Lords and Ladies of the West, all those ruled by the Element of Water, I*
> *bid you peacefully depart. My thanks, and farewell.*

This Witch passes the snuffer to the Witch in the North who extinguishes the candle flame and traces the banishing pentagram in the air over the candle, while saying:

> *Lords and Ladies of the North, all those ruled by the Element of Earth, I*
> *bid you peacefully depart. My thanks, and farewell.*

This last Witch returns the snuffer to the HPS, who lays it aside.

HPS: *Ground!*

All within the circle lay both hands, palms down, on the floor, while the HPS and HP do so on the altar to ground any remaining power.

HPS raises her arms as she says:

Fairies, Spirits, Elementals, and all in the invisible, we give our thanks and our blessings. May we always work in harmony together. Blessed be.

Entire coven: *Blesséd be!*

HP takes his dagger and goes to the eastern edge of the circle. He sweeps the dagger across the invisible circle from right to left and says:

The circle is cut, but the blessings long remain. Merry meet and merry part and merry meet again. Blesséd be!

Entire coven: *Blesséd be!*

Study Work

Do a self-initiation. Record how your feelings may have changed from the beginning to the end of the initiation and how it now feels to be a fully dedicated, consecrated Witch.

CHAPTER 36

The Charge of the Goddess

Before you start using the Charge of the Goddess in ritual work, you should understand what is being said and why you are saying it. It is a beautiful, solemn, and sacred part of the ritual, one that actively invokes the Goddess more than any other part of the ceremony.

The Charge of the Goddess was originally used in Western Europe among Gardnerians and Alexandrians, but now has spread into other Wiccan groups. Gerald Gardner wrote his version of the Charge by adapting it from the book *Aradia: Queen of Witches* by Leland, and including material from Aleister Crowley. Doreen Valiente rewrote it later and deleted the Crowley material. She first wrote it in rhyme, then in prose. Many covens use one of her versions still today.

Since then, the Charge of the Goddess has been rewritten to suit any solitary Witch or coven using it. Although the basics remain the same, the wording may vary from Witch to Witch, or group to group.

In most covens, the Charge is spoken immediately after the circle casting, the opening portion of the ritual ceremony, and the Drawing Down the Moon ceremony. When a High Priestess speaks the Charge, she says the words as if the Goddess Herself were speaking. The priestess is actually invoking the Goddess into her body.

This wording works well for coven gatherings. However, it becomes a little awkward for the solitary Witch, although the solitary female Witch can do this without much trouble. If a male Witch is practicing alone and speaks the Charge, it is best if he uses the third person status when vocalizing it. He says the words as if the Goddess is standing in the circle with him, listening to his rendition, for he is invoking Her into his circle, not his body.

The following Charge is one of my personal renditions of this writing. It is not written in the first person, as with the coven Charge, but as if the priest/priestess is talking directly to Her, and then telling what the Goddess wishes done.

THE CHARGE OF THE GODDESS

Great Goddess, I call upon You by all Your names, known and unknown. Be here within this sacred circle that I might feel Your power and love. Hear my words, all you creatures of this world. The Goddess is the Great Mother of all! I am never alone or abandoned. She hears every secret longing of my heart, sees every step I take along my life's path. She is everywhere, in everything. Nothing and no one exists without Her.

The Goddess is the beauty of this earth and everything upon it. She reflects Herself in the glowing moon, the brilliant sun, and every star in the heavens. Nothing is born without Her plan and power, and all things return to Her at the end of their life cycle. Although the Goddess is the gatherer Crone, She is also the Maiden of desire. All acts of love and joy and pleasure are rituals in Her eyes.

I cast my circle at each Full Moon in accordance with Her ancient worship that I may honor Her and ask for what I need. I follow Her words that say I must value my freedom and strive for the highest of ideals, without being hindered or turned aside. For if I do not learn to value myself, others may lead me into slavery.

The Goddess is the gateway to the ancient Inner Mysteries. Her secret teachings lead me through the spiritual labyrinth to the Sacred Center. All who seek Her must understand Her ancient words. "All your seeking and yearning will avail you nothing, unless you know the Mystery: For if what you seek you find not within, you will never find without." For behold, the Goddess has been with us from the beginning, and She will gather us to Her breast at the end of all things.

All of the Charge is fairly straightforward, except the lines that say: *All who seek Her must understand Her ancient words. All your seeking and yearning will avail you nothing, unless you know the Mystery: For if what you seek you find not within, you will never find without.* Many new Witches, and some of the older ones as well, become confused about this statement. However, it is simple to understand, and has been part of Goddess worship and the ancient Mysteries for thousands of years.

The Goddess resides within each person, as well as being within everything in the universe. You cannot find Her by looking outside yourself. She doesn't exist in religions or schools or expensive courses. You can take instructional courses forever and never encounter the true Goddess. You will not find Her by parading your spiritual ideas in public, by wearing Pagan jewelry with every outfit, or recruiting members for your coven. She appears and answers only on an individual basis in meditation, prayer to Her, and heartfelt, sincere rituals. The Goddess does not make personal appearances to large gatherings, but chooses to greet Her followers one at a time in the silence of their own hearts.

Belonging to a group will not draw you closer to the Goddess. Your own life must be in order to be worthy of Her arrival. All the exterior physical acts you do, the words you say, and the masks you put on to hide your true self from others are no barriers to the Goddess. She instantly knows who you truly are inside. No truth can be hidden from Her.

Before you invoke the Head Mistress of the Universal Mysteries, take a close, realistic, and truthful look at yourself. If you have bad habits, change them. If you are constantly putting down other people, engaging in malicious acts, holding onto the idea of revenge, and blaming others for everything you do, you must change these behaviors if you call upon the Goddess. You can lie to yourself and everyone else, but you can't lie to Her.

There is also another truth contained in these words. The power for magic and communication with the Otherworld lies within each person, regardless of their status in life or position in a Wiccan group. Magical power does not come from ritual tools or spell materials, belonging to the "right" Wiccan group, or anything else. The power is within each Witch. You discover this power by reaching deep within yourself during ritual and spellwork, in meditation and prayer to the Goddess. Place your complete trust in Her, and She will teach you how to access and use this power to accomplish and create anything you want.

Study Work

Write what the Charge of the Goddess means to you. If there are parts you do not quite understand, meditate upon them until you receive an answer.

CHAPTER 37

Drawing Down
the Moon and Sun

The moon and the Goddess have been linked since early practices of human rituals. Moon rituals were entirely a female celebration at first. The moon was recognized as a mysterious agency that brought about the menstrual cycles of women, and thus were associated with childbearing. When women and men finally made the connection that both female and male are necessary to make a child, they began to include the Goddess as the moon in worship involving both sexes. The priest of the ritual celebrated the Moon Goddess by invoking Her essence and spirit into the body of the priestess. The priestess often went into a trance of varying depths, and became the Goddess for a short period of time. While the priestess and the Goddess were one, she gave advice, teachings, and future predictions from the Goddess to the assembled worshippers. We do not know what those ancient people called this ritual. Today it is known as Drawing Down the Moon.

The Drawing Down the Sun ceremony probably evolved later when the cultures began to base their calendars on the solar year. In the Drawing Down the Sun, it is the priest who invokes the God into his body with the priestess honoring the God within. This rite is performed less often than the Drawing Down the Moon.

Not all Wiccan groups use the Drawing Down the Moon or the Sun rites. Solitary Witches cannot perform these ceremonies as they are written; they must work with a Witch of the opposite sex. However, I have rewritten them to use in solitary ritual, as well as giving them in the full form for group work. If you wish, you can choose to not use these two rituals.

Most Witches agree that the modern rite generally comes from that found in *Aradia: Queen of the Witches* by Charles Godfrey Leland. Those who use the Drawing

Down the Moon ceremony insert it just before the Charge. It can be included during any New or Full Moon celebration or on the holy days.

The High Priest says the rite while kneeling before the High Priestess and invoking the Goddess to be present in the woman before him.

For the High Priestess, or any priestess, to properly entrance the Goddess, she must try to attune herself with the Lady and act as a channel for any messages the Goddess wishes to give. All sense of self, pride, and ego must be set aside, or a true invocation will not occur. This invocation is possible, because the Power of the Female Principle can easily transcend and penetrate the Veil between the Worlds. If there are any problems, they will arise on this end of the Otherworld connection because of an impeding imperfection within the vessel, or person, being used. The same principles apply to the priest during the Drawing Down the Sun ritual.

The priest must also make himself a vessel for the God's essence and spirit to properly perform his essential part of this rite. This process is aided by the priest when he honors the Goddess within the physical woman. He must fully believe and understand that the Goddess *is* standing before him. And that it is the God within him who is actually doing the honoring.

The primary obstacle to correctly doing this rite is usually in the mental attitude of the priestess and/or priest involved. They must learn to set aside their hopes, fears, and any other emotional baggage they carry, and open themselves without reservation to the Otherworld consciousness. At no time will the entire essence of the Goddess inhabit the priestess, or the God inhabit the priest, for this is impossible without permanently damaging the physical and mental bodies of the humans.

The Gardnerian tradition has very elaborate Drawing Down the Moon and Drawing Down the Sun ceremonies, complete with the five-fold kiss gesture. However, it is not necessary to follow that example if a group does not work nude, or skyclad, or is not comfortable with that version.

Because there is equality in Witchcraft, there is also a Drawing Down the Sun ritual that can be used on the eight holy days. These days are strongly connected with the God, and the sun and its yearly cycle. This time it is the priestess containing the Goddess who invokes the God into the priest and honors the transformation. Drawing Down the Sun usually occurs after the Drawing Down the Moon ceremony.

Because it is essential for the apprentice, indeed, all Witches, to understand the importance and antiquity of both of these ceremonies, I have included it here, with the New and Full Moon rituals following.

COVEN DRAWING DOWN THE MOON

EXTRA ITEMS NEEDED: The High Priestess wears a crown with a crescent moon on it, while the High Priest wears a crown with antlers on it.

Just before the Charge is said, the HPS stands with her back to the altar. She stands in the Osiris pose with the wand in her right hand and the dagger in her left. Her wrists should be crossed, and the ritual tools she holds also should cross. The HP kneels before her.

HP: *I bless thy feet that walk the sacred path. I bless thy knees that kneel before the Old Ones. I bless thy womb, the symbol of Goddess fertility. I bless thy breasts, the symbol of the Goddess and Her nurturing power. I bless thy lips that sing praises to the Goddess and the God. I honor the Goddess within you.*

The HPS moves into the Isis pose, with her arms outstretched and her feet apart. The HP stands and kisses her.

The HP kneels again and says:
I call You, Great Goddess, to come through the Veil and be among us. Fill the body of this woman, Your Priestess. Bless us with Your presence and power. Through Your wisdom and Your great Otherworld energy, fill our lives with renewing power. As seed becomes bud, and bud becomes flower, and flower becomes fruit, so shall we flower and fruit with good health, prosperity, happiness, and spiritual growth. We give You honor, Great Goddess!

Entire coven: *We honor You!*

HP raises his arms and says:
Proud and beautiful as the moon on high that races across the midnight sky, the Goddess blesses our joyful rite. Her glory fills our inner sight. She shows Her signs in fire and smoke, in chalice wine. Her we invoke into this Priestess at the altar, a transformed being, Goddess-daughter. We kneel in awe and chant the rune.

Entire coven kneels and says: *All honor to the Lady of the Moon!*

Coven stands again. HP stands facing the HPS.

HPS draws an invoking pentagram in the air with the wand and says:

(Full Moon) *The five-point star of love and power I bless you with this holy hour. Pray to me when the moon is round, and good things I promise will abound. I charge you follow my ancient ways with joy and bliss through all your days. (If the HPS has Otherworld messages, she gives them at this time.)*

(New Moon) *Darkened moon in blackest sky, as Crone and Dark One I hear your cry. All barriers I sweep away. No evil will I allow to stay. I bless and comfort my children all and answer when I hear your call.*

This completes the Drawing Down the Moon.

Solitary Drawing Down the Moon

EXTRA ITEMS NEEDED: The Priestess needs a crown with a crescent moon on it, while the Priest needs a crown with antlers on it.

This ceremony is said just before the Charge. Lay the wand and dagger on the altar, crossing them. Stand facing the altar in the Osiris pose, with your wrists crossed.

Say: *Blesséd Goddess, I call to you across the Veil between the Worlds! Enter this sacred space that I may feel Your presence and know that You are truly here!*

Kneel before the altar and say:

Bless my feet that walk the sacred path. Bless my knees that kneel before the Old Ones. (If you are a woman: *Bless my womb, the symbol of Goddess fertility. Bless my breasts, the symbol of the Goddess and Her nurturing power.*) (If you are a man: *Bless my phallus, the symbol of the God's fertile blessings.*) *Bless my lips that sing praises to the Goddess and the God. I honor the Goddess within me.* (This is entirely appropriate for men, as the Goddess and the God are present in both sexes.)

Move into the Isis pose, with your arms outstretched and your feet apart. Say:

We are each male and female. Therefore, the Goddess and the God inhabit all creatures, just as They do all creation. The Goddess within me empowers my soul.

Kneel again and say:

> *I call You, Great Goddess, to come through the Veil and be with me here. Fill my body with Your holy presence. Bless me with Your presence and power. Through Your wisdom and Your great Otherworld energy, fill my life with renewing power. As seed becomes bud, and bud becomes flower, and flower becomes fruit, so shall I flower and fruit with good health, prosperity, happiness, and spiritual growth. I give You honor, Great Goddess!*

Raise your arms and say:

> *Proud and beautiful as the moon on high that races across the midnight sky, the Goddess blesses my joyful rite. Her glory fills my inner sight. She shows Her signs in fire and smoke, in chalice wine. (If a woman: Her I invoke into this Priestess at the altar, a transformed being, Goddess-daughter.) (If a man: Her I invoke into this Priest at the altar. A follower strong, I never falter.) I kneel in awe and chant the rune. All honor to the Lady of the Moon!*

Stand, draw an invoking pentagram in the air with the wand, and say:

> (Full Moon) *The five-point star of love and power I bless you with this holy hour. Pray to me when the moon is round, and good things I promise will abound. I charge you follow my ancient ways with joy and bliss through all your days.*

> (New Moon) *Darkened moon in blackest sky, as Crone and Dark One I hear your cry. All barriers I sweep away. No evil will I allow to stay. I bless and comfort my children all and answer when I hear your call.*

This completes the Drawing Down the Moon.

COVEN DRAWING DOWN THE SUN

EXTRA ITEMS NEEDED: The High Priestess wears a crown with a crescent moon on it, while the High Priest wears a crown with antlers on it.

Just after the Drawing Down the Moon and before the Charge is said, the HP stands with his back to the altar. He stands in the Osiris pose with the dagger in his right hand with the point upward. His wrists should be crossed. The HPS kneels before him.

HPS: *I bless thy feet that walk the sacred path. I bless thy knees that kneel before the Old Ones. I bless thy phallus, the symbol of the God's fertile blessings. I bless thy lips that sing praises to the Goddess and the God. I honor the God within you.*

The HP moves into the Blessing pose, with his arms outstretched and his feet apart, still holding the dagger point upward. The HPS stands and kisses him.

The HPS kneels again and says:

I call upon You, Great God, to come through the Veil and be among us. Fill the body of this man, Your Priest. Bless us with Your presence and power. Through Your wisdom and Your great Otherworld energy, join with the Goddess to fill our lives with renewing power. As God to Goddess, lightning to earth, dagger to chalice, and man to woman, thus shall our lives be fruitful with good health, prosperity, happiness, and spiritual growth. We give You honor, Great God!

Entire coven: *We honor You!*

HPS raises her arms and says:

Oh, Hornéd One of ancient fame, we invoke You by Your secret name that echoes down through history, hidden in the Mystery of life and death, love and rebirth. As sun lights moon, sky touches earth, and moving sea touches shore, we see You in the ancient lore as Lover of the Holy Mother, the Co-creator, Holy Father. Enter this Priest; transform his soul, that through him we may see the whole, of vision great that is Your plan to transform all the souls of man. We kneel in awe and chant the rhythm.

Entire coven kneels and says: *All honor to the God divine!*

Coven stands again. HPS stands facing the HP.

HP draws an invoking pentagram in the air with the dagger and says:

The five-point star, the secret sign of God and Goddess, of love divine, I make, and show you yet one more, an ancient sign of ancient lore. (Priest makes the sign of the horns with his free hand.) *Behold! I give this sign to you, to call My presence, strong and true, whenever you have need of Me. This is my will, so shall it be!*

Entire coven makes the sign of the horns and says: *Hail to the Hornéd One!*

(If the HP has Otherworld messages, he gives them at this time.)

This completes the Drawing Down the Sun.

SOLITARY DRAWING DOWN THE SUN

EXTRA ITEMS NEEDED: The Priestess needs a crown with a crescent moon on it, while the Priest needs a crown with antlers on it.

Just after the Drawing Down the Moon and before the Charge is said, stand facing the altar in the Osiris pose with the dagger in your power hand with the point upward. Your wrists should be crossed. Say:

Great God, I call to you across the Veil between the Worlds! Enter this sacred space that I may feel Your presence and know that You are truly here!

Kneel before the altar and say:

I bless my feet that walk the sacred path. I bless my knees that kneel before the Old Ones. (If a man: *I bless my phallus, the symbol of the God's fertile blessings.*) (If a woman: *I bless my womb, symbol of the cauldron that receives the God's fertilizing seed.*) *I bless my lips that sing praises to the Goddess and the God. I honor the God within me.* (This is entirely appropriate for women, as the Goddess and the God are present in both sexes.)

Move into the Blessing pose, with your arms outstretched and your feet apart, still holding the dagger point upward. Say:

We are each male and female. Therefore, the Goddess and the God inhabit all creatures, just as They do all creation. The God within me empowers my soul.

Kneel again and say:

> *I call upon You, Great God, to come through the Veil and be with me. (If a man: **Fill the body of this man, Your Priest.**) (If a woman: **Fill this body of this woman, Your Priestess.**) Bless me with Your presence and power. Through Your wisdom and Your great Otherworld energy, join with the Goddess to fill my life with renewing power. As God to Goddess, lightning to earth, dagger to chalice, and man to woman, thus shall my life be fruitful with good health, prosperity, happiness, and spiritual growth. I give You honor, Great God!*

Raise your arms and say:

> *Oh, Hornéd One of ancient fame, I invoke You by Your secret name that echoes down through history, hidden in the Mystery of life and death, love and rebirth. As sun lights moon, sky touches earth, and moving sea touches shore, we see You in the ancient lore as Lover of the Holy Mother, the Co-creator, Holy Father. Enter this Priest (Priestess); transform my soul, that through You I may see the whole, of vision great that is Your plan to transform all the souls of man. I kneel in awe and chant the rhythm, all honor to the God divine!*

Stand, draw an invoking pentagram in the air with the dagger, and say:

> *The five-point star, the secret sign of God and Goddess, of love divine, I make, and show you yet one more, an ancient sign of ancient lore. (Make the sign of the horns with your free hand.) Behold! I give this sign to you, to call My presence, strong and true, whenever you have need of Me. This is my will, so shall it be! Hail to the Hornéd One!*

This completes the Drawing Down the Sun.

Study Work

In your notebook write down what each of the above ceremonies means to you on a personal level. Do they help bring you closer to the Goddess and the God? When you read them, do you feel a surge of deity power flow through you?

CHAPTER 38

New Moon Ritual

TIME: The night of the New Moon.

ITEMS NEEDED: Regular ritual items. However, use a black pillar candle for the altar instead of white.

Create the circle using the method described in Chapter 34.

After the circle is cast, lay the wand and dagger on the altar, crossing them. Stand facing the altar in the Osiris pose, with your wrists crossed. Say:

> *Blesséd Goddess, I call to you across the Veil between the Worlds! Enter this sacred space that I may feel Your presence and know that You are truly here!*

Kneel before the altar and say:

> *Bless my feet that walk the sacred path. Bless my knees that kneel before the Old Ones.* (If you are a woman: *Bless my womb, the symbol of Goddess fertility. Bless my breasts, the symbol of the Goddess and Her nurturing power.*) (If you are a man: *Bless my phallus, the symbol of the God's fertile blessings.*) *Bless my lips that sing praises to the Goddess and the God. I honor the Goddess within me.* (This is entirely appropriate for men, as the Goddess and the God are present in both sexes.)

Move into the Isis pose, with your arms outstretched and your feet apart. Say:

> *We are each male and female. Therefore, the Goddess and the God inhabit all creatures, just as They do all creation. The Goddess within me empowers my soul.*

Kneel again and say:

> *I call You, Great Goddess, to come through the Veil and be with me here. Fill my body with Your holy presence. Bless me with Your presence and power. Through Your wisdom and Your great Otherworld energy, fill my life with renewing power. As seed becomes bud, and bud becomes flower, and flower becomes fruit, so shall I flower and fruit with good health, prosperity, happiness, and spiritual growth. I give You honor, Great Goddess!*

Raise your arms and say:

> *Proud and beautiful as the moon on high that races across the midnight sky, the Goddess blesses my joyful rite. Her glory fills my inner sight. She shows Her signs in fire and smoke, in chalice wine.* (If a woman: *Her I invoke into this Priestess at the altar, a transformed being, Goddess-daughter.*) (If a man: *Her I invoke into this Priest at the altar. A follower strong, I never falter.*) *I kneel in awe and chant the rune. All honor to the Lady of the Moon!*

Stand, draw an invoking pentagram in the air with the wand, and say:

> *Darkened moon in blackest sky, as Crone and Dark One I hear your cry. All barriers I sweep away. No evil will I allow to stay. I bless and comfort my children all and answer when I hear your call.*

Lay aside any ritual tools you are holding. Stand facing the altar with your arms raised high and say:

> *Great Goddess, I call upon You by all Your names, known and unknown. Be here within this sacred circle that I might feel Your power and love. Hear my words, all you creatures of this world. The Goddess is the Great Mother of all! I am never alone or abandoned. She hears every secret longing of my heart, sees every step I take along my life's path. She is everywhere, in everything. Nothing and no one exists without Her.*
>
> *The Goddess is the beauty of this earth and everything upon it. She reflects Herself in the glowing moon, the brilliant sun, and every star in the heavens. Nothing is born without Her plan and power, and all things return to Her at the end of their life cycle. Although the Goddess is the gatherer Crone, She is also the Maiden of desire. All acts of love and joy and pleasure are rituals in Her eyes.*

I cast my circle at each New Moon in accordance with Her ancient worship that I may honor Her and ask for what I need. I follow Her words that say I must value my freedom and strive for the highest of ideals, without being hindered or turned aside. For if I do not learn to value myself, others may lead me into slavery.

The Goddess is the gateway to the ancient Inner Mysteries. Her secret teachings lead me through the spiritual labyrinth to the Sacred Center. All who seek Her must understand Her ancient words. All your seeking and yearning will avail you nothing, unless you know the Mystery: For if what you seek you find not within, you will never find without. For behold, the Goddess has been with us from the beginning, and She will gather us to Her breast at the end of all things.

Kneel before the altar and say:

It is right that I thank the Gods for what I have. Yet also may I ask Them for what I feel I need. So be it.

(Silently thank the Goddess and the God and ask for help.)

With your dagger in your power hand, go to the East. Raise the dagger in salute and say:

All negatives that are sent against me, or that dwell within my own mind, I order you to depart and never return!

Go to the South, salute, and say:

All negatives that disrupt my spiritual path, whatever their origin or purpose, I order you to depart and never return!

Go to the West, salute, and say:

All negatives that influence my emotions, whether from my own misguided desires, or the influences of others who wish me ill, I order you to depart and never return!

Go to the North, salute, and say:

All negatives that have taken root in my body, whether from the will of others or my own faults, I order you to depart and never return!

Return to the altar and say:

> *Dark Mother of the darkened moon, I beg Your aid and ask a boon.*
> *Reveal to me the Mysteries deep, of karma and life plan. Keep me safe*
> *from evil of all kind, soul or body, emotions, mind. Within Your hands I*
> *place the ill that others send. Do as You will. Keep me safe and by Your*
> *side, and by Your will I shall abide.*

Now is the time for any spellworking that needs done. End the work by saying:

> *Air to vitalize it. Fire to purify it. Water to consecrate it. Earth to ground*
> *it. Spirit to blend all Elements together into an unbreakable link with the*
> *Goddess and the God. So mote it be.*

Set the chalice of wine on the pentacle. Take the dagger and gently touch the tip to the wine/juice, saying:

> *As this athame is the male, so this cup is the female, and joined they*
> *bring blessings.*

Raise the chalice high over the altar and say:

> *To the Old Ones! Merry meet and merry part and merry meet again!*
> *Blessèd be!*

Close the circle as described in Chapter 34.

Study Work

Perform a New Moon ritual. What thoughts, feelings, or experiences did you have? Was there a greater sense of peace and protection after the ritual than before?

CHAPTER 39

Full Moon Ritual

TIME: The night of the Full Moon.

ITEMS NEEDED: The regular ritual items, plus a small bell.

Cast the circle as described in Chapter 34.

After the circle is cast, lay the wand and dagger on the altar, crossing them. Stand facing the altar in the Osiris pose, with your wrists crossed. Say:

> *Blesséd Goddess, I call to you across the Veil between the Worlds! Enter this sacred space that I may feel Your presence and know that You are truly here!*

Kneel before the altar and say:

> *Bless my feet that walk the sacred path. Bless my knees that kneel before the Old Ones.* (If you are a woman: *Bless my womb, the symbol of Goddess fertility. Bless my breasts, the symbol of the Goddess and Her nurturing power.*) (If you are a man: *Bless my phallus, the symbol of the God's fertile blessings.*) *Bless my lips that sing praises to the Goddess and the God. I honor the Goddess within me.* (This is entirely appropriate for men, as the Goddess and the God are present in both sexes.)

Move into the Isis pose, with your arms outstretched and your feet apart. Say:

> *We are each male and female. Therefore, the Goddess and the God inhabit all creatures, just as They do all creation. The Goddess within me empowers my soul.*

Kneel again and say:

> *I call You, Great Goddess, to come through the Veil and be with me here. Fill my body with Your holy presence. Bless me with Your presence and power. Through Your wisdom and Your great Otherworld energy, fill my life with renewing power. As seed becomes bud, and bud becomes flower, and flower becomes fruit, so shall I flower and fruit with good health, prosperity, happiness, and spiritual growth. I give You honor, Great Goddess!*

Raise your arms and say:

> *Proud and beautiful as the moon on high that races across the midnight sky, the Goddess blesses my joyful rite. Her glory fills my inner sight. She shows Her signs in fire and smoke, in chalice wine.* (If a woman: *Her I invoke into this Priestess at the altar, a transformed being, Goddess-daughter.*) (If a man: *Her I invoke into this Priest at the altar. A follower strong, I never falter.*) *I kneel in awe and chant the rune. All honor to the Lady of the Moon!*

Stand, draw an invoking pentagram in the air with the wand, and say:

> *The five-point star of love and power I bless you with this holy hour. Pray to me when the moon is round, and good things I promise will abound. I charge you follow my ancient ways with joy and bliss through all your days.*

Lay aside any ritual tools you are holding. Face the altar with your arms raised high and say:

> *Great Goddess, I call upon You by all Your names, known and unknown. Be here within this sacred circle that I might feel Your power and love. Hear my words, all you creatures of this world. The Goddess is the Great Mother of all! I am never alone or abandoned. She hears every secret longing of my heart, sees every step I take along my life's path. She is everywhere, in everything. Nothing and no one exists without Her.*
>
> *The Goddess is the beauty of this earth and everything upon it. She reflects Herself in the glowing moon, the brilliant sun, and every star in the heavens. Nothing is born without Her plan and power, and all things return to Her at the end of their life cycle. Although the Goddess is the*

gatherer Crone, She is also the Maiden of desire. All acts of love and joy and pleasure are rituals in Her eyes.

I cast my circle at each Full Moon in accordance with Her ancient worship that I may honor Her and ask for what I need. I follow Her words that say I must value my freedom and strive for the highest of ideals, without being hindered or turned aside. For if I do not learn to value myself, others may lead me into slavery.

The Goddess is the gateway to the ancient Inner Mysteries. Her secret teachings lead me through the spiritual labyrinth to the Sacred Center. All who seek Her must understand Her ancient words. All your seeking and yearning will avail you nothing, unless you know the Mystery: For if what you seek you find not within, you will never find without. For behold, the Goddess has been with us from the beginning, and She will gather us to Her breast at the end of all things.

Kneel before the altar and say:

It is right that I thank the Gods for what I have. Yet also may I ask Them for what I feel I need. So be it.

(Silently thank the Goddess and the God and ask for help.)

Stand facing the altar, ring the bell once, and say:

Lady of the Full Moon bright, be here with me on this night. Guide my hands, my head, my heart that, from Your path I never part. Lead me to the ancient power to aid me in this magical hour. Teach me how to spell and cast a magic future that will last. An ancient power since time begun, Oh Ancient Beauty, Powerful One.

Go to the East. Salute with the dagger and say:

I open myself to the Lady's power of strong thought and clear ideas.

Go to the South, salute, and say:

I open myself to the Lady's power of bright spiritual fire and dedication to Her.

Go to the West, salute, and say:

I open myself to the Lady's power of healing and love.

Go to the North, salute, and say:

> *I open myself to the Lady's power of a healthy body, prosperous life, and strong friendships.*

Return to the altar, say:

> *All hail the unending power and beauty of the Goddess!*

(Now is the time for any spellworking that needs to be done.) End the work by saying:

> *Air to vitalize it. Fire to purify it. Water to consecrate it. Earth to ground it. Spirit to blend all Elements together into an unbreakable link with the Goddess and the God. So mote it be.*

Set the chalice of wine on the pentacle. Take the dagger and gently touch the tip to the wine/juice, saying:

> *As this athame is the male, so this cup is the female, and joined they bring blessings.*

Raise the chalice high over the altar and say:

> *To the Old Ones! Merry meet and merry part and merry meet again! Blesséd be!*

When the complete ritual is finished, take your dagger in your power hand and the candlesnuffer in the other.

Close the circle as described in Chapter 34.

Study Work

Perform a Full Moon ritual. If you did spellwork or divination, was it stronger within the circle than when you did it outside the circle? Did you feel a strong presence of the Goddess? What physical, emotional, or psychic experiences did you have?

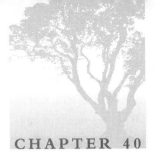

CHAPTER 40

Imbolc

The names used for these holy days are Celtic in origin.

TIME: February 2.

ITEMS NEEDED: The regular ritual items, plus a white candle, green candle, and a small cauldron. The cauldron is placed in the center of the altar with the white candle inside it. The green candle is placed beside the cauldron. Put tarot cards or rune stones on the altar if you plan to do a divination or guidance. Incense: earthy-smelling incense, such as patchouli.

HISTORY: This is the first holy day after the beginning of the solar year at Winter Solstice. It is a traditional time of cleansing and purifying in preparation for a new cycle of life. Often, it is the time chosen by Wiccan groups for initiations.

Cast the circle as described in Chapter 34.

After the circle is cast, say:

> *The earth is restless with the first stirring with renewed energy and life. Awake, Maiden! Hear the voice of the Lord, as he calls to You to join with Him in the dance of life. Prepare the fields and forests, all creatures large and small, for the coming of Spring!*

Tap the altar three times with your dagger or wand and say:

> *This is a time of growing sunlight. It signals to all followers of the Lady and the Lord that we must purify our minds and spirits for new cycles of life. At this time and in this place, I ask the Goddess and the God to give me guidance for the future.*

Silently ask for guidance as you shuffle the tarot cards or stir the rune stones. If you have particular goals in mind, ask about these. Carefully note which cards or runes are drawn so that you can meditate upon them later. When you are finished, again lightly tap the altar three times. Say:

> Oh Lady and Lord, I place my dreams for the future within Your keeping. If the goals I choose are not to my benefit, if You foresee a better future for me, send clear messages that I may change my path. I do thank You.

Using the taper, light the white candle in the cauldron from the altar candle. Say:

> I salute the Goddess as the sacred Maiden, who now returns from Her resting place in the creative abyss of the Crone's cauldron. The Maiden's joyful dance releases a cycle of renewal in the world. As She spreads Her blessings upon all lands and all creatures, so am I touched by Her gentle hand.

Light the green candle beside the cauldron. Say:

> I salute the Lord as the young Sun King, the one who calls to the Maiden and awakens Her from slumber. By blending Their powers, the Goddess and the God pour a stream of creative energy into this world, energy that permeates everything. Regeneration begins anew, and all things are blessed.

(Any spellwork for renewal or new cycles can be done at this time.)

Set the chalice of wine on the pentacle. Take the dagger and gently touch the tip to the wine/juice, saying:

> As this athame is the male, so this cup is the female, and joined they bring blessings.

Raise the chalice high over the altar and say:

> To the Old Ones! Merry meet and merry part and merry meet again! Blesséd be!

Drink a little of the wine/juice, saving some for the nature spirits.

Take your dagger in your power hand and the candlesnuffer in the other.

Close the circle as described in Chapter 34.

CHAPTER 41

Spring Equinox

TIME: Approximately March 21.

ITEMS NEEDED: The regular ritual tools, plus a small piece of paper and a pen, the cauldron, and the wand. You can decorate the altar with colored eggs and spring flowers if you wish. Incense: flowery or herbal. Take time before the ritual to consider what goals you would like fulfilled for the year. Write them on the paper and place it next to the cauldron on the altar.

HISTORY: Eggs colored red have been used at the Spring Equinox as far back as the Mesopotamian cultures. Red is the color of the blood and life, while the egg itself represents birth and regeneration.

Create the circle as described in Chapter 34.

After the circle is cast, take the wand in your power hand, raise your arms in greeting, and say:

> *Hear me, Lady and Lord. I ask Your sacred presences in this place while I celebrate the ancient festival of the Spring Equinox.*

Tap the cauldron three times gently with the wand. Say:

> *Oh, joyful Goddess of new beginnings and the promise of good things to come, bring warmth and love to this circle.*

Tap the cauldron three times again, and say:

> *Oh, laughing God of the forest and regeneration, bring anticipation and power to this circle.*

Tap the cauldron three times again, and say:

Now I cast behind me the darkness of winter and the past. I look ahead to that which lies before me. Now is the time of planting of seeds in the physical, mental, and spiritual planes.

Fold your paper in half, hold it up over the altar, and say:

This represents the seeds of my goals and desires.

Light the paper from the altar candle and drop it into the cauldron. Say:

I place my dreams and desires into the keeping of the Goddess and the God. May these goals manifest and become part of my physical life.

(Now is the time for any spellworking you wish to do.)

Set the chalice of wine on the pentacle. Take the dagger and gently touch the tip to the wine/juice, saying:

As this athame is the male, so this cup is the female, and joined they bring blessings.

Raise the chalice high over the altar and say:

To the Old Ones! Merry meet and merry part and merry meet again! Blesséd be!

Drink a little of the wine/juice, saving some for the nature spirits.

Take your dagger in your power hand and the candlesnuffer in the other.

Close the circle as described in Chapter 34.

CHAPTER 42

Beltane

TIME: May 1.

ITEMS NEEDED: The regular ritual tools, plus a symbol(s) of your house guardian(s). The wand and/or dagger may be decorated with colored ribbons. Incense: a woodsy blend, such as pine.

HISTORY: This was an ancient fertility festival and was connected with the Sacred Marriage between Goddess and God, Priestess and Priest, King and Goddess. The maypole was a phallic symbol, the colored ribbons representing the life-giving energy that flows forth from sacred copulation. It is also a good time to honor the guardian house spirits.

Cast the circle as described in Chapter 34.

After the circle is cast, tap the wand on the altar three times. Raise your wand in greeting, and say:

> *I call upon the Goddess, She who was once called Lady of the*
> *Greenwood, Mistress of Love and Fertility. Greetings, Lady of all things*
> *wild and free. I welcome You, and rejoice in Your presence. Blesséd be!*

Tap the wand on the altar three times. Raise it in greeting, and say:

> *I call upon the God; He who was once called Lord of the Greenwood,*
> *Pan of the Forest, the Hornéd One. Greetings, Lord of all things wild*
> *and free. I welcome You, and rejoice in Your presence. Blesséd be!*

Lay aside the wand. Dance or walk deosil around the circle, beginning in the East. Pause at each quarter. Raise your arms in greeting, saying:

> *The Two are One, and the One is all!*

When finished, return to the altar, and say:

> *I am a follower of the Lady and the Lord. Through me They make Themselves known upon the earth. I have pledged myself to Their service. Fill me as a cup with knowledge and understanding. Let my ears hear Your blesséd words. Let my hands do Your work, and my feet follow Your path forever. For I am a follower of the Old Ways!*

Pass incense smoke around the symbol(s) of your house guardian(s). Say:

> *Lord and Lady, I present to You the guardian(s) of this house. I thank them for all they have done for me, and ask that You also bless them. Spirit-guardians, I ask you to continue your good work. Blesséd be.*

(Now is the time for any spellworking you wish to do.)

Set the chalice of wine on the pentacle. Take the dagger and gently touch the tip to the wine/juice, saying:

> *As this athame is the male, so this cup is the female, and joined they bring blessings.*

Raise the chalice high over the altar and say:

> *To the Old Ones! Merry meet and merry part and merry meet again! Blesséd be!*

Drink a little of the wine/juice, saving some for the nature spirits.

Close the circle as described in Chapter 34.

CHAPTER 43

Summer Solstice

TIME: Approximately June 21.

ITEMS NEEDED: The regular ritual tools, plus a cup of fresh water placed in the cauldron, a green candle, and a gold candle. Set the cauldron in the center of the altar, with the green candle on the left and the gold on the right. Incense: flower scents, such as rose, lily, or lilac.

HISTORY: This holy day is connected strongly with nature spirits, such as Elves and Fairies. The Vikings called it Sonnenwende, or Sun's Turning, because there is a balance of light and dark, just before the sun begins its slide into shorter days.

Create the circle as described in Chapter 34.

After the circle is cast, light the green candle, and say:

> *Lady of the stars, Spinner of fates, I call upon You by all Your ancient names and welcome You to my circle. All you Fairies, Elves, and other friendly nature spirits, welcome, welcome! The tides of magical power flow strong. I ask for your friendship, for I too walk the path of magical power.*

Light the gold candle, and say:

> *Hail, Sun King, the Golden Lord of light and love. Welcome! Your dazzling robes bless the land. Under Your gentle reign, the Small Folk are abroad, reveling in the kiss of summer power. I ask Your blessing upon this house and all within it.*

Place your palms over the water in the cauldron, and say:

> *Bless this water with Your touch, Oh Lady and Lord. May it be an earthly connection with the hidden Well of Wisdom.*

Hold your hands between the green and the gold candles and make a wish for your future. With the forefinger of your power hand, touch the cauldron water and then your forehead, lips, and heart. Kneel before the altar and rededicate your life.

> *I will serve the Lady and the Lord with all my heart. I choose to be a Pagan, a stone in the ancient circle of power and Mysteries. I will stand firm in my love of the Old Ones, enduring through all time. May the Goddess and the God witness my words!*

(Now is the time for any spellworking you wish to do.)

Set the chalice of wine on the pentacle. Take the dagger and gently touch the tip to the wine/juice, saying:

> *As this athame is the male, so this cup is the female, and joined they bring blessings.*

Raise the chalice high over the altar and say:

> *To the Old Ones! Merry meet and merry part and merry meet again! Blesséd be!*

Drink a little of the wine/juice, saving some for the nature spirits.

Close the circle as described in Chapter 34.

CHAPTER 44

Lughnasadh

TIME: August 1.

ITEMS NEEDED: The regular ritual tools, plus a yellow or orange candle in the cauldron, and a plate of bread. The cauldron is set in the center of the altar, with the plate of bread beside it. Autumn leaves and flowers can be used for decoration. Incense: an herbal scent.

HISTORY: This Celtic holy day was one of the four Great Sabbats. The later Saxon word for this festival was Lammas (loaf mass). Another name is Lunasa. In the northern regions, this was the time of harvest, while to areas farther south this day was one of two harvest festivals, the other being Autumn Equinox in September.

Create the circle as described in Chapter 34.

After creating the circle, breathe deeply for a few minutes. Concentrate on the cleansing power that you draw into your body. As you exhale, concentrate on expelling all negatives from your life.

When you are ready, light the cauldron candle and say:

This candle represents the harvest within my life. Those goals I have worked on this year are now nearing completion. I accept the harvest of all those that work to my good, and reject any harvest of those that would work against me. I prepare myself—body, mind, and soul—for the time of winter and rest.

Set the chalice of wine on the pentacle. Take the dagger and gently touch the tip to the wine/juice, saying:

As this athame is the male, so this cup is the female, and joined they bring blessings.

Raise the chalice high over the altar and say:

To the Old Ones! Merry meet and merry part and merry meet again! Blesséd be!

Lift the plate of bread high over the altar. Set it down and briefly raise the chalice of juice. Say:

Every seed of grain, every fruit, is imprinted with a record of ancient times and a promise of all that will come. This bread and this juice are symbols of life eternal through the regenerating cauldron of the Goddess.

Eat a piece of the bread and drink some of the juice. Save some of both for the nature spirits. Say:

As in the bread and wine, so it is within me. The grain that made this bread carries with it the imprint of every grain that has grown upon this earth. The fruit that produced this juice (wine) holds within itself the history of every fruit that ever grew. The Mysteries of ancient times and all my ancestors are imprinted upon my soul. May the coming season of waning light and increasing darkness not be heavy for me. Let the approaching dark days be ones of resting, planning, waiting, until once more the Goddess and the God open the doors to new beginnings. I am blessed, guided, and loved by the Old Ones. Blesséd be!

(Now is the time for any spellworking you wish to do.)

When the complete ritual is finished, take your dagger in your power hand and the candlesnuffer in the other.

Close the circle as described in Chapter 34.

CHAPTER 45

Autumn Equinox

TIME: Approximately September 21.

ITEMS NEEDED: The regular ritual tools, plus the cauldron, a white, a red, and a black candle. Ribbons of autumn colors can be tied to the dagger. Set the cauldron in the center of the altar with the three candles arranged around it.

HISTORY: This festival was celebrated by those cultures whose harvests came later than that at Lughnasadh. This is the final harvesting of the year's crops, the time when fruits, vegetables, and grains were stored for the winter season. This is the second balancing of light and darkness found in each year. This festival was a thanksgiving for the food stored against the barren months.

Create the circle as described in Chapter 34.

After the circle is created, light the white candle by the cauldron and say:

> *I call upon the Maiden. May She give me joy and hope.*

Light the red candle by the cauldron and say:

> *I call upon the Mother. May She give me prosperity and happiness.*

Light the black candle by the cauldron and say:

> *I call upon the Crone. May She give me courage and strength.*

Salute the cauldron with your dagger. Say:

> *I give honor to the threefold God, the Divine Child, the Lover, the Lord of the Hunt. May He give me guidance. I rejoice in the turning of the year wheel and the changing seasons.*

Take the dagger in your power hand and the wine chalice in the other. Say:

Each life fulfills its proper cycle, laying aside the old and embracing the new. This is the way of the eternal chain of living. I celebrate the fullness of my life and the harvest of this year's lessons.

Walk three times deosil around the circle, carrying the dagger and chalice. As you go, say:

The year wheel turns, and bounty comes.

Stand before the altar. Set the chalice of wine on the pentacle. Take the dagger and gently touch the tip to the wine/juice, saying:

As this athame is the male, so this cup is the female, and joined they bring blessings.

Raise the chalice and say:

To the good seasons that have gone, and the good ones yet to come. To good friends and the beauty of autumn. To the Lady and the Lord!

Drink a toast. Then raise the chalice high again over the altar and say:

To the Old Ones! Merry meet and merry part and merry meet again! Blesséd be!

Drink a little more of the wine/juice, saving some for the nature spirits.

(Now is the time for any spellworking you wish to do.)

Take your dagger in your power hand and the candlesnuffer in the other.

Close the circle as described in Chapter 34.

CHAPTER 46

Samhain

TIME: October 31.

ITEMS NEEDED: The regular ritual tools, plus a plate of bread and salt, the cauldron with white, black, and red candles around it, and a green candle to put inside it.

HISTORY: The Celtic word Samhain actually means "Summer's End." It is one of the four great Sabbats of Celtic countries. Today it is called Halloween, which is derived from All Hallows Eve, a name given it by the Christian Church when people refused to stop using this day to honor the ancestors. Tradition says that the Veil between the worlds is thinnest at this time, making possible communication with the dead. It is also an excellent time for all divination. The Crone aspect of the Goddess rules now.

Create the circle as described in Chapter 34.

After creating the circle, light the white candle beside the cauldron and say:

I honor the Maiden of new beginnings and the planted seed.

Light the red candle beside the cauldron and say:

I honor the Mother of magic, prosperity, and fertility.

Light the black candle beside the cauldron and say:

I honor the Wise Crone of wisdom, death, and rebirth. I welcome the Goddess in all Her aspects.

Light the green candle inside the cauldron and say:

I honor the God, Lord of the Wild Hunt, who gathers souls at the time of destiny. With love, He guides those souls into the Otherworld, where they will again be born at the proper time and place.

Raise your arms and say:

> This is the Feast of the Dead, the night of the ever-turning year wheel, the night of the Thin Veil. The gates between the worlds are open this night. The footsteps of my ancestors rustle in the fallen autumn leaves. The winds carry their voices into this world. All those who wish me well are welcome within this sacred circle.

Place the plate of bread and salt on the pentacle, saying:

> The Veil is lifted that my loved ones and friends in the Otherworld may know I have not forgotten them. I await their voices that I may know they have not forgotten me.

Dip a piece of bread into the salt, saying:

> Bread of the earth and salt of the sea, all creatures are born of these Elements. The bread gives strength and form to our bodies, while the salt reminds us of the magical blood of the Goddess that creates us within Her cauldron of rebirth. Eat the bread.

Set the chalice of wine on the pentacle. Take the dagger and gently touch the tip to the wine/juice, saying:

> As this athame is the male, so this cup is the female, and joined they bring blessings.

Raise the chalice high over the altar and say:

> To the Old Ones! Merry meet and merry part and merry meet again! Blesséd be!

Drink a little of the wine/juice, saving some for the nature spirits.

Gaze at the cauldron and the four colored candles. Say:

> Life is an unending circle of birth, death, and rebirth. Those who are called to the Otherworld are never lost to us forever. The Goddess gives us this night to open our inner ears and hear our loved ones once more. The Lady and the Lord protect me with Their gentle hands, guide my steps, hear my desires. For this I give Them honor and love.

Tap the pentacle gently with your wand or dagger. Say:

Give me true inner vision so that I may see into the future and the past.
Lead me to wisdom and truth.

(Now is the time to do any type of divination that you wish to do. Listen carefully for any messages you may get from your loved ones in the Otherworld.)

Take your dagger in your power hand and the candlesnuffer in the other.

Close the circle as described in Chapter 34.

CHAPTER 47

Winter Solstice

TIME: Approximately December 21.

ITEMS NEEDED: The regular ritual tools, plus a yellow candle in the cauldron, a red, black, and white candle to place around the cauldron, and a bell or chimes.

HISTORY: Celebrations on the Winter Solstice have long been religious customs of many ancient civilizations, particularly those whose holy days revolved around the solar calendar. The Norse knew this celebration as the Night of the Three Mothers, or Mother Night. This is the time of the newborn sun, the shortest day of the year before the light begins to increase. The earth energy tides turn once more. The Full Moon right after the Winter Solstice is considered the strongest of the entire year.

Create the circle as described in Chapter 34.

After creating the circle, ring the bell three times. Say:

> *I call upon the Goddess in all Her aspects. I call upon the Maiden, the Mother, and the Wise Crone to be here with me this night. The darkness that has held sway is retreating before the increasing light. The God is once more born from the cauldron as the newborn Solstice sun.*

Hold your hands over the cauldron and say:

> *I stand in the stillness behind all motion. It is here that all energy comes together before it can manifest in the physical. The power of the Goddess and the wisdom of Her ancient Mysteries await all seekers who enter the vast stillness of the Otherworld cauldron.*

Light the white candle and say:

> *White is for the Maiden, the bringer of hope and new life. White is for the Divine Child, who teaches us how to begin anew.*

Light the red candle and say:

> *Red is for the Mother, the creatrix who teaches the weaving of magic threads into manifestation. Red is for the Father, the creator who blends His energy with the Mother to create all things.*

Light the black candle and say:

> *Black is for the Wise Crone, who gives wisdom to understand the ancient magical and spiritual Mysteries. Black is for the Lord of the Wild Hunt, who protects us from enemies and, at the last, returns us to the Goddess.*

Light the yellow candle inside the cauldron and say:

> *Divine Child of love and joy and hope for the future, I welcome you once more into life. Shine Your spiritual life upon me that I may become stronger in my spiritual path and wiser in my life.*

Take the bell to the East. Ring it once and say:

> *All you Elementals of the East, you of tender beginnings and the joy of life, I ask that you bless me with ideas and goals that I may improve my life.*

Go to the South. Ring the bell once and say:

> *All you Elementals of the South, you of strength and prosperity, I ask that you bless me with good health and security.*

Go to the West. Ring the bell once and say:

> *All you Elementals of the West, you of love and beautiful happenings, I ask that you bless me with happiness and pleasant friendships.*

Go to the North. Ring the bell once:

> *All you Elementals of the North, you of deep spiritual wisdom and magical knowledge, I ask that you bless me with insight and the truth of the ancient Mysteries.*

Return to the altar. Ring the bell five times for the Elements and say:

> *Hail to the most ancient Three in One, the bringer of light out of darkness, new life out of the cauldron of rebirth, new beginnings out of the ashes of an old year. I ask the blessing of the Goddess and the God in all Their aspects.*

Stand quietly while awaiting the blessing.

Set the chalice of wine on the pentacle. Take the dagger and gently touch the tip to the wine/juice, saying:

> *As this athame is the male, so this cup is the female, and joined they bring blessings.*

Raise the chalice high over the altar and say:

> *To the Old Ones! Merry meet and merry part and merry meet again! Blesséd be!*

Drink a little of the wine/juice, saving some for the nature spirits.

(Now is the time for any spellworking you wish to do.)

Take your dagger in your power hand and the candlesnuffer in the other.

Close the circle as described in Chapter 34.

CHAPTER 48

Naming Ritual

Most of the rites of passage in this and following chapters do not have to be performed within a cast, consecrated circle, although you may if you wish. If you choose to do these rites within a circle, cast the circle and do the ritual as always, inserting the rite just before you consecrate and present the wine/juice. In some Wiccan groups, it is traditional that a Wiccan handfasting be done within a circle.

What is now called a Wiccaning is the formal presentation of a baby or small child to the Goddess and the God. I prefer to call it a Naming ceremony instead.

The last ritual (Chapter 55), one for protection, is not actually a rite of passage. However, it is of value to any Witch, and is included for that reason. It is performed within a cast circle as added security while the Witch is fighting off negative forces.

ITEMS NEEDED: The regular ritual tools, plus the wand, a white candle with the child's name carved into it, the cauldron, a special piece of jewelry, and a plate of cookies. The carved candle is placed inside the cauldron, which is set in the center of the altar.

INSTRUCTIONS: This same ceremony can be used when a couple adopts a child. The couple can be joined by supportive family and friends.

Cast the circle as usual. However, when calling the quarter guardians, you can say:

> *Welcome, Lords and Ladies of the East (or whatever direction). Join us as we welcome a new soul into our midst.*

The Priestess stands before the altar and touches the carved candle with the wand, and says:

This candle represents this child, who has been given by the Lady and the Lord to (names of the parents). *May* (child's name) *always walk the ancient path of light and love.*

The parents come to the altar with the child. One of them lights the carved candle from the altar candle. They both say:

This child is born of our love and joy. We freely bring (child's name) *to this altar to thank the Goddess and the God. We will share with* (child's name) *our love, our faith in the Old Way, and the light of our spiritual path.*

(If the child is adopted, substitute the following, instead of the above paragraph.) The parents both say:

We chose this child above all others. We freely bring (child's name) *to this altar to thank the Goddess and the God for joining* (child's name) *with us. We will share with* (child's name) *our love, our faith in the Old Way, and the light of our spiritual path.*

The Priest or the one officiating says: *Have you named this child?*

The parents answer: *Yes. This child is named* (the legal name).

Priest: *Is it your will that this child be raised in the Old Way?*

Parents: *It is our will that* (child's name) *follow the ancient path to the Goddess and the God.*

The Priestess or one of the parents gently sprinkles the child's head with consecrated water from the chalice. She says:

We bless you with Water and Earth. We name you (child's legal name), *and welcome you into this life. May your life be one of joy and love. May the sacred circle always bring you peace and comfort. And may your heart always cleave to the Lady and Her Lord.*

The Priest carefully passes a lighted candle over the child. He says:

We bless you with Fire.

The Priest waves incense smoke gently toward the child. He says:

We bless you with Earth, Air, Fire, Water, four Elements do we freely give. The fifth is Spirit. That comes only from the Lady and the Lord.

The Priestess takes the piece of jewelry out of the cauldron and hands it to the parents. The parents may put it on the child, or hold it for her/him.

Priestess: *Rejoice, all spirits of nature and the Elements! Rejoice, all Pagans, near and far! Come, all guardians and teachers in spirit! We welcome* (child's name) *within this circle with all our love, for* (child's name) *is a gift from the Old Ones!*

(The wine/juice is blessed as usual.)

The Priestess raises the juice chalice high over the altar, and says:

To the Lord of the harvest!

Circle members: *To the Lord of the harvest!*

A drop of the juice is placed in the child's mouth. Then the others within the circle drink.

The Priest raises the plate of cookies high over the altar, and says:

To the Earth Mother!

Circle members: *To the Earth Mother!*

If possible, a tiny crumb of cookie is given to the child. Then the plate is passed around the circle and shared, finally being replaced on the altar.

The Priestess raises her arms, and says:

We thank You, Lady and Lord, for this new life within our circle. May (child's name) *walk in light and gladness all her/his days! Blesséd be!*

Circle members: *Blesséd be!*

The ritual is finished, and the circle broken.

CHAPTER 49

Puberty Rites

FEMALE PUBERTY RITES

ITEMS NEEDED: The regular ritual tools, plus a calendar with the moon phases and a red candle with the girl's name carved into it.

INSTRUCTIONS: This rite is done soon after the onset of menstruation. Two women of the girl's family (including the mother), or two close adult female friends, are needed to take the part of the Mother and the Crone.

After the circle is cast, the Priestess opens it briefly for the Mother to take the girl's hand and lead her to the altar. The Priestess returns to the altar and stands facing the girl who is flanked by the Mother and the Crone.

Priestess: *Who is this who comes into the presence of the Goddess?*

Mother: *I bring* (girl's name) *who no longer has the body of a child, but has blossomed into a woman.*

Priestess: *We welcome her into this circle of women.*

Mother: *Great Mother Goddess, who flows with the wise blood, I present to You* (girl's name). *She has passed through the gates of childhood, and now takes her place in the never-ending circle of women. Bless her, Goddess, and guide her along her life's path.*

Crone: *Great Mother Goddess, who knows the secret and wisdom of releasing or holding back the wise blood, I present to You this newly made woman. Bless her, Goddess, that she may learn responsibility and self-control of this new phase of life.*

Priestess: *We welcome you (girl's name) as a Goddess-daughter into life's circle of all women. We are joined with all our sisters, past, present, and future.*

Girl: *I stand with pride and joy before the Goddess and this circle of women. I am made in the Mother's image and rejoice that I, too, hold Her creative powers within my body.*

Mother: *Every woman has great value in the eyes of the Lady. She gives us the gifts of physical love and pleasure. But we must be wise in using these gifts. We must never give away our freedom and pride.*

Crone: *The wise blood creates children when a woman joins with a man. Choose the father of your children wisely, that your children, and you, will have no cause for regret.*

The Mother touches the moon calendar on the altar. She says:
> *Ancient woman-magic teaches that all the faces of the Goddess are revealed by the waxing and waning faces of the moon. The rhythms of your body, the coming and going of the wise blood, follow the moon and its phases. Watch and learn of this Mystery. The flowing of the wise blood is a Mystery shared only by women. It is a woman-gift from the Goddess.*

The Crone touches the red candle on the altar. She says:
> *As you kindle the flame of this candle, may your spirit kindle to the Mysteries of the Goddess. We welcome you to this circle of women.*

The girl lights the candle from the altar candle. She says:
> *May my life be as bright as the flame of this candle.*

The ritual is completed, and the circle broken. The red candle is saved for the girl to use during meditation. Those within the circle may now celebrate.

MALE PUBERTY RITES

ITEMS NEEDED: The regular ritual tools, plus a green candle with the boy's name carved into it and a calendar containing the phases of the moon.

INSTRUCTIONS: This rite is usually done at the age of thirteen. Two men of the boy's family (including the father), or two close adult male friends, are needed to take the part of the Father and the Lord of the Hunt. If possible, the man taking the part of the Lord of the Hunt should wear a crown with antlers.

After the circle is cast, the Priest opens it briefly for the Father to take the boy's hand and lead him to the altar. The Priest returns to the altar and stands facing the boy who is flanked by the Father and the Lord of the Hunt.

Priest: *Who is this who comes into the presence of the God?*

Father: *I bring* (boy's name) *who has reached the age of manhood.*

Priest: *We welcome him into this circle of men.*

Father: *Great Father God, who is the consort and companion of the Goddess, I present to You* (boy's name). *He has passed through the gates of childhood, and now takes his place in the never-ending circle of men. Bless him, Lord, and guide him along his life's path.*

Lord of the Hunt: *Great Father God, the Keeper of the Laws of the Goddess, I present to You this newly made man. Bless and guide him, Lord, that he may learn responsibility and self-control of this new phase of life.*

Priest: *We welcome you* (boy's name) *as a son of the Goddess and the God. You have now entered into life's circle of all men. Remember, we are joined with all our brothers, past, present, and future. It is the responsibility of all men to become like the God. Do nothing that will shatter your pride in yourself, or cause you regret when you face the God, within a circle or within your own heart.*

Boy: *I stand with pride and joy before the God and this circle of men. I am made in the God's image. I rejoice that I have left childhood behind, and now take my place within the circle as a man.*

Father: *Every man has great value in the eyes of the Lord. He gives us the gifts of physical love and pleasure. But we must be wise in using these gifts. We must never give away our sense of responsibility and pride.*

Lord of the Hunt: *As the God is the co-creator, so is He also the Lord of the Hunt, the One who carries out the laws of the Goddess. As with Him, so it is with mortal man. We co-create with women, yet are we also responsible for living within the sacred laws. Choose the mother of your children wisely, that your children, and you, will have no cause for regret.*

The Father touches the moon calendar on the altar. He says:
The phases of the God and the Goddess are revealed by the waxing and waning faces of the moon. So, too, are the energies of the earth and all upon it. This secret is part of the ancient Mysteries. Watch and learn of this Mystery.

The Lord of the Hunt touches the green candle on the altar. He says:
As you kindle the flame of this candle, may your spirit kindle to the ancient Mysteries of the God and the Goddess. We welcome you to this circle of men.

The boy lights the candle from the altar candle. He says:
May my life be as bright as the flame of this candle.

The ritual is completed, and the circle broken. The green candle is saved for the boy to use during meditation. Those within the circle may now celebrate.

CHAPTER 50

Eldering

ELDERING FOR WOMEN

ITEMS NEEDED: The regular ritual tools, plus a black candle with the person's name carved into it, the cauldron in which the candle is set, and a special piece of magical jewelry.

INSTRUCTIONS: Women enter this phase when menopause occurs. Women may choose to undergo this ceremony if they have had a hysterectomy. Two women are needed to take the part of the Maiden and the Mother. Gifts may be piled within the circle, or set on a table along with refreshments for after the ceremony.

After the circle is cast, the Priestess briefly opens the circle for the Maiden to bring in the woman for whom the ceremony will be done. They all go to the altar, where the woman is flanked by the Maiden and the Mother. The Priestess faces the three women.

Priestess: *Three faces has the Goddess: Maiden, Mother, and Crone. As above, so below. Each woman holds within her these three faces. We celebrate all aspects of the Goddess.*

Maiden: *I bring* (woman's name), *that she may be initiated into a new phase of her life cycle.*

Priestess: *Welcome! We honor you in your new phase of life!*

Circle women: *Welcome,* (woman's name)*!*

The Maiden turns to the woman, and says:

As once you were the Maiden, so do I now stand. As the Maiden becomes the Mother, so must she eventually become the Wise Crone. For the cycle of life must flow, and our lives must turn with the wheel of time. I am honored to stand here with you.

The Mother turns to the woman, and says:

As once you were the Mother, so do I now stand. The Mother must always give way to the carrier of wisdom, the Wise Crone. For the cycle of life must flow, and our lives must turn with the wheel of time. I am honored to stand here with you.

Woman: *I have ridden the wheel of time and known both joy and sorrow. I bring my hopes and fears before the Goddess, trusting Her to guide my steps. I accept this new phase of my life.*

Priestess: *The Goddess is wise and loving. To understand Her in all Her glory and complexity, all women must experience each of Her three faces. Rejoice, (woman's name)!*

Maiden: *The Maiden must give way to the Mother, as the Mother must give way to the Wise Crone. Accept the well-earned mantle of Her elder Priestess, for you still have great value in the eyes of the Goddess.*

Priestess: *The Goddess is wise and loving. Each of Her three faces is powerful in its own way. Rejoice, (woman's name)!*

Mother: *There comes a time when childbearing must end, and the wise blood of the moon is withheld. Know that within you is the power to do even greater things. You still have great value in the eyes of the Goddess.*

The woman lights the black candle, and says:

Goddess, I accept the new cycle in my life. As the Wise Elder and Crone of Wisdom, I take up this responsibility with joy and love.

The Maiden hugs her, and says:

Welcome, elder sister. Within you I see the Wise Crone of great wisdom of life. I am honored by your presence.

The Mother hugs her, and says:

> *Welcome elder sister. Within you I see the place that I will take someday. I am honored by your presence.*

The women of the circle all hug her, and say:

> *Welcome, Wise One.*

The Priestess takes up the magical jewelry and places it on the woman. She says:

> *Elder sister, may all your days be filled with the presence of the Goddess.*

Woman: *I am one of three, the three that are made one by the ancient Mysteries. Inside me are the Maiden and the Mother, but the face I turn to the world is that of the Crone. May the Goddess bless me by revealing more of Her ancient Mysteries.*

Priestess raises her arms, and says:

> *We give thanks to the Goddess, and rejoice with* (woman's name) *in her new cycle of life.*

The ritual is finished, and the circle broken.

ELDERING FOR MEN

ITEMS NEEDED: The regular ritual tools, plus a black candle with the person's name carved into it, the cauldron in which the candle is set, and a special piece of magical jewelry.

INSTRUCTIONS: Although women enter this phase when menopause occurs, men do not have such a bodily change to mark their transition. Therefore, men can choose to undergo the ceremony of eldering at the age of fifty or beyond. Two men are needed to take the parts of the Son and the Father. Gifts may be piled within the circle, or set on a table along with refreshments for after the ceremony.

After the circle is cast, the Priest briefly opens the circle for the Son to bring in the man for whom the ceremony will be done. They all go to the altar, where the man is flanked by the Son and the Father. The Priest faces the three men.

Priest: *Three faces has the Goddess: Maiden, Mother, and Crone. But also does the God have three faces: that of Son, Father, and Lord of the Hunt. As above, so below. Each man holds within him these three faces. We celebrate all aspects of the God.*

Son: *I bring* (man's name), *that he may be initiated into a new phase of his life cycle.*

Priest: *Welcome! We honor you in your new phase of life!*

The Son turns to the man, and says:

As once you were the Son, so do I now stand. As the Son becomes the Father, so must he eventually become the Lord of the Hunt, the Keeper of the Laws. For the cycle of life must flow, and our lives must turn with the wheel of time. I am honored to stand here with you.

The Father turns to the man, and says:

As once you were the Father, so do I now stand. The Father must always give way to the carrier of wisdom, the wise Keeper of the Laws. For the cycle of life must flow, and our lives must turn with the wheel of time. I am honored to stand here with you.

Man: *I have ridden the wheel of time and known both joy and sorrow. I bring my hopes and fear before the God, trusting Him to guide my steps. I accept this new phase of my life.*

Priest: *The God is wise and loving. To understand Him in all His glory and complexity, all men must experience each of His three faces. Rejoice,* (man's name)*!*

Son: *The Son must give way to the Father, as the Father must give way to the Keeper of the Laws. Accept the well-earned mantle of His elder Priest, for you still have great value in the eyes of the God.*

Priest: *The God is wise and loving. Each of His three faces is powerful in its own way. Rejoice,* (man's name)*!*

Father: *There comes a time when a man moves beyond the energy and strength of youth, and the responsibilities of fatherhood. Know that within you is the power to do even greater things. You still have great value in the eyes of the God.*

The man lights the black candle, and says:

Great God, I accept this new cycle in my life. As the Keeper of the Laws, I take up this responsibility with joy and love.

Son: *Welcome, elder brother. Within you I see the wise Keeper of the Laws, one who has learned great wisdom of life. I am honored by your presence.*

Father: *Welcome elder brother. Within you I see the place that I will take someday. I am honored by your presence.*

The men of the circle all greet him, and say:

Welcome, Wise One.

The Priest takes up the magical jewelry and places it on the man. He says:

Elder brother, may all your days be filled with the presence of the God.

Man: *I have endured the trials of life and earned my mantle of age. I am one of three, the three that are made one by the ancient Mysteries. Inside me are the Son and the Father, but the face I turn to the world is that of the wise Keeper of the Laws. May the God bless me by revealing more of His ancient Mysteries.*

The Priest raises his arms, and says:

We give thanks to the God and the Goddess, and rejoice with (man's name) *in his new cycle of life.*

The ritual is finished, and the circle broken.

CHAPTER 51

Handfasting and Marriage

HANDFASTING

ITEMS NEEDED: The regular ritual tools, plus two white candles (one carved with each name) with holders, a broom, a bell, rings or magical jewelry, the cauldron, and white, red, and black ribbons within the cauldron.

INSTRUCTIONS: Handfasting is not a legal marriage. It is a Wiccan agreement to stay together without benefits under civil law. The old period of a handfasting was for a year and a day, at which time it could be renewed. Any time that the couple wants to end this agreement, they should go through a handfasting separation. If the handfasting couple are the same sex, have one take the man's part in the ceremony.

Cast the circle as usual, with assigned people calling upon the quarter guardians. When all is done, the Priestess opens the circle to admit the couple being handfasted. After the Priestess closes the circle, she sweeps outward around the entire edge of the circle with the broom. Then, she places the broom on the floor before the altar. The couple stands to one side of the altar.

The Priestess stands before the altar, raises her arms, and says:

> *Lord and Lady, bless all those gathered within this circle. For this is a happy time of rejoicing!*

The Priest stands before the altar, raises his arms, and says:

> *Lord and Lady, this couple has come before Your altar to make a vow of togetherness. As it was in ancient times, so is it now!*

Person assigned to the East: *Rejoice, all Lords and Ladies of the East, for these two have chosen to begin a new life together.*

Person assigned to the South: *Rejoice, all Lords and Ladies of the South, for love has bound these two people together.*

Person assigned to the West: *Rejoice, all Lords and Ladies of the West, for a new companionship of heart and spirit has been forged.*

Person assigned to the North: *Rejoice, all Lords and Ladies of the North, for these two people chose to walk the Old Way together.*

The Priestess rings the bell three times, and says:

> *I call upon the guardians of* (the names of the couple). *By the power of the Goddess and the God, I charge you to bless this couple anew each day. Honor them with love and compassion.*

The Priest speaks to the couple, saying:

> *The sharing of a life path is not to be lightly undertaken. It requires much love, commitment, trust, work, and compromise. It may experience difficult periods where your love, faith, and devotion are tested. Each of you is giving your heart and dreams into the keeping of the other. Be compassionate and loving with this trust. If you can speak in sincerity of your devotion before the Goddess and the God, answer, "I will."*

The couple: *I will.*

The woman takes up her gift of magical jewelry, and says:

> *As a symbol of my love, I give you this token. I will comfort and honor you all our days.*

She puts it on the man.

The man takes up his gift of magical jewelry, and says:

> *As a symbol of my love, I give you this token. I will protect and honor you all our days.*

He puts it on the woman.

The Priestess touches the carved, white candles, and says:

> *These candles are symbols of your love. Let their fire never be quenched by harsh words or hasty, ill-thought deeds. Before these witnesses, light your candle from the altar fire and pledge your troth.*

The Priest hands them the candle bearing their name, and says:

> *A pledge of handfasting is a solemn vow, not to be given lightly. May the candle of your spirits light your way through dark times and light, through sorrow and joy, as you walk life's path together.*

The woman lights her candle from the altar candle, and says:

> *I have chosen you above all others. I will share with you my love and the light of the Goddess.*

The man lights his candle from the altar candle, and says:

> *I have chosen you above all others. I will share with you my love and the light of the God.*

They set the lighted candles on the altar.

The Priestess takes the three ribbons, one by one, out of the cauldron as she says:

> *These ribbons are symbols of the three faces of the Goddess and the God.* (She takes up the white ribbon.) *White is for the Maiden and the Son, who bring new life cycles and potentials.* (She takes out the red ribbon.) *Red is for the Mother and the Father, who create new growth and changes.* (She takes out the black ribbon.) *Black is for the Wise Crone and the Keeper of the Laws, for they decree the turn of life's wheel, marking all endings in preparation for new beginnings. Can you accept this?*

The couple: *I can.*

The couple holds out their left hands, while the Priestess wraps the ribbons around their wrists, loosely binding them together. She says:

> *May you always stand together, but not so close together that you lose what is uniquely you. May you be as one, but keep each the freedom that is theirs by right. May you love fully, but not smother with that love. And may you walk the path of the Goddess and the God together. So mote it be!*

Circle members: *So mote it be!*

The Priestess removes the ribbons and places them on the altar. The wine/juice is now consecrated. The Priestess holds the chalice high over the altar, and says:

> *As a Priestess of the Old Ones, I call down blessings upon this newly made couple. Blesséd be!*

The Priest joins his hands on the chalice, and says:

> *As a Priest of the Old Ones, I call down the gifts of love, patience, and wisdom upon this newly made couple. Blesséd be!*

The Priestess gives the chalice to the couple, who drink and hand it back to her. Then all in the circle drink. After the chalice is returned to the altar, the Priestess lays the broom on the floor where the couple can easily jump over it.

Priestess: *Over the broom and into new life!*

The couple holds hands and jumps over the broom.

Priest: *The Goddess and the God are honored by celebrations of joy and love. Let us rejoice in this handfasting!*

The ritual is finished, and the circle broken.

Marriage

ITEMS NEEDED: The regular ritual tools, plus a bell, two white candles each with one of the couple's names carved into it, and red, black, and white ribbons threaded through the rings.

INSTRUCTIONS: All legal marriages must be performed by a state-licensed minister, and registered with the state in which the license was obtained and the marriage took place. Either the Priest or the Priestess should be an ordained minister. At least two witnesses are required. There is no "giving away" of the bride, since it is a patriarchal custom that signifies that the woman is a piece of property. This ceremony is written without a cast circle. However, one may be used.

When the altar is ready, and the guests assembled, the couple walks in together. They stand before the altar with their two witnesses behind them. The Priest and Priestess stand directly before the altar facing the couple.

Priest: *Come, Goddess and God. Be with us as we celebrate this sacred joining in love of* (the names of the couple). *Pour out upon all gathered here Your blessings.*

The Priestess rings the bell three times, and says:
Harken, all you in spirit. Hear me, all you guides and guardians of (the names of the couple). *Today, this man and this woman make a commitment to live their lives together, through sickness and health, through sorrow and joy. Give them the love, patience, and compassion to endure all the tests that life will send their way.*

Priest: *Each of you is giving your heart into the keeping of the other. Do not break the trust you have been given, for it is sacred to the Goddess and the God.*

Priestess: *This commitment is a solemn vow that should not be made lightly. If you can speak in honesty before the Goddess, answer "I will."*

The couple: *I will.*

The Priestess points to the white, carved candles, and says:
These candles are the outward symbol of your vow. Light your candles and pledge your troth.

The woman lights her candles from the altar candle. She turns to the man and says:
I have chosen you above all others. I vow to you my love and the light of the Goddess.

The man lights his candle from the altar candle. He turns to the woman and says:
I have chosen you above all others. I vow to you my love and the light of the God.

The Priestess picks up the rings, holding the ribbons threaded through them. She says:
There are three faces of both the Goddess and the God. (She removes the white ribbon and lays it on the altar.) *White is for the Maiden and the*

Son, who bring new beginnings of events and new cycles to life. (She removes the red ribbon and lays it on the altar.) *Red is for the Mother and the Father, whose joining of creative energy gives birth to everything in the universe.* (She removes the black ribbon and lays it on the altar.) *Black is for the Wise Crone and the Keeper of the Laws. These aspects of the Goddess and the God represent endings and preparation for new beginnings. Each life runs in a cycle through these three aspects. Can you accept this?*

The couple: *I can.*

The Priestess gives the woman's ring to the man, and says:
With this ring, pledge your troth.

The man places the ring on the woman's finger, and says:
I give to you my love and my hand, for you are my beloved, the keeper of my heart.

The Priest gives the man's ring to the woman, and says:
With this ring, pledge your troth.

The woman places the ring on the man's finger, and says:
I give to you my love and my hand, for you are my beloved, the keeper of my heart.

Priestess: *Hold to your pledge, for such a vow is not given lightly. Honor each other in all ways.*

Priest: *Hold to your pledge, for such a vow is not given lightly. Walk the path of the Old Ones together, and Their light will always guide you.*

(The wine/juice is consecrated.)

The Priestess raises the chalice high, and says:
As the Lord and the Lady join in the Sacred Marriage, so does this couple. Blesséd be!

The ordained Priest and/or Priestess says:

By the power of the Goddess granted to me by Her as Her earthly representative, and by the civil authority granted to me by temporal powers, I declare to all here that this couple is legally joined in marriage. Blessèd be!

The Priestess hands the chalice to the couple, and says:

This symbolic joining of athame and chalice seals your vows.

The couple drinks. Then all others gathered drink. The chalice is returned to the altar.

Priest: *Now is a time of rejoicing with our friends. Let us celebrate this happy and sacred occasion, for the Goddess and the God are honored by joy and love.*

The couple takes the ribbons to use as part of each anniversary celebration. If a divorce ever occurs, the ribbons are used in the separation ceremony.

CHAPTER 52

Divorce or Separation

ITEMS NEEDED: The regular ritual tools, plus the following items. If possible, use the three colored ribbons from the Pagan handfasting or marriage ceremony. If the marriage was not Pagan, use some symbol from the actual wedding. Also have two pictures with both people in the pictures, as well as two black candles, a cauldron, a pair of scissors, two long pieces of red yarn or thread, and white candles carved with a name of the couple. Use both a black and a white altar candle. The two smaller black candles are set behind the cauldron in the center of the altar.

INSTRUCTIONS: If only one person is taking part in this ceremony, omit the parts for the other person, and change the pronoun to the proper one. The person for whom the ceremony is held should stand to one side of the altar. If two people are present, have one stand at each end of the altar, facing each other.

In this case, the circle should be cast counterclockwise, beginning and ending in the East. The quarter guardians should also be called counterclockwise.

This ceremony is inserted just before the consecration of the wine/juice.

Priest: *Now is a time of separation. What was once one life now must become two. There are always endings in life, if two people do not grow together. It is better that these two people,* (names of the couple), *release unconditionally and move on to new beginnings.*

Priestess: *The outer physical ties of this life have been severed. Now we come before the Dark Mother, the Wise Crone of the cauldron, to ask that She sever any remaining mental and emotional ties.*

Priest: *Wise One, we ask that You guide these people into a deeper understanding of this separation. Let them leave bitterness and sorrow behind as they seek out new beginnings.*

The Priestess hands each of the couple a photo, and says:
By the power of the Goddess and the God, you each have the right and the will to sever the last remaining ties between you.

The Priestess hands the scissors to the woman, who cuts the figures in one of the photos apart. She then gives the scissors to the man, who does the same.

Priest: *The tie is shattered! The vows are broken! The one is made two again!*

The woman lights the man's part of the photo and drops it into the cauldron to burn. The man does the same.

The Priest ties one piece of the red yarn to the woman's wrist and the other end to one of the black candles. The Priestess ties the other piece of the red yarn to the man's wrist and the other end to the other black candle.

Priestess: *Red is the color of passion and life. The tie to passion and life between you is finished. Now you must sever any remaining ties.*

The Priestess hands the scissors to the woman, who cuts the yarn. Then she gives the scissors to the man, who does the same.

The Priestess says to the woman: *You are yourself, a Goddess-daughter. Begin a new life with joy and expectation for only good in the future, for the Goddess will never disappoint you in Her gifts.*

The Priest says to the man: *You are yourself, a son of the God. Begin a new life with joy and expectation for only good in the future, for the God will never disappoint you in His gifts.*

The woman lights her white candle, and says:
I cast off the old. I welcome new beginnings. So have I said, so shall it be.

The man lights his white candle, and says:
I cast off the old. I welcome new beginnings. So have I said, so shall it be.

The Priest takes the woman's arm, and the Priestess the man's arm. They stand the couple back to back.

Priest: *As once you walked together, now must you walk apart. Depart from each other.*

The couple walks to opposite sides of the circle where they stand.

The Priestess picks up the pieces of red yarn, and says:

We solemnly commit these ties to the cauldron.

She places the yarn into the cauldron. Later, the yarn can be burned or buried.

The ritual is finished, and the circle broken.

CHAPTER 53

Death or Remembrance

ITEMS NEEDED: A photo of the deceased person or pet, a white candle carved with the name, and a personal item belonging to the deceased. Cremated ashes in an urn may also be set on the altar. Have a chalice of consecrated water on the altar, and burn patchouli or frankincense incense.

INSTRUCTIONS: This ceremony does not have to be held within a cast circle. A personal friend, one of the family, a Priest, or a Priestess may direct the memorial service. Change the identity of the speakers' parts as needed.

Light the carved white candle.

Priestess: *Goddess and God, we give* (name of the deceased) *into Your keeping. May she/he rest within Your renewing cauldron until another cycle of life is decreed.*

Priest: *Our sorrows come from physical absence. Yet we know that the spirit is not ended at death. It transforms into a different body, to live again in the Otherworld.*

The Priestess lightly sprinkles the photo, personal item, and cremation urn with consecrated water. The Priest waves incense smoke around these items.

Priestess: *Lord and Lady, we ask for Your comforting power to fall upon us that our sorrows may ease. Farewell,* (name of the deceased). *Go in peace. May our future meetings be filled with love and joy.*

Friends and family: *Go in peace. We love you.*

Now is a time to share happy memories. This is a necessary part of healing.

CHAPTER 54

Blessing a House or Property

ITEMS NEEDED: A white candle, consecrated water, burning frankincense incense, and a small dish of consecrated salt. Either carry these items on a tray, or have someone carry them for you.

INSTRUCTIONS: No cast circle is necessary. If you cannot walk around the entire outside of your house, plan to go through every room, including the basement, if you have one. Begin and end at the main entry door. The word *house* can be changed to boat or whatever property you are blessing.

Stand before the main entry door, and say:

> *Spirits of this house, I call upon you to be present. I ask that the blessings of the Lady and the Lord be upon you and upon this dwelling place. I would have only peace, joy, and love enter here.*

Circle the room clockwise while carrying the lighted white candle. Set it back on the tray, and lightly sprinkle salt around the room. Repeat with the consecrated water. End by carrying the smoking incense around the room.

When you return to the room's door, say:

> *Blessings upon you and upon the dwellers of this house.*

Repeat this with every room in the house. When your circuit returns you to the main entry door, put aside the tray.

Raise your arms, and say:

> *Only those spirits of light and truth may dwell here. I call upon the Elements fourfold to bless this house and all who dwell within. May we know only blessings and joy. So mote it be.*

CHAPTER 55

Protection Ritual

ITEMS NEEDED: The regular ritual items, plus a sword, bell, and patchouli or exorcism incense. Also, a black votive or taper candle placed inside the cauldron is set in the center of the altar.

INSTRUCTIONS: This ritual can be used when you have an unusual streak of bad luck, or feel under psychic attack. Never mention the names of people you think may be responsible. Instead, trust in the Dark Mother and the Lord of the Hunt to know the truth and take care of the culprits. You must feel strongly about experiencing the negative forces, or the ritual will not work properly.

The circle is cast widdershins, or counterclockwise. The circle must not be broken until the ritual is entirely finished.

Stand before the altar. Close your eyes, breathe deeply, and center your thoughts on the upcoming ritual and the reason behind it. Ring the bell once, and say:

> *This ritual has begun.*

Next, move to the eastern edge of the ritual area, holding your dagger in your power hand. Visualize a blue-white flame issuing from the tip of the dagger. Point it at the floor in the East. Walk counterclockwise around the circle, drawing the circle mark in the air as you go. Be sure to overlap the ends in the East as you finish.

As you walk, say:

> *I consecrate this circle to the Dark Mother and the Lord of the Hunt.*
> *Here may they manifest and bless their child.*

Return to the altar and stand facing it. Raise your arms with the dagger in your power hand, and say:

This is a time that is not a time, in a place that is not a place, on a day that is not a day. I stand at the threshold between the worlds, before the Veil of the Mysteries. May the Old Ones protect me that I may walk the true path forever. By the bright circle of the golden sun, by the bright courses of the glorious moon, by the dread potency of every star in the mysterious zodiac's burning girth, by each and all of these supernal signs, I do call and command you with this sacred blade. Guard me in this time and place from all evil and unbalanced forces.

Lay the dagger on the altar, raise your arms in greeting, and say:

Come, all those who would help me here this night. I give you welcome within this sacred circle. Join your powers with my desires that I may crush the negative atmosphere around me.

Take up the dagger and hold it point down over the chalice of water. (Some Witches believe the dagger should actually touch the water, salt, and incense.) Say:

The blessings of the Goddess be upon this water, symbol of Water. May it ever remind me of the endless cauldron waters of rebirth.

Hold the dagger with the point down over the container of salt. Say:

The blessings of the Goddess be upon this salt, symbol of Earth. May I ever honor the blesséd earth that is Her body in the physical world.

With the tip of your dagger, scoop up a little of the salt and tip it into the chalice of water. Put the dagger aside and take up the chalice in your power hand. Swirl it gently three times in a counterclockwise movement.

Hold the chalice high over the altar and say:

Water and Earth, Elements of birth. By touch, purify. By power, sanctify. Great Goddess, be you adored!

Using the fingers of your power hand, lightly sprinkle the water around the edge of the circle, beginning and ending in the East, and moving counterclockwise.

Replace the chalice on the altar, and take the dagger in your power hand. Hold it point down over the burning charcoal and say:

May the blessings of the God be upon this charcoal, symbol of Fire. May I ever honor the sacred Fire that dances within me.

Hold the dagger point down over the incense and say:

> *May the blessings of the God be upon this incense, symbol of Air. May I always listen to the spiritual inspiration that whispers to my soul.*

Lay the dagger aside. Put a small amount of the incense on the burning charcoal. Hold the burner high over the altar and say:

> *Fire and Air, Elements so fair. By touch, purify. By power, sanctify. Great God, be you adored!*

Carry the burning incense around the circle, beginning and ending in the East, and moving clockwise. Return the censer to the altar.

Stand facing the altar and say:

> *Round and round, the power has bound, this circle tonight in Otherworld light. No evil may enter, no harm befall me. For this is my will, and so shall it be.*

Take the small taper candle and light it from the white pillar candle. With your dagger in your power hand and the taper in the other, go to the East. Light the yellow candle. Say:

> *Lords and Ladies of the East, all you warriors and guardians of the Element of Air, I do summon you to witness this ritual and to guard this circle.*

Go to the North; light the green candle. Say:

> *Lords and Ladies of the North, all you warriors and guardians of the Element of Earth, I do summon you to witness this ritual and to guard this circle.*

Go to the West; light the blue candle. Say:

> *Lords and Ladies of the West, all you warriors and guardians of the Element of Water, I do summon you to witness this ritual and to guard this circle.*

Go to the South; light the red candle. Say:

> *Lords and Ladies of the South, all you warriors and guardians of the Element of Fire, I do summon you to witness this ritual and to guard this circle.*

Return to the altar, snuff out the taper candle, and lay it and the dagger aside. Take up the sword and raise it in salute to the altar. Breathe deeply several times.

Go to the eastern quarter and hold the sword up in salute. Then hold it straight out in a threatening stance, and say:

> *You warriors and guardians of the East, repel and destroy all evil and unbalanced forces that come from the East! May they never touch my mind!*

Go to the northern quarter. Repeat the movements, and say:

> *You warriors and guardians of the North, repel and destroy all evil and unbalanced forces that come from the North! May they never touch my body!*

Go to the western quarter. Repeat the movements, and say:

> *You warriors and guardians of the West, repel and destroy all evil and unbalanced forces that come from the West! May they never touch my emotions!*

Go to the southern quarter. Repeat the movements, and say:

> *You warriors and guardians of the South, repel and destroy all evil and unbalanced forces that come from the South! May they never touch my spirit!*

Return to the altar and say:

> *Dark Mother, there are those who work against me, those who fill my life with misfortune and chaos. Protect me, Dark Mother! Let the efforts of my enemies fail! Let them taste their just rewards! Lord of the Hunt, You who keeps the Sacred Laws and the balance of karma, protect me! Destroy the barriers my enemies have erected to cause me to fail and falter in my life! Fill their mouths with words condemning of themselves! Let their evil thoughts return to the maker! So mote it be!*

Draw a banishing pentagram with the sword in the air over the altar, and say:

> *It is done!*

When the complete ritual is finished, take your dagger in your power hand and the candlesnuffer in the other.

Go to the East. Extinguish the candle flame. Say:

Lords and Ladies of the East, all warriors and guardians of the Element of Air, I bid you peacefully depart. My thanks, and farewell.

Go to the North. Extinguish the candle flame. Say:

Lords and Ladies of the North, all warriors and guardians of the Element of Earth, I bid you peacefully depart. My thanks, and farewell.

Go to the West. Extinguish the candle flame. Say:

Lords and Ladies of the West, all warriors and guardians of the Element of Water, I bid you peacefully depart. My thanks, and farewell.

Go to the South. Extinguish the candle flame. Say:

Lords and Ladies of the South, all warriors and guardians of the Element of Fire, I bid you peacefully depart. My thanks, and farewell.

Return to the altar. Lay aside the candlesnuffer. Lay both hands, palms down, on the altar to ground any remaining power.

Raise your arms in greetings as you say:

Fairies, Spirits, Elementals, and all in the invisible, I give my thanks and my blessings. May we always work in harmony together. Blessèd be.

Take your dagger and go to the eastern edge of the circle. Sweep the dagger across the invisible circle from right to left. Say:

The circle is cut, but the blessings long remain. Merry meet and merry part and merry meet again. Blessèd be!

Part IV
THE BOOK OF SPELLS

CHAPTER 56

What Is Magic?

Magic has been known and used successfully for thousands of years, and is still being used today. The word magic probably comes from the Greek phrase *Magiké techné*, which translates as "the art of the Magi." The Magi were learned people who studied a variety of subjects, including astrology, alchemy, the power of stones, the unlimited powers of the mind and the spirit, and the astral planes.

The prospect of doing magic attracts many people to Wicca. However, magic is not actually part of the Wiccan religion. In fact, magic is not a part of any religion, but can be performed on its own without believing in any deity, although belief in deities aids the magician in this work. Magic is a system of using certain words, gestures, devices, and techniques to acquire what is desired. In fact, every act of strong-willed thought and every emotion-filled prayer are acts of magic.

In occult language, magic is finding a pressure point in the web of the world's energy and knowing how to gently apply mental energy and will to change the outcome of an event or desire. Magic is the mental art of changing consciousness so as to alter physical reality at will. One can tap into this web of energy through the practice of self-control, meditation, and certain techniques, such as candle burning. Learning how and where to apply the pressure takes much practice and patience.

Knowledge equals power equals energy equals matter equals mass, and mass distorts space. In other words, by learning everything you can, you accumulate power. All power can be shaped into energy. All matter is made of energy. Matter itself has mass. Mass will distort space so that it can take a form. When space is distorted, or moved, the mass can materialize from one plane of existence into another.

Witches and ceremonial magicians realize the truth behind magic, and apply the above equation, even subconsciously, whenever they perform the magic. They go one step beyond the commonplace use of candles and stones, however, to assure success with their magic. They perform their magical spells within a cast and consecrated circle. When a Witch is standing in the center of her magical circle, she is literally in a position of power unequalled anywhere in the physical world. The cast circle creates a space that is on the boundary between this world and the Otherworld. While working in this space between the worlds, the magician can more easily tap into the universal energy needed to make a spell work. Magicians can also call upon the Elements for power and aid in manifesting their desires through magic. They can expect to see those desires manifested into their physical world.

Magic is not instantaneous, nor does it violate the laws of nature. For example, you can do all the magical spells you want, but you will never change lead into gold. Lead by nature is not gold, nor does it have the composition or nature of gold. Also, the results of a spell must build up over a period of time until the willed desire manifests. To increase the rate of success, the Witch should never count on one performance of a spellworking. The spell must be done consecutively for three, five, seven, or nine days.

Magic not only can produce manifested physical results, it is a technique that is valuable because it opens the inner door to the hidden parts of the self. It can also connect the inner self of a Witch with the inner selves of all other humans, including the ancestors and deceased Witches from the past.

The stereotyped image of an old Witch with warts casting curses is merely negative propaganda. People who pray for someone's death are just as guilty of cursing. The magic lies within the person and their intent. Strong emotional thoughts are capable of manifesting the thought-of desire. You do not have to be a Witch or practice magic to be guilty of producing negative actions.

Magic, correctly taught, always comes with the warning to avoid deliberately harming anyone. An experienced Witch may feel compelled to take on the removal by natural means of evil people, but does not put death curses on someone because of disagreements or because, for example, two people desire the same man or woman. Witches know that irresponsible actions come home to roost, frequently with devastating consequences. Karma does not care whether you believe in it or not.

The art of magic is learned by study, practice, patience, and persistence. You do not acquire skill in magic instantaneously.

Isaac Bonewits, in *Real Magic*, writes that the only difference between magic and science is that magical knowledge hasn't been confirmed yet or accepted by scientists.

Many of the things we take for granted today, such as astronomy, chemistry, medicine, physics, reading, mathematics, and writing, were all once occult secrets.

So, in a fashion, everyone who works magic is stretching the limits of knowledge and delving into new frontiers, which someday will be acknowledged as ordinary.

CHAPTER 57

The Art of Spellcasting

Like any art or skill, spellcasting is acquired by work and study. Many cowans, or non-Witches, believe that Wiccans use secret words that, by simply uttering them, produce anything the Witch desires without any effort, practice, or patience. This is rather like thinking that the words *hocus pocus*, a phrase from old ceremonial magic grimoires, will drop gold into your lap.

The only way you will attract your desire into your life is to make your vibrations match the frequency of the desired object. For example, if you wish prosperity, you must think of positive, prosperous things and avoid all negative thoughts that dwell on lack or poverty. Then, you do spellwork for prosperity and hold to the belief that it is yours, while waiting for it to manifest. Most of the time, the desired object is not dropped into your path, but produces opportunities to gain what you want.

The words spellwork and magic are connected. Whenever Witches or magicians do a spell, they draw down energy from another plane of existence and weave it into a desired visualized form through the use of certain words, gestures, thoughts, and practices. The whole idea behind magic is to contact specific energy pools called deities. By tapping into these pools, Witches can add a great amount of power to their personal inner energy. This produces a physical manifestation of the spell. The primary purpose of every ritual or spell is to create a change.

This takes us back to the equation given in the last chapter: Knowledge equals power equals energy equals matter equals mass, and mass distorts space.

Witches who are successful study constantly to refine their rate of success. Witches know that by using certain colors of candles, herbs, stones, oils, incenses, numbers, and actions they raise the success rate constantly.

Witch magicians must go deep into their subconscious mind before they can reach the doorway to other dimensions. Without reaching this doorway, effective magic cannot be performed. The practice of self-discipline, self-knowledge, and self-control are the only things that will enable the Witch to pass unharmed into the Otherworld. Because Witches have few preconceived ideas about what they will discover there, they are open to discoveries that can revolutionize thinking, science, and humankind's relationship with the universe and everything in it. Wiccan training enables one to find, see, and understand universal symbols. This understanding allows Witches to apply these symbols and Otherworld knowledge to everyday life.

The Four Laws of the Magus are very ancient. These laws are part of ceremonial magic, but have great value to Witches as well. Tradition says that these Laws came from Hermes Trigmegistus in ancient Egypt. I suggest every new Witch make a copy of these Laws and put them up in a prominent place in the ritual room or on the altar.

The Four Laws are matched to the Elements and give good advice for any magician: to know (Air); to dare (Water); to will (Fire); and to keep silent (Earth). To know means to study and learn everything you can about magic and the way it can be used. Then, magicians must dare to practice what they have learned. They must have the will to do the magic, and will with all their being for the result desired. At the end of this comes the most important part of the Laws. Magicians must keep quiet about the work they are doing and what they are doing it for. Every time magicians talk about their magical work, part of the energy is given away. Also, the magician may be telling someone who, for whatever reason, does not want the magician to succeed. That person, knowing what is being done, can counteract the results. This is not a usual occurrence, but it can, and does, happen. In silence there is knowledge.

CHAPTER 58

Planetary Influences

Ancient cultures as far back as Mesopotamia knew of, and used, only seven of the planets we know today. These astrological bodies were the Sun, Moon, Mercury, Venus, Mars, Jupiter, and Saturn.

Certain powers and attributes were associated with each planet. These seven planets were also connected with certain days of the week and certain hours of the day and the night. This knowledge was applied to both ceremonial rituals and magical spells.

Surviving historical information reveals that such religious bodies as the Persian Mithraic Mysteries used the same method of planetary power and correspondence that was later used in the medieval times by ceremonial magicians and the Qabalists. There is also reference to planetary energies in the ancient writings of Hermes Trismegistus, used by both the Egyptians and the Greeks.

These reservoirs of astral energy are actually archetypal pools of power. They can be tapped and used by any magician or Witch. Using planetary influences in magic sharpens the magician's focus on a desired result. The more correspondences used in a spell, the more focused the intent, and the higher the rate of success.

The waxing and waning of the moon was also taken into consideration when planning the time of a spell. The waxing moon was used for increase, building, and growth, while the waning moon was used for decrease, release, removal, destruction, and binding. The use of planetary hours for both the day and the night is discussed in the next chapter.

When using the planetary power system, find that planet that corresponds to the spellwork you plan to do. Select several correspondences from that planet's attributes, and incorporate them into the spell. For example, if you plan a success ritual using the Sun, you might choose a yellow or gold candle, Kyphi or frankincense incense and oils, a picture of a lion or phoenix, and the four sixes (six of pentacles, wands, swords, and cups) from a tarot deck. You might also place a picture or image of a sun disk or the god Horus on the altar.

The following list of planets and their elements does not provide all the correspondences. However, the examples will aid you in making other associations, such as different but similar deities.

The Sun: Sunday is the day of the week associated with the Sun. The word Sunday is derived from the words "Sun's day." Its color is bright yellow or gold. The metal traditionally listed is yellow gold; however, anything that is a true shining gold will work. Use the tarot cards the Sun and the four sixes. Associated stones are goldstone, topaz, and chrysoleth. The Sun is said to rule the sign of Leo. Oils and incenses associated with the Sun are Egyptian Kyphi, heliotrope, cloves, frankincense, cinnamon, and vanilla. Creatures connected with the Sun are the hawk, phoenix, and lion. Among the Sun deities are Horus, Ra, Adonis, Bel, Lugh, Sekhmet, Sol, Bast, Apollo, and Helios. Use for rituals involving healing and health, prosperity and success, confidence, physical vitality, quick money, honor, friendships, and active change.

The Moon: The weekday of the Moon is Monday; the word Monday is derived from "Moon's day." Corresponding colors are silver, pearl-white, light blue, and lavender. The metal is silver. Use the tarot cards the Moon and the four nines; nine has always been a magical Moon number. Stones are the moonstone, clear quartz crystal, and beryl; some list the pearl also. The Moon rules the sign of Cancer. Oils and incenses would be lily, jasmine, lotus, and white rose. Creatures connected with the Moon are the hare, hart, boar, horse, and elephant. Moon deities are Isis, Khensu, Neith, Diana, Hecate, Selene, and the Mórrígan. Use for rituals involving visions, divination, dreams, love, birth, emotional problems, and domestic and family situations.

Mercury: The weekday for Mercury is Wednesday; the modern word Wednesday comes from "Odin's or Wodan's day." Mercury is associated with changeable colors, or colors connected with changeable ideas or emotions, such as orange, violet, and multi-colors. The traditional metal is quicksilver, which is unsafe to handle; substitute an alloy metal such as aluminum instead. Use the tarot cards the Magician and the four eights. Associated stones are the carnelian, fire opal, and agate. Mercury is said to rule the signs of Gemini and Virgo. Oils and incenses can be white sandalwood and storax. Associated creatures are the ibis, twin serpents, swallows, and the jackal. Mercury deities are Mercury, Thoth, Hermes, Anubis, Maat, Odin, and Ogma. Use for rituals involving creativity, scientific reasoning, business, divination, eloquence, writing and speeches, inspiration of all kinds, and healing nervous disorders.

Venus: The weekday of Venus is Friday; the modern day is associated with the Old Norse "Frigg's day" or "Freyja's day." Colors can be light green, light blue, and pink. Use the tarot cards the Empress and the four sevens. The metal is copper, and the stones are amber, malachite, jade, peridot, and turquoise. Venus rules Taurus and Libra. Corresponding oils and incenses are apple blossom, verbena, rose, and red sanders or sandalwood. Venus deities are Venus, Aphrodite, Astarte, Hathor, and Freyja. Corresponding creatures are all cats, lynx, leopard, dove, and swan. Use for rituals involving love, marriage, artistic creativity, fertility, partnerships, spiritual harmony, and children.

Mars: The weekday of Mars is Tuesday; the modern word comes from the Old Norse "Tiw's day." The metal is iron or steel. The associated color is red, and the tarot cards are the Tower and the four fives. Mars rules Aries and Scorpio. Corresponding stones are garnet, bloodstone, red agate, ruby, and red topaz. Oils and incenses would be dragon's blood and any peppery scents. Creatures are the wolf, bear, horse, ram, and basilisk. Mars deities are Ares, Mars, Tyr, and Horus. Use for rituals involving energy, courage, conflicts, surgery, physical strength, endurance, destruction, defense, and winning.

Jupiter: The weekday of Jupiter is Thursday; the word comes from the Old Norse "Thorr's day." The metal is tin, and the colors are blue and purple. Corresponding stones are lapis lazuli, amethyst, turquoise, and sapphire, while the tarot cards are the Wheel of Fortune and the four fours. Oils and incense would be lilac, storax, saffron, cedar, and nutmeg. Jupiter rules Sagittarius and Pisces. Associated creatures are the eagle and unicorn. Jupiter deities are Jupiter, Zeus, Amun, the Dagda, Thorr, and Marduk. Use for rituals involving honor, prosperity, success, good health, friendships, good luck, religion, legal matters, trade, and employment.

Saturn: The weekday of Saturn is Saturday, or "Saturn's day." Colors are black and indigo, while associated stones are onyx, obsidian, jet, and star sapphire. The metal is lead. The tarot cards are the Universe or World and the four threes. Corresponding oils and incense would be myrrh, storax, and civet. Saturn rules Aquarius. Associated creatures are the dragon, goose, crocodile, and goat. Saturn deities are Saturn, Cronus, Nephthys, Isis, Demeter, Ceres, Nut, Cerridwen, Danu, and Hecate. Use in rituals involving knowledge, death, reincarnation, binding, overcoming curses, protection, intuition, and dealing with karma.

The chart of planetary symbols shows the astrological marking signs used to identify the planets. These signs appear on the charts for the planetary hours in the next chapter.

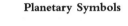

Planetary Symbols

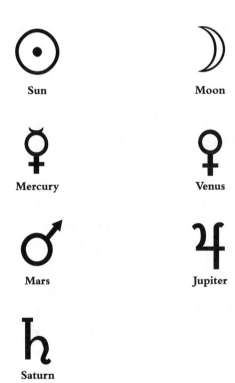

Sun   Moon

Mercury   Venus

Mars   Jupiter

Saturn

CHAPTER 59

The Days and Hours

Just as the days of the week are connected with the seven planets, so is each hour of the day and the night. By carefully considering the phase of the moon, the planetary day, and the planetary hour, a magician can fine tune spells, thus making the rate of success much higher.

The rare books once available on this knowledge made the subject of planetary hours very difficult to understand and learn. They required the use of the latitude where the magician lived, along with the day of the week and the hour of the day or night, before the correct calculation could be reached. We know that consideration of the planets, their days, and their hours was part of ancient Mesopotamian and Egyptian magic. The surviving records of these magicians never mention anything about latitude. In fact, it is highly unlikely that they knew of or recognized anything remotely similar to latitude. From my own experience, I have found that one can use the planetary hours quite satisfactorily without taking latitude into consideration.

When working with planetary hours, one should not think of them in the same manner as one thinks of clock hours. Planetary-day hours technically are measured from sunrise to sunset, while planetary-night hours are measured from sunset to sunrise. Each span of time (sunrise to sunset or sunset to sunrise) is then divided into twelve equal parts. Each part is then considered to be a planetary hour. No consideration need be given to time zones. However, this calculation can become very involved and time-consuming, as the span of time measured changes each day.

Planetary hours do not remain the same from one day to the next through any given week. The calculations begin with Sunday and end with the following Saturday. The sequence of the planetary hours are rotated so that at the end of twenty-four hours the next planetary hour on the next day will be that of the planet ruling that day.

According to astrological and magical users, the influence of a planetary hour would be strongest on the week day of its corresponding planet. For example, Mars hours would be strongest on Tuesday. In addition, the planetary hours and days would be strongest during the month ruled by that planet. Therefore, Mars would be most influential on Tuesdays in the astrological month of Aries, March 21 to April 19.

This calculation becomes far too complicated for the average, busy Witch and magician. Rather than become mired in endless calculations, most modern magicians do not use planetary hours in their magic. An acceptable alternative is the charts provided in this book.

The simplified charts given in this chapter are effective, easy to use, and work just as well as spending hours calculating according to the old method. If you decide to use planetary hours in your magical work, I suggest you make copies of these charts and keep them handy in your ritual/magical area. Then, you can refer to them as needed.

When using the charts for the day- and the night-planetary hours, remember to adjust the hours for daylight savings time. The accompanying chart giving the astrological symbols for each planet will help in deciphering the markings on the planetary hour charts.

When choosing planetary hours, the magician should recognize that the meanings for the hours can be slightly different than the meanings for the planetary days.

The Sun: Sun influences tend to be full of activity and dealing with those in a position of authority. Use Sun hours for business advancement, quick money, working on stalled enterprises, entertaining for social purposes, and dealing with any governmental agency.

The Moon: Many people consider the moon unstable and negative. However, this is not necessarily true. Moon influences may be changeable and emotional, but this is not bad. Use Moon hours for domestic affairs, short journeys, making changes that will be temporary in nature, and anything of an emotional nature. I find Moon hours also beneficial in divination of all types.

Mercury: Mercury influences deal primarily with the intellect, memory, understanding, and expression. Use Mercury hours for work dealing with speeches, writing, business conferences, study, advertising matters, publishers, printers, scientific studies, newspapers, and lawyers.

Venus: Venus influences are associated with happiness, love, friendships, the arts, beauty, dinners and banquets, houses, furnishings, and land. Use Venus hours for starting exercise programs, to go on a diet, get a new hairstyle, learn to use cosmetics, meet with friends, settle disagreements, hold low-key business conferences, and make travel arrangements.

Mars: Mars influences tend to boldness, aggressiveness, and ambition. Use Mars hours for anything that requires physical energy to accomplish or anything that needs courage and resolution to gain what you desire.

Jupiter: Jupiter influences always have a beneficial effect. Use Jupiter hours for studying religious materials, advancing spiritual growth, beginning new enterprises, applying for a loan, healing and health matters, and working with anything that requires justice.

Saturn: Saturn influences tend to be conservative, organizational, cautious, and karmic in nature. Use Saturn hours for anything to do with building, leasing, property improvement, mental healing, working out karmic relationships and issues, endurance, breaking up blockages, delays, and hindrances, and reaching or getting decisions that have been a long time in consideration.

The first five planets, excluding the Sun and the Moon, are sometimes called the "physical" planets, as they are associated with the five physical senses. Mercury rules sight, Venus the emotions and sensations, Mars taste, Jupiter smell, and Saturn hearing. The Sun is connected with the life force or physical vitality, while the Moon rules the body in general and the form it takes, and emotional reactions to people and events.

Although the planets Uranus, Neptune, and Pluto are not given space in planetary hour charts, or assigned to week days, they do have influence upon humans and events. The three outer planets play an important part in human life, as they affect less physical, and more spiritual, matters. They can be used through the hours of other specific planets.

Uranus rules the human aura, intuition, and clairvoyance. It can cause sudden, unexpected events, as well as anything odd, unique, and rather revolutionary in nature. It rules the occult sciences, metaphysics, telepathy, inventions, reforms, natural healing (no chemical drugs), and the fields of radio, television, and computers. It is applied through the hours of Mercury.

Neptune is associated with mental perception and reasoning ability, psychometry, psychic phenomena, séances, perfumes, chemicals, brewers, and all parts of the fishing industry. It is applied through the hours of Venus.

Pluto is associated with exposing injustice, revitalizing ideas, astral and dream experiences, hypnotism, surgery, legacies, taxes and insurance, exposing crimes, and spiritual laws. It is applied through the hours of Mars.

There are, however, some additional rules of planetary hours about which you hear little. To observe these rules, you must have a correct natal chart and understand which planets in your chart might be considered adversely aspected. Adversely aspected planets are primarily those in opposition or squared to other planets. For example, if you have an adversely aspected Saturn or Mars in your natal chart, some astrologers believe it is best to avoid using Saturn or Mars hours. These astrologers believe that the hours of these planets are not fortunate to anyone. They teach that the best planetary hours are those that fall between ten A.M. and noon, provided the hours are not those of Saturn and Mars. This has not been my experience.

When worked with a proper attitude and caution, any planetary hour can be used to benefit the magician, regardless of the chart's adverse planets. The magician, however, must be well aware of the adverse planets and plan the energy use in strictly positive ways. This is particularly true of Saturn, which rules karma and karmic events. If you have an adversely aspected Saturn, and are working in that hour and/or on that day to help other people feel their karma immediately, you will find yourself dealing with your unsolved karmic issues first.

When choosing a planetary hour, wait at least fifteen minutes into that hour before you begin your magical work. This will put you safely within the desired time regardless of whether you are north or south of the equator, or what latitude you live in.

It is best to work first by doing any magical spellwork on a specific planetary day. It is easiest for apprentices to start with this method. Then, work with both the day and a specific planetary hour. These two combinations will usually be sufficient for most magical needs. If you have enough preplanning and foresight, you can add the correct planetary month to the equation.

If you find that the spell did not work correctly according to the planet you chose, carefully consider the planetary energy needed for the magic. You may need to choose a different planet and plan the spellwork to approach the result from a different angle.

Hours of the Day

	Monday	Tuesday	Wednesday	Thursday	Friday	Saturday	Sunday
1	☽	♂	☿	♃	♀	♄	☉
2	♄	☉	☽	♂	☿	♃	♀
3	♃	♀	♄	☉	☽	♂	☿
4	♂	☿	♃	♀	♄	☉	☽
5	☉	☽	♂	☿	♃	♀	♄
6	♀	♄	☉	☽	♂	☿	♃
7	☿	♃	♀	♄	☉	☽	♂
8	☽	♂	☿	♃	♀	♄	☉
9	♄	☉	☽	♂	☿	♃	♀
10	♃	♀	♄	☉	☽	♂	☿
11	♂	☿	♃	♀	♄	☉	☽
12	☉	☽	♂	☿	♃	♀	♄

Hours of the Night

	Monday	Tuesday	Wednesday	Thursday	Friday	Saturday	Sunday
1	♀	♄	☉	☽	♂	☿	♃
2	☿	♃	♀	♄	☉	☽	♂
3	☽	♂	☿	♃	♀	♄	☉
4	♄	☉	☽	♂	☿	♃	♀
5	♃	♀	♄	☉	☽	♂	☿
6	♂	☿	♃	♀	♄	☉	☽
7	☉	☽	♂	☿	♃	♀	♄
8	♀	♄	☉	☽	♂	☿	♃
9	☿	♃	♀	♄	☉	☽	♂
10	☽	♂	☿	♃	♀	♄	☉
11	♄	☉	☽	♂	☿	♃	♀
12	♃	♀	♄	☉	☽	♂	☿

CHAPTER 60

Magical Alphabets

In the beginnings of the world's cultures, all alphabets were sacred. The Celts used the Ogham alphabet, composed of certain glyphs or lines against a central stem. The Viking cultures gave the world the Runic alphabet, sometimes called the *futhork*, a name taken from the first six letters. The names of the alphabet letters often contained hidden religious secrets. The division of an alphabet into consonants and vowels also held arcane knowledge. Many of these ancient alphabets had, or at least began with, twenty-two letters.

In some cultures, in which the alphabet came first and numbers second, each alphabet letter was assigned a numerical meaning. This early association of numbers and alphabet letters is the basis for modern numerology. We find this association still in the Hebrew alphabet and its use in the sacred system called the Qabala. The word *Qabala* literally means, "traditional knowledge." This system became an important part of Western mysticism and magic during the Middle Ages. The Sufis and other Eastern mystical groups used the Arabic alphabet in much the same manner, as did the ancient Greeks with their alphabet.

The Celtic Druids had several forms and versions of the Ogham alphabet. Some of these versions are mentioned in Celtic lore, but their specific meanings have been lost. Because of the structure of the Ogham alphabet, it could be used as a secret sign language, as well as a form of writing, and had magical and spiritual uses. The Welsh Bardic alphabet and the Gaelic alphabet are lesser known forms of the Ogham.

When the Vikings, and later the Angles and Saxons, settled in the British Isles, they brought with them the Runic alphabet of the Norse culture. The word *rune* means "a magical rhyme." Certain runes were carved on sword hilts to give power and victory to the owner. Often daggers were also carved with runes. The carvings were done by the magically trained blacksmiths who originally forged the weapons. Magically endowing a dagger and a sword by carving runes upon it carried into ceremonial magic, then into modern Witchcraft.

Because of the magical and sacred connections of various alphabets, the Christian church forcibly replaced them with the Latin alphabet in all territories they conquered. However, the Ogham alphabet continued to be used by Welsh Bards, who eventually evolved their own Bardic alphabet, which is slightly different from the original Ogham.

During the Middle Ages in Europe, several other created alphabets came into existence. These secret alphabets, usually based on the twenty-two letter Hebrew alphabet, were invented and used by ceremonial magicians, alchemists, and some Witches. Frequently, these medieval alphabets are a combination of alchemical marks, astrological signs, and the inventor's imagination. A few are modified scripts of such known alphabets as those of the Hebrews, Greeks, and Romans; on rare occasions one finds evidence that Slavonic letters were influential in the construction of an alphabet.

One can find these "invented" alphabets written down in the remnants of ancient alchemical and magical books. They seem to have been used in preparing talismans and ceremonial magic circles. Any deity names mentioned are always a form of the Hebrew/Christian god. Other names in these texts are those of angels and demons.

The Theban alphabet of Honorius, for example, was based on the Latin alphabet. This alphabet was preferred by the European Witches, as they did not do Qabalistic magic. Its name comes from a great magician called Honorius the Theban.

Many of these medieval alphabets were first published in 1801, in *The Magus* by Francis Barrett. He copied them from much older books, many of which were handwritten and not available to just anyone.

In the past, these alphabets were used to write out everything of a magical, mystical nature. This prevented the Witch or magician from being detected and persecuted if the writings were found by Witch hunters. The only reason for Witches to write anything out in a secret, magical alphabet today is that the writing makes Witches concentrate entirely upon what they are doing. The more concentrated thought that is poured into a spell, the more power it gains to materialize. Letters from one of these alphabets can be carved into candles or written out on paper for spellwork, thus endowing the material used and/or burned with mystical power to increase the efficiency of the spell.

I do not recommend that the Book of Shadows or any book of spellwork be written out in an ancient, secret alphabet. Without daily use, Witches will find themselves trying to translate each word letter by letter, thus taking vital energy away from the ritual or spell. However, Witches or magicians should be fairly well acquainted with the secret, magical meanings of the letters in these alphabets so that they can use them correctly in spellwork.

We have lost the magical knowledge behind some of the alphabets listed here, but they still hold power. Enough information remains on a few alphabets, such as the Runes and Ogham, for us to correctly comprehend the mystical knowledge behind them. On others, such as the Greek and Egyptian, there are enough clues that one knowledgeable in ancient lore can deduce what was meant.

There are charts in this chapter for the following alphabets: Runes, Ogham, Greek, Egyptian Hieroglyphs, Malachim, Celestial, Passing the River, and Theban.

THE RUNES

The Runic alphabet is very ancient. Like the Celtic Ogham, the runes have few curved lines as they were originally carved in wood or stone. Although there are a few variations in other Viking-settled countries, enough similarities are there for any knowledgeable rune-master to read the message. A rune-master was an important person in the Norse society and was considered to be a powerful magician.

Carved runes were frequently painted red. Originally, the red coloring came from blood. This red coloring endowed the writing with magical power. The Old Germanic word for "to make red" and "to give magical power" was the same word.

The word *rune*, which means "a magical rhyme," came into the languages of other cultures through contact with the Norse people. In Old Norse, the word *run* meant both "secret wisdom" and "magical power." The word *run* in both Old Saxon and Old English meant "mystery, secret." When the Vikings settled in northern Germany, the word *runa* entered the Old High German language, where it meant "to whisper a secret."

The number of letters in a Runic alphabet depends upon which Viking-influenced culture you are studying. Also, there are other frequently used Norse symbols found primarily in rock carvings. Although these are not considered to be part of the Elder Runes, they are of power and importance. On the Rune chart, you will see

Runes

F	U, V	Th	A	R
C, K	G	W	H	N
I	J	Ei, Y	P	Z
S	T	B	E	M
L	Ng	D	O	Triskelion
Battle Axe	World Tree	Sun Wheel	Moon	Ship

seven picture runes at the bottom. These powerful symbols do not represent alphabet letters, but rather are a type of shorthand communication for an entire series of words or ideas.

There is one similarity between the Runic alphabet and the Celtic Ogham. The letters in both are associated with specific trees.

The Rune chart lists what are called the twenty-four Elder Runes. These are traditionally divided into three groups of eight runes each. The first group, which consists of *fehu, uruz, thurisaz, ansuz, raidho, kaunaz, gebo,* and *wunjo,* is called Freyja's Eight. Hagal's Eight are *hagalaz, naudhiz, isa, jera, eihwaz, perdhro, elhaz,* and *sowilo.* Tyr's Eight are *tiwaz, berkano, ehwo, mannaz, laguz, ingwaz, dagaz,* and *othalaz.*

F is connected with the elder tree, and the Aesir deities. Its Norse names are *fehu, feoh,* and *fe.* The literal meaning is "cattle, money, gold, a fee." The magical and divination meanings are wealth, property, good luck, fulfillment of desires, and power.

U, V are connected with the birch tree, and the Vanir deities. The Norse names are *uruz* and *ur.* The literal meaning is "ox, drizzle, rain." The magical and divination meanings are good fortune, advancement of plans and life, happiness, and the power to manifestation desires.

TH are combination letters connected with the oak tree, and the god Thorr. The Norse names are *thurisaz, thorn,* and *thurs.* The literal meaning is "giant, thorn, the good one, the strong one." The magical and divination meanings can be a journey across water, good news that comes from afar, strength to wait, and strength to break up a resistance.

A is connected with ash tree, and the god Odin. The Norse names are *ansuz, oss,* and *ass.* The literal meaning is "god, one of the Aesir, and ancestral deity." The magical and divination meanings are transformation of the self and/or life, information that will create great changes, or new goals.

R is connected with oak tree, and the god Forseti. The Norse names are *raidho, reidh, rit,* and *rad.* The literal meaning is "a long journey on horseback, a chariot, or riding by wagon." The magical and divination meanings are making a physical journey, arriving at the hidden truth, and seeing through illusions.

C, K are connected with the pine tree, and the goddess Freyja and the gods Weland and Loki. The Norse names are *kenaz, kaon, cen,* and *kaun.* The literal meaning is "torch, swelling, boil, forge, hearth, or pyre." The magical and divination meanings are life-strength, ambition, determination, willpower, inspiration, and energy for dissolving a situation.

G is connected with the ash and elm trees, and the god Odin and the goddesses Freyja and Gefion. The Norse names are *gebo, gifu, gyfu,* and *gipt.* The literal meaning is "blessings, generosity, or gifts from the gods." The magical and divination meanings are weddings, legacies, windfalls, promotions, and the exchange of power between the gods and humans.

W is connected with the ash tree, and the god Freyr. The Norse names are *wunjo, wynn, wunna,* and *vend.* The literal meaning is "joy, hope, pleasure, or pasture." The magical and divination meanings are security, comfort, and happiness.

H is connected with the yew and ash trees, and the god Ymir. The Norse names are *hagalaz, haegl,* and *hagal.* The literal meaning is "hail or snow." The magical and divination meanings are delays while waiting for the proper timing, and the ability to reconcile opposites in power.

N is connected with the beech tree, and the three fate goddesses called the Norns. The Norse names are *naudhiz, nyd, naut,* and *naudhr.* The literal meaning is "need, distress, or necessity." The magical and divination meanings are a past conditioning that drives you now, use caution if you wish success, and emotional distress clouds your vision.

I is connected with the alder tree, and the gods known as the Frost Giants. The Norse names are *isa, iss,* and *eis.* The literal meaning is "ice." The magical and divination meanings are a static period of no action, the freezing of motion, and taking care what you say to anyone.

J is connected with the oak tree, and the god Freyr. The Norse letter "j" is always pronounced "y." The Norse names are *jera, ger, yer, ar,* and *jer.* The literal meaning is "good harvest, good year." The magical and divination meanings are a cycle of time and no quick results.

EI, I, Y are connected with the yew tree, and the gods Odin and Ull. The Norse names are *eihwaz, eoh, yr,* and *ihwar.* The literal meaning is "yew tree or mountain ash." The magical and divination meanings are end of a cycle, situation, or problem or a drastic change.

P is connected with the beech tree, and the three fate goddesses called the Norns. The Norse names are *perdhro, perodh, peorth,* and *pear.* The literal meaning is "fate or dice cup." The magical and divination meanings are a surprise, unexpected material gain, or a turn of luck.

Z is connected with the yew tree, and the goddesses known as the Valkyries. The Norse names are *elhaz, eolh, aquizi,* and *ihwar.* The literal meaning is "elk, stone axe, yew bow, or protection." The magical and divination meanings are blockages removed and visible movement.

S is connected with the juniper tree, and the god Balder. The Norse names are *sow-ilo, sigil, sig,* and *sol.* The literal meaning is "sun or sun wheel." The magical and divination meanings are drastic changes, unexpected guidance, advancement of plans, and a period of renewal.

T is connected with the oak tree, and the god Tyr. The Norse names are *Tiwaz, Tyr, Tiu,* and *Tir.* These are all variations of the name of the god Tyr. The literal meaning is "sky god or the god Tyr." The magical and divination meanings are wisdom, justice, the law, justified victory, and success.

B is connected with the birth tree, and the goddesses Frigg, Nerthus, and Hel. The Norse names are *berkano, beorc,* and *birca.* The literal meaning is "birch tree or birch goddess." The magical and divination meanings are creativity, fertility, new beginnings, marriage, and birth.

E is connected with the oak and ash trees, and the god Freyr and the goddess Freyja. The Norse names are *ehwo, eoh, ehwaz,* and *eh.* The literal meaning is "horse, steed, or stallion." The magical and divination meanings are a new attitude, self-transformation, a new home, new goals in life, and steady progress is seen.

M is connected with the holly tree, and the gods Heimdall and Odin. The Norse names are *mannaz, man,* and *madhr.* The literal meaning is "mankind, human being, or the physical world." The magical and divination meanings are a male influence in life, new career opportunities, and developing a link with the deities.

L is connected with the willow tree, and the gods Njord and Balder. The Norse names are *laguz, lagu,* and *logr.* The literal meaning is "lake or water." Sometimes, the word *laukaz,* or "leek," is attached to this rune. The magical and divination meanings are below the surface movement that is difficult to detect, primal creative energy, and waiting for manifestation to come from the spiritual into the physical.

NG is a combination letter connected with the apple tree, and the god Freyr, who was also known as the god Ing. The Norse names are *ingwaz, ingvi,* and *ing.* The literal meaning is "the god Ing, or kin." The magical and divination meanings are blood relationships or family relatives, and creative energy at work.

D is connected with the spruce tree, and the god Odin. The Norse names are *dagaz, dag,* and *daeg.* The literal meaning is "day." The magical and divination meanings are sudden understanding, spiritual illumination, and mystic light that reveals hidden knowledge.

O is connected with the hawthorn tree, and the gods Odin and Thorr. The Norse names are *othalaz, ethel, odal, odhal,* and *othala.* The literal meaning is "inherited land, property, the home country, or sacred enclosure." The magical and divination meanings are tangible, personal possessions, and inborn talents.

The **Triskelion** rune is actually another form of the Sun Wheel rune. It represents movement and motion in life. It also can mean changing residences or advancement of plans and goals.

The rune marked "Unknown" symbolizes wealth, prosperity, and material gain.

The **Battle Axe** symbol is tied to the god Thorr and his magical hammer Mjollnir. It represents total protection, increase, controlled magical power, and increase or fertility in all things. This rune can be used to overpower all negative magic.

The **World Tree** rune, symbol of the sacred tree that connects all the worlds in Norse lore, means a total, general protection, particularly through the use of magic. It can overpower any negative magic. It also represents the guidance one receives from the deities in everyday life.

The **Sun Wheel** represents the eight-spoked year wheel, a symbol of cycles and time; it is associated with the gods Odin and Balder. It also represents spiritual and/or intuitive guidance, the seeking out of mystical knowledge, and protection.

The **Moon** glyph symbolizes the powers of divination, the Norns or Fates, and the goddess Freyja. It represents orderly change in life and the strengthening of psychic abilities.

The **Ship** symbol signifies journeys, whether of the mind, the body, or the spirit; it can also represent the ship said to take the dead into the Otherworld. It symbolizes movement in life and affairs of life, physical journeys, and the ability to transmute difficulties into positive solutions.

The runes can be used for divination as well as magical inscriptions. Paint each rune on a small flat stone or a piece of thin wood one-inch square. Keep these rune stones in a bag large enough to insert your hand and freely draw a rune. Lay out three stones, placing the left one first. The left rune represents the past, the middle the present, and the right one the future.

OGHAM ALPHABET

The Celtic Ogham (pronounced *oh'-ahm*) alphabet was especially sacred to the Druids. All of the letters, except two, were associated with trees. Each letter was also connected with a calendar month, and was classified as a chieftain, peasant, or shrub. These classifications had nothing to do with the tree's physical form, but rather the importance attached to its energy and aura.

The last five letters of this alphabet are what is known as the Crane Bag. The mythic Crane Bag belonged to the sea god Manannán mac Lir, in which he stored powerful, secret treasures. Among the Crane Bag letters are the only two that are not associated with trees: the Sea and the Grove.

At one time, the hidden secrets of this alphabet were taught only to initiates in the Druidic orders. For ordinary correspondences and messages, the ancient Celts used the Greek alphabet, with which they were quite familiar. They used the Ogham letters for sacred records, histories, and genealogies. They also used their alphabet for magical purposes and, when the letters were carved or painted onto sticks, for divination.

B was associated with the birch tree, which was called Beth. It represented the month of November, and was of the peasant class. This month was the beginning of the Celtic year. The divinatory meaning is changes, purification, and new beginnings.

L was associated with the rowan tree, which was called Luis. It represented the month of December, and was of the peasant class. The divinatory meaning is protection against control by others, and being responsible for your own life.

Ogham Alphabet

├	╞	╞	╞	╞
B	L	F, V	S	N
┤	┤	╡	╡	╡
H	D	T	C, K	Q
⊬	⊬	⊬	⊬	⊬
M	G	Ng	R	St, Z Ss
┼	╪	╪	╪	╪
A	O	U. W	E	I, J, Y
⅄	◇	⋈	ρ	⊞
Ea, Ch, Kh	Oi, Th	Ui, P, Pe	Ph, Io	Ae, X, Xi

F, V were associated with the alder tree, which was called Fearn. It represented the month of January, and was of the chieftain class. The divinatory meaning is spiritual guidance, and receiving help in making choices.

S was associated with the willow tree, which was called Saille. It represented the month of February, and was of the peasant class. The divinatory meaning is to gain balance in life.

N was associated with the ash tree, which was called Nuin. It represented the month of March, and was of the chieftain class. The divinatory meaning is feeling constricted in your choices, and finding oneself locked into a chain of events.

H was associated with the hawthorn tree, which was called Huathe. It represented the month of April, and was of the peasant class. The divinatory meaning is a period of time where no movement or momentum is possible.

D was associated with the oak tree, which was called Duir. It represented the month of May, and was of the chieftain class. The divinatory meaning is security and strength.

T was associated with the holly tree, which was called Tinne. It represented the month of June, and was of the peasant class. The divinatory meaning is finding the energy and guidance for problems.

C, K were associated with the hazel tree, which was called Coll. It represented the month of July, and was of the chieftain class. The divinatory meaning is drawing on creative energies to complete projects.

Q was associated with the apple tree, which was called Quert. It represented no month and was of the shrub class. The divinatory meaning is resolving a choice that has to be made.

M was associated with the vine, which was called Muin. The Celts considered the vine as a tree. However, since grapes did not grow wild in Ireland or the British Isles, the vine may have meant the blackberry. It represented the month of August, and was of the chieftain class. The divinatory meaning is although inner growth is occurring, one should take time to relax.

G was associated with the ivy, which was called Gort. The ivy is also not a tree, but was held as sacred by the Celts. It represented the month of September, and was of the chieftain class. The divinatory meaning is to take your time in reaching a decision, or you will make a mistake.

NG were combined letters associated with the reed, which was called Ngetal. Although not a tree, the Celts classified it as such. It represented the month of October, and was of the shrub class. The divinatory meaning is sudden surprises or upsets.

SS, ST, Z were associated with the blackthorn tree, which was called Straif. It represented no month, and was of the chieftain class. The divinatory meaning was refusal to look at the truth, confusions, and resentment.

R was associated with the elder tree, which was called Ruis. It represented the three days that made up the thirteenth Celtic month at the end of the Celtic year, and was of the shrub class. The divinatory meaning was the end of a cycle or situation.

A was associated with the silver fir tree, which was called Ailim. It represented no month, and was of the shrub class. The divinatory meaning was to learn from past experiences, and take care in making a choice.

O was associated with the furze bush, which was called Ohn. It represented no month, and was of the chieftain class. The divinatory meaning was to be alert for information that can change your life.

U, W were associated with two plants, which were the heather and the mistletoe. They were both known under the month name of Ur. These plants represented no month; heather was of the peasant class, while mistletoe was a chieftain. The divinatory meaning was healing and growth is taking place on a spiritual level.

E was associated with the white poplar or aspen tree, which was called Eadha. It represented no month, and was of the shrub class. The divinatory meaning was doubts, fears, and problems arise.

I, J, Y were associated with yew tree, which was called Ioho. It represented no month, and was of the chieftain class. The divinatory meaning was a complete change of goals, attitude, or direction in life.

CH, KH, EA were associated with the symbol called the Grove, which was known as Koad. It represented no month, and had no class. The divinatory meaning was knowledge gained by looking past illusions.

OI, TH were associated with spindle tree, which was called Oir. It represented no month, and was of the peasant class. The divinatory meaning was no forward movement in life until one finished with obligations and duties.

P, PE, UI were associated with honeysuckle, which was called Uilleand. It represented no month, and was of the peasant class. The divinatory meaning was to be cautious in moving forward with plans.

PH, IO were associated with beech tree, which was called Phagos. It represented no month, and was of the chieftain class. The divinatory meaning was the arrival of new experiences and information.

AE, X, XI were associated with the sea, which was called Mor. It represented no month, and had no class. The divinatory meaning was travel and movement.

GREEK ALPHABET

The Greek alphabet, with its twenty-four letters, has a complete assignment of attributions that can be used in divination, much as the Norse runes. It was only later, during the practice of Mithraism, that some of the letters took on strong patriarchal qualities.

The Greek letters, like those of the Hebrews, were also associated with numerical values. This numbering symbolism was later used in the practice of *gematria* and modern numerology. The number value of each letter was added together, and then reduced to a single number.

To use the Greek alphabet in divination, imprint the letters on small clay or wood squares, or write them on blank cards. Without looking, select five squares or cards. Lay them out left to right before you. The two squares on the left represent the past that influences your question. The single middle square is the present, while the last two on the right are the future.

The meanings of each letter can be applied to both divination and magical uses.

Alpha: Money made through employment job or by creations done with your hands. Does not apply to land or property.

Beta: A time of new beginnings and new life cycles. New opportunities arise. In the Mithraic religion, this sign was used to symbolize the demonic God of Wrongdoing, who challenged and destroyed unity.

Greek Alphabet

⊿	β	γ	△	ε
Alpha	Beta	Gamma	Delta	Epsilon
ζ	η	ϑ	ι	κ
Zeta	Eta	Theta	Iota	Kappa
λ	μ	ο	π	ρ
Lambda	Mu	Omicron	Pi	Rho
σ	τ	υ	φ	χ
Sigma	Tau	Upsilon	Phi	Chi
ψ	♏			
Psi	Omega			

Gamma: Searching for the sacred. Opening oneself to inspiration.

Delta: There is a need for balance in life or events. This symbol signifies the four Elements and the four directions.

Epsilon: Open yourself to seeking along a new spiritual path. To the Greeks, the aion, or ether, was symbolized by this sign. In alchemy, the fifth Element was known as the Quintessence.

Zeta: A sacrifice, such as giving up one thing to gain something better. The loss of someone or something important to you.

Eta: Joy, love, and harmonious events. To the Greeks, this sign referred to the harmony of the seven planets.

Theta: Security and stability.

Iota: Working out a karmic problem or relationship. This letter was associated with the Three Fates.

Kappa: Bad luck, illness, misfortune. This letter was sacred to Rhea in her aspect of the Dark Mother.

Lambda: A cycle of life marked by order and growth.

Mu: You are faced with making decisions that will have a strong influence on life.

Nu: Stubbornness about listening to good advice. Making the wrong use of magic. Refusing to let go of a bad relationship.

Xi: Avoiding responsibility. Moving through life with no goals.

Omicron: Gaining the good things in life: love, good health, success, and prosperity.

Pi: A number of opportunities present themselves, but you have difficulty making a choice.

Rho: Growth, fertility, creativity, pregnancy.

Sigma: The end of a relationship, job, or problems.

Tau: The influence of family and friends, for good or ill.

Upsilon: Strong emotions are affecting your life. A spiritual initiation is coming.

Phi: An opportunity to learn new talents that will affect your life.

Chi: Unexpected gifts come from the gods.

Psi: Spiritual guidance; further development of psychic abilities; visions.

Omega: The very best of everything opens to you.

EGYPTIAN HIEROGLYPHS

Many Pagans feel a deep fascination with ancient Egyptian practices and lore. Therefore, I have included a table of Egyptian hieroglyphs.* Unfortunately, we do not have the original key to unravel all of the hidden mysteries of this alphabet. However, it is possible to deduce many of the meanings from old records.

Hieroglyphic characters were written either in columns or horizontal lines. These lines were usually read from the left to the right, but on occasion were read from the right to the left. Although hieroglyphs represented sounds and sometimes whole words, they also represented certain powers, most often symbolized by the creature painted. Except for foreign words, the Egyptians did not write out the vowels. This has created controversy about how many of the Old Egyptian words were actually spelled.

Egyptian hieroglyphs were used as amulets or good luck charms, and to write out magical spells while chanting. They can be used today as mystical alphabets when writing out requests, or in divinatory methods.

A is the forearm. The magical and divinatory meanings are events involving books, documents, or accounts; read these carefully before making any decisions.

B is the foot. The magical and divinatory meanings are progress is seen; possibly a new cycle starts.

C, S is the folded cloth. The magical and divinatory meanings are reaping the rewards of labor; working to join energy and ideas.

D is the hand. The magical and divinatory meanings are guidance and aid from the gods; learning to form astral energies in order to manifest in the physical.

---

* The basis for these hieroglyphs comes from a book published by the Metropolitan Museum of Art in New York.

Egyptian Hieroglyphics

A	B	C, S	D	E, O
F, Ph, V	G	H	I, Y	J
K	L, R	M	N	P
Q	T	U, W	X	Z
Ch	Sh	Th		

E, O is the vulture. The magical and divinatory meanings are drastic changes, either good or bad. These are brought about by your own choices. It can also mean the end of a project, relationship, job, or life cycle.

F, PH, V is the horned viper. The magical and divinatory meanings are you will create serious problems if you are not careful about what you do or say.

G is the pot stand. The magical and divinatory meanings are you attract a new life cycle, new relationship, or a spiritual initiation and rebirth.

H is the rope. The magical and divinatory meanings are you will be given an opportunity to pull yourself out of trouble, whether this be physical, mental, or emotional; a sudden, unexpected turn of events.

I, Y is the one reed leaf. The magical and divinatory meanings are a need to communicate with someone or calm troubled waters; a need to rectify past mistakes.

J is the cobra. The magical and divinatory meanings are spiritual growth and enlightenment are offered.

K is the basket. The magical and divinatory meanings are gaining or uncovering information that will benefit you.

L, R is the open mouth. The magical and divinatory meanings are communications with others; possible gossip.

M is the owl. The magical and divinatory meanings are having or keeping a secret; discovering mystical secrets.

N is the water. The magical and divinatory meanings are being faced with emotional issues; detaching your emotions from unproductive situations or people.

P is the stool. The magical and divinatory meanings are working with someone who has a position of authority; a challenging job is offered.

Q is the basket and quail chick. The magical and divinatory meanings are the opportunity to explore new ideas or visit new surroundings, thus gaining a reward of some kind.

T is the bread loaf. The magical and divinatory meanings are life's needs are being met; wealth and prosperity are within reach.

U, W is the quail chick. The magical and divinatory meanings are the discovery of hidden information, but beware how you use it. Your inexperience and naiveté may lead you into trouble.

X is the basket and folded cloth. The magical and divinatory meanings are reaching a satisfactory outcome to a problem or event; ending one cycle and beginning another.

Z is the door bolt. The magical and divinatory meanings are successfully closing the door on negative past events or people.

CH, TSH is the hobble rope. The magical and divinatory meaning is the stopping of all progress or forward movement, a static period of neutrality in life; a period of confusion where one does not know what to do next.

SH is lake. The magical and divinatory meanings are a period when one needs quiet and solitude.

TH is considered unknown. However, this symbol could well be the teardrop. The magical and divinatory meanings are establishing boundaries to keep others from demanding too much; coming to a hard decision; a period of upheaval and strong emotions, good or bad.

Since all ancient alphabets were originally sacred, you can use any of them in your magical work, even the modern ones. However, using an ancient alphabet with which you are not familiar makes you concentrate harder on your goal while writing out a request or carving your desire into a candle. The harder you concentrate, the more energy goes into the manifestation.

Malachim Alphabet or Language of the Magi

A	B	G	D
H	I, J	K	I,
M	N	O	P
Q	R	S	T
V	Z	Ch	Tz
Sh	Th		

Celestial or Angelic Alphabet

A	B	D	G
H	I	K	L
M	N	O	P
Q	R	S	T
V	Z	Ch	Sz
Th	Tz		

A	B	D	G
H	I	K	L
M	N	O	P
Q	R	S	T
V	Z	Ch	Sh
Th	Tz		

Theban or Witches' Alphabet

A	B	C	D
E	F	G	H
I	J	K	L
M	N	O	P
Q	R	S	T
U	V	W	X
Y	Z	end of sentence	

CHAPTER 61

Breaking a Spell

Along with how to cast a spell it is important for Witches to know how to break a spell, or dismantle it, if necessary. If Witches create a ball of astral energy to act as a watcher or protector, they should know how to return that energy to the cosmic void when the watcher's task is finished. The last thing you want wandering around your environment is an energy ball without a purpose.

One way to avoid this is to end all spells by saying: "In no way will this spell cause me or mine to suffer any negative effects. When the time of this spell is finished, all unused energy will return harmless to the cosmic void."

This statement will also protect you from the effects of a spell that might not be worded exactly right. For example, if you are selling your house, but living in another place at the time you cast the spell, you want to sell the old house, not the new one.

There may also come a time when you find yourself the victim of an unwanted spell from another magician. If the guilty magician has only average spellworking ability, you can deflect the magic by simply doing your monthly New Moon protection rituals. If, however, the magician in question is adept at creating powerful spells and knows how to prevent a rebound, you may be able to deflect the spell but, because of the proficiency of the magician, the spell will continue to return to you even though you have successfully deflected it. Therefore, you should end every spell with the above protection, or at least something similar. By this time you should have absorbed the admonition to avoid working spells against other people or trying to curse them.

Another time you will need to know how to break a spell is if a spell is ever sent against you. The easiest method for doing this is to keep up your New Moon protection rituals without fail, cleansing and blessing your entire home as needed, and adopting a positive attitude in your life.

If you are contending with an adept magician, you certainly do not want to end up playing tennis with a spell. Some innocent person could get hurt if the energy bounces their way. The best method for dealing with a situation like this is to trap the spell and neutralize it by sending it back into the cosmic void.

One way to do this is to set up a mirror trap on your altar. Set three mirrors at equal distances around your cauldron, all slightly facing inward. You need to have the mirrors angled in this way to draw in the spell and bounce it into the cauldron. Hold a fairly large piece of black onyx or black obsidian in your hands and instruct it to absorb the energy of any incoming spell and neutralize it. Then, place the stone inside the cauldron, in the center of the three mirrors. The spell energy will hit one of the mirrors, circle the cauldron by hitting each angled mirror several times, and, when momentum decreases, it will fall into the cauldron. At intervals, you will need to clean the mirrors, the stone, and the cauldron to keep them in top operating condition.

CHAPTER 62

Moon Magic

It is vital that a Witch have an astrological calendar that accurately lists the times and days for each time zone when the moon reaches each quarter. It makes little sense to use this finely tuned method of moon magic if one is off by too many hours. Do take care that the calendar you use *is* an accurate one, as some calendars list the New and Full Moons a day late.

The New Moon and the Full Moon are well known to most people who observe the night sky. These two moon phases are the ones most frequently mentioned in magical books and most often seen on calendars. A knowledgeable Witch, however, knows that there are more secrets to moon magic than these two phases.

New Moon: The New Moon phase is connected with the Dark Mother, the Wise One who controls the cauldron of unending cosmic energy. The Sacrificed Savior, who was the Old King, goes into the cauldron, and the reborn Divine Child comes out of it. Use this phase of the moon for protection spells, ending projects or relationships, changing your career, deep meditations on karma, past lives, and spiritual knowledge, and contacting deceased loved ones. It is also good for certain types of divination, such as serious questions about spiritual growth or immediate problems in your life. Cut your hair and nails during this time to slow down their growth.

First Quarter: The first quarter of the moon is associated with the Maiden, the virgin aspect of the Goddess. She is the Huntress and the Keeper of the Keys to the labyrinth that leads to the Divine Center of being. Her companion is the Lord of the Forests. He is the Lover, who entices the Maiden to explore her potential. Use this phase of the moon to start a diet or exercise program, begin new projects, friendships, or relationships, begin a new study or schooling, do a makeover of your appearance (hair styles, clothing, and so on), plan a vacation or trip, pay off bills, set up a new life in a new place or a new house, gain creative inspiration, and do divinations on your future.

Full Moon: The Full Moon phase is the Great Mother, the Creatrix who bonds with the Great Father to produce all creation. Cut your hair and nails during this time to speed up their growth. Use this phase of the moon for prosperity, success in a new job, healing, making decisions about relationships, selling or buying a house or vehicle, and planning complicated projects. Divinations on all types of questions work well at this time.

Fourth Quarter: The fourth quarter of the moon is connected with the Ancient Grandmother phase of the Goddess. Her companion is the Old King, the Grandfather of Wisdom. Use this phase of the moon for cleansing and purifying your ritual area or house to raise the vibrations, smoothing over family or relationship problems, removing obstacles, working for any kind of change, and doing spells for stubborn illnesses that resist healing. Divinations work well at this time for questions on uncovering hidden secrets, finding lost articles or people, and getting answers to questions that were not clearly answered before.

The four Elements can also be used in association with the four phases of the Moon. Sometimes, one has a project that cannot wait until the moon changes into the most auspicious phase. With the moon running through the cycle of zodiac signs as it does, a Witch can connect with the zodiac sign and, with forethought and care, successfully launch a magical project. For example, if the moon is in the New Moon phase, but you need to work a spell for prosperity, check to see if the moon is in an Earth sign.

If the Moon phase is in an Air sign, such as Gemini, Libra, or Aquarius, begin new projects or end old ones, work on any project that requires logic and perhaps categorizing of ideas.

If the Moon phase is in a Fire sign, such as Aries, Leo, or Sagittarius, work on transformations, creativity, love, courage, inspiration, or clearing out old or negative vibrations.

If the Moon phase is in a Water sign, such as Cancer, Scorpio, or Pisces, work to remove opposition, discover knowledge on a needed subject, healing, meditation, or overcoming obstacles.

If the Moon phase is in an Earth sign, such as Taurus, Virgo, or Capricorn, work on spells for security, prosperity, comfort, love, career, journeys, or raising oneself on a spiritual level.

CHAPTER 63

Sun Magic

In order to take full advantage of sun-seasonal energy, the Witch should have a very good astrological calendar that lists not only all eight of the Sabbats, but the times, according to time zones, when the sun changes into each astrological sign and when it arrives on the Solstices and Equinoxes.

Generally speaking, the spring is good for beginnings, while the summer is for actively working for material benefits. Autumn calls for spells of harvesting and winnowing out spells that did not work properly. Winter is the time for reflection and meditation in preparation for beginning a new solar year.

The Solstices and Equinoxes are set by the sun's movements and, although they may deviate by a day in one direction or the other from year to year, they are essential set times. The holy days, or Greater Sabbats according to Celtic Witches, are arbitrarily set on calendar dates. Originally, this was probably not the case. However, there have been several major calendar changes that have affected these dates, so these days are no longer celebrated on the same dates as were used hundreds or thousands of years ago.

The last major calendar change occurred in 1582. The Western world was using the Julian, or Roman, calendar at that time. The Julian calendar was instituted on January 1, 45 B.C.E. By 1477, however, the Christian Church decided to change the existing calendar because it no longer had Easter on the day they wished. Pope Gregory XIII abolished the Julian calendar in March, 1582, and dropped eleven days, so that the new calendar would match the date that the Council of Nicae met. Thereby Thursday, October 4, was immediately followed by Friday, October 15.

Some writers suggest that Pagans and Witches at one time calculated the four holy days by degrees into a zodiac sign. This would put these days halfway between each Solstice and Equinox. Thus, Imbolc would be at fifteen degrees of Aquarius, Beltane at fifteen degrees of Taurus, Lughnasadh at fifteen degrees of Leo, and Samhain at fifteen degrees of Scorpio.

Logically speaking, however, it is very doubtful that the typical, commonplace Witch or Pagan calculated anything by degrees of a sign, or were aware how to calculate such a thing. Their learned leaders, though, may have been able to do this for them. This might explain the eight-spoked wheel, which has all the days equidistant from each other. No one is absolutely certain who began to use these four holy days on the first day of certain months. These set dates have been used at least since the early 1900s, if not before.

The Solstices and Equinoxes also mark the turnings of the solar tides of energy. With the Solstices and Equinoxes marking the sun's energy tides, and the other four days marking the halfway points between, like the four phases of the moon, followers of the Old Way knew when they could tap into powerful flows of universal energy to make things happen. The ancient Celtic cultures realized this, and set their holy days to mark these turnings. This is why the eight holy days are so powerful for magic and connecting with universal and spiritual energy.

Imbolc: Traditionally on February 2, this festival might be called the Tide of New Light. It can be used for study of hidden knowledge, strengthening spiritual growth, preparing for initiations, and deep meditation.

Spring Equinox: This occurs approximately March 21, and can be called the Tide of Beginnings. It can be used for self-improvement, motivation, new beginnings, material status, changes in career or housing, and strengthening the spiritual.

Beltane: The traditional date is May 1, and is the Tide of Fertility. It can be used for relationships, love, prosperity, healing, success, career advancement, and changing jobs.

Summer Solstice: This day is celebrated on approximately June 21, and is the Tide of Nature Spirits. It can be used for communicating with Fairies and other nature spirits, general healing, herbs, divination, astral travels, plant and animal healing, and studying the occult knowledge of stones and herbs.

Lughnasadh: Traditionally, this date is August 1, and can be called the Tide of Ebb and Flow. It can be used for any situation that needs change, releasing obstructions in spells, removing obstacles in life, reaping the rewards of spells already in motion, and casting long-range spells that will not manifest quickly.

Autumn Equinox: This day falls on approximately September 21, and is the Tide of Preparation. It can be used for accumulating spell energy for the darker times of the year, cleansing and purifying your ritual area and home, working on renewing yourself and making personal changes, and dispersing and re-doing spells that have not worked.

Samhain: This day falls on October 31, and can be called the Tide of Static Movement. It can be used for communication with the dead and the Otherworld, learning divination, meditation on karma and past lives, and ending unproductive projects or relationships. Among the Celtic clans, Samhain was the end of one year and the beginning of the next.

Winter Solstice: This day is celebrated on approximately December 21, and is the Tide of Rest and Rebirth. It can be used for healing of the body, mind, emotions, and spirit, doing an inventory of your spiritual and physical progress for the year, and meditation. Among some Pagan cultures, particularly those that did not observe a lunar calendar, this was the end of the year.

CHAPTER 64

Herbal Powders and Brews

Powders and brews made of herbs have been used successfully for thousands of years. They should be an important part of the modern Witch's magical arsenal. If you wondered about all the "extra equipment" I mentioned in Chapter 17, now you will learn why you need it and how to use it.

When working magic with herbs and oils, there are certain items you will need: a mortar and pestle to grind up the herbs, a non-metallic pot, a non-metallic bowl for mixing, wooden spoons for mixing, a number of eyedroppers for oils, a non-metallic pan for heating herbal brews, sterilized bottles with lids for storing dry herbal mixtures, sterilized small dark-colored bottles with lids for storing mixtures of oils, small funnels to pour the oils into the bottles, labels for the bottles, and small strainers and cheesecloth if you need to strain the brews.

In purchasing a mortar and pestle, it is best to consider those made of metal or marble. However, copper or brass should not be exposed to certain substances as they can create dangerous vapors. Glass or ceramic mortars and pestles are too easily broken, while wooden ones tend to absorb odors and can splinter. You will use the mortar and pestle for grinding and crushing dried herbs.

The non-metallic pot or kettle should be heat resistant, and can be of glass, enamel, or Corning Ware. A two-quart or larger pan with a tight-fitting glass lid is best. If you need to carry the brew around your house, sometimes it is better to use a cast iron cauldron with a bail. You will use this pot whenever you need to heat an herbal brew. The lid prevents the escape of steam and essential oils.

The broad classification of "herbs" includes not only the traditionally known plant herbs, but also tree gums and resins, all of which have been used from the earliest recording of religion and magic. If you have garden space, you can grow the more common herbs, such as basil, chamomile, rosemary, sage, and thyme. However, if you do not have the time or space for a garden, you can purchase some herbs at your local markets. Often, Pagan supply shops, herbal stores, and catalog suppliers can furnish such uncommon ingredients as frankincense, sandalwood powder, and acacia gum. Purchase all gums and resins in a powder form, as they are extremely sticky and difficult to grind. Be sure that the herbs, gums, and resins have a strong fragrance. If they do not, they are not very fresh and should not be purchased.

Following is an alphabetical listing of those ingredients that are not too expensive or difficult to find. They all have their uses in magic, whether made into powders, brews, or incense. A list of important oils and their magical uses is given in the next chapter. I do not list any ingredient that can be dangerous, such as asafetida, foxglove, or sulfur. Many old recipes from medieval grimoires call for ingredients that are definitely harmful if burned in an enclosed area. If you read some of the ingredients contained in old magical incenses and such, it's no wonder that some ceremonial magicians were considered more than a little strange or saw demons coming out of the walls.

I do not list mandrake root, as what is sold on the market under that name is false ninety-nine percent of the time. These false roots also come with a very expensive price tag. There are other herbal and tree roots that are acceptable substitutes for true mandrake.

Although exact formulas for mixtures are given later in this chapter, I have included some magical uses within the descriptions as well.

HERBS

Absinthe: See wormwood.

Acacia gum (*Acacia senega*): Folk names for this gum are gum arabic, gum senegal, Egyptian thorn, Cape gum, and just plain acacia. The gum is used. Use it in protection mixtures, or for psychic development, such as clairvoyance. If you are fortunate enough to get acacia flowers, they can be burned as incense during love rituals. This is associated with the Sun.

Allspice (*Pimento officinalis*): Folk names are clove pepper, Jamaica pepper, and pimento. The immature fruit, particularly the shell or rind, which smells like a combination of cloves, juniper berries, cinnamon, and pepper, is used. Use it for protection, money, and to increase energy. This is associated with Mars and Mercury.

Aloe, Lignum (*Aquilaria agallocha*): Folk name is aloeswood. The resinous wood is used. Use for love and offerings to the deities. This is associated with Venus.

Angelica (*Angelica archangelica* or *Angelica officinalis*): Folk names are masterwort, archangel, and garden angelica. The leaves, roots, and seeds are used. Use it for exorcism and protection. Carry a piece of the root as an amulet. Burn the dried leaves to exorcise negative spirits. Add to the bath to remove curses and bad luck. This is associated with the Sun.

Anise (*Pimpinella anisum*): Folk names are anneys and aniseed. The seed is used. Use it for purification and protection. A small pillow of anise keeps away nightmares. This is associated with Jupiter, and sometimes Mercury.

Apple (*Pyrus malus*): Folk names are Silver Bough, fruit of the Underworld, and the tree of love. The blossoms, fruit, and cider is used. Use for love, healing, and binding. Apple cider can be substituted for blood in rituals and spells. This is associated with Venus.

Artemisia: See mugwort.

Ash (*Fraxinus excelsior* or *Fraxinus Americana*): Folk name is nion. The leaves, roots, and wood are used. Use for protection, prophecy, and healing. Scatter the leaves to the four directions while chanting for wealth, success, and healing. Poppets carved of ash root can be substituted for mandrake. This is associated with the Sun.

Avens (*Geum urbanum*): Folk names are herb bennet, star of the earth, yellow avens, golden star, and blessed herb. The entire herb is used. Use for protection, cleansing, and exorcism. Carry the root as an amulet against evil spirits. This is associated with Jupiter.

Balm (*Melissa officinalis*): Folk names are sweet balm, lemon balm, and melissa. The entire herb is used. Use for love and luck. This is associated with Jupiter.

Balm of Gilead (*Icica carana, Populus candicans, P. balsamifera, P. nigra,* or *Commiphora opobalsamum*): Folk names are Balm of Mecca and Balsam of Gilead. The buds are used. Use for protection, love, and spiritual manifestations. Carry to help mend a broken heart. This is associated with Saturn.

Balsam of Peru (*Myroxylon pereirae*): No folk names. The resin is used. Use for success. This is associated with the Sun.

Balsam of Tolu (*Myrospermum toluiferum*): Folk name is Balsamum Americanum. The liquid resin is used. Use for success. This is associated with the Sun.

Basil (*Ocimum basilicum*): Folk names are American dittany, alabahaca, and St. Joseph's wort. The entire herb is used. Use for purification, protection, exorcism, and love. Burn basil leaves to exorcise negative spirits. This is associated with Mars.

Bay laurel (*Laurus nobilis*): Folk names are bay, Grecian laurel, Indian bay, Roman laurel, Sweet Bay, and baie. The leaf is used. Use for protection, clairvoyance, exorcism, purification, and healing. Sleep with bay leaves under your pillow to attract prophetic dreams. This is associated with the Sun.

Bdellium (*Commiphora spp.*): There are no folk names. The gum resin is used. Use for protection and charms against diseases. This is associated with Mars.

Benzoin (*Styrax benzoin*): Folk names are Benjamen, gum benzoin, and Siam benzoin. The gum resin is used. Use for purification, business success, and séances. This is associated with the Sun.

Bergamot, Wild (*Monarda didyma*): Folk names are bee balm, horsemint, Oswego tea, and monarda. The leaves and flowers are used. Use for friendship and health. This is associated with Jupiter.

Bethroot (*Trillium pendulum and T. erectum*): Folk name is John the Conqueror, Wake Robin, Southern John, Lamb's quarters, and Indian shamrock. The root is used. Use for success, prosperity, and good luck. Carry a piece of root as a good fortune talisman. This is associated with the Sun. See John the Conqueror oil.

Betony (*Stachys officinalis, Betonica officinalis, Stachys betonica*): Folk names are bishopwort, lousewort, wood betony, and purple betony. The entire herb is used. This was a sacred herb to the Druids. Use for protection and purification. Sprinkle the crushed herb near all doors and windows to build up a wall of protection. It is associated with Jupiter.

Bistort (*Polygonum bistorta*): Folk names are patience dock, snakeweed, dragonwort, sweet dock, osterick, English serpentary, red legs, and Easter giant. The herb and root are used. Use for clairvoyance, divination, and psychic powers. This is associated with Saturn.

Boneset (*Eupatorium perfoliatum*): Folk names are thoroughwort, agueweed, teasel, feverwort, and Indian sage. The entire herb is used. Use for stuffing poppets. This is associated with Saturn.

Borage (*Borago officinalis*): Folk names are nepenthe, burrage, and bugloss. The leaves and flowers are used. Use for health and clairvoyance. This is associated with Jupiter.

Briar rose (*Rosa rubiginosa* or *Rosa canina*): Folk names are sweet briar, eglantine, dog rose, and Witches' brier. The flowers and hip fruit are used. Use for love, luck, honor, and riches. This is associated with Jupiter.

Broom (*Cytisus scoparius*): Folk names are genista, Scotch broom, and Irish broom. The entire herb is used. Use for purification and protection. Use branches to sweep an outdoor ritual area. Hang a sprig in your indoor ritual area as protection. Burn the herb to calm winds. This is associated with the Sun and Mars.

Burdock (*Arctium lappa*): Folk names are beggar's buttons, clotburr, happy major, burrseed, great burdock, and cocklebur. The herb and root are used. Use for protection and purification. This is associated with Mars.

Calamus (*Acorus calamus*): Folk names are sweet flag, sweet sedge, sweet rush, and aromatic rush. The ground root is used. Use for protection, binding, and wisdom. This is associated with the Moon.

Caraway (*Carum carvi*): Folk names are careum and carvi. The seed is used. Use for protection and love. Carry the seeds for protection and to strengthen the memory. This is associated with Mercury.

Cardamom (*Elettaria cardamomum*): Folk names are ebil, capalaga, ilachi, and Grains of Paradise. The dried, ripe seed is used. Use for love, creativity, and divination. This is associated with Mercury.

Carnation (*Dianthus caryophyllus*): Folk names are gilliflower and Jove's flower. The flower is used. Use for energy and protection. Place on the altar for added energy. This is associated with the Sun.

Cassia (*Cinnamomum cassia*): There are no folk names. The bark is used. Use for protection, healing, and success. Cinnamon is a substitute. This is associated with the Sun and Mercury.

Cedar (*Cedrus libani*, [*Cedar of Lebanon*—the Old World species], *Thuja occidentalis, Yellow cedar,* or *Arbor vitae*): Folk names are tree of life, arbor vitae, and cedar of Lebanon. The wood and needles are used. Use for exorcism and protection. Cedar was widely used by the ancient Babylonians, Egyptians, and Greeks. This is associated with Jupiter.

Chamomile (*Anthemis noblis, Matricaria chamomilla*): Folk names are maythen, manzanilla, camayle, ground apple, Roman chamomile, and vulgar or dog chamomile. The Roman chamomile has the scent of apples. The flowers are used. Use for prosperity, meditation, and sleep. Brew as a tea to help sleep. This is associated with the Sun.

Cinnamon (*Cinnamonum zeylanicum* or *Cinnamonum lauraceae*): Folk names are sweet wood and cassia. The bark and oil are used. Use for protection, healing, clairvoyance, raising spiritual vibrations, and prosperity. Burn to stimulate clairvoyance, heal, and attract money. This is associated with the Sun.

Cinquefoil (*Potentilla canadensia* or *Potentilla reptans*): Folk names are five fingers, five leaf grass, and sunfield. The entire herb is used. Use for protection, love, prosperity, and healing. Hang above the door for protection. This is associated with Jupiter.

Clary sage (*Salvia sclarea*): There are no folk names. The seeds and oil are used. Use for love. It can be used as a substitute for ambergris. This is associated with the Moon.

Clove (*Eugenia caryophyllata, Caryophyllus aromaticus* or *Syzygium aromaticum*): There are no folk names. The undeveloped flowers and buds are used. Use for protection, to stop gossip, to attract the opposite sex, and to strengthen the memory. This is associated with the Sun.

Copal gum (*Copalquahuitl*): There are no folk names. This pale yellow gum comes from Mexico, Central America, West Africa, and Zanzibar. It has an odor that smells rather like a mixture of lemon and pine. The resin is used. Use it for protection, exorcisms, purification, prosperity, and to enhance spirituality. This is associated with Jupiter.

Coriander (*Coriandrum sativum*): Folk names are cilantro, culantro, and Chinese parsley. The seed is used. Use for love and long life. This is associated with Mars.

Cubeb (*Piper cubeba*): Folk names are Java pepper and tailed pepper. The unripe fruit is used. Use for protection and physical attraction. This is associated with Mars.

Dandelion (*Taraxacum officinale*): Folk names are cankerwort, piss weed, wild endive, lion's tooth, and blow ball. The leaves and root are used. Use for divination and summoning spirits. This is associated with Jupiter.

Deerstongue or Deer's Tongue (*Frasera speciosa* or *Liastris odoratissima*): Folk name is wild vanilla. The leaf is used. Use for love and repelling gossip. This is associated with Venus.

Dill (*Anethum graveolens* or *Peucedanum graveolens*): Folk names are aneton, dilly, and dill weed. The entire herb and the seeds are used. Use for protection and love. This is associated with Mercury.

Dittany of Crete (*Origanum dictamnus*): Folk name is hop marjoram. The entire herb is used. Use for divination and spiritual manifestations. This is associated with Mercury.

Dock (*Rumex spp.*): Folk name is yellow dock. The seeds and root are used. Use it for healing, money, and business success. This is associated with Jupiter.

Dragon's blood (*Daemonorops draco* or *Dracaena draco*): Folk name is calamus draco. The red gum is used. Use for protection, purification, love, and energy. Put a piece under the mattress to treat impotency. A stick of dragon's blood can be used to draw protective runes. This is associated with Mars.

Elder (*Sambucus canadensis*): Folk names are yakori benestro, devil's eye, lady elder, Frau Holle, Hollunder, pipe tree, tree of doom, and elderberry. The leaves, berries, and flowers are used. Use for purification, cursing, seeing Fairies, visions, exorcism, and protection. Elder has a mixed reputation, according to various cultures. Scatter leaves to the four directions to bless or curse. This is associated with Venus.

Eucalyptus (*Eucalyptus globules*): Folk name is blue gum. The leaves, pods, and oil are used. Use for healing, cleansing, and stuffing poppets. Hang the leaves in a sickroom for healing. This is associated with the Moon.

Fern; *all spp.*: There are no folk names. Use the entire herb. Use for protection and rain. Burn outdoors to bring rain. This is associated with Saturn.

Frankincense (*Boswellia carterii* or *Boswellia thurifera*): Folk names are olibanum, olibans, and incense tree. The gum is used. Use for protection, purification, consecration, exorcism, and meditation. This is associated with the Sun.

Galangal (*Alpinia officinarum* or *Kaempferia galanga*): Folk names are catarrh root, Indian root, colicroot, chewing John, and low John. The root is used. Use for good luck, energy, and communicating with spirit teachers. This is associated with Mars and Jupiter.

Gardenia (*Gardenia spp.*): There are no folk names. The flower is used. Use for love and passion. Wear a fresh flower to attract a lover. This is associated with the Moon.

Ginger (*Zingiber officinale*): Folk names are African ginger and black ginger. The root is used. Place a root on the altar to attract Fairies and elemental spirits. This is associated with Mars and the Sun.

Grains of Paradise (*Ampelopsis grana paradisi* or *habzeli*): Folk names are Hungarian pepper, paprika, and sweet pepper. The pods and seeds are used. Use for protection. This is associated with Mars and sometimes Jupiter.

Graveyard Dust: See valerian and mullein.

Hazel (*Corylus spp.* and *Corylus avellana*): Folk name is coll. The nuts and wood are used. Use for fertility, protection, healing, good luck, and divination. String hazel nuts and hang in the house for good luck. This is associated with the Sun.

Heather (*Erica vulgaris* and *Calluna vulgaris*): Folk names are heath, common heather, and Scottish heather. The entire herb is used. Use for love, protection, and rainmaking. Burn with fern to attract rain. This is associated with Venus.

Heliotrope (*Heliotropium preuviana, H. europaeum,* or *H. arborescens*): Folk names are turnsole and cherry pie. Use for exorcism and clairvoyance. Put the flowers under your pillow for prophetic dreams. This is associated with the Sun.

High John the Conqueror Root (*Impomoea purga, Convolvulus jalapa,* or *Ipomea jalapa*): Folk name is jalap. The root is used. Use for prosperity and protection. Add the root to candle oils to strengthen them. Carry the root as a talisman against danger and trouble. This is associated with Saturn.

Honeysuckle (*Lonicera caprifolium* or *Lonicera periclymenum*): Folk name is woodbine. The flower is used. Use for prosperity and clairvoyance. Anoint a green candle with money oil (recipe in Chapter 65), then ring the candle with honeysuckle flowers. This is associated with Jupiter.

Horehound (*Marrubium vulgare*): Folk names are eye of the star, horehound, white horehound, maruil, soldier's tea, seed of Horus, bull's blood, haran haran, and Llewyd y cwn (Wales). The entire herb is used. Use for protection. This herb was revered by the ancient Egyptians and Romans. This is associated with Mercury.

Hyssop (*Hyssopus officinalis*): Folk names are ysopo, isopo, and holy herb. The entire herb is used. Use for purification, making holy water, and protection. Use a sprig to sprinkle the consecrated water around the circle. This is associated with Jupiter.

Jasmine (*Jasminum officinale* or *J. odoratissimum*): Folk names are moonlight on the grove and Jessamime. The flower is used. Use for love and prosperity. The flowers of *J. odoratissimum* retain their scent when dried. This is associated with Jupiter.

Juniper berries (*Juniperus communis*): There are no folk names. The berries and needles are used. Use for protection, love, and shamanic journeys. Put a sprig of juniper in your car or purse to protect from accidents. String the mature berries as a charm to attract a lover. This is associated with the Sun.

Khus-khus: See Vetiver.

Labdanum: See Rock rose.

Lavender (*Lavendula officinale* or *Lavendula vera*): Folk names are spike and elf leaf. The flower is used. Use for love, protection, healing, and purification. Carry a sachet of dried lavender flowers to see ghosts. Add to baths for healing and sleep. This is associated with Mercury and Jupiter.

Lemon (*Citrus limon*): Folk names are citrus medica, citronnier, and leemoo. The rind, juice, and oil are used. Use for divination, prophecy, and eloquence. Use the dried, grated peel in incenses. This is associated with Mercury.

Lemon verbena (*Lippia citriodora*): Folk names are yerba Louisa and cedron. The entire herb is used. Wear for protection and attracting the opposite sex. This is associated with Venus.

Low John: See Galangal.

Marigold (*Calendula officinalis*): Folk names are calendula, summer's bride, holigold, marybud, bride of the sun, pot marigold, and ruddes. The flower is used. Use for love, seeing Fairies, and clairvoyant dreams. Pick the flowers while the moon is in Virgo and a dream will reveal who stole something from you. Place the flower under the bed for prophetic dreams. This is associated with the Sun.

Marjoram (*Origanum marjorana*): Folk names are joy of the mountains, wintersweet, sweet marjoram, pot marjoram, and mountain mint. The entire herb is used. Use for love, protection, and purification. Put a little of the herb in each room for protection; change once a month. This is associated with Mercury.

Mastic (*Pistachia lentiscus*): Folk names are masticke and gum mastic. The gum resin is used. Use for clairvoyance, opening the Third Eye, and manifestations. The Egyptians were very fond of this gum in incenses. This is associated with the Sun.

Moonwort (*Botrychium lunaria*): Folk name is martagon. The crescent-shaped leaflets and the fronds are used. Use for love, divination, and breaking locks. It is similar to adder's tongue. This is associated with the Moon.

Motherwort (*Leonurus cardiaca*): Folk names are lion's ear, lion's tail, and throwwort. The flowering tops and the leaves are used. Use for protection. Stuff small pillows with this herb to ward off evil spirits. This is associated with Venus.

Mugwort (*Artemisia vulgaris*): Folk names are naughty man, old man, artemisia, Witch herb, muggons, sailor's tobacco, and felon herb. The entire herb is used. Use for protection, scrying, divination, and opening the Third Eye. Rub fresh leaves on magic mirrors and crystal balls to aid in scrying. Gather at Summer Solstice to protect against disease and misfortune. This plant's powers are strongest when picked on a Full Moon. This is associated with Venus.

Mulberry (*Morus nigra and M. rubra*): Folk names are black mulberry and red mulberry. The fruit and bark are used. Use for gaining wisdom and understanding the deeper Mysteries. This is associated with Mercury.

Mullein (*Verbascum thapsus*): Folk names are hag's taper, feltwort, doffle, candlewick plant, Aaron's rod, velvet plant, Jupiter's staff, shepherd's herb, flannel plant, and blanket leaf. The entire herb is used. Use for protection and healing. You can substitute mullein in any old magical recipes calling for "graveyard dust." Wear for courage. This is associated with Saturn.

Myrrh (*Commiphoria myrrha*): Folk names are karan, mirra balsom odendron, and gum myrrh tree. The gum or resin is used. Use for purification, consecration, protection, and healing. This resin is sacred to the Great Goddess and was once considered to be Her tears. This is associated with the Sun.

Nasturtium (*Nasturtium officinale* and *Tropaeolum majus*): Folk name is Indian cress. The flowers, leaves, and seeds are used. Use for protection, uncrossing, study, and psychic sight. This is associated with Saturn.

Nettle (*Urtica dioica* [the Greater] and *Urtica urens* [the Lesser]): Folk names are common nettle and stinging nettle. The entire herb is used. Use for protection and exorcism. Stuff poppets with this herb to remove a curse. This is associated with Mars.

Nutmeg (*Myristica fragrans*): Folk names are mace, macis, and arillus myristicae. Part used is the seed. Use for clairvoyance and divination. The dried kernel of this herb is the nutmeg, while the dried arillus of the seed is mace. This is associated with Jupiter and Mercury.

Oakmoss (*Evernia pruastri*): There are no folk names. Harvested from oak and spruce trees in central and southern Europe, this is a lichen. It has a slightly spicy smell. Use it in money spells and as a fixative in herbal mixtures for bags. Oakmoss was the base of the ancient Egyptian body powder called Chypre. This is associated with Mercury.

Onycha: See Rock rose.

Orris (*Iris florentina*, *Iris germanica*, or *Iris pallida*): Folk names are Queen Elizabeth root, Florentine iris, and yellow flag. The root is used. Use for love, wisdom, and power. This is associated with Venus, the Sun, and Jupiter.

Patchouli (*Pogostemon cablin* or *Pogostemon patchouli*): Folk name is pucha-pot. The entire herb is used. Use for passion, love, divination, clairvoyance, and remembrance of the dead. It also is helpful for protection. This is associated with the Sun and Mars.

Pennyroyal (*Mentha pulegium*): Folk names are squaw mint, run-by-the-ground, lurk-in-the-ditch, pudding grass, tickweed, and mosquito plant. The entire herb is used. Use for protection and exorcism. Can be used in summer incenses. This is associated with Venus.

Pepper (*Capsicum spp.*): Folk names are cayenne, red pepper, and capsicum. The berry is used. Use for protection and exorcism. Very stinging smoke when burned. This is associated with Mars.

Peppermint (*Mentha piperita*): Folk names are lammint and brandy mint. The entire herb is used. Use for healing, cleansing an area, and purification. Drink peppermint tea when you are cold or tired. This is associated with Venus and the Moon.

Pine (*Pinus spp.*): There are no folk names. The needles and cones are used. Use for purification, energy, fertility, and dreams. Burn crushed, dried pine needles to purify a room. Add to a bath sachet for cleansing. This is associated with Mars.

Red Saunders: See Sandalwood.

Rock Rose (*Cistus creticus*): Folk names are European rock rose, labdanum, onycha, and frostwort. The gum resin is used. Use for success and prosperity. The oil smells like ambergris. The gum resin is a natural exudation, and burns with a clear flame. This is associated with the Sun.

Rose (*Rosa spp.*): There are no folk names. The flower is used. Use for love, fertility, clairvoyant dreams, and healing. The rose was said to be one of the flowers that sprang from the blood of Adonis. The most fragrant of the species are the *Rosa centifolia* (cabbage rose), *R. damascena* (damask rose), and *R. indica* (the old-fashioned tea rose). Burn dried petals to produce clairvoyant dreams. This is associated with Venus.

Rosemary (*Rosemarinus officinalis*): Folk names are dew of the sea, incensier, sea dew, ros maria, and guardrobe. The needles are used. Use for purification, healing, intellectual pursuits, love, and protection. Burn the dried needles to clean, purify, and exorcise. Rosemary yields its oil to heated white wine better than to water. This is associated with the Sun, and sometimes the Moon.

Rowan (*Fraxinus aucuparia, Pyrus aucuparia,* or *Sorbus aucuparia*): Folk names are mountain ash, Witchwood, quickbane, wicken tree, roynetree, wiggin ran tree, sorb apple, and roden-quicken. The wood and twigs are used. Use for protection, divination, summoning spirits, and healing. The seeds are poisonous, as they contain cyanide. This is associated with the Sun.

Rue (*Ruta graveolens*): Folk names are ruta, bashoush, German rue, garden rue, hreow, herbygrass, and herb of grace. The entire herb is used. Use for protection, intellectual pursuits, exorcism, and purification. This herb is traditionally an antidote against spells and curses. This is associated with the Sun and Saturn.

Saffron (*Crocus sativus*): Folk names are autumn crocus, Spanish saffron, and crocus. The flower is used. Use for purification, clairvoyance, and healing. Saffron is very expensive. Dried marigold petals are a substitute. Drink saffron tea to increase clairvoyant powers. Cleanse the hands with the tea before healing rituals. This is associated with the Sun and Jupiter.

Sage (*Salvia officinalis* varieties): Folk names are garden sage, red sage, and white sage. The entire herb is used. Use for healing, wisdom, and prosperity. Hang over the door to absorb negativity. This is associated with Jupiter.

St. John's Wort (*Hypericum perforatum*): Folk names are Herba Jon, Goat Weed, Tipton Weed, and Klamath Weed. The entire herb is used. Use for protection and exorcism. Hang in the house to protect. Wear to strengthen your will power. This is associated with the Sun and Mercury.

Sandalwood (*Santalum album*): Folk names are santal and white saunders. This is best purchased in a powdered form. The white to light brown variety is known as white sandalwood, while the red color is often called red saunders. It has a deep, clean scent, and is usually imported from India and the Far East. The wood is used. Use it for exorcism, protection, healing, and enhancing spirituality. The white is associated with the Moon and Mercury. Red sandalwood (*Pterocarpus santalinus* and *S. rubrum*) is a different tree, and is associated with Venus.

Savory, Summer (*Satureia hortensis*): Folk name is bean herb. The entire herb is used. Use for love, sexual attraction, dreams, and creativity. This is associated with Venus.

Savory, Winter (*Satureia montana*): The uses are the same as summer savory.

Silverweed (*Potentilla anserine*): Folk names are prince's feathers, trailing tansy, goosewort, silvery cinquefoil, moor grass, and wild agrimony. The entire herb is used. Use for success and prosperity. This is associated with Jupiter.

Spearmint (*Menta spicata* or *M. viridis*): Folk names are garden mint, lamb mint, green spine, and spire mint. The entire herb is used. Use for healing and love. This is associated with Venus.

Squill (*Urginea scilla*): Folk names are white squill, red squill, and maritime squill. The bulb is used. Use for prosperity, success, and psychic visions. This is associated with Mars.

Star anise (*Illicium verum* or *Illicium anisatum*): Folk name is Chinese anise. The seed is used. Use for clairvoyance. Use a seed to make an herbal pendulum. This is associated with Jupiter.

Storax (*Liquidamber orientalis* or *L. styraciflua*); the American species is called sweet gum: The folk name is sweet gum. The wood and inner bark are used. Use for purification and success. The storax mentioned in ancient manuscripts was the *Styrax officinale*, a close relative of benzoin. This is associated with the Sun, and sometimes Mercury and Saturn.

Thistle (*Sonchus spp., Carbenia benedicta, Cnicus benedictus,* or *Carduus benedictus*): Folk names are holy thistle and blessed thistle. The entire herb is used. Use for protection and energy. This is associated with Mars.

Thyme, Garden (*Thymus vulgaris*), or **Wild Thyme** (*Thymus serpyllum*): Folk names are common thyme and mother of thyme. The entire herb is used. Use for clairvoyance, cleansing, pleasant dreams, and purification. Burn to purify a magical room. Use in small pillows to avoid nightmares. Wear a sprig to funerals to avoid being contaminated with negative emotions. This is associated with Venus.

Tobacco (*Nicotiana tabacum*): There are no folk names. The leaf is used. Use for exorcism. Can be used as a substitute for sulfur in old magical recipes. This is associated with Mars.

Tonka beans (*Coumarouna odorata* or *Dipsteryx odorata*): Folk names are tonqua, tonquin bean, and coumara nut. The bean is used. These usually come from Venezuela. Although they have a vanilla scent, they must not be eaten or used in place of vanilla extract! Use whole in spells for money and love attraction. Carry as a love talisman, and to attract good fortune. This is associated with Venus.

Uva Ursi (*Arctostaphylos uva-ursi* or *Arbutus uva-ursi*): Folk names are bearberry and kinnikinnick. The leaf is used. Use for astral projection and any magic work. This is associated with Venus.

Valerian (*Valeriana officinalis*): Folk names are phu, all heal, amatilla, set well, capon's tailor, garden heliotrope, vandal root, and St. George's herb. The herb and root are used. Use for love, harmony, sleep, and purification. Some cats find valerian as enticing as catnip. This is associated with Mercury and Saturn.

Vanilla (*Vanilla aromatica* or *Vanilla planifolia*): There are no folk names. The bean is used. The bean is poisonous if ingested in large quantities. Use for love. This is associated with Jupiter.

Vervain (*Verbana officinalis* or *Verbana hastate*): Folk names are Juno's tears, herb of grace, pigeon's grass, enchanter's plant, holy herb, verbena, van-van, and herb of enchantment. The entire herb is used. Use for love, purification, and protection. The Druids used a sprig to sprinkle consecrated water at rituals. Carry to ward off psychic attack. Hang on the bed to repel nightmares. This is associated with Venus and Mercury.

Vetiver (*Vetiveria zizanioides*): Folk names are khus-khus, vetivert, and vertivert. The root is used. Use for love, protection, and prosperity. The root of this herb smells like faded violets. This is associated with Venus.

Violet (*Viola tricolor* or *Viola odorata*): Folk names are blue violet and sweet violet. The flower is used. Use for love, healing, good fortune, and protection. Carry the flower to attract good fortune. This is associated with Venus.

Wormwood (*Artemisia absinthium*): Folk names are old woman, absinthe, and crown for a king. This herb is poisonous if too much is ingested; better not to swallow it or drink it in anything. The entire herb is used. Use for clairvoyance, scrying, divination, prophecy, astral projection, and protection. The scent of this herb comes only when it is dried. Carry a leaf when you want to change your life or your outlook on it. This is associated with Mars.

Yarrow (*Achillea millefolium*): Folk names are seven year's love, sanguinary, old man's pepper, soldier's woundwort, knight's milfoil, thousand seal, arrow root, wound wort, stanch weed, devil's bit, snake's grass, and stanch grass. The flower is used. Use for love, clairvoyance, exorcism, divination, prophetic dreams, and protection. Wear to ward off negativity and stop all fear. Put under the pillow for dreams of a future spouse. This is associated with Venus.

Yerba Buena (*Satureja douglasii*): No folk name. The leaf is used. Use for binding and protection. This is associated with Saturn.

WICCAN AND COMMON NAMES OF HERBS

Sometimes you will encounter an herbal name that makes no sense to you, and you can't find it in books. This may be because the writer is using a Wiccan name for an herb, instead of a common name. The following list will help you sort through such discoveries.

WICCAN NAME	COMMON NAME
Adam and Eve	Lungwort
Adder's Mouth	Stitch Wort
Adder's Tongue	Dogstooth Violet
Ass's Ear	Comfrey
Bear's Ear	Auricula
Bear's Foot	Stinking Hellebore
Beehive	Snail Plant
Beggar's Tick	Cuckhold
Bird's Eye	False Hellebore
Bird's Tongue	European Ash
Black Boy Resin	Xanthorrhaea Arborea
Bloody Fingers	Foxglove
Bulls' Eyes	Marsh Marigold
Bull's Foot	Coltsfoot
Calf's Snout	Toadflax
Candlemas Maiden	Snowdrop
Candlewick Plant	Mullein
Catgut	Hoary Pea
Cat's Eye	Star Scabious
Cat's Foot	Canada Snake Root
Cat's Foot or Paw	Ground Ivy
Cat's Milk	Wartwort
Chicken Toe	Crawley Root
Cock's Comb	Yellow Rattle
Cow's Tail	Canada Fleabane
Crow Foot	Cranesbill
Crown for a King	Wormwood
Devil's Bit	True Unicorn Root
Devil's Milk	Wartwort
Dew of the Sea	Rosemary
Dog's Tongue	Hound's Tongue
Donkey's Eyes	Cowage Plant
Dove's Foot	Cranesbill

Dragon's Claw	Crawley Root
Dragon's Eye	Nephalium Loganum
Dragonwort	Bistort
Duck's Foot	American Mandrake
Dwale	Deadly Nightshade
Earth Smoke	Fumitory
Elfwort	Elecampane
Enchanter's Plant	Vervain
Eye of the Star	Horehound
Fairy Fingers/Gloves	Foxglove
Five Finger Grass	Cinquefoil
Flesh and Blood	Tormentil
Fox Tail	Club Moss
Foal's Foot	Coltsfoot
Frog's Foot	Bulbous Buttercup
Goat's Beard	Vegetable Oyster
Goat's Foot	Ash Weed
Golden Star	Avens
Graveyard Dust	Valerian, mullein
Hare's Foot	Clover
Hedgehog	Medicago Intertexta
Honey Lotus	Melilot
Horse Tail	Scouring Rush
Horse Tongue	Hart's Tongue
Hound's Tongue	Vanilla Leaf
Jew's Ear	Fungus on Elder or Elm
John the Conqueror	Bethroot
Joy of the Mountains	Marjoram
Lamb's Tongue	Ribwort Plantain
Little Dragon	Tarragon
Lizard's Tail	Breast Weed
Lizard's Tongue	Sauroglossum
Love-In-Idleness	Pansy
Love Parsley	Lovage

Loveroot	Orris Root
Low John	Galangal
Lucky Hand	Satyrion, Male Fern
Maiden's Ruin/Lad's Love	Southernwood
Master of the Woods	Woodruff
Masterwort	Angelica
May Lily	Lily of the Valley
Mistress of the Night	Tuberose
Mother's Heart	Shepherd's Purse
Mouse Ear	Mouse Blood Wort
Mouse Tail	Common Stonecrop
Negro Head	Vegetable Ivory
Old Man's Beard	Fringe Tree
Ox Tongue	Bugloss
Password	Primrose
Queen of the Meadow	Meadowsweet
Rabbit's Foot	Field Clover
Ram's Head	American Valerian
Seven Years' Love	Yarrow
Shepherd's Heart	Shepherd's Purse
Sleep Wort	Lettuce
Snake Head	Balmony
Snake Milk	Blooming Spurge
Snake's Tongue	Adder's Tongue Fern
Sorcerer's Violet	Periwinkle
Squirrel Ear	White Plantain
Stag Horn	Club Moss
Starflower	Borage
Star of the Earth	Avens
Starweed	Chickweed
Starwort	Aster
Stinking Goose Foot	Chenopodium Foetidum
Swine Snout	Dandelion
Thousand Seal	Yarrow

Thunder Plant	Houseleek
Toad	Toadflax
Unicorn Horn	True Unicorn Root
Wax Dolls	Fumitory
Witch Grass	Dog Grass
Witch Herb	Mugwort
Witches' Aspirin	White Willow Bark
Witches' Bells	Foxglove
Witches' Briar	Brier Rose
Witchwood	Rowan
Wolf's Claw	Lycopodium
Wolf's Foot	Bugle Weed

SUBSTITUTIONS

Frequently, you will find that you are out of a certain herb or oil, but need to make up an incense, powder, or oil, or, you want to try a recipe in another book and either don't have what the writer calls for, or the recipe names herbs that could be dangerous. In any of these instances, you can always substitute another product. The following list will help you determine what you need.

RECIPE CALLS FOR	SUBSTITUTION
Acacia	Gum Arabic, Mimosa
Ambergris	Clary Sage
Arabic Gum	Frankincense, Gum Mastic
Asafoetida	Tobacco, Valerian
Balm of Gilead	Rose Buds, Gum Mastic
Belladonna	Tobacco
Benzoin	Gum Arabic, Gum Mastic
Camphor Oil	Lavender Oil
Carnation	Rose Petals with Clove Oil
Cassia	Cinnamon
Cactus	Pepper
Cedar	Sandalwood

Cinquefoil	Clover
Clove	Mace, Nutmeg
Copal	Frankincense, Cedar
Deerstongue	Woodruff, Vanilla
Dittany of Crete	Gum Mastic
Dragon's Blood	Frankincense and Red Sandalwood
Eucalyptus Oil	Lavender Oil
Galangal	Ginger Root
Gum Bdellium	Dragon's Blood
Hellebore	Tobacco
Hemlock	Tobacco
Hemp	Nutmeg, Star Anise, Bay
Henbane	Tobacco
Hyssop	Lavender
Jasmine Oil	Rose Oil
Lemongrass	Lemon Peel
Mace	Nutmeg
Mandrake	Tobacco
Mastic, Gum	Gum Arabic, Frankincense
Mistletoe	Mint, Sage
Neroli Oil	Orange Oil
Nightshade	Tobacco
Oakmoss	Patchouli
Red Sandalwood	Sandalwood and Dragon's Blood
Rose Geranium	Rose
Saffron	Orange Peel
Sulfur	Tobacco, Club Moss
Wolfsbane	Tobacco
Wood Aloe	Sandalwood
Wormwood	Mugwort
Yew	Tobacco

TREES AND WANDS

It has long been the custom that the woods of certain trees are used in ritual fires and for magic wands. What were called Sabbat needfires were traditionally made of nine different kinds of wood: oak, ash, cherry, rowan, birch, holly, hawthorn, fir, and pine. The wood of the elder and willow were never burned, as it was thought such a practice brought bad luck. On Samhain, a special fire for seeing visions was kindled with juniper, cedar, and sandalwood.

If you plan to harvest wood from a tree for a wand, be certain to ask permission of the nature spirits, dryads, or Fairies that live in the tree before doing so. Tradition says that if the branches and leaves of the tree suddenly stir or shake, the answer is "No."

Almond: Wands are for general magic. This is associated with the Sun.

Ash: Wands are used for general magic, plus healing and solar. This is associated with the Sun.

Elder: A tree with a mixed reputation for good and ill, wands are used for exorcising evil spirits. This is associated with the planet Venus.

Hawthorn: Wands are powerful for all spells. Never cut hawthorn without leaving an offering of milk and honey poured out onto the ground. This is associated with the planet Mars.

Hazel: Wands are the most powerful and are used for white magic and healing. Forked hazel twigs are made into divining rods. This is associated with the Sun.

Laurel: Wands counteract negativity and restriction. This is associated with the Sun.

Oak: This was the high holy tree of the Druids. Wands are for protection and inspiration, as well as being all-purpose. This is associated with both the Sun and Jupiter.

Rowan: Wands of this very magical tree are for knowledge, divination, and summoning spirits. This is associated with the Sun.

Willow: Wands are used for moon magic, divination, healing, and poetic inspiration. Also, a forked twig can be used as a divining rod, particularly when seeking water. This is associated with the Moon.

Herbal Powders

When making up herbal powders, you will need to grind the herbs as fine as possible in your mortar and pestle. While you are grinding, you must concentrate upon and visualize the goal for which you are making the powder. Both the act of grinding and the concentration strengthen the power of the herbs to fulfill your desire. Use the chant (see page 388) when mixing the herbs and oils together.

It is best to make up only a cup or less of the mixture at any time, although if you plan to share the powder with a friend, you could make two cups. Making the herbal powder in small quantities keeps it from being stored too long and losing some or all of its creative energy.

To make powders, you will need a mortar and pestle, a non-metallic bowl, a wooden spoon, an eyedropper, alcohol for cleansing the eyedropper if you use more than one essential oil, and measuring spoons or a small scale for measuring out the herbs. To store the powder, use dry, clean jars with tight lids. Be sure to label each jar and date it. Many herbal powders look very similar when mixed, thus making it difficult to know which is which.

When mixing and working with herbs, be aware that some herbs and resins, such as dragon's blood and yellow dock, will stain carpets, clothes, and such. The stains often cannot be removed.

Magical powders are made to sprinkle around the house, in your wallet or purse, in the mailbox, or put into little bags to carry or hang in specific areas. They are not meant to be consumed.

To make a magical powder, first collect all the supplies you will need. As you grind the herbs in your mortar and pestle, and then mix them with the oils, focus on the goal you desire. Grind the herbs as fine as you can. They should be powdery when finished. Chant the following verse while you do the last mixing.

When a "pinch" of an herb is called for in a magical recipe, this means the tiny amount you can hold between your thumb and forefinger.

You should use separate eyedroppers for each essential oil. If you do not have enough eyedroppers, flush the inside of the dropper with alcohol when you switch from one oil to another.

When you use the powder, sprinkle it on the altar in a heart for love, a dollar sign for money and success, a circle for working with the psychic and divination, a pentagram for protection, a knot for binding, or an equal-arm cross for healing. You may choose other symbols if you wish. Just remember to keep their shapes simple. While you sprinkle the powder, chant the verse appropriate to the mixture and desire. A chanting verse is given at the end of each magical mixture recipe.

EMPOWERING CHANT FOR MIXING

CHANT:

Elements of Wind and Fire, bring to me my heart's desire.
Water, Earth, my wish fulfill. Strong my magic, strong my will.
Within these Elements fourfold, the power grows and so will hold.

☽ Business Success Powder

TIME: The waxing moon or Full Moon; or on a Wednesday or Sunday.

> *Herbs:*
> 1/2 teaspoon cinnamon
> 1 tablespoon sage
> 5 tablespoons yellow dock
> 2 tablespoons squill
> 2 teaspoons crumbled bay leaves
>
> *Oils:*
> 5 drops honeysuckle oil
> 4 drops violet oil

INSTRUCTIONS: Sprinkle this around your place of business, particularly at the door, the cash register, and the mailbox.

CHANT:

Tides of business, flow my way.
Bring me money that will stay.

☽ Divination Powder

TIME: The Full Moon or New Moon; or on a Monday or Wednesday.

> *Herbs:*
> 2 tablespoons acacia

1/2 teaspoon cardamom
1/4 cup Dittany of Crete
1/2 teaspoon grated lemon peel
1/4 cup gum mastic
pinch of nutmeg

Oils:
6 drops lotus oil
3 drops heliotrope oil

INSTRUCTIONS: Sprinkle this lightly on your altar, or on the table where you plan to lay out cards or the runes. You can also sprinkle a little in the box or drawer where you keep your divination tools.

CHANT:

I see the future and the past.
The answers come both true and fast.

☾ Exorcism Powder

TIME: The waning moon or New Moon; or on a Saturday.

Herbs:
1 teaspoon bay
1/8 cup cedar powder
1/2 cup frankincense powder
pinch of black pepper
1/4 cup rue
1/2 cup sandalwood powder
1 tablespoon dragon's blood
1/4 cup vervain

Oils:
7 drops bay oil
2 drops cedar oil

INSTRUCTIONS: Sprinkle this around a home or a building that is troubled by negative spirits.

CHANT:

I call upon the psychic tide
That nothing evil here abide.

☽ General Healing Powder

TIME: The waxing moon or Full Moon; or on a Sunday or Wednesday.

Herbs:
1/2 cup lavender
1 tablespoon spearmint
2 tablespoons bay

Oils:
6 drops frankincense oil
2 drops apple cider (apple blossom oil may be substituted for cider)

INSTRUCTIONS: Sprinkle this lightly in each corner of the room belonging to a sick person. Or, it can be sprinkled on your altar when you do healings.

CHANT:

Cleanse the body. Cleanse the heart.
Cleanse the soul. All ill depart.

☽ Good Luck Powder

TIME: The waxing moon or Full Moon; or on a Sunday or Thursday.

Herbs:
1/4 teaspoon allspice
1/2 cup angelica
1/2 cup yellow dock
1/2 cup vetiver
1 cup lemon balm

Oils:
7 drops apple blossom oil
2 drops bergamot oil

INSTRUCTIONS: This powder can be sprinkled lightly into your purse or wallet, as well as in your mailbox and near your main entry door. You can also put some in a small bag and carry it with you.

CHANT:

Good luck, come in. Bad luck, depart.
Good fortune, enter my life and heart.

☾ Love Powder

TIME: The waxing moon or Full Moon; or on a Monday or Friday.

Herbs:
1/2 cup lavender
1/2 cup ground orris root
1 cup rose petals

Oils:
4 drops gardenia oil
3 drops jasmine oil

INSTRUCTIONS: Put some of this powder in a small bag and carry it with you.

CHANT:

I call into the mists of time
To bring to me a love sublime.

☾ Meditation Powder

TIME: The waxing moon or Full Moon; or on a Monday or Saturday.

Herbs:
1/2 cup chamomile
1/8 cup frankincense powder
1/2 cup hyssop
1/8 cup gum mastic

Oils:
7 drops lilac oil
3 drops acacia oil
3 drops heliotrope oil

INSTRUCTIONS: Sprinkle a little of this powder around the room when you meditate.

CHANT:

Oh, door of wisdom, open for me,
Show me the truth and set me free.

☽ Money Powder

TIME: The waxing moon or Full Moon; or on a Thursday or Sunday.

Herbs:
1/4 teaspoon cinnamon
1/4 cup cinquefoil
1 cup oakmoss

Oils:
2 drops bayberry oil
2 drops cinnamon oil
1 drop mint oil

INSTRUCTIONS: This powder can be sprinkled lightly into your purse or wallet, as well as in your mailbox and near your main entry door. You can also put some in a small bag and carry it with you.

CHANT:

Coins and paper, silver and gold,
Give me all my life can hold.

☽ Prosperity Powder

TIME: The waxing moon or Full Moon; or on a Sunday or Thursday.

Herbs:
1/8 cup sage
1/2 cup squill
1/2 cup oakmoss
1/8 cup vetiver
1/2 cup chamomile
1 teaspoon cinnamon

Oils:
2 drops honeysuckle oil
2 drops jasmine oil
7 drops styrax oil
5 drops vanilla oil

INSTRUCTIONS: Use this in the same manner as you do the Money Powder. This powder, however, attracts not only money, but also good luck, good health, and positive opportunities.

CHANT:

Balance my life, and give to me
The greatest, fullest prosperity.

☾ Protection Powder

TIME: The waning moon or New Moon; or on a Tuesday or Saturday.

Herbs:
1 tablespoon dragon's blood
1/4 teaspoon anise seed
1/4 cup marjoram
1/4 cup betony
1/2 cup calamus root
1/2 cup patchouli
1 tablespoon pennyroyal
1/8 cup wormwood

Oils:
6 drops carnation oil
7 drops sandalwood oil

INSTRUCTIONS: Lightly sprinkle this powder in your vehicle as well as your home.

CHANT:

Keep me safe from evil and harm.
I ask protection as I speak this charm.

HERBAL BREWS

Herbal brews are made by simmering herbal mixtures in a pot. These mixtures are then carried through the house while still steaming, or cooled, strained, and bottled to use for sprinkling. A list of herbal teas is given separately at the end of this chapter.

To make brews, you will need a mortar and pestle, a non-metallic pot with a tight lid, a cast-iron cauldron with a lid (if the recipe stipulates), a wood spoon, measuring cups or a small scale for measuring the herbs, and a supply of spring water. Avoid using tap water if at all possible, as it is contaminated with chlorine and other pollutants. If you cannot collect rainwater, buy good bottled water.

Herbal brews may also be simmered in a ceramic-lined potpourri pot, or a small crockpot. However, if you want to spread the herbal fumes into every room of your house, it is best to heat the brew in a cast-iron cauldron or a kettle, and then carry the cauldron through the entire house while it is still steaming.

Visualize your desired goal while grinding and mixing the herbal mixture of your choice. As you mix the herbs together the last time, say the empowering chant. Heat two cups of spring or bottled water to a boil in your cauldron or kettle. Slowly stir the herbs into the boiling water while chanting the verse given at the end of the herbal mixture. Remove the kettle from the heat. Quickly add any oils you need, and put on the lid. Let the brew stand for about five to ten minutes. Remove the lid, and carry the brew slowly through your house. When you have finished, set the cauldron or kettle on your altar until it is cool. Pour the remaining liquid and herbs outside onto the ground, if possible.

It is not advantageous to keep a brew after using it. It is best to make up a new brew as you need it.

An appropriate chanting verse is given at the end of each magical mixture recipe. Say this chant as you carry the brew throughout the house.

EMPOWERING CHANT FOR MIXING

CHANT:
Elements of Wind and Fire, bring to me my heart's desire.
Water, Earth, my wish fulfill. Strong my magic, strong my will.
Within these Elements fourfold, the power grows and so will hold.

☾ *Calmness Brew*
TIME: Best mixed on a Wednesday, Thursday, or Friday.

> *Herbs:*
> 1/2 cup chamomile
> 1 cup hyssop
> 2 tablespoons grated lemon peel

Oil:
7 drops frankincense oil

CHANT:

Calm as the eye of a storm I stand.
Spiritual magic is in my hand.

☾ Exorcism Brew

TIME: Best mixed on a Tuesday or Saturday.

Herbs:
1/2 teaspoon anise seed
1 tablespoon dragon's blood
1/4 cup bay leaves
1 cup vervain

Oils:
2 drops bay oil
5 drops clove oil

CHANT:

Be gone, foul evil spirits, all.
This is my word, so heed the call.

☾ God Brew

TIME: Best mixed on a Sunday.

Herbs:
1 cup lemon balm
1/4 cup cedar powder
1/4 cup bay leaves
1 teaspoon nutmeg

Oil:
7 drops pine oil

CHANT:

Honor to You, Hunter, Lover,
Consort to the Holy Mother.

☾ Goddess Brew

TIME: Best mixed on a Monday.

Herbs:
1 cup rose petals
1 cup lavender
1/2 cup marigold petals
1 tablespoon powdered myrrh

Oil:
5 drops jasmine oil

CHANT:
Honor to the One in Three,
My love I give You. Please bless me.

☾ Healing Brew

TIME: Best mixed on a Sunday, Wednesday, or Thursday.

Herbs:
1 cup hyssop
1/4 cup spearmint
1/4 cup sage

Oils:
4 drops violet oil
9 drops sandalwood oil

CHANT:
Erase the illness. Remove the pain.
Let those sick be whole again.

☾ Love Brew

TIME: Best mixed on a Monday or Friday.

Herbs:
1 cup lemon balm
1 teaspoon basil
1/2 cup vetiver
1 tonka bean

Oils:
6 drops apple blossom oil
10 drops ambergris oil

Chant:
Spiritual love is in this brew,
Send me love, I do ask you.

☾ Prosperity Brew

TIME: Best mixed on a Sunday or Thursday.

Herbs:
1/4 cup sage
1/4 cup oakmoss
1/4 cup hazel leaves, if possible
1 High John root
1 cup chamomile

Oils:
4 drops bayberry oil
2 drops mint oil

CHANT:
Send jingling money, happiness, health,
Satisfaction, joy, and wealth.

☾ Protection Brew

TIME: Best mixed on a Tuesday or Saturday.

Herbs:
1/8 cup rosemary
1 tablespoon dragon's blood
1/2 cup pennyroyal
1 cup nettles

Oils:
4 drops sandalwood oil
3 drops bergamot oil

CHANT:

Tie and bind all negativity.
Reverse all spells sent against me.

☾ Purifying Brew

TIME: Best mixed on a Sunday or Monday.

> *Herbs:*
> 1 cup hyssop
> 1 cup rue
> 1 cup pine needles
>
> *Oils:*
> 6 drops frankincense oil
> 6 drops myrrh oil

CHANT:

Pure as a primal ocean, pure as a gentle rain,
This water will cleanse and purify all again.

HERBAL TEAS

Herbal teas as opposed to herbal brews are meant to be drunk. If you suspect you might be allergic to any herbal ingredients, be cautious about using herbal teas. Do not make up too much of the herbal tea mixture at one time.

To make teas, you will need a mortar and pestle, measuring spoons for measuring the herbs, a ceramic teapot, and pieces of cheesecloth or a similar item for enclosing the herbs while in the pot. It is not necessarily to grind the herbs for tea as finely as you do for herbal powders. If you store the tea mixture in tightly closed containers, you can make up larger amounts at a time.

As you grind the herbs, say the empowering chant. Heat the teapot by filling it with hot water. Empty this water, put in the herbs, and fill the pot again with hot water. Let it steep for about ten to thirteen minutes. While the tea is steeping, hold your hands around the teapot and chant the appropriate verse for the goal desired. Do the chanting three or five times. Then drink the tea.

An appropriate chanting verse is given at the end of each magical mixture recipe.

EMPOWERING CHANT FOR MIXING

CHANT:

Elements of Wind and Fire, bring to me my heart's desire.
Water, Earth, my wish fulfill. Strong my magic, strong my will.
Within these Elements fourfold, the power grows and so will hold.

☽ Calmness Tea

TIME: Best mixed on a Monday or Wednesday.

Herbs:
1/4 cup chamomile
1/4 cup lemon balm

CHANT:

Stillness. Peacefulness. Calm.
Restfulness. Quiet. Soothing balm.

☽ Love Tea

TIME: Best mixed on a Monday or Friday.

Herbs:
1 tablespoon jasmine blossoms, or jasmine tea
pinch of grated orange peel
1/4 cup rose petals

CHANT:

Joy and love will replace strife.
Bring a love into my life.

☽ Prophetic Dreams Tea

TIME: Best mixed on a Monday.

Herbs:
4 tablespoons anise seed
1 tablespoon mugwort

Dreams of the future, I ask of thee.
This is my will, and so mote it be.

☾ Psychic Abilities Tea

TIME: Best mixed on a Monday or Saturday.

Herbs:
1/2 cup borage blossoms
1/2 teaspoon cinnamon
1/8 teaspoon thyme

CHANT:

Open the gate that has no key.
Open my psychic senses for me.

☾ Spiritual Healing Tea

TIME: Best mixed on a Sunday, Wednesday, or Thursday.

Herbs:
1 cup bergamot
pinch of grated orange peel
2 tablespoons spearmint

CHANT:

Light of healing, strong and bright,
Bring me healing now tonight.

CHAPTER 65

Incenses and Oils

In my opinion, the best magical incenses are blends that can be burned on charcoal blocks. These special blocks can be purchased at any Pagan shop. Do not in any circumstances use barbecue briquettes, as they create dangerous fumes in enclosed spaces. Make only small amounts of herbal incenses at a time, and keep them in jars with tight-fitting lids.

The incense burner for mixtures needs to have chains attached to it so you can carry it. Fill the censer one-third full of clean sand. This makes it easy to remove the buildup of ashes with a spoon. The first time you use the censer, purify it by burning frankincense or rosemary in it.

Although many apprentices to magic think spells or incenses made using a ceremonial magic grimoire will work better, this isn't true, and could bring the apprentice into immediate trouble with some of the dubious ingredients. Many such spells call for blood or noxious or dangerous ingredients. The use of blood always can be replaced with incense, such as the incense of Abramelin, or dragon's blood and frankincense combined. For materializations, use the herb known as Dittany of Crete.

Some believe oils should be made from a real herb or animal, and you should never use synthetic oils. An authentic jasmine oil will cost you hundreds of dollars for a very tiny bottle, and if you use ambergris or civet oil you are promoting the slaughter of whales and civet cats. Good synthetic oils will work just as well as the high priced authentic oils, so don't waste your money.

Take care in using some of the following oils as some people may develop a rash if they get the oil on their skin. Also, some oils, such as bergamot and vervain, will take the varnish off furniture if spilled on it.

Some oils are easier to find, and cheaper in price, than other oils. Take your time finding a reliable supplier. Also, start out with just a few essential oils.

By using a good quality almond oil as a base, a magician can mix essential oils with it and thus stretch the mixture. Almond oil by itself protects from evil influences and raises vibrations. It is also an oil of the Sun.

ESSENTIAL OILS

Acacia: Has very high vibrations and is helpful when worn for meditation and developing psychic powers. This oil also aids in divination. Use it for anointing the altar and candles. An oil of the Sun.

Ambergris: Since the authentic product comes from whales, please buy the synthetic or use clary sage, which resembles ambergris in scent. It promotes pure love and high spiritual vibrations. An oil of Jupiter.

Apple blossom: Anoint candles for love rituals, and wear to attract happiness and success. An oil of Venus.

Basil: This oil creates harmony of all kinds. An oil of Mars.

Bay: This is a very powerful scent that helps with protection, visions, meditation, divination, exorcism, and purification. It also draws power in general. Now you know why some men love bay rum aftershave. An oil of the Sun.

Bayberry: Use for protection and to become receptive to the psychic. Anoint green candles with this oil to bring prosperity into the home. An oil of Mercury.

Bergamot: Another powerful scent, it is used for protection and attracting prosperity. An oil of Jupiter.

Carnation: This is another oil that attracts power. Use for producing energy, healing, and consecration. An oil of the Sun.

Cedar wood: Traditionally, this oil is said to repel demons and negative spirits, while it attracts good spirits. Use it for peace, wealth, and good fortune. An oil of Jupiter.

Cinnamon: It increases the power of any incense to which it is added, as it has high vibrations. Use it for spiritual magic, clairvoyance, healing, wealth, problem-solving meditations, and protection. An oil of the Sun.

Clove: Use this oil to drive away illnesses and evil influences. An oil of the Sun.

Cypress: This Saturn oil vibrates on high astral planes. Use it for blessing, consecration, protection, peace, controlling the will, and screening out negative vibrations.

Fir: This promotes peace and contentment. It also cleanses an atmosphere. An oil of Jupiter.

Frangipani: This erotic scent is used for physical love. An oil of the Moon.

Frankincense: This is one of the most powerful and sacred of all oils. Use it to anoint yourself and the altar. Also use it for exorcism, protection, blessing, meditation, and visions. An oil of the Sun.

Gardenia: This highly magnetic oil is useful for protection, mending marital problems, and attracting pure love. An oil of the Moon.

Heliotrope: This oil has very high spiritual vibrations. Use it for peace, harmony, clairvoyance, meditation, and psychic development. An oil of the Sun.

High John the Conqueror: Although this oil can be used for power, justice, and courage, its primary influence is to gain success in court cases. An oil of Saturn.

Honeysuckle: This oil stimulates the mind and creativity. Also use it for prosperity and love. An oil of Jupiter.

Hyacinth: Use it for peace, sleep, and psychic dreams. An oil of Venus.

Hyssop: This is an excellent oil to use for all kinds of rituals and spells. It is also said to increase finances and purify. An oil of Jupiter.

Jasmine: An oil of the Moon and Jupiter, jasmine is highly spiritual. It has many magical and mystical qualities. Use it for psychic protection, balance, peace, restful sleep, meditation, and astral projection. The authentic oil comes from *Jasminum officinale*.

Lavender: Lavender can be used for anointing, cleansing, exorcism, and good health. An oil of Mercury.

Lemon: The oil, oleum limonis, is very fragrant. Use for divination, prophecy, and eloquence. An oil of Mercury.

Lilac: Sometimes called the Far Memory oil, lilac is used when working on past lives, either to remember them or to learn from them. Use it also for clairvoyance, creativity, and peace. An oil of Venus.

Lotus: This was a very sacred oil to the Egyptians, and was an oil of the Moon and magic. Use it for anointing, psychic protection, happiness, good health, fertility, good fortune, blessing, visions, astral travel, and harmony.

Magnolia: This is excellent for meditation, psychic development, and harmony. An oil of the Moon.

Mimosa: Use it for prophetic dreams and healing. An oil of Saturn.

Mint: This scent is said to be very magnetic for attracting money and good fortune. Use it for prosperity and business success. An oil of Mercury.

Musk: Traditionally called the sex scent, this oil attracts both sexes. Also use it for courage, determination, and anointing. An oil of Saturn.

Myrrh: This very sacred oil has extremely high spiritual vibrations, and is ruled by both Saturn and the Great Goddess. Use it for exorcism, protection, purification, meditation, and healing. Sweet cicely smells similar. An oil of the Sun and Saturn.

Orange blossom: Also called neroli, this oil attracts love and is said to induce proposals of marriage. An oil of the Sun.

Orris root: The oil of this root is used for love and desire, concentration, creativity, and strengthening the will power. An oil of Venus, the Sun, and Jupiter.

Patchouli: This is a very powerful scent, with occult qualities. Use it for a peaceful separation in a relationship, to ward off negativity and evil, and to keep away unwanted persons. An oil of the Sun and Mars.

Pine: An oil of the Horned God, pine is excellent for exorcism and defense, as well as purifying an atmosphere. An oil of Mars.

Rose: An oil of Venus, use it for love, beauty, artistic creativity, health, peace, dispelling anger, and anointing.

Rosemary: This is one of the most powerful of herbal oils for protection and exorcism. Put it on the doors and windows of a house to purify and bless. Use it also for peace, good health, determination, courage, psychic development, prophetic dreams, and healing. An oil of the Sun and the Moon.

Sandalwood: This is a very powerful and spiritual oil that raises vibrations and purifies. Use it for good health, meditation, visions, protection, and opening the doors to past lives. The white is an oil of the Moon and Mercury; red is an oil of Venus.

Strawberry: This attracts wealth and good fortune. An oil of Venus.

Styrax: This oil is very difficult to find, but is excellent, as it vibrates on a high spiritual plane. Use it for spiritual growth and meditation. An oil of the Sun, Mercury, and Saturn.

Vanilla: Traditionally, this is said to be arousing to women. Also use it for restoring energy and gaining extra power during rituals. An oil of Jupiter.

Vervain: This was a very magical herb to the Celts. Use it for protection, anointing, attracting material good fortune, stimulating creativity, exorcism, and purification. An oil of Venus and Mercury.

Violet: At one time, violets were said to be sacred to the Fairy Queen and the Goddess of the Witches. Use it to ward off evil, for healing and good health, to promote reunions of separated families, and to attract wealth. An oil of Venus.

Wisteria: This oil creates a bridge between this earth plane and the higher spiritual planes. It is very powerful for divination, illumination, astral travel, and psychic work. An oil of Saturn.

Ylang ylang: Sometimes called the Flower of Flowers, this oil attracts the opposite sex and love. It also can soothe marital problems. Also use it to help find a job. An oil of Venus and Mercury.

HERBAL INCENSES

The following incenses are meant to be burned on charcoal blocks. To avoid setting off smoke alarms or causing breathing problems in a ritual room, burn only small amounts of the incense mixtures at a time.

Larger amounts of incense mixtures can be made at a time, if the mixtures are stored in glass jars with very tight lids. Be sure to label each jar with the name of the mixture. These incenses may be burned during both rituals and spellwork.

Grind the herbs for the incense you choose. In a non-metallic bowl, mix the herbs with the oils while saying the empowering chant. As you spoon the incense into a clean jar, say the verse appropriate to the incense mixture.

When a "pinch" of an herb is called for in a magical recipe, this means the tiny amount you can hold between your thumb and forefinger.

An appropriate chanting verse is given at the end of each magical mixture recipe.

EMPOWERING CHANT FOR MIXING

CHANT:
Elements of Wind and Fire, bring to me my heart's desire.
Water, Earth, my wish fulfill. Strong my magic, strong my will.
Within these Elements fourfold, the power grows and so will hold.

☾ Imbolc

TIME: Best mixed the week prior to February 2.

Herbs:
1/2 cup acacia gum
1/2 cup hyssop
1/4 cup lavender

Oils:
7 drops apple blossom oil
5 drops bergamot oil

CHANT:
New beginnings. New goals. New life.

☾ Spring Equinox

TIME: Best mixed the week prior to March 21.

Herbs:
1/4 teaspoon allspice
1/2 cup bergamot
1/2 cup lemon balm
1/8 teaspoon grated lemon peel

Oils:
10 drops hyssop oil
2 drops lemon oil
3 drops rosemary oil

CHANT:
Growing Sun, the year's well begun.

ℂ *Beltane*

TIME: Best mixed the week prior to May 1.

Herbs:
1/4 cup lavender
1/2 cup rose petals
1 cup sandalwood powder

Oils:
6 drops ambergris oil
9 drops magnolia oil
4 drops musk oil

CHANT:
Lord of the Forest, Lady of May.

ℂ *Summer Solstice*

TIME: Best mixed the week prior to June 21.

Herbs:
1/4 teaspoon ginger
1 cup mastic gum
1/4 cup marigold petals
1/2 cup mugwort

Oils:
9 drops heliotrope oil
9 drops lilac oil
5 drops honeysuckle oil

CHANT:
High time of the Fairies. High time of the Sun.

☽ Lughnasadh

TIME: Best mixed the week prior to August 1.

Herbs:
1/2 cup benzoin gum
1/4 teaspoon cloves
1/2 cup juniper berries
2 tablespoons myrrh

Oils:
7 drops frankincense oil
7 drops sandalwood oil

CHANT:
Prepare for the harvest of fields and of thoughts.

☽ Autumn Equinox

TIME: Best mixed the week prior to September 21.

Herbs:
3 tablespoons cedar
1/4 cup juniper berries
1 cup sandalwood powder
3 tablespoons sage

Oils:
10 drops frankincense
6 drops myrrh

CHANT:
The year wheel turns, and harvest comes.

☽ Samhain

TIME: Best mixed the week prior to October 31.

Herbs:
1/4 cup Dittany of Crete
1/2 cup mastic gum
1/4 cup mugwort
1/2 cup patchouli

1/4 cup squill
1/2 cup wormwood
1/4 cup yarrow

Oils:
9 drops lotus oil
3 drops patchouli oil
5 drops wisteria oil

CHANT:
The Veil between the worlds is thin. I hear the ancestors speak again.

☾ Winter Solstice

TIME: Best mixed the week prior to December 21.

Herbs:
1 cup sandalwood powder
1/2 cup crushed pine needles
1/2 cup vervain

Oils:
3 drops clove oil
3 drops fir or pine oil

CHANT:
The old Sun dies. The new is born.

☾ Sun

TIME: Best mixed on a Sunday.

Herbs:
1/2 cup acacia gum
1/4 teaspoon bay
1/4 cup benzoin gum
3 tablespoons frankincense
4 tablespoons patchouli
1/4 cup rue
1/4 cup yarrow

Oils:
7 drops acacia oil
2 drops bay oil
3 drops cinnamon oil

CHANT:
Brightness. Glory. The God.

☾ *Moon*

TIME: Best mixed on a Monday.

Herbs:
1 cup sandalwood powder
3/4 cup rose petals

Oils:
7 drops gardenia oil
7 drops jasmine oil

CHANT:
Silver shine. Mysteries. The Goddess.

☾ *Binding*

TIME: Best mixed on a Tuesday or Saturday.

Herbs:
1/2 cup acacia gum
5 tablespoons calamus root
2 tablespoons dragon's blood
1/4 cup patchouli
1/4 cup vervain

Oils:
10 drops patchouli oil
4 drops vervain oil

CHANT:
Bind. Restrain. Restrict.

☽ Breaking a Curse

TIME: Best mixed on a Saturday.

Herbs:
1/2 cup sandalwood powder
1/2 cup blessed thistle
1 tablespoon tobacco
1/8 cup valerian
1/4 cup wormwood

Oils:
10 drops frankincense oil

CHANT:

Break. Dissolve. Obliterate.

☽ Communication with Spirits

TIME: Best mixed on a Monday or Saturday.

Herbs:
1/2 cup acacia gum
5 tablespoons benzoin gum
1/2 cup Dittany of Crete
1/2 teaspoon ginger
1/2 cup juniper berries

Oils:
6 drops acacia oil
4 drops Balm of Gilead oil
1 drop bay oil
9 drops lotus oil

CHANT:

Spirits of the Otherworld, speak.

☽ Consecration

TIME: Best mixed on a Monday.

Herbs:
1/8 cup acacia gum

1 teaspoon cardamom
1/2 cup hyssop
1 cup sandalwood powder

Oils:
7 drops frankincense oil
9 drops lotus oil

CHANT:

Bless. Consecrate. Make holy.

☾ *Divination*

TIME: Best mixed on a Monday, Wednesday, or Saturday.

Herbs:
4 tablespoons bistort
1 teaspoon cinnamon
1/2 cup mastic gum
1 cup sandalwood powder
1/2 cup yarrow

Oils:
12 drops sandalwood oil
9 drops wisteria oil

CHANT:

Foretell the future, oh sacred Ones.

☾ *Exorcism*

TIME: Best mixed on a Tuesday or Saturday.

Herbs:
1/2 cup acacia gum
1/4 cup angelica
1/4 cup calamus root
2 tablespoons cedar
1 teaspoon clove

Oils:
5 drops bay oil
10 drops myrrh oil

CHANT:
Return to the Otherworld realm of darkness.

☽ *Funeral*

TIME: Best mixed on a Saturday.

Herbs:
1 tablespoon cedar
4 tablespoons frankincense
1 cup sandalwood powder
1 teaspoon thyme

Oils:
12 drops cypress oil
7 drops styrax oil

CHANT:
Death. Rest. Rebirth.

☽ *Handfasting*

TIME: Best mixed on a Friday.

Herbs:
1/2 cup bergamot
1 teaspoon coriander
1/2 cup lavender
5 tablespoons orris root
1/2 cup rose petals
1 cup red saunders or sandalwood powder
1 teaspoon savory

Oils:
5 drops rose oil
9 drops violet oil
7 drops vanilla oil

CHANT:

Two become one.

☽ Healing

TIME: Best mixed on a Sunday, Wednesday, or Thursday. If the healing is for a surgery, mix on a Tuesday.

> *Herbs:*
> 1 teaspoon bay
> 5 tablespoons juniper berries
> 1 cup lavender
> pinch of rosemary
> 1/2 cup sandalwood powder
>
> *Oils:*
> 12 drops apple blossom oil
> 2 drops cinnamon oil

CHANT:

Balance. Purify. Heal.

☽ House or Vehicle Blessing

TIME: Best mixed on a Monday or Thursday.

> *Herbs:*
> 1 cup sandalwood powder
> 2 tablespoons rosemary
> 1 teaspoon thyme
> 1/2 cup vervain
>
> *Oils:*
> 4 drops bay oil
> 4 drops cedar oil

CHANT:

Bless. Protect.

☾ *Initiation*

TIME: Best mixed on a Monday.

Herbs:
1/8 cup betony
1/2 cup hyssop
1/8 cup calamus root
1 cup sandalwood powder

Oils:
7 drops frankincense oil
9 drops heliotrope oil

CHANT:
New path. New life.

☾ *Karma*

TIME: Best mixed on a Saturday.

Herbs:
4 tablespoons avens
1/8 cup calamus root
1/2 cup hyssop
1/2 cup patchouli

Oils:
9 drops myrrh oil
9 drops patchouli oil

CHANT:
Balance the scales. Set free.

☾ *Love*

TIME: Best mixed on a Monday or Friday.

Herbs:
1 cup red saunders or sandalwood powder
4 tablespoons valerian
1/2 cup vervain

Oils:

9 drops carnation oil

9 drops violet oil

CHANT:

Joy. Happiness. Love.

☾ Meditation

TIME: Best mixed on a Monday, Friday, or Saturday.

Herbs:

1/2 cup mastic gum

1/4 cup mugwort

1 teaspoon nutmeg

1/2 cup wormwood

1/2 cup yarrow

Oils:

5 drops jasmine oil

10 drops lilac oil

CHANT:

Calm center. Open the heart.

☾ Money

TIME: Best mixed on a Sunday or Thursday.

Herbs:

1 teaspoon allspice

1/2 cup benzoin gum

1/4 cup squill

1/2 cup vetiver

Oils:

3 drops bayberry oil

6 drops bergamot

6 drops honeysuckle oil

CHANT:

Silver. Gold. Security.

☾ Prophecy

TIME: Best mixed on a Monday, Wednesday, or Saturday.

Herbs:
1/2 cup acacia gum
1 teaspoon cardamom
1 teaspoon cinnamon
1/4 cup mastic gum
1/4 cup mugwort
1/2 cup sandalwood powder

Oils:
7 drops acacia oil
4 drops cinnamon oil

CHANT:
The past. The future. Guidance.

☾ Prosperity

TIME: Best mixed on a Sunday or Thursday.

Herbs:
2 teaspoons cinnamon
1/2 cup hyssop
1 cup sandalwood powder

Oils:
12 drops strawberry oil

CHANT:
Desires. Goals. Plans.

☾ Protection

TIME: Best mixed on a Tuesday or Saturday.

Herbs:
1/4 cup acacia gum
1/4 cup patchouli
1 cup sandalwood powder

Oils:
9 drops patchouli oil
2 drops rosemary oil

CHANT:
Boundaries of protection, build.

☾ *Psychic Opening*

TIME: Best mixed on a Monday.

Herbs:
1/8 cup acacia gum
1 teaspoon nutmeg
1 cup sandalwood powder

Oils:
4 drops acacia oil
9 drops honeysuckle oil

CHANT:
As in the body, so in the soul. Open the doors.

☾ *Purifying*

TIME: Best mixed on a Monday or Saturday.

Herbs:
1/4 teaspoon anise
1/8 cup angelica
1/2 cup hyssop
3/4 cup sandalwood powder

Oils:
7 drops frankincense oil
9 drops lotus oil

CHANT:
Make all clean again.

☾ Scrying

TIME: Best mixed on a Monday.

Herbs:
1/8 cup benzoin gum
1/2 cup Dittany of Crete
1/2 cup mastic gum
1/4 cup mugwort

Oils:
5 drops Balm of Gilead oil
10 drops heliotrope oil

CHANT:
All is clear, far and near.

☾ Spiritual Awareness

TIME: Best mixed on a Monday, Friday, or Saturday.

Herbs:
1/8 cup frankincense
1/2 cup mugwort
1 cup sandalwood powder

Oils:
9 drops lotus oil
9 drops wisteria oil

CHANT:
My inner eyes are open. I see the truth.

☾ Success

TIME: Best mixed on a Sunday or Thursday.

Herbs:
1/8 cup benzoin gum
1/2 cup lemon balm
1 cup sandalwood powder

Oils:
2 drops bay oil
7 drops High John oil

CHANT:
Goals are met. Success at last.

☾ *Celtic*

TIME: Best mixed during a waxing moon, during any of the eight holy day rituals.

Herbs:
4 tablespoons cedar
1/2 cup lavender
1/2 cup mastic gum
1/2 cup vervain

Oils:
9 drops lavender oil
13 drops lilac oil

CHANT:
Circles of stone. Runes of bone.

☾ *Egyptian*

TIME: Best mixed during a waxing moon, during any of the eight holy day rituals.

Herbs:
1/2 cup acacia gum
1/4 cup frankincense
1/8 cup myrrh

Oils:
14 drops lotus oil

CHANT:
Lotus pools so still. Sistrum music fill.

☾ *Norse*

TIME: Best mixed during a waxing moon, during any of the eight holy day rituals.

Herbs:
1/2 cup calamus root
3 tablespoons cinnamon
1/2 cup juniper berries

Oils:
4 drops bayberry oil
2 drops pine oil

CHANT:

Thorr's hammer. Freyja's necklace. Odin's ravens.

OIL MIXTURES

Mixing blends of oils is much easier than mixing up herbal mixtures. For example, you can measure the drops of oil directly into a dark-colored, sterilized bottle with a tight lid. Take care that the bottle is large enough for the one tablespoon of almond oil you put in first. Be sure to label the bottles.

You will need eyedroppers, alcohol for cleansing the eyedropper when using different essential oils, and a number of dark-colored bottles with tight-fitting lids. Bottles that come with eyedroppers make dispensing much easier. You can use the oil mixtures to coat candles for spells, add to herbal mixtures for amulet bags, or even to add in small amounts to bath water.

Add one tablespoon of good quality almond oil to each recipe of essential oils. This extends the essential oils, and also makes them blend together more smoothly. Some writers suggest adding a drop of benzoin as a preservative to the oils. However, benzoin has a sharp odor that I do not find appealing. If the bottles are sterilized before use, and tightly capped afterward, you should have no trouble with mold.

As you carefully measure each oil into the dark-colored bottle, say the following empowering chant. When the oil mixture is finished, hold the bottle in your hands and say the verse appropriate to the oil mixture.

An appropriate chanting verse is given at the end of each magical mixture recipe.

EMPOWERING CHANT FOR MIXING

CHANT:

Elements of Wind and Fire, bring to me my heart's desire.
Water, Earth, my wish fulfill. Strong my magic, strong my will.
Within these Elements fourfold, the power grows and so will hold.

☽ *Anointing Oil*

TIME: The waxing moon or the Full Moon.

> *Oils:*
> 13 drops lotus oil
> 7 drops frankincense oil
> 15 drops sandalwood oil

CHANT:

Purification, sanctity,
Bless this oil. So mote it be.

☽ *Binding Oil*

TIME: The waning moon or the New Moon.

> *Oils:*
> 10 drops patchouli oil
> 9 drops vervain oil
> 2 drops pine oil

CHANT:

Forever tie, forever bind,
The powers of body, soul, and mind.

☽ *Breaking a Spell Oil*

TIME: The waning moon or the New Moon.

> *Oils:*
> 10 drops frankincense oil
> 2 drops cedar oil
> 13 drops lotus oil

CHANT:

The spell that was made is unmade.
The words that were said are not said.

☽ Divination Oil

TIME: The waxing moon or the Full Moon.

> *Oils:*
> 10 drops heliotrope oil
> 10 drops magnolia oil
> 12 drops wisteria oil

CHANT:

Lords of the future, let me see.
Open the inner doors to me.

☽ Exorcism Oil

TIME: The waning moon or the New Moon.

> *Oils:*
> 2 drops cedar oil
> 14 drops patchouli oil
> 1 drop rosemary oil
> 14 drops myrrh oil

CHANT:

Be gone, you spirits of doubt and fear.
Return to your plane. You can't stay here.

☽ Fast Money Oil

TIME: The waxing moon or the Full Moon.

> *Oils:*
> 5 drops bayberry oil
> 2 drops cinnamon oil
> 10 drops bergamot oil
> 13 drops vervain oil

CHANT:

Money, money, beautiful money.
Make my life as sweet as honey.

☾ Healing Oil

TIME: The waxing moon or the Full Moon.

> *Oils:*
> 9 drops lavender oil
> 15 drops lotus oil
> 10 drops mimosa oil

CHANT:

Powers of healing and purity,
Enter this oil. Set illness free.

☾ Initiation Oil

TIME: The waxing moon or the Full Moon.

> *Oils:*
> 9 drops frankincense oil
> 7 drops hyssop oil
> 15 drops lotus oil
> 9 drops myrrh oil

CHANT:

Sacred blessings come to me.
This is my will. So shall it be.

☾ Karma Oil

TIME: The waning moon or the New Moon.

> *Oils:*
> 20 drops sandalwood oil
> 10 drops lilac oil

CHANT:

Karmic laws of good and ill,
Set me free. This is my will.

☾ Love Oil

TIME: The waxing moon or the Full Moon.

> *Oils:*
> 10 drops ylang ylang oil
> 10 drops gardenia oil
> 5 drops rose oil

CHANT:

Companion and lover, hear my cry.
I seek you now. Our time is nigh.

☾ Meditation Oil

TIME: The waxing moon or the Full Moon; if for past lives, the waning moon or the New Moon.

> *Oils:*
> 3 drops cinnamon oil
> 15 drops jasmine oil
> 15 drops lilac oil
> 4 drops frankincense oil

CHANT:

In the silence, there is wisdom.
In the quiet, there is guidance.

☾ Opening the Psychic Oil

TIME: The waxing moon or the Full Moon; if for communication with spirits, the waning moon or the New Moon.

> *Oils:*
> 15 drops heliotrope oil
> 2 drops frankincense oil
> 15 drops lotus oil

CHANT:

Strengthen my psychic senses.
Open my inner eyes.

☾ *Prosperity Oil*

TIME: The waxing moon or the Full Moon.

> *Oils:*
> 10 drops honeysuckle oil
> 7 drops violet oil
> or
> 10 drops strawberry oil
> 1 drop mint oil

CHANT:

Happiness, prosperity,
Riches of life, please bring to me.

☾ *Protection Oil*

TIME: The waning moon or the New Moon.

> *Oils:*
> 6 drops bergamot oil
> 7 drops cypress oil
> 15 drops vervain oil

CHANT:

Protect! Deflect!
Guard! Ward!

☾ *Purifying Oil*

TIME: The waxing moon or the Full Moon.

> *Oils:*
> 10 drops hyssop oil
> 7 drops jasmine oil
> 10 drops lavender oil

CHANT:

Purify! Sanctify!
Cleanse my soul. Make me whole.

☾ Sabbat Oil

TIME: The waxing moon or the Full Moon.

> *Oils:*
> 7 drops acacia oil
> 3 drops carnation oil
> 7 drops hyssop oil
> 10 drops lotus oil
> 7 drops myrrh oil

CHANT:

Ancient Witches of the past,
Bring me power that will last.

☾ Scrying Oil

TIME: The waxing moon or the Full Moon; if for past events, the waning moon or the New Moon.

> *Herbs:*
> 1/4 teaspoon of ground mugwort
>
> *Oils:*
> 10 drops acacia oil
> 7 drops heliotrope oil
> 10 drops lilac oil

CHANT:

Into the future I cast my sight
That I may read the signs tonight.

☾ *Success Oil*

TIME: The waxing moon or the Full Moon.

> *Oils:*
> 1 drop bay oil
> 15 drops High John oil
> 2 drops mint oil

CHANT:

Success and joy accompany me,
Whatever I say, wherever I be.

☾ *Spring Oil*

TIME: The waxing moon or the Full Moon.

> *Oils:*
> 10 drops apple blossom oil
> 12 drops hyssop oil
> 7 drops lavender oil

CHANT:

Spring is here!
Be of good cheer!

☾ *Summer Oil*

TIME: The waxing moon or the Full Moon.

> *Oils:*
> 12 drops ambergris oil (or substitute)
> 7 drops magnolia oil
> 3 drops musk oil
> 2 drops rose oil

CHANT:

Time of the Fairies, time of the Sun,
Bring in the Sunshine. Summer's begun!

☽ *Autumn Oil*

TIME: The waxing moon or the Full Moon.

> *Oils:*
> 4 drops cedar oil
> 7 drops cinnamon oil
> 14 drops sandalwood oil

CHANT:

Bless the harvest! Bless the workers!

☽ *Winter Oil*

TIME: The waxing moon or the Full Moon.

> *Oils:*
> 3 drops clove oil
> 6 drops fir or pine oil
> 10 drops vervain oil

CHANT:

The Sun lies low. The cold is here.
Winter Solstice is almost here.

☽ *Sun Oil*

TIME: The waxing moon or the Full Moon.

> *Oils:*
> 14 drops acacia oil
> 3 drops bay oil
> 3 drops cinnamon oil

CHANT:

Lord of the Sun, your power's begun.

☾ Full Moon Oil

TIME: The waxing moon or the Full Moon.

Oils:
2 drops frangipani oil
5 drops gardenia oil
9 drops jasmine oil
12 drops sandalwood oil

CHANT:

Lady of the Moon, grant me a boon.

☾ New Moon Oil

TIME: The waning moon or the New Moon.

Oils:
7 drops cypress oil
9 drops lotus oil
9 drops sandalwood oil

CHANT:

Orb of black, send the power I lack.

☾ Celtic Oil

TIME: Any time.

Oils:
1 drop cedar oil
9 drops lavender oil
2 drops mint oil
10 drops vervain oil

CHANT:

Ancient gods of the Celtic way,
Give me wisdom now, I say.

☽ Egyptian Oil

TIME: Any time.

> *Oils:*
> 9 drops frankincense oil
> 9 drops lotus oil
> 9 drops myrrh oil

CHANT:

Ancient gods of the Egyptian way,
Give me wisdom now, I say.

☽ Norse Oil

TIME: Any time.

> *Oils:*
> 8 drops bayberry oil
> 5 drops cinnamon oil
> 3 drops pine oil

CHANT:

Ancient gods of the Viking way,
Give me wisdom now, I say.

CHAPTER 66

Candle Magic

Certain types of magic can be accomplished by chanting and burning colored candles. This is a very old magical practice, mentioned in surviving records of ancient Egypt. Candle magic is one of the easiest forms of magic for the apprentice to learn and practice. It requires a minimum of supplies and knowledge.

The Witch should have a supply of different-colored candles on hand at all times, and a basic variety of essential oils, herbs, oil mixtures, non-flammable candleholders, and a knife to carve words into the surface of the candle. To attract things into your life, burn the candles during the waxing moon. To repel energy or get rid of things in your life, burn the candles during the waning moon.

To further empower a candle, cut a pentagram or a few words about the basic spell into the side of it. Coat the candle with an oil mixture before burning it. To attract a certain desire to you, rub the oil on the candle from the wick to the end. To repel certain events or energies, rub the oil from the end to the wick. Choose an appropriate and complementary incense to burn during the spell. An appropriate chanting verse is given with each candle spell.

All candle spells should be repeated for three, five, seven, or nine consecutive days. Place the candle in a safe place where it is not near anything flammable, and sits sturdily in a metal or other nonflammable holder.

For certain spells, you can use a seven-day candle that comes in a tall glass. Scratch a few words of your desire in the top of the wax and then put a few drops of appropriate oil on it. These candles usually come in green, white, or red wax only, although on rare occasions you will find one that has several colors in layers.

Some writers recommend burying any remaining candle wax or throwing it into running water after a spell. The writers say that burying the wax is necessary because of spell power still in the wax. However, if a spell is done properly, the power will be disseminated into the astral by the time the spell is finished. Therefore, there is nothing wrong with dispensing of the remaining wax in the garbage can.

Candles can also be used to communicate with spirits. In this type of candle burning, the magician asks that the spirit make the candle flame flicker or change color in response to questions. A flame with a bluish tinge means a spirit is present.

CANDLE COLORS

Black: Although many people are uncomfortable using black candles, this is one of the most powerful colors available for magic. Black can absorb and remove any vibration or spellwork. It can repel any dark magic or negativity, even thought forms. Black can be used to reverse, uncross, bind, protect, release, and break up blockages. It also is useful for creating confusion and discord among your enemies. However, misuse with selfish or evil intent can cause spells or energy to backlash.

Blue: Use light blue for inspiration, gaining wisdom, finding the truth, good health, inner peace, harmony in the home, and working on your personal spiritual growth. Use royal blue for loyalty, group success, and occult power.

Brown: This color always attracts Earth Elementals. Use for communicating with nature spirits, attracting money, financial success, intuition, study, and grounding.

Gold or light yellow: Use for good fortune, quick money, divination, knowledge, healing, happiness, intuition, a change of luck, working with those in positions of authority, and contacting higher powers.

Green: Use for abundance, fertility, material gain, success, good fortune, marriage, healing, communing with nature, a fresh outlook on life, and wealth in general. This color is especially good for balancing an unstable situation.

Indigo: Use it to stop gossip and lies, balance karma, neutralize negative magic or energy, meditation, or unfair competition.

Magenta: This high vibrational color is usually burned with candles of other colors to speed up the action. When burned alone, it influences quick changes.

Orange: This color brings about major changes. Use it for encouragement, sudden changes, prosperity, creativity, success, energy, and when studying.

Pink: This color attracts the purest form of love, friendship, spiritual awakening, healing, and warm familial situations.

Purple: Use this color to remove curses and bad luck, drive away evil, and influence people who have power over you. It also is good for success, higher psychic ability, wisdom, progress, protection, gaining magical knowledge from the Otherworld, and making contact with spirits.

Red: Use for energy, sexual potency, passionate love, strong will power, and good health. It can also be used to counter psychic attack.

Silver or light gray: This color can neutralize any situation and repel destructive forces. Also use it for stability, meditation, and the development of psychic abilities.

White: Use this color for purity, truth, spirituality, contacting your spirit helpers, raising the vibrations, balancing the aura, and destroying negative energy. Whenever in doubt about a candle color, use white.

Yellow: This color is useful for strengthening the intellect, creativity, confidence, concentration, mental clarity, knowledge, counseling, business ventures, and studying medicine.

Planetary Colors

The energies of the planets are also used in magical candle spells. When working with this type of energy, choose a candle according to the following list.

Earth: brown and shades of brown.

Jupiter: royal blue, purple.

Mars: all shades of red.

Mercury: yellow, orange.

Moon: silver, pink, light gray, white, pale blue.

Saturn: black, very dark blue, very dark purple.

Sun: gold, deep yellow.

Venus: pink, green, pale blue.

CANDLE SPELLS

Candle spells are governed by the same Wiccan laws and morals as other spells. Do not use them to gain control over someone, harm another creature, or try to take something or someone away from another person.

☽ Attracting Love

TIME: Best done on a Friday during a waxing moon.

ITEMS NEEDED: Two light green, light blue, or pink candles; Love or rose oil; Love powder; Love incense; a few rose petals.

INSTRUCTIONS: It is best to never do magic to make another person love you. Not only will you invite negative karma, but you will have great difficulty getting that person to stay in love with you. Instead, scratch your name on one of the candles, and "unknown lover" on the other candle. Oil the candles, and set them side by side on your altar. Sprinkle the powder in a heart shape about the candles. Scatter the rose petals within the heart shape. Light the candles. Chant the verse three times. Leave the candle to burn out.

CHANT:

Kissed by the stars in the heavens,
Warmed by the sun above,
All spirits of joy and happiness,
Bring me my own true love.

☽ Binding

TIME: Best done on a Saturday during a waning moon.

ITEMS NEEDED: One black candle; one foot of black thread; patchouli or Binding oil; Protection powder; Binding incense.

INSTRUCTIONS: Never do magic to control another person, unless that person is attempting to harm you and yours. Before doing a binding spell, however, you must be certain that your actions are not contributing to the problem. If you are part of the problem, you will bind yourself as well as the offending person.

Oil the black candle, and place it on your altar. Sprinkle protection powder in each corner of every room of your house. Also, sprinkle it on the altar in a double-circle around the black candle. Tie seven knots in the black thread as you chant the verse. Begin at one end of the thread, and end at the other. Place the thread near the candle. Leave the candle to burn completely out. If there is any wax left, bury it and the black knotted thread. You can dispose of the wax in the garbage can, but never leave it inside your house when the spell is finished. The thread can be burned.

CHANT:

What I bind stays bound.
What goes out comes back around.
Black to black, white to white,
My words have power on this night.

❨ *Breaking a Spell or Curse*

TIME: Best done on a Tuesday or Saturday during a waning moon.

ITEMS NEEDED: One indigo candle; a foot of black thread; myrrh, Breaking a Spell or Exorcism oil; Exorcism powder; Breaking a Spell or Exorcism incense.

INSTRUCTIONS: Scratch your name onto the indigo candle. Tie the black thread around the candle, about one inch from the top. Oil the candle, and then roll it in the powder. Put the candle in a secure holder on your altar. Light the candle, and chant the verse five times. Leave the candle to burn out.

CHANT:

What was made is broken. What was sent is returned.
Reap the rewards of your planting, as this candle is burned.

❨ *Buying a House or Vehicle*

TIME: Best done on a Sunday during a waxing moon.

ITEMS NEEDED: One green or gold candle; a description of the kind of house or vehicle you desire; bayberry or Success oil; Success powder; Money, Prosperity, or Success incense.

INSTRUCTIONS: Oil the candle and roll it in the powder. Put it in a holder on your altar. Place paper containing the description of your ideal house or vehicle under the candleholder. Meditate for a few moments on what you want and need. As you lightly sprinkle the powder around the candle in three circles, chant the verse. Leave the candle to burn out.

CHANT:

Candle of plenty, candle of fire,
Bring to me my heart's desire.

☾ Changing Your Luck

TIME: Best done on a Thursday during a waxing moon.

ITEMS NEEDED: Three orange candles; one green candle; Success oil; Good Luck powder; Prosperity or Success incense.

INSTRUCTIONS: Oil the candles and place them all in safe holders. Scratch your name onto the green candle. Set the orange candles equidistant around the green candle. Sprinkle the altar with the powder as you chant. Leave the candle to burn out.

CHANT:

Like the tides of wind and weather,
Bad luck leaves and good luck gathers.

☾ Contacting Spirits

TIME: Best done on a Monday during a waxing moon.

ITEMS NEEDED: One indigo and one white candle; sandalwood or Opening the Psychic oil; Divination powder; Communication with Spirits or Psychic Opening incense.

INSTRUCTIONS: This candle spell is best done for a meditation in which you seek your spiritual guides and teachers. Place the indigo candle on the left side of your altar or table, and the white candle on the right. Sprinkle the divination powder in a circle around each candle as you chant the verse. If the candle flame flickers without a draft or burns blue, spirits are present in the room. Then do your usual meditation. Leave the candle to burn out.

CHANT:

Open the door to the Otherworld. Teachers, come to me.
Guide me to greater knowledge. Help me the truth to see.

☾ Divination

TIME: Best done on a Monday or Saturday during a waxing moon.

ITEMS NEEDED: One violet candle; Divination or wisteria oil; Divination powder; Communication with Spirits, Divination, or Psychic Opening incense.

INSTRUCTIONS: Oil the candle and set it in the center of your altar or table. Sprinkle the powder in a circle around the candle, and chant the verse while doing this. Light the candle, and let it burn while reading the cards or runes.

CHANT:

Show me a portent. Give me a sign.
Show me the future that's no will of mine.

☾ Exorcism

TIME: Best done on a Tuesday or Saturday during a waning moon.

ITEMS NEEDED: Two indigo candles and one black candle; Exorcism or patchouli oil; Exorcism powder; Breaking a Curse or Exorcism incense.

INSTRUCTIONS: Oil the candles with the oil. Then, set the black candle in the center of your altar or table, with an indigo candle on each side of it. Carry the incense through the entire house and also wave it over each person present. Sprinkle a little Exorcism powder in the corners of each room. Return to the altar. Look at the candles while holding the palms of your hands toward them. Then, you, and everyone present, chants the verse. Leave the candle to burn out.

CHANT:

I call upon the powers of Light to cleanse this house and people tonight.
Cast out all darkness and distress, and fill this atmosphere with rest.

☾ Fast Money

TIME: Best done on a Sunday during a waxing moon.

ITEMS NEEDED: Two magenta candles and one green candle; cinnamon or Fast Money oil; Good Luck, Money, or Prosperity powder; Money, Prosperity, or Success incense.

INSTRUCTIONS: Carve a large dollar sign into the green candle. Oil the candles. Place the green candle in the center of your altar with a magenta candle on each side of it. Sprinkle the powder on each of the four altar corners. Make a small dollar sign with the powder directly onto the altar in front of the green candle. Light the green candle first, then the magenta candles. Chant the verse. Leave the candle to burn out.

CHANT:

Money fall into my hand. Having riches is my plan.
Fill me with prosperity. Instant money is my plea.

☾ Finding a Job

TIME: Best done on a Sunday, Wednesday, or Thursday during a waxing moon.

ITEMS NEEDED: One gold or bright yellow candle; paper detailing the kind of job you want; sandalwood or Success oil; Good Luck or Prosperity powder; Money, Prosperity, or Success incense.

INSTRUCTIONS: Carve a pentagram into the gold candle. Oil it, and roll it in the powder. Place it in a holder in the center of your altar. Read aloud what you wrote on the paper, and then move it through the incense smoke. Sprinkle a little powder on the paper. Put the paper under the candleholder. Circle your altar three times while chanting the verse. Leave the candle to burn out.

CHANT:

The job I'm seeking, I shall find.
I claim it now, for the job is mine.

☾ Finding the Truth

TIME: Best done on a Monday, Tuesday, or Wednesday during a waxing moon.

ITEMS NEEDED: One silver or light gray candle; lotus or Opening the Psychic oil; Good Luck or Meditation powder; Karma, Meditation, or Success incense.

INSTRUCTIONS: Use the powder to draw an arrow on your altar from the south to the north (————➤). Oil the silver candle and place it on your altar, directly on the arrow. Moisten the tip of your forefinger with the oil, and touch the center of your forehead. After chanting the verse three times, sit quietly and think about the truth you seek. The answer may come in meditation, dreams, or in some unexpected manner. Leave the candle to burn out.

CHANT:

I seek the truth both far and near.
Oh, Great Ones, make the truth appear.

☾ General Prosperity

TIME: Best done on a Sunday or Thursday during a waxing moon.

ITEMS NEEDED: One brown or green candle; bayberry, honeysuckle, or Prosperity oil; Prosperity powder; Prosperity or Success incense.

INSTRUCTIONS: Carve your name into the candle. Oil it, and place it in a holder on your altar. Sprinkle the powder onto the altar in the shape of a pentagram and a dollar sign. Chant the verse. Sit quietly and think of what prosperity means to you and what you desire to make your life better. Chant the verse again. Leave the candle to burn out.

CHANT:

Good health and happiness is my goal. Prosperity is my plan.
Contentment with life and spiritual growth. Give me a helping hand.

☾ Getting Justice

TIME: Best done on a Thursday during a waxing moon.

ITEMS NEEDED: One purple candle; cedar or Karma oil; Good Luck powder; Karma or Success incense. One High John root and a small bag.

INSTRUCTIONS: Oil the candle, coat it with the powder, and place it on your altar. Light the candle. Sprinkle a little of the powder into the small bag. Wave the High John root through the incense smoke, and then put it into the bag. Place the bag in front of the candle. Hold your hands over the bag while you chant the verse five times. Leave the bag on the altar overnight. Carry the bag with you. Leave the candle to burn out.

Be very certain that you are not in the wrong when using this spell. If you are, the result may not be what you wanted. This spell covers any problem connected with justice. And balancing justice is touchy at best because of personal involvement in the problem. This is best left to the Lords of Karma.

CHANT:

Oh Lords of Karma, hear my plea.
Balance the scales of justice for me.

☾ Healing

TIME: Best done on a Sunday, Monday, or Wednesday during a waxing moon.

ITEMS NEEDED: If healing from surgery, one red candle. Other healings, one gold or bright yellow candle. A photo of the sick person, or a paper with their name written on it. Three pieces of clear quartz crystal and three pieces of black obsidian or black onyx. Dragon's blood, frankincense, or Healing oil; General Healing powder; Healing incense.

INSTRUCTIONS: Oil the candle, coat it with the powder, and place it in the center of your altar. Put the photo of the sick person directly in front of the candle, and put the crystal and onyx in alternating positions around it. Sprinkle a little of the powder onto the photo while you say the chant. Concentrate on seeing white light and healing flooding over the sick person. Leave the candle to burn out.

CHANT:

The bad goes out, the good comes in. The healing is here to stay.
All illness vanishes like a mist. Let healing be now, I say.

☽ *Protection*

TIME: Best done on a Tuesday or Saturday during a waning moon.

ITEMS NEEDED: One red candle and one black candle; myrrh or Protection oil; Protection powder; Protection or Success incense. Two sharp pins.

INSTRUCTIONS: Oil the candles and put them side by side in holders on your altar. Stick a pin in each candle, about a quarter of an inch from the top. Sprinkle the powder in a counterclockwise circle around the black candle, and in a clockwise circle around the red candle. Chant the verse. Visualize yourself surrounded by great walls of protection that nothing and no one can cross. When the candle flames reach the pins, extinguish the candles. The next night, move the pins down another quarter of an inch and repeat the spell. Do this for seven nights. Then, on the last night, leave the candles to burn out completely. Bury or flush the remaining wax.

CHANT:

Great barriers of shining light protect me from all harm that's near.
Eternal light surrounds my soul, dissolving harm and dread and fear.

☽ *Releasing Negative Situations or People*

TIME: Best done on a Tuesday or Saturday during a waning moon.

ITEMS NEEDED: One indigo and one black candle; Karma or lavender oil; Protection powder; Karma or Protection incense. A black thread three feet long. A photo or a paper with the person's or persons' names with whom you wish to break contact. A cauldron. A pair of scissors.

INSTRUCTIONS: Place the cauldron in the center of your altar. Carve your name onto the indigo candle. Carve the name or names of the person or people with whom you wish to end any type of relationship. Oil the candles, and roll them in the powder;

put them in holders. Place the indigo candle on the left side of the cauldron, and the black candle on the right. Tie one end of the thread to the indigo candle and the other end to the black candle. Look at the photo or paper while you chant the verse five times. Then, light the photo or paper from the black candle and put it in the cauldron. Cut the thread between the candles with the scissors, saying, "It is finished!"

CHANT:

The ties between us are no more. All relationship is ended.
Our karmic ties are all dissolved. They cannot be mended.

☾ *Repelling Psychic Attack*

TIME: Best done on a Tuesday or Saturday during a waning moon.

ITEMS NEEDED: One indigo, one black, and one red candle; Breaking a Spell, Exorcism, or frankincense oil; Exorcism powder; Breaking a Curse or Exorcism incense. A piece of jewelry that you can bless and wear for protection.

INSTRUCTIONS: Oil the candles and place them in holders on your altar. Set the black candle in the middle, with the indigo candle on the left and the red candle on the right. Sprinkle the powder in a circle around them. Light the candles. Then, sprinkle a little of the powder at each window and door of the house. Return to the altar. Moisten the tip of your forefinger with the oil and touch the center of your forehead. Move the piece of jewelry through the incense smoke, and then put it on. Say the chant three times.

CHANT:

All doors are barred on all the planes.
No way is found to enter here.
All evil returns unto the sender.
I live my life in joy, not fear.

☾ *Selling a House or Vehicle*

TIME: Best done on a Sunday, Wednesday, or Thursday during a waxing moon.

ITEMS NEEDED: One green or blue candle; Fast Money, honeysuckle or Success oil; Good Luck or Prosperity powder; Money, Prosperity, or Success incense. A photo of the house or vehicle being sold. A sheet of white typing paper, adhesive tape, and a green felt pen.

INSTRUCTIONS: Oil the candle and put it into a holder in the center of your altar. Using the tape, fasten the photo to the center of the sheet of white paper. With the green felt pen, write "Sold" just below the photo, including the price for which you want to sell it. Then draw dollars signs and pentagrams all around the photo. Place the paper in front of the candle, and sprinkle it with the powder. Chant the verse. Light the candle and burn it for five minutes, while concentrating on the word "sold." Extinguish the candle. Repeat the spell, burning the candle each night for five minutes until it is burned out.

CHANT:

To sell this (house, car) *is my plan.*
A buyer comes with money in hand.
All love and light, the sale is done.
And I shall prosper, the battle won.

❰ *Stopping Gossip or Lies*

TIME: Best done on a Tuesday or Saturday during a waning moon.

ITEMS NEEDED: One black, one red, and one magenta candle; Binding, Exorcism, or myrrh oil; Exorcism powder; Binding, Karma, or Protection incense. Three sharp pins. A paper with the names of those gossiping.

INSTRUCTIONS: Don't do this spell if you have a bad habit of gossiping yourself, or it will likely rebound on you.

Oil the candles and roll them in the powder. Place the black candle in the center of your altar, with the red candle on the left side and the magenta candle on the right. Take the paper with the names of the gossips; stick each of the pins into every name. Stick one of the pins in the black candle about a quarter of an inch from the top. Stick the second pin below this at another quarter inch, and the third pin below the second at the same distance. Chant the verse three times. Leave the candles to burn out.

CHANT:

Each time your tongue recites my name,
Each time your ugly thoughts defame me,
Your tongue and mind will feel the pain
Of pricking needles. So shall it be.

CHAPTER 67

The Knotted Cord

Binding through the tying of knots is a very ancient practice. The Egyptian goddess Isis is connected with the magic of knots. Her sacred symbol, the Tat, was called the Knot of Fate. Surviving Egyptian texts say that her priestesses could control the weather by braiding or unbraiding their hair, as well as tying and blowing on knots. Isis herself could bind up the actions and events in a human life by making a knot in a cord; she could remove the binding by blowing on the knot. The Holy Mysteries of Isis were known as *shetat*, or "she-knots."

The Greek goddess Circe was also associated with the magic of knots. She controlled the forces of creation and destruction by placing knots and braids in her hair. When the sacred king married the Magna Mater, or Great Goddess, priestesses fastened a great knot to the yoke on his chariot to signify the Sacred Marriage, or "tying the knot."

In most Pagan religions, the Fate Goddesses were associated with the magical tying and loosing of knots. In this way they were said to be able to bind or loose the energy for creation and destruction, and the length of human lives. The Triple Fate Goddesses of the Norse, the Norns, held the same powers.

Using magic knots to control rain and wind was a common practice used by certain women in Finland, Lapland, and Scotland. Sailors often went to these women for wind-knots, which they carried with them on board ship. If the wind died, the sailor would untie the knot to raise the wind again. To call up a storm and rain, Scottish women would tie a knot in a wet rag and then beat it on a rock. British witches were thought to be able to control a nosebleed by tying knots in a red thread.

Special cords are sometimes presented to initiates for use in ceremonies and magic. These cords are worn around the waist until needed during a ritual. Some groups weave these cords temporarily together during ritual for spellwork. However, most cord and knot magic is done with smaller, more flexible cords or thread.

Witches need a number of special, colored cords and spools of thread for this purpose. Choosing cord colors according to the list of candle colors is a good reference. To do knot magic, Witches chant a verse while tying the knot and thinking of the energy or person they want to bind up. To loose the knot, Witches again chant a verse while untying the knot. An appropriate chanting verse is given with each knot spell.

Knot magic is also used to store magical power to use at another time. For example, Full Moon magic is knotted into a cord and released during a spell during the New Moon days, and vice versa.

(Binding Action or an Event

TIME: Best done during a waning moon.

ITEMS NEEDED: Binding incense; black thread.

INSTRUCTIONS: Cut a piece of thread about a foot long. Hold the thread in the incense smoke before beginning. While tying the knots, concentrate on the action or event you want to become static and not progress. Begin by tying the first knot slightly off center in the middle of the thread. Tie the next knot near one end of the thread, and the third knot near the other end of the thread. The next two knots are tied in between these knots. The sixth knot is tied near the first knot, in the center of the thread. Tie the ends of the thread together to make the last and seventh knot.

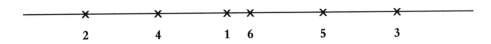

2	4	1	6	5	3

CHANT:

Bind, bind, tie and bind. Nothing moves but me and mine.
Static movement is my will. These knots will thus my wish fulfill.

(Binding Full Moon Energy

TIME: Best done during a Full Moon. However, you can also do this during the first quarter of the moon.

ITEMS NEEDED: Moon or Success incense; a silver or dark purple cord at least two to three feet long.

INSTRUCTIONS: Stored Full Moon energy can be used during waxing moon or New Moon times when the Witch needs to perform prosperity, healing, or similar spells.

Move the cord through the incense smoke until every inch of the cord has been smoked. Take the cord out into the moonlight to do this knot spell, or at least stand where the moonlight falls unimpeded through a window. Turn the cord over and over in your hands so that the moonlight touches every inch of the cord. You will tie nine knots in the cord, as nine has long been a magical moon number. Tie the knots in the cord by beginning at one end and finishing at the other end. Chant the verse as you tie the knots.

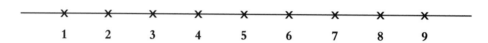

1   2   3   4   5   6   7   8   9

CHANT:
Knot of one, this spell's begun.
Knot of two, the power is true.
Knot of three, my will shall be.
Knot of four, I gather more.
Knot of five, moon power is alive.
Knot of six, the power I fix.
Knot of seven, moon magic leaven.
Knot of eight, this spell is fate.
Knot of nine, the threes are trine.
I gather moonbeams in this cord,
According to my magic words.
Moon power is stored here on this night
For magic good and strength so bright.

☽ Binding New Moon Energy

TIME: Best done during a New Moon. However, you can also do this spell during the third quarter of the moon.

ITEMS NEEDED: Moon or Success incense; a black or dark purple cord at least two to three feet long.

INSTRUCTIONS: New Moon energy can be stored to use during waxing moon or Full Moon times when the Witch needs to do a protection spell, exorcism, or something similar.

Hold the cord over the incense smoke so that every inch of it has been touched. Go out under a New Moon, or at least stand near a window where the black night sky is seen. Tie thirteen knots in the cord, beginning at one end and finishing at the other. Chant the verse as you tie the knots.

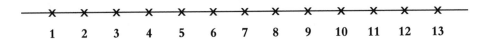

| 1 | 2 | 3 | 4 | 5 | 6 | 7 | 8 | 9 | 10 | 11 | 12 | 13 |

CHANT:

I bind the New Moon energy as it flows through my hands and into the knots I tie. The power is caught within each knot. I control each knot and the power stored within it. I weave moon power with my hands.

☾ Binding a Person

TIME: Best done during a waning moon.

ITEMS NEEDED: Binding, Karma, or Protection incense; three pieces of thread three feet long (one black, one red, and one white); a black votive candle.

INSTRUCTIONS: This spell should be used on a person who is willfully causing you problems; an ex-husband, ex-lover, malicious neighbor, jealous coworker, etc. Remember, if you use magic against another person simply because you do not like them or want something that person has, it can rebound and gather karma to yourself.

Scratch the name of the person you are binding into the top or side of the votive candle. Light the incense and the black candle. Hold the threads over the incense smoke. With the first knot, tie one end of the three threads together. Continue to tie the threads together with each knot. After the last knot is tied and the verse chanted, burn the thread in the flame of the black votive candle. Leave the candle to burn out. The remaining wax and any knotted thread should be buried, burned, or thrown into running water. If you can't do any of these, break up the remains and flush them.

To finish the spell, tie the ends of the threads together.

CHANT:

(One) *In the name of the Maiden and the Divine Child I bind you.*

(Two) *In the name of the Great Mother and Her Lover, I bind you.*

(Three) *In the name of the Crone and the Lord of the Hunt, I bind you.*

(Four) *I bind your bodily energy that it cannot be used against me.*

(Five) *I bind your mental energy that you send no harmful thoughts my way.*

(Six) *I bind your astral energy that no magic of yours will find me.*

(Seven) *Six times I bind you. With the seventh knot, the spell is done.*

☾ *Releasing and Using Full Moon Energy*

TIME: Best done during a waxing moon.

ITEMS NEEDED: Moon or Success incense; a previously tied silver or dark purple cord.

INSTRUCTIONS: To use the stored moon energy, you should do this spell at your altar just before you begin your spellwork or certain types of healing.

You will untie the nine knots in the cord that you tied when you stored the Full Moon energy. Untie the knots in the cord by beginning at one end and finishing at the other end. Chant the verse as you untie the knots. Visualize the moon energy flowing into your hands as you untie each knot.

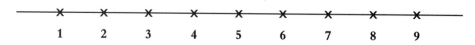

CHANT:

I open the door to the power beyond,
The moon gate that has an Otherworld key.
Unending power flows into my hands.
This is my will, and so shall it be.

☾ *Releasing and Using New Moon Energy*

TIME: Best done during a waxing moon.

ITEMS NEEDED: Moon or Success incense; a previously tied silver or dark purple cord.

INSTRUCTIONS: Untie the thirteen knots in the cord, beginning at one end and finishing at the other. Chant the verse as you untie the knots. Feel the moon energy flowing into your hands and body as you untie each knot.

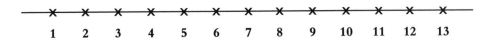

| 1 | 2 | 3 | 4 | 5 | 6 | 7 | 8 | 9 | 10 | 11 | 12 | 13 |

CHANT:

Dark moon magic, pure and bright,
I gather your energy here tonight.
Your powers of the Air and Earth and Sea
Are mine to command. So shall it be.

CHAPTER 68

Talismans and Amulets

There is a magical difference between an amulet and a talisman, although some writers speak as if they were the same thing. An amulet is an ornamental charm or symbol that is worn to avert danger and evil influences. It is usually magically charmed for the protection of a particular person. For thousands of years, the world's civilizations used amber as a protective amulet against bad luck, illness, and evil. Amber's ancient name was *amuletum* or *amoletum*, which means "method of defense." Originally amulets were natural objects, not manmade ones, such as certain stones, clovers, and the rabbit foot.

The charm bracelet, which is not a modern innovation, is an example of an amulet or several amulets worn together. Examples of charm bracelets have been discovered in ancient Greek ruins, dated over two thousand years ago.

The word charm is derived from the Latin *carmen*, which means "a chanted or sung incantation." The charm in this sense would be a word, phrase, or complete verse.

A talisman is an object that is inscribed or carved to protect from the evil eye and danger and to attract good fortune. These are manmade items, such as the little Arabic cases containing papers written from the Koran.

It is common today for many people to wear what they consider to be a "lucky" shirt, coat, dress, or jewelry on special occasions. They also wear engraved belt buckles, bracelets, and pendants, all remnants of ancient talismans and amulets. The wearing of specific stones in all kinds of jewelry is also popular.

All Witches eventually accumulate magical jewelry. They find that the jewelry and stones impart a certain energy to their aura and aid in accomplishing certain objectives.

Even if you are only moderately proficient with tools you can create your own talismans and amulets. You will need a strong glue, a small pair of needle-nose pliers, a small, non-electric drill found in hobby shops, jeweler's wire or filament, and an assortment in size of caps, clasps, and jump-rings.

The stone carnelian has long been known for its healing and protective powers. You can make your own talisman by purchasing carnelian beads and stringing them on jeweler's wire or clear filament for a necklace or bracelet. Add a clasp to the ends of the wire. If you don't want an entire string of beads, you can center one large carnelian bead on the wire and then small silvertone or goldtone beads on each side of it until the desired length is reached.

If you decide you want a stone other than carnelian, read Chapter 30. There are many stones available on the market, either tumbled smooth or cut into beads. Stones such as quartz crystal come in their natural long shape with a point on one end.

If you decide you want only a single stone to attach to a silver or gold chain, you may wish to glue a cap and clasp directly onto the chosen stone, as is done with purchased charms for bracelet. This makes it possible for you to fasten the stone to any neck chain, or change stones whenever you feel the need.

You can also use tumbled stones for pendants by enclosing them in a cage of heavy silver jeweler's wire. The cage is made by winding the flexible wire several times around the stone until it is securely held. Attach the cage to a neck-chain by fastening the ends of the wire through a jump-ring.

To create earrings, glue a cap onto a small bead or stone. Then, add a jump-ring through the bail on the clasp. Attach the stone onto the earring wire.

Small cowry shells can be made into a love amulet. To do this, you will need a small, non-electric hand drill. These are usually found in hobby shops. This tool allows you to carefully and slowly drill a small hole in shells so that a jump-ring or necklace clasp can be attached. String three cowry shells together on a necklace. The cowry shell and the number three are both sacred to the Goddess, with the shell particularly connected with the love aspect of the Goddess.

When finished, pass the jewelry nine times through incense smoke. A good incense for this is frankincense and myrrh. While you do this, chant: "By the power of Sun and Moon, I cleanse this magic charm for protection. May it never fail me as long as the stars hang in the sky, and the ocean rolls in to meet the shore." The word "protection" can be replaced by any word appropriate to the charm, such as love, prosperity, good health, and so on. Repeat this chant and cleansing at each Full Moon.

CHAPTER 69

Poppets

Most people associate poppets with voodoo dolls stuck with pins, although images of humans have been used for magic for centuries in other cultures besides Africa. These images were made of wax, clay, or cloth, to represent a person, and used for healing, love, or cursing. This practice dates back to the ancient Middle East, where clay figures of babies were anointed with menstrual blood to promote a pregnancy. The practice survived into Old England, where the country word for poppet was "mommet."

Poppets are not toy dolls, although they might resemble these. Poppets are made to represent a specific person in a magical sense. Centuries-old magical spells for poppets taught that each "doll" must contain something personal of the human whom the poppet represented, such as blood, fingernails, hair, earth from a footprint, or a personal piece of clothing. The poppet itself could be made of clay, wax, or cloth. During ancient times, poppets were primarily used to curse or force someone to fall in love with you.

Today, the use of poppets has been refined. Most poppets are simple figures made out of cloth in various colors to match the magical need. In fact, their basic shape closely resembles a gingerbread man cookie. Their facial features, and sometimes the hair, is drawn or embroidered onto the cloth doll.

Modern Witches frequently use poppets to perform distance healings. They write the sick person's name on the doll's body or glue a photo of the person's face to the head of the doll. These healing poppets are often made of blue or white cloth, and stuffed with healing herbs, stones, and/or crystals.

Instead of cursing someone today, the Witch is more likely to work magic with poppets in a more positive manner. For example, dolls to stop gossip are of black cloth with their mouths stitched closed.

A few Pagan shops offer poppets for sale under the name "voodoo dolls." They come in various colors. Some of the poppets you can buy are stuffed with cotton batting. If you use pre-made poppets, you will need to loosen a seam on one side of the doll and pull out part or all of the cotton. Then, you can stuff the doll with the appropriate herbs, adding certain stones if you wish.

If you want to make your own poppets, it is not difficult. You will need cloth in various colors, thread and needle, and a pattern from which to cut the doll. The easiest pattern is made by using a gingerbread boy cookie cutter. Simply draw around the cutter, enlarging it into the size you want. Cut out two pieces of cloth for every poppet you make. Stitch the two pieces together, leaving a temporary opening along one side of the body. Using a black felt pen, you can draw on the facial features, write on a person's name, and mark the site of an illness. You will need a bright white or silver marker when you use black cloth. Stuff in appropriate herbs via the body opening; then stitch closed.

Choosing the cloth color will depend upon what magical use you plan to make of the poppet. The power of the magic affecting the poppet is dependent upon the emotional energy you pour into the spell. Take care that you are not hateful or spiteful when working poppet magic, or you will accrue negative karma.

Black can be used to stop gossips, bind someone who is harming you, create confusion among your enemies, to reverse hexes and spells sent against you, or to break someone's control over you.

Blue is for good health, harmony in the home, mental and emotional healing, or to help someone see the truth of a situation.

Brown can attract money and financial success, as well as encourage someone to study.

Green can be used for prosperity, fertility, material gain in general, marriage, or healing of many kinds.

Orange is for major changes in a life, success, or energy.

Pink is for a true love, compassion, harmony, mending the family, or physical fertility for conceiving a child.

Purple is used for influencing people who have power over you, driving away evil, promoting psychic ability, or removing bad luck.

Red can be used for courage, blood diseases, anemia, strength, or passion.

White is for any spell, but is also helpful in balancing someone's aura and destroying negative energies and influences.

Yellow can be used for healing of mental illnesses, such as those of an organic nature. It also is good for business ventures.

An example of poppet magic is a general love spell. No person is named in this work, except the one for whom the doll is made. In this case, we will call the person Ann. Make the poppet from pink cloth. Draw facial features on the doll, and write Ann's name across the body portion. Stuff the poppet loosely with dried rose petals and any other love herbs you wish. Include a rose quartz stone. Stitch the doll closed. Ann can now take the poppet to her altar and chant any of the love chants in this book. She should keep the poppet under her pillow to encourage prophetic dreams of her future love life. When Ann's love arrives, she either can keep the poppet and tuck it away in her drawer, or carefully take it apart and burn the herbs and cloth.

Stopping a gossip is often necessary, but often verbal reminders to the offending person are not likely to work. Sew a poppet from black cloth. Partially stuff it with cotton batting, finishing with patchouli and any other binding herbs. Put a piece of black onyx inside the doll, and stitch it closed. Instead of facial features, write the offender's name on a small piece of paper. Take a needle and thread and stitch closed the facial parts where the eyes and mouth would be. Light a black candle, and drip wax over these places until they are covered. Now, pin the paper with the name to the doll's face. Use one of the binding chants in this book, but also tell the "doll" exactly what you think of the offender's gossipy habits. Finish the ritual by throwing the poppet on the floor and stamping on it. Then, put it inside a small plastic bag, tie the bag shut, and put it in your freezer. When the gossip's nasty words backfire on them, take the doll out of the freezer. Either burn it in your barbecue grill or fireplace, or throw it into the garbage.

If you use poppets for healing, you should put the doll on your altar. Go there each day and visualize the sick person well. When the person is recovered, and if they would not be shocked by the action, you could give them the healing poppet.

If you do not care to use any of the chants previously given in this book, you can use the short Poppet Chant.

POPPET CHANT

Poppet dolly, do my will. Please my magic words fulfill.
Make my powers bright and strong that this spell will linger long.

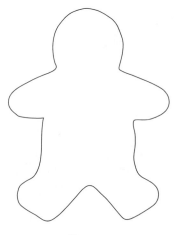

Poppet

CHAPTER 70

Chants

Chanting is often used during circle magic to build up the astral power, which is then released to manifest a certain goal. The chanting, or repetition of certain words or phrases, often puts Witches into a self-hypnotized state. This state creates a change of consciousness, the most powerful state of mind for working magic.

Sounds and musical tones have been part of religious gatherings for thousands of years. However, unless the sounds are made with a specific intent in mind, they are useless. Intoning certain sounds with intent can heal, balance, and manifest desires.

To intone properly, the apprentice must learn to control the breath and practice deep breathing. A common exercise is to breathe in for the count of five, hold the breath for a count of five, and breathe slowly out for a count of five. This breathing is never hurried. Allow the diaphragm muscles to expand during breathing, as this will let your lungs take in the most air.

When you intone vowels or sounds, do it in your natural voice. Never adopt an artificial voice, as that will not work in coordination with your normal vibrations. The voices of some people will automatically be lower or higher than the musical sound recommended. However, if you have a harsh, strident, or squeaky sounding voice, you should work to make it more harmonious and modulated.

When intoning, you should be able to feel the sounds reverberating within your chest cavity and throat. When sound vibrates in this manner, it affects the aura of the body, as well as the astral energy immediately around you.

Some Wiccan groups have certain sounds that are part of every ritual. A few of these date back to ancient religions, such as those in Greece and India. One of these is the call "I-o-evoe-ee." This sound is long and drawn out. Another call is A-E-O, pronounced as "ah-ee-oh."

Vowel sounds give a more soothing vibration than the more explosive sounding consonants. Some writers divide these into the Goddess sounds (the vowels) and the God sounds (the consonants). However, some consonants, such as mm, belong to the Goddess. The vowels in particular can set up a sonic reverberation that can open the doors to the Otherworld if properly done.

The "a," as in "ahh," was considered to be the most powerful of the Goddess sounds in ancient cultures. It is creative and soothing, yet powerful for forming universal energy into a desired form and speeding manifestations.

The "e," as in "emit," prepares both the physical and astral bodies for action, as well as consolidating any available energy. This sound also helps to strengthen astral energy after it is formed into a desire.

The short "e," as in "echo," affects the astral body. It increases the strength of astral senses, as well as creating an alertness valuable when astral traveling.

The long "o," as in "ocean," is a more neutral sound than most others. However, it has a direct effect on the immediate environment. It can be used when purifying and cleansing an area or house.

The "oo" sound, as in "tool," cleans an area or an aura of physical or psychic germs that cause problems. It will repel small negative spells, or rid an area of lingering negative particles. It also helps to connect the conscious and subconscious minds.

The "mm" sound is another powerful Goddess sound. When properly intoned, the "mm" note balances both the physical and astral bodies. It is another creating tone.

The "ss," or hissing sound, is a protective, warning tone in both the physical world and in the Otherworld. It instantly strengthens the aura.

The "shh" tone can restore harmony and peace, and soothes the nerves, as well as the mind and aura. It is valuable in changing the vibrations of a person or area from activity to quiet and preparation for the next step in ritual.

An "uh" tone, as in "huh," arouses the emotions, usually on a survival or sexual level.

"Aye," as in "hay," will balance and help open the Third Eye in the center of the forehead, while the "eee," as in "feel," will work on the chakra at the top of the head.

The sound "eye" added to any intonation will empower the sounds made. If you add "ah," as in "hah," to this, the sounds are balanced on emotional, psychic levels. This will prevent any negatives from being created accidentally.

Often, sounds are combined to produce a balanced Goddess/God energy. The Sanskrit mantra of *Om mani padme hum* is an example of this. The phrase literally translates as "the jewel within the lotus" or could be translated as "the penis within the vagina."

However, there are lesser known tonal phrases that are far more helpful to the Wiccan magician. "Ahh eh" can be used in spellwork for love and relationships. "Shoo maa" aids when working for manifestation of material goals. "Paa maa eye oh" is a combination of sounds valuable when doing protective spells. The explosive sound "pah" is very helpful in defense work.

Chants of ordinary words can also create a change of consciousness, thus making the Witch more powerful and effective in performing spells. These are usually worded in rhyme and refer to specific actions or ideas. The phrases are repeated many times, until the person saying them feels a change. Examples would be:

1. Earth, Air, Water, Fire, bring to me my heart's desire.
2. I cast this spell within my heart that love will come and not depart.
3. My hands fill with prosperity. This is my will, so mote it be.
4. Round the circle now I go. As above, so below. The power builds to my demand and forms itself so I can swiftly draw this goal to me. As I wish so shall it be.

CHAPTER 71

Other Spells

There are a number of ways to do magic that have not been discussed thus far in this book. In fact, there are so many methods that I cannot cover them all. This chapter discusses a few such methods.

Never do a magic spell just once and assume that it should work. Magic requires a commitment of time, energy, and deep concentration over a period of days, in order to form enough energy for your desire to manifest in the physical world. The use of numbers goes far back beyond recorded history. Certain numbers, such as three, five, seven, nine, and thirteen are connected with both the Goddess and magic. If the magician repeats a charm or spell a minimum of three times, the power is much stronger than if it was said only once. This multiple repetition was a cornerstone of ancient magic. It holds true today.

LOVE

Love spells and charms have always been popular in the magical community. Even those people who say they do not believe that magic works will approach a Witch and ask for such a spell. If you are approached or plan to do a love spell for yourself, be certain you adhere to the magical laws. These spells should be used to attract love, not to command another person to love you.

The Chinese crushed coriander seeds and added them to wine for love spells.

To become irresistible in love, steep a handful of rosemary and thyme in boiling water with orris root and lovage root. Strain and stir into your bathwater.

To attract love, fill a small bag with sage, rosemary, and thyme. Keep it in a drawer or under your pillow. Every seven days, moisten the bag with seven drops of bergamot oil.

Mirrors

Mirrors can also be used for magic, even though it is more frequently used for scrying. The mirror is used to reflect negative or dark magic back to the sender. To do this, rub a clean, one-sided, hand mirror with a little fresh mugwort. Then, move the mirror through patchouli incense smoke. Go to the East in your ritual room. Hold up the mirror with the reflecting side away from you. Say: *I return all evil to the sender.* Go clockwise around the room to the other directions, and repeat the chant while holding up the mirror. Then wash the mirror carefully with warm water and soap.

General Desires

Many old formulas require "dove's blood" ink, such as the one that follows. To gain a desire, rub a paper with lavender and write your wishes on the paper with crimson "dove's blood" ink. This spell does not require that anyone kill a bird and use its blood. "Dove's blood" is only a bright red ink. Any bright red ink can be used.

Friendships

For enduring friendship, fill two small bags with cloves. Carry one and give the other to a friend.

Home Exorcism

To get rid of negative energy in your home, put a quarter of an onion in each corner of your room overnight. The next day, wearing gloves, chop up the onions and bury them. Repeat this for three to seven days.

Banners

A banner can be made to visually form images of a desired result. You will need a piece of long paper (or two sheets of typing paper taped together end to end), and colored felt markers. Make your banner so that the long edge will hang downward when you finish. You can draw pictures of your desire on the paper, glue on pictures (such as of vacation spots or a house), or a photo. Draw magical symbols on the paper wherever you please. Also, write various words that describe what you want. Pin up the banner in your bedroom or ritual area.

An example would be a vacation banner. Glue a picture of the resort area from a travel brochure. Surround it with hearts, money signs, pentagrams, and words, such as "warm sand, cool water," "a wonderful time," and "best vacation ever." Put all your emotions into making the banner. When you hang it up, say, *"This is my will, so shall it be."* Look at the banner every day, and imagine yourself at your destination.

Wish Posters

Wish posters are different than banners. The wish poster is made on a sheet of poster board and covers more than one area of your life. You will need a large sheet of poster board, a black felt marker, and magazine pictures that illustrate what you want to accomplish with this project. At the top of the poster, print the words, "My Life Goals." Divide the poster board into four equal sections, drawing the lines with the black pen. In one section, write "Personal Life," in another print "Career." The other two sections will be "Spiritual Goals" and "Health." Cut out all the illustrations that remind you of each section of your goals, and glue them onto the proper area. Hang this in a place where you can see it every day. Visualize yourself accomplishing the goals in each section.

Wish Books

Most Witches I know, and many who are not Witches, keep a wish book. This is usually a little spiral notebook into which Witches write in detail all their desires and needs. When the desires and needs are met, Witches joyfully cross out that page and give thanks at their altar. When you get despondent over your magical success, or lack of it, it boosts the spirits to look through your wish book and realize everything you have accomplished.

BIBLIOGRAPHY

Abergel, Matthew. *Work Your Stars*. NY: Fireside Book, 1999.

Abraham, Sylvia. *How to Read the Tarot*. St. Paul, MN: Llewellyn Publications, 1994.

Achterberg, Jeanne. *Imagery in Healing: Shamanism and Modern Medicine*. Boston, MA: Shambhala, 1985.

Adams, Evangeline. *Astrology For Everyone*. NY: Dodd, Mead & Co., 1931.

_____. *Astrology, Your Place Among the Stars*. NY: Dodd, Mead & Co., 1930.

Adler, Margot. *Drawing Down the Moon*. NY: Penguin, 1986.

Aima. *The Ancient Wisdom and Rituals*. Hollywood, CA: Foibles Publications, no date.

_____. *Perfume, Oils, Candles, Seals & Incense*. USA: Foibles Publications, 1971.

Ali Shah, Sirdar Ikbal. *Occultism: Its Theory & Practice*. NY: Dorset Press, 1993.

Alleau, Rene. *History of Occult Sciences*. UK: Leisure Arts, 1965.

Altman, Nathaniel. *Palmistry Workbook*. NY: Sterling, 1990.

Anderson, Mary. *Colour Healing*. UK: Aquarian Press, 1981.

Anderson, Rosemarie. *Celtic Oracles*. NY: Harmony Books, 1998.

Anderson, William. *Green Man: The Archetype of Our Oneness with the Earth*. San Francisco, CA: HarperCollins, 1990.

Andrews, Lynn. *Teachings Around the Sacred Wheel*. NY: Harper & Row, 1990.

Andrews, Ted. *Animal-Speak: The Spiritual and Magical Powers of Creatures Great and Small*. St. Paul, MN: Llewellyn Publications, 1993.

_____. *Enchantment of the Faeire Realm*. St. Paul, MN: Llewellyn Publications, 1993.

_____. *How to Meet & Work With Spirit Guides*. St. Paul, MN: Llewellyn Publications, 1995.

_____. *How to Uncover Your Past Lives*. St. Paul, MN: Llewellyn Publications, 1996.

_____. *The Magical Name*. St. Paul, MN: Llewellyn Publications, 1991.

_____. *Simplified Magic: A Beginner's Guide to the New Age Qabala*. St. Paul, MN: Llewellyn Publications, 1989.

Angus, S. *The Mystery-Religions*. NY: Dover Publications, 1975.

Arnold, Margaret. *How to Use Numerology for Career Success*. St. Paul, MN: Llewellyn Publications, 1996.

Arrowsmith, Nancy & George Moorse. *A Field Guide to the Little People*. NY: Pocket Books, 1977.

Arroyo, Stephen. *Astrology, Karma & Transformation: The Inner Dimensions of the Birth Chart*. Sebastopol, CA: CRCS Publications, 1992.

_____. *Exploring Jupiter: The Astrological Key to Progress, Prosperity & Potential*. Sebastopol, CA: CRCS Publications, 1996.

Asano, Michael. *Hands: The Complete Book of Palmistry*. NY: Japan Publications, 1985.

Ashcroft-Nowicki, Dolores. *The Shining Paths*. UK: Aquarian Press, 1983.

Aswynn. Freya. *Leaves of Yggdrasil*. St. Paul, MN: Llewellyn Publications, 1990.

Atkinson, W. W. *Reincarnation and the Law of Karma*. Yogi Publication Society, 1936. (Originally published 1908.)

Atwater, P. M. H. *Goddess Runes*. NY: Avon Books, 1996.

Avalon, Arthur. *Shakti and Shakta*. NY: Dover, 1978.

Avery, Jeanne. *The Rising Sign: Your Astrological Mask*. NY: Doubleday, 1982.

Aviza, Edward A. *Thinking Tarot*. NY: Simon & Schuster, 1997.

Ayto, John. *Arcade Dictionary of Word Origins*. NY: Arcade Publishing, 1990.

Bachofen, J. J. *Myth, Religion & Mother Right*. Translator, Ralph Manheim. Edited by Joseph Campbell. Princeton, NJ: Princeton University Press, 1992.

Baer, Randall & Vicki. *Windows of Light: Quartz Crystals & Transformation*. San Francisco, CA: Harper & Row, 1984.

Bailey, Alice. *A Treatise on White Magic*. NY: Lucis, 1951.

Balcombe, Betty F. *Everyone's Guide for Using Psychic Ability*. York Beach, ME: Samuel Weiser, 1995.

Baring, Anne & Jules Cashford. *The Myth of the Goddess: Evolution of an Image*. NY: Viking Arkana, 1991.

Baring-Gould, Sabine. *Curious Myths of the Middle Ages*. NY: University Books, 1967.

Barrett, Clive. *The Norse Tarot: Gods, Sagas & Runes From the Lives of the Vikings*. UK: Aquarian Press, 1989.

Barrett, Francis. *The Magus*. Secaucus, NJ: Citadel Press, 1980.

Barstow, Anne Llewellyn. *Witchcraze: A New History of the European Witch Hunts*. San Francisco, CA: Pandora/Harper Collins, 1994.

Barthell, Edward E., Jr. *Gods & Goddesses of Ancient Greece*. Coral Gables, FL: no publisher, 1971.

Barton, Tamsyn. *Ancient Astrology*. UK: Routledge, 1998.

Bary, William Theodore, editor. *Sources of Chinese Traditions*. NY: Columbia University Press, 1960.

Baumgartner, Anne S. *A Comprehensive Dictionary of the Gods*. NY: University Books, 1984.

Bayley, Harold. *The Lost Language of Symbolism: An Inquiry into the Origin of Certain Letters, Words, Names, Fairy Tales, Folklore & Mythologies*. 2 vols. NY: Citadel Press, 1993. (Originally published 1912.)

Beal, George. *Playing-Cards and Their Story*. NY: Arco Publishing, 1975.

Beck, Renee & Sydney Barbara Metrick. *The Art of Ritual*. Berkeley, CA: Celestial Arts, 1990.

Beckwith, Martha. *Hawaiian Mythology*. Honolulu, HI: University Press of Hawaii, 1971.

Beer, Robert Rudiger. Translated by Charles M. Stern. *Unicorn: Myth & Reality*. UK: Van Nostand Reinhold Co., 1977.

Belhayes, Irish with Enid. *Spirit Guides*. San Diego, CA: ACS, 1985.

Bell, Jessie Wicker. *The Grimoire of Lady Sheba*. St. Paul, MN: Llewellyn Publications, 1972.

Bell, Pamela Hobs & Jordan Simon. *Astronumerology*. NY: Avon Books, 1998.

Bennett, Florence Mary. *Religious Cults Associated With the Amazons*. NY: AMS Press, 1967. (Originally published 1912.)

Berger, Pamela. *The Goddess Obscured: Transformation of the Grain Protectress from Goddess to Saint*. Boston, MA: Beacon Press, 1985.

Berndt, C. H. & R. M. *The World of the First Australians*. Australia: Angus & Robertson, 1965.

Besant, Annie. *The Ancient Wisdom*. UK: Theosophical Publishing House, 1905.

Bethards, Betty. *The Dream Book: Symbols for Self-Understanding*. Petaluma, CA: Inner Light Press, 1992.

Bett, Henry. *English Myths & Traditions*. UK: Batsford, 1952.

Beyerl, Paul. *The Master Book of Herbalism*. Custer, WA: Phoenix Publishing, 1984.

Bhattacharya, A. K. *Gem Therapy*. Calcutta, India: Firma KLM Private Ltd., 1992.

Bias, Clifford. *Ritual Book of Magic*. NY: Samuel Weiser, 1981.

Bibb, Benjamin O. & Joseph J. Weed. *Amazing Secrets of Psychic Healing*. West Nyack, NY: Parker Publishing, 1976.

Bierhorst, John. *The Mythology of Mexico and Central America*. NY: William Morrow & Co., 1990.

_____. *The Mythology of South America*. NY: Wm. Morrow, 1988.

Bierlein, J. F. *Parallel Myths*. NY: Ballantine Books, 1994.

Birren, Faber. *The Symbolism of Color*. Secaucus, NJ: Citadel Press, 1988.

Black, Jeremy & Anthony Green. *Gods, Demons and Symbols of Ancient Mesopotamia*. Austin, TX: University of Texas Press, 1992.

Blanchard, Robert. *The Stone Missal: A Grimoire on the Magick of the Gargoyles*. Palm Springs, CA: International Guild of Occult Sciences, 1993.

Blavatsky, H. P. *The Secret Doctrine*. Wheaton, IL: Theosophical Publishing, 1979.

_____. *Isis Unveiled*. Pasadena, CA: Theosophical University Press, 1976.

Blum, Ralph. *The Book of Runes*. NY: St. Martin's, 1982.

_____. *The Rune Cards: Ancient Wisdom for the New Millennium*. NY: St. Martin's, 1997.

Bonewits, P. E. I. *Real Magic*. Berkeley, CA: Creative Arts Books, 1979.

Bonfanti, Leo. *The Witchcraft Hysteria*. 2 vols. Wakefield, MA: Pride Publications, 1971, 1977.

Bord, Janet & Colin. *Earth Rites*. UK: Paladin, 1983.

Borgeaud, P. *The Cult of Pan in Ancient Greece*. Chicago, IL: University of Chicago Press, 1988.

Boulding, Elise. *The Underside of History*. Boulder, CO: Westview Press, 1976.

Bowers, Barbara. *What Color is Your Aura?* NY: Simon & Schuster, 1989.

Bowman, Catherine. *Crystal Awareness*. St. Paul, MN: Llewellyn Publications, 1996.

Brady, Linda & Evan St. Lifer. *Discovering Your Soul Mission: Karmic Astrology*. NY: Three Rivers Press, 1998.

Branston, Brian. *Gods of the North*. UK: Thames & Hudson, 1955.

Breasted, James H. *Development of Religion and Thought in Ancient Egypt*. NY: Charles Scribner's Sons, 1912.

Brennan, J. H. *Experimental Magic*. UK: Aquarian Press, 1984.

Brenner, Elizabeth. *Hand In Hand*. Millbrae, CA: Celestial Arts, 1981.

Briffault, Robert. *The Mothers: A Study of the Origins of Sentiments and Institutions*. 3 vols. NY: Macmillan, 1952. (Originally published 1927.)

Briggs, Katherine, editor. *British Folktales*. NY: Dorset Press, 1977.

_____. *An Encyclopedia of Fairies, Hobgoblins, Brownies, Bogies, & Other Supernatural Creatures*. NY: Pantheon Books, 1976.

_____. *The Fairies in Tradition and Literature*. UK: Routledge & Kegan Paul, 1967.

_____. *Pale Hecate's Team*. UK: Routledge & Kegan Paul, 1962.

_____. *The Vanishing People: Fairy Lore and Legends*. NY: Pantheon Books, 1978.

Briggs, Robin. *Witches & Neighbors*. NY: Viking, 1996.

Broekman, Marcel. *The Complete Encyclopedia of Practical Palmistry*. Englewood Cliffs, NJ: Prentice-Hall, 1972.

Bromage, B. *The Occult Arts of Ancient Egypt*. UK: Aquarian Press, 1953.

Bromley, Michael. *Spirit Stones*. Boston, MA: Journey Editions, 1997.

Brown, Cheever Mackenzie. *God as Mother: A Feminine Theology in India*. Harford, VT: Claude Stark & Co., 1974.

Bruce-Mitford, Miranda. *The Illustrated Book of Signs and Symbols*. NY: DK Publishing, 1996.

Buckland, Raymond. *Advanced Candle Magick*. St. Paul, MN: Llewellyn Publications, 1996.

_____. *Anatomy of the Occult*. NY: Samuel Weiser, 1977.

_____. *Gypsy Love Magick*. St. Paul, MN: Llewellyn Publications, 1991.

_____. *The Magick of Chant-o-Matics*. West Nyack, NY: Parker Publishing, 1978.

_____. *Practical Color Magick*. St. Paul, MN: Llewellyn Publications, 1983.

_____. *Practical Candleburning Rituals*. St. Paul, MN: Llewellyn Publications, 1981.

_____. *Scottish Witchcraft*. St. Paul, MN: Llewellyn Publications, 1991.

_____. *Secrets of Gypsy Fortunetelling*. St. Paul, MN: Llewellyn Publications, 1988.

_____. *The Tree: The Complete Book of Saxon Witchcraft*. NY: Samuel Weister, 1981.

Budapest, Z. *The Holy Book of Women's Mysteries*. Oakland, CA: Susan B. Anthony Coven No. 1, 1979.

Budapest, Zsuzsanna E. *Grandmother Moon*. San Francisco, CA: Harper & Row, 1991.

Budge, E. A. Wallis. *Amulets and Superstitions*. NY: University Books, 1968.

_____. *The Egyptian Language*. NY: Dover, 1977.

_____. *Egyptian Magic*. NY: Dover, 1971.

_____. *The Gods of the Egyptians*. 2 vols. NY: Dover, 1969.

Bunker, Dusty. *Numerology & Your Future*. Atglen, PA: Whitford Press, 1980.

Buoisson, M. *Magic: Its History and Principal Rites*. Translator, G. Almayrac. NY: Dutton, 1961.

Burland, Cottie A. *North American Indian Mythology*. NY: Peter Bedrick Books, 1985.

Butler, Bill. *Dictionary of the Tarot*. NY: Schocken Books, 1977.

Butler, W. E. *How to Read the Aura, Practice Psychometry, Telepathy and Clairvoyance*. NY: Warner Destiny Books, 1978.

_____. *Magic and the Qabala*. UK: Aquarian Press, 1964.

_____. *The Magician: His Training and Work*. UK: Aquarian Press, 1969.

Cabot, Laurie & Jean Mills. *Celebrate the Earth: A Year of Holidays in the Pagan Tradition*. NY: Dell Publishing, 1994.

_____. *Love Magic*. NY: Delta Books, 1992.

_____. *Power of the Witch*. NY: Delta Books, 1989.

Camp, Robert. *Destiny Cards*. Naperville, IL: Sourcebooks, 1998.

Campanelli, Dan & Pauline. *Circles, Groves, & Sanctuaries: Sacred Spaces of Today's Pagans*. St. Paul, MN: Llewellyn Publications, 1992.

Campanelli, Pauline. *The Ancient Ways*. St. Paul, MN: Llewellyn Publications, 1991.

_____. *Wheel of the Year*. St. Paul, MN: Llewellyn Publications, 1990.

Campbell, Florence. *Your Days Are Numbered*. Ferndale, PA: The Gateway, 1975.

Campbell, Joseph. *The Masks of God: Primitive, Oriental, Occidental and Creative Mythology*. UK: Penguin Books, 1968.

_____. *Transformation of Myth Through Time*. NY: Harper & Row, 1990.

_____. *The Way of the Animal Powers*. San Francisco, CA: Harper & Row, 1983.

Campbell, Joseph & Charles Muses. *In All Her Names: Explorations of the Feminine in Divinity*. San Francisco, CA: Harper & Row, 1991.

Campbell, Joseph & Richard Roberts. *Tarot Revelations*. San Anselmo, CA: Vernal Equinox Press, 1982.

Carlyon, Richard. *A Guide to the Gods*. NY: William Morris & Co., 1982.

Carr, A. H. Z. *How to Attract Good Luck*. No. Hollywood, CA: Wilshire Book Co., 1965.

Carrington, Hereward. *Your Psychic Powers and How to Develop Them*. NY: Newcastle Publishing, 1975.

Carrol, David. *The Magic Makers*. NY: Arbor House, 1974.

Carter, Mildred. *Hand Reflexology: Key to Perfect Health.* West Nyack, NY: Parker Publishing, 1975.

_____. *Helping Yourself With Foot Reflexology.* West Nyack, NY: Parker Publishing, 1969.

Case, Paul Foster. *Book of Tokens.* Los Angeles, CA: Builders of the Adytum Publishers, 1968.

_____. *The Tarot: A Key to the Wisdom of the Ages.* Los Angeles, CA: Builders of the Adytum Publishers, 1970.

Cavendish, Marshall, editor. *Paths to Prediction.* UK: Marshall Cavendish, 1991.

Cavendish, Richard. *The Black Arts.* NY: G. P. Putnam's Sons, 1967. (Not a book of black magic.)

_____, editor. *Mythology: An Illustrated Encyclopedia.* NY: Rizzoli, 1980.

Cayce, Edgar. *Twenty-Two Gems, Stones & Metals.* Virginia Beach, VA: A.R.E. Press, 1974.

Cayce, Hugh Lynn. *Edgar Cayce's Story of Karma.* NY: Berkeley Books, 1972.

Chadwick, Gloria. *Discovering Your Past Lives.* Chicago, IL: Contemporary Books, 1988.

Chandu, Jack F. *The Pendulum Book.* Translated by Tony Langham & Plym Peters. UK: The C. W. Daniel Co., 1997.

Chaney, Robert. *Akashic Records: Past Lives and New Directions.* Upland, CA: Astara, 1996.

Chappell, Helen. *The Waxing Moon: A Gentle Guide to Magick.* NY: Links Books, 1974.

Cheetham, E. *The Prophecies of Nostradamus.* UK: Corgi, 1981.

Cheiro. *Cheiro's Book of Numbers.* NY: Prentice-Hall, 1988.

_____. *The Language of the Hand.* NY: Prentice-Hall, 1987.

Chocron, Daya Sarai. *Healing With Crystals and Gemstones.* York Beach, ME: Samuel Weiser, 1986.

Christie, Anthony. *Chinese Mythology.* UK: Paul Hamlyn, 1973.

Chung, Lily. *The Path to Good Fortune.* St. Paul, MN: Llewellyn Publications, 1997.

Church, W. W. *Story of the Soul.* Virginia Beach, VA: A.R.E. Press, 1989.

Churchward, James. *The Sacred Symbols of Mu.* NY: Paperback Library, 1972.

Cicero, Chic & Sandra T. *The Golden Dawn Journal: Book I.* St. Paul, MN: Llewellyn Publications, 1994.

Cirlot, J. E. *A Dictionary of Symbols.* NY: Philosophical Library, 1978.

Clarkson, Rosetta E. *Green Enchantment: The Magic and History of Herbs and Garden Making.* NY: Collier Books, 1991. (Originally published 1940.)

Clayton, Peter. *Great Figures of Mythology.* NY: Crescent Books, 1990.

Clough, Nigel R. *How to Make & Use Magic Mirrors.* NY: Samuel Weiser, 1977.

Connolly, Eileen. *Tarot: A New Handbook for the Apprentice.* No. Hollywood, CA: Newcastle Publishing, 1990.

_____. *Tarot: The First Handbook for the Master.* No. Hollywood, CA: Newcastle Publishing, 1994.

_____. *Tarot: The Handbook for the Journeyman.* No. Hollywood, CA: Newcastle Publishing, 1987.

Conway, D. J. *Advanced Celtic Shamanism*. Freedom, CA: The Crossing Press, 2000.

———. *The Ancient & Shining Ones*. St. Paul, MN: Llewellyn Publications, 1993.

———. *Animal Magick*. St. Paul, MN: Llewellyn Publications, 1996.

———. *By Oak, Ash & Thorn*. St. Paul, MN: Llewellyn Publications, 1995.

———. *The Celtic Book of Names*. Secaucus, NJ: Carol Publishing, 1999.

———. *Celtic Magic*. St. Paul, MN: Llewellyn Publications, 1990.

———. *Crystal Enchantments*. Freedom, CA: The Crossing Press, 1999.

———. *Falcon Feather & Valkyrie Sword*. St. Paul, MN: Llewellyn Publications, 1995.

———. *Flying Without a Broom*. St. Paul, MN: Llewellyn Publications, 1995.

———. *Laying on of Stones*. Freedom, CA: The Crossing Press, 1999.

———. *A Little Book of Altars*. Freedom, CA: The Crossing Press, 2000.

———. *A Little Book of Candle Magic*. Freedom, CA: The Crossing Press, 2000.

———. *A Little Book of Pendulums*. Freedom: CA: The Crossing Press, not yet released.

———. *Lord of Light & Shadow*. St. Paul, MN: Llewellyn Publications, 1997.

———. *Magick of the Gods & Goddesses*. St. Paul, MN: Llewellyn Publications, 1993. (Originally titled *The Ancient & Shining Ones*.)

———. *Magickal, Mythical, Mystical Beasts*. St. Paul, MN: Llewellyn Publications, 1996.

———. *Maiden, Mother, Crone: The Myth & Reality of the Triple Goddess*. St. Paul, MN: Llewellyn Publications, 1994.

———. *Moon Magick*. St. Paul, MN: Llewellyn Publications, 1995.

———. *The Mysterious, Magickal Cat*. St. Paul, MN: Llewellyn Publications, 1998.

———. *Norse Magic*. St. Paul, MN: Llewellyn Publications, 1990.

———. *Perfect Love*. St. Paul, MN: Llewellyn Publications, 1996.

Conway, D. J. & Lisa Hunt. *Celtic Dragon Tarot*. St. Paul, MN: Llewellyn Publications, 1999.

Conway, D. J., Sirona Knight, & Lisa Hunt. *Shapeshifter Tarot*. St. Paul, MN: Llewellyn Publications, 1998.

Conway, David. *Magic: An Occult Primer*. NY: E. P. Dutton & Co., 1973.

Cooksley, Valerie Gennari. *Aromatherapy: A Lifetime Guide to Healing With Essential Oils*. Paramus, NJ: Prentice Hall, 1996.

Cooper, D. Jason. *The Power of Dreaming: Messages From Your Inner Self*. St. Paul, MN: Llewellyn Publications, 1996.

Cooper, J. C. *The Aquarian Dictionary of Festivals*. UK: Aquarian Press, 1990.

———. *Symbolic and Mythological Animals*. UK: Aquarian/Thorsons, 1992.

———. *Symbolism, the Universal Language*. UK: Aquarian Press, 1982.

Cooper, Phillip. *Basic Magick: A Practical Guide*. York Beach, ME: Samuel Weiser, 1996.

Cosimano, Charles. *Psychic Power: Techniques & Inexpensive Devices that Increase Your Psychic Powers*. St. Paul, MN: Llewellyn Publications, 1992.

Cotterell, Arthur. *A Dictionary of World Mythology*. NY: Perigee Books, 1979.

_____. *The Macmillan Illustrated Encyclopedia of Myths & Legends*. NY: Macmillan, 1989.

Coulton, G. G. *Inquisition and Liberty*. Boston, MA: Beacon Press, 1959.

Coxhead, David and Susan Hiller. *Dreams: Visions of the Night*. NY: Thames & Hudson, 1976.

Cranston, Sylvia. *H.P.B.: The Extraordinary Life and Influence of Helena Blavatsky*. Los Angeles, CA: Jeremy P. Tarcher, 1992.

Crawford, O. G. S. *The Eye Goddess*. NY: Macmillan, 1956.

Crow, W. B. *A History of Magic, Witchcraft, and Occultism*. UK: Aquarian Press, 1969.

Crowley, Aleister. *777 & Other Qabalistic Writings of Crowley*. York Beach, ME: Samuel Weiser, 1986.

_____. *The Book of Thoth*. York Beach, ME: Samuel Weiser, 1981.

_____. *Magick in Theory and Practice*. NY: Dover Publications, 1976.

Crowley, Vivian. *Principles of Wicca*. UK: Thorsons, 1997.

Crowther, Patricia. *Lid Off the Cauldron*. York Beach, ME: Samuel Weiser, 1985.

_____. *The Witches Speak*. NY: Samuel Weiser, 1976.

Csikszentmihalyi, Mihaly. *Finding the Flow*. NY: BasicBooks, 1997.

Cuddon, Eric. *The Meaning and Practice of Hypnosis*. NY: Citadel Press, 1965.

Cumont, Franz. *Astrology and Religion Among the Greeks and Romans*. NY: Dover, 1960.

Cunningham, Scott. *The Art of Divination*. Freedom, CA: The Crossing Press, 1993.

_____. *The Complete Book of Incense, Oils, and Brews*. St. Paul, MN: Llewellyn Publications, 1991.

_____. *Cunningham's Encyclopedia of Crystal, Gem & Metal Magic*. St. Paul, MN: Llewellyn Publications, 1985.

_____. *Cunningham's Encyclopedia of Magical Herbs*. St. Paul, MN: Llewellyn Publications, 1985.

_____. *Earth Power*. St. Paul, MN: Llewellyn Publications, 1983.

_____. *Earth, Air, Fire and Water*. St. Paul, MN: Llewellyn Publications, 1992.

_____. *Living Wicca*. St. Paul, MN: Llewellyn Publications, 1993.

_____. *Magical Aromatherapy*. St. Paul, MN: Llewellyn Publications, 1992.

_____. *Magical Herbalism*. St. Paul, MN: Llewellyn Publications, 1982.

_____. *The Magical Household*. St. Paul, MN: Llewellyn Publications, 1991.

_____. *Wicca: A Guide for the Solitary Practitioner*. St. Paul, MN: Llewellyn Publications, 1992.

Cunningham, Scott & Harrington, David. *Spell Crafts: Creating Magical Objects*. St. Paul, MN: Llewellyn Publications, 1993.

Curtin, Jeremiah. *Myths & Folk-Tales of the Russians, Western Slavs & Magyars*. Boston, MA: Little, Brown & Co., 1890.

D'Alviella, Count Goblet. *Migration of Symbols*. UK: Aquarian Press, 1979.

_____. *The Mysteries of Eleusis: The Secret Rites & Rituals of the Classical Greek Mystery Tradition.* UK: Aquarian Press, 1981.

Dale, Cyndi. *New Chakra Healing: The Revolutionary 32-Center Energy System.* St. Paul, MN: Llewellyn Publications, 1996.

Daly, Mary. *Beyond God the Father.* Boston, MA: Beacon Press, 1973.

Daniels, Cora Linn & Stevans, C. M., editors. *Encyclopedia of Superstitions, Folklore and the Occult Sciences of the World.* Detroit: Gale Research, 1971.

Daniels, Estelle. *Astrological Magick.* York Beach, ME: Samuel Weiser, 1995.

Davidson, Gustav. *A Dictionary of Angels, Including the Fallen Angels.* NY: The Free Press, 1967.

Davidson, H. R. Ellis. *The Journey to the Other World.* Totowa, NJ: D. S. Brewer Ltd. and Rowman and Littlefield for The Folklore Society, no date.

_____. *Myths and Symbols in Pagan Europe.* Syracuse, NY: University Press, 1988.

Davies, Rodney. *Fortune-Telling With Numbers.* UK: Aquarian Press, 1986.

Davis, Audrey Craft. *Metaphysical Techniques That Really Work.* Malibu, CA: Valley of the Sun, 1996.

Davis, Patricia. *Aromatherapy.* UK: C. W. Daniel Co., 1988.

Day, Laura. *Practical Intuition.* NY: Villard, 1996.

De A'morelli, Richard & Reavis, Sharana. *The Book of Magickal & Occult Rites & Ceremonies.* West Nyack, NY: Parker Publishing, 1980.

de Givry, G. *A Pictorial Anthology of Witchcraft, Magic & Alchemy.* NY: University Books, 1958. Originally published in 1931.

de Laurence, L W. *The Great Book of Magical Art, Hindu Magic and Indian Occultism.* Chicago, IL: The deLaurence Co., 1915.

_____. *The Greater Key of Solomon.* Chicago, IL: The deLaurence Co., 1914.

_____. *The Sixth & Seventh Books of Moses.* Chicago, IL: The deLaurence Co., no date.

De Lubicz, Isha Schwaller. *Her-Bak, Egyptian Initiate.* NY: Inner Traditions International, 1978.

_____. *Her-Bak, The Living Face of Ancient Egypt.* NY: Inner Traditions International, 1978.

de Saint-Germain, Comte C. *The Practice of Palmistry.* No. Hollywood, CA: Newcastle Publishing, 1973.

Deaver, Korra. *Rock Crystal: The Magic Stone.* York Beach, ME: Samuel Weiser, 1985.

Decoz, Hans. *Numerology: Key to Your Inner Self.* Garden City Park, NY: Avery Publishing Group, 1994.

Delsol, Paula. *Chinese Astrology.* NY: Warner Books, 1976.

Denning, Melita & Osborne Phillips. *Astral Projection.* St. Paul, MN: Llewellyn Publications, 1990.

_____. *Creative Visualization For the Fulfillment of Your Desires.* St. Paul, MN: Llewellyn Publications, 1991.

_____. *The Development of Psychic Powers.* St. Paul, MN: Llewellyn Publications, 1992.

_____. *The Magical Philosophy.* 4 vols. St. Paul, MN: Llewellyn Publications, 1974–1981.

_____. *Magical States of Consciousness*. St. Paul, MN: Llewellyn Publications, 1985.

_____. *The Magick of the Tarot*. St. Paul, MN: Llewellyn Publications, 1983.

_____. *Planetary Magick*. St. Paul, MN: Llewellyn Publications, 1989.

Dennys, Rodney. *The Heraldic Imagination*. NY: Charles N. Potter, 1975.

Devereux, Charla. *The Aromatherapy Kit*. Boston, MA: Charles E. Tuttle Co., 1993.

Dexter, W. W. *Ogam, Consaine and Tifinag Alphabets*. VT: Academy Books, 1984.

Dey, Charmaine. *The Magic Candle*. NY: Original Publications, 1989.

Diagram Group. *Predicting Your Future*. NY: Ballantine, 1983.

Diner, Helen. Translated by John Philip Lunden. *Mother and Amazons: The First Feminine History of Culture*. NY: Doubleday/Anchor, 1973.

Dixon, Jeane. *Jeane Dixon: My Life and Prophecies*. NY: Morrow, 1969.

Doane, Doris Chase & King Keyes. *Tarot-Card Spread Reader*. West Nyack, NY: Parker Publishing, 1967.

Dolak, George. *The Religious Beliefs & Practices of the Ancient Slavs*. Springfield, IL: Concordia Theological Seminary, 1949.

Dossey, Larry. *Healing Words: The Power of Prayer and the Practice of Medicine*. NY: HarperCollins, 1993.

Douglas, Ray. *Palmistry and the Inner Self*. UK: Blandford, 1998.

Dowson, John. *A Classical Dictionary of Hindu Mythology*. UK: Routledge & Kegan Paul, 1950.

Drury, Neville. *Dictionary of Mysticism and the Esoteric Traditions*. UK: Prism Press, 1992.

Dubats, Sally. *Natural Magick: Inside the Well-Stocked Witch's Cupboard*. NY: Kensington Books, 1999.

Ducie, Sonia. *Do It Yourself Numerology*. UK: Element Books, 1998.

Duer, Hans Peter. Translator, Felicitas Goodman. *Dreamtime: Concerning the Boundary Between Wilderness & Civilization*. UK: Basil Blackwell, 1985.

Dunwich, Gerina. *Candlelight Spells*. NY: Citadel Press, 1990.

_____. *The Wicca Source Book: A Complete Guide for the Modern Witch*. Secaucus, NJ: Citadel Press, 1999.

_____. *A Wiccan's Guide to Prophecy and Divination*. NY: Carol Publishing, 1997.

Durdin-Robertson, Lawrence. *The Cult of the Goddess*. Ireland: Caesara Publications, 1974.

_____. *God the Mother*. Ireland: Cesara Publications, 1982.

_____. *Goddesses of Chaldea, Syria and Egypt*. Ireland: Caesara Publications, 1975.

_____. *Goddesses of India, Tibet, China and Japan*. Ireland: Caesara Publications, 1976.

Dynamo House. *Dream Studio*. Australia: Dynamo House, 1999.

Eason, Cassandra. *The Handbook of Ancient Wisdom*. NY: Sterling Publishing, 1997.

Eclipse. *The Moon in Hand: A Mystical Passage*. Portland, ME: Astarte Shell Press, 1991.

Edmonds, I. G. *D. D. Home: The Man Who Talked with Ghosts*. Nashville, TN: Thomas Nelson, 1978.

Edwards, Gillian. *Hobgoblin and Sweet Puck*. UK: Bles, 1974.

Edwards, Paul. *Reincarnation: A Critical Examination*. NY: Prometheus Books, 1996.

Ehrenrich, Barbara & Deirdre English. *Witches, Midwives & Nurses: A History of Women Healers*. Old Westbury, NY: Feminist Press, 1973.

Eliade, Mircea. Translated by Willard R. Trask. *A History of Religious Ideas: Vol. 1: From the Stone Age to the Eleusinian Mysteries*. Chicago, IL: University of Chicago Press, 1978.

_____. *Rites & Symbols of Initiation: The Mysteries of Birth & Rebirth*. NY: Harper & Row, 1965.

_____. *Shamanism: Archaic Techniques of Ecstasy*. Princeton, NJ: Princeton University Press, 1964.

Eliseev, S. *Asiatic Mythology: The Mythology of Japan*. UK: Harrap, 1932.

Ellis, Hilda Roderick. *The Road to Hel*. NY: Greenwood Press, 1968.

Elsbeth, Marguerite. *Crystal Medicine*. St. Paul, MN: Llewellyn Publications, 1997.

Elsworthy, Frederick. *The Evil Eye*. NY: Julian Press, 1958.

Epstein, Perke. *The Way of the Jewish Mystic*. Boston, MA: Shambhala, 1988.

Escobar, Thyrza & J. Allen Jones. *Chalden Cycles Revealed*. AZ: American Federation of Astrologers, 1997.

Evans-Wertz, W.Y. *The Fairy Faith in Celtic Countries*. NY: Citadel, 1990.

_____. *Tibet's Great Yogi, Milarepa: A Biography from the Tibetan*. UK: Oxford University Press, 1951.

Evers, Ona C. *Everybody's Dowser Book*. San Rafael, CA: Onaway Publications, 1977.

Farrar, Janet & Stewart. *Eight Sabbats for Witches*. UK: Robert Hale, 1981.

_____. *The Witches' God*. Custer, WA: Phoenix Publishing, 1989.

_____. *The Witches' Goddess*. UK: Robert Hale, 1987.

_____. *The Witches' Way*. UK: Robert Hale, 1984.

Farrar, Stewart. *What Witches Do*. Custer, WA: Phoenix Publishing, 1983.

Ferguson, Anna-Ferguson. *Legend: The Arthurian Tarot*. St. Paul, MN: Llewellyn Publications, 1995.

Ferguson, Sibyl. *The Crystal Ball*. NY: Samuel Weiser, 1979.

Fernie, William T. *The Occult & Curative Powers of Precious Stones*. San Francisco, CA: Harper & Row, 1973.

Fiery, Ann. *The Book of Divination*. San Francisco, CA: Chronicle Books, 1999.

Finch, Bill. *The Pendulum and Possession*. Cottonwood, AZ: Esoteric Publications, 1975.

Finch, Elizabeth & Bill. *The Pendulum and Your Health*. Cottonwood, AZ: Esoteric Publications, 1980.

_____. *Photo-Chromotherapy*. Cottonwood, AZ: Esoteric Publications, no date.

Fitch, Ed. *Magical Rites From the Crystal Well*. St. Paul, MN: Llewellyn Publications, 1984.

Flanders, Angela. *Aromatics*. NY: Clarkson N. Potter, 1995.

Flint, Valerie I. J. *The Rise of Magic in Early Medieval Europe*. Princeton, NJ: Princeton University Press, 1991.

Flowers, Stephen E. *The Secret of the Runes*. Rochester, VT: Destiny Books, 1988.

Fontana, David. *The Secret Language of Dreams*. San Francisco, CA: Chronicle Books, 1994.

_____. *The Secret Language of Symbols: A Visual Key to Symbols and Their Meanings*. San Francisco, CA: Chronicle Books, 1994.

Ford, Arthur and Marguerite Harmon Bro. *Nothing So Strange*. NY: New American Library, 1973.

Fortune, Dion. *The Mystical Qabalah*. NY: Ibis Books, 1981.

_____. *Psychic Self-Defence*. York Beach, ME: Samuel Weiser, 1982.

Fox, Judy, Karen Hughes, and John Tampion. *An Illuminated I Ching*. NY: Arch, 1984.

Fox, Oliver. *Astral Projection: A Record of Out-of-the-Body Experiences*. Secaucus, NJ: Citadel Press, 1962. Original 1920.

Fowler, W. Warde. *Roman Ideas of Deity*. UK: Macmillan, 1914.

Franck, Adolphe. *The Kabbalah*. NY: Bell, 1978.

Frankfort, Henri. *Ancient Egyptian Religion*. NY: Harper & Row Torchbooks, 1961.

Frater A.H.E.H.O. *Angelic Images*. The Sorcerers Apprentice Press, 1984.

Frater Malak. *The Mystic Grimoire of Mighty Spells & Rituals*. West Nyack, NY: Parker Publishing, 1976.

Frazer, James G. *Adonis, Attis, Osiris: Studies in the History of Oriental Religion*. NY: University Books, 1961.

Frazer, Sir James G. *The Illustrated Golden Bough*. NY: Simon & Schuster, 1996. (Originally published 1890.)

Friedrich, Johannes. *Extinct Languages*. NY: Barnes & Noble, 1993.

Frost, Gavin & Yvonne. *A Witch's Grimoire of Ancient Omens, Portents, Talismans, Amulets & Charms*. West Nyack, NY: Parker Publishing, 1979.

_____. *The Magic Power of Witchcraft*. West Nyack, NY: Parker Publishing, 1976.

Funk, Wildred. *Word Origins & Their Romantic Stories*. NY: Bell Publishing, 1978.

Galde, Phyllis. *Crystal Healing: The Next Step*. St. Paul, MN: Llewellyn Publications, 1991.

Gamache, Henri. *The Master Book of Candle Burning*. NY: Original Publications, 1984.

Gardner, Gerald B. *The Meaning of Witchcraft*. NY: Magickal Childe, 1982.

_____. *Witchcraft Today*. NY: Citadel Press, 1970.

Gardner, Joy. *Color and Crystals*. Freedom, CA: The Crossing Press, 1988.

Garen, Nancy. *Tarot Made Easy*. NY: Fireside Book/Simon & Schuster, 1989.

Garfield, Laeh Maggie & Jack Grant. *Companions in Spirit*. Berkeley, CA: Celestial Arts, 1984.

Garfield, Patricia. *Healing Power of Dreams*. NY: Fireside Books, 1991.

_____. *The Dream Messenger*. NY: Simon & Schuster, 1997.

Gaster, Moses. *The Wisdom of the Chaldeans*. Edmonds, WA: Holmes Publishing Group, 1999.

George, Demetra. *Mysteries of the Dark Moon: The Healing Power of the Dark Goddess*. San Francisco, CA: Harper & Row, 1992.

George, Llewellyn. *The Planetary Hour Book*. St. Paul, MN: Llewellyn Publications, 1975.

Gerald, John. *The Herball, or Generall Historie of Plants*. NY: Dover, 1975. (Originally published 1597.)

Gettings, Fred. *Palmistry Made Easy*. No. Hollywood, CA: Wilshire Books, 1966.

Gilchrist, Cherry. *The Circle of Nine*. NY: Penguin/Arkana, 1991.

Gile, Robin & Lisa Lenard. *The Complete Idiot's Guide to Palmistry*. NY: Alpha Books, 1999.

Giles, Cynthia. *The Tarot: History, Mystery and Lore*. NY: Paragon House, 1992.

Gimbutas, Marija. *The Goddesses & Gods of Old Europe: Myths & Cult Images*. Berkeley, CA: University of California Press, 1992.

_____. *The Language of the Goddess*. San Francisco, CA: Harper & Row, 1989.

Ginsburg, C. D. *The Kabbalah*. UK: Routledge & Kegan Paul, 1955. (Originally printed 1863.)

Giovetti, Paola. *Angels: The Role of Celestial Guardians and Beings of Light*. York Beach, ME: Samuel Weiser, 1993.

Glass, Justine. *Witchcraft, the Sixth Sense*. No. Hollywood, CA: Wilshire Book Co., 1965.

Goddard, David. *The Sacred Magic of the Angels*. York Beach, ME: Samuel Weiser, 1996.

Godwin, David. *Godwin's Cabalistic Encyclopedia*. St. Paul, MN: Llewellyn Publications, 1979.

Godwin, Joscelyn. *Mystery Religions in the Ancient World*. NY: Harper & Row, 1981.

Goldenberg, Naomi R. *The Changing of the Gods: Feminism & the End of Traditional Religions*. Boston, MA: Beacon Press, 1979.

Goldman, Jonathan. *Healing Sounds: The Power of Harmonics*. UK: Element Books, 1999.

Goldschneider, Gar & Elffers, Joost. *The Secret Language of Destiny*. NY: Viking Studio, 1999.

Gonzalez-Wippler, Migene. *The Complete Book of Amulets & Talismans*. St. Paul, MN: Llewellyn Publications, 1991.

_____. *The Complete Book of Spells, Ceremonies and Magic*. St. Paul, MN: Llewellyn Publications, 1988.

Goodman, Morris C. *Modern Numerology*. No. Hollywood, CA: Wilshire Books, 1945.

Goodrich, Norma Lorre. *Priestesses*. NY: HarperCollins, 1989.

Gordon, Cyrus H. *Forgotten Scripts*. NY: Basic Books, 1968.

Gordon, Stuart. *The Book of Spells, Hexes & Curses: True Tales From Around the World*. NY: Citadel Press, 1995.

Graves, F. D. *The Windows of Tarot*. NY: Morgan & Morgan, 1973.

Graves, Robert. *The White Goddess*. NY: Farrar, Straus & Giroux, 1980.

Graves, Tom. *The Dowser's Workbook*. NY: Sterling Publishing, 1990.

Gray, Louis Herbert., editor. *The Mythology of All Races*. 13 vols. Boston, MA: no publisher, 1918.

Gray, William G. *Inner Traditions of Magic*. York Beach, ME: Samuel Weiser, 1984.

_____. *Magical Ritual Methods*. NY: Samuel Weiser, 1980.

_____. *The Magician: His Training & Work*. UK: Aquarian Press, 1969.

Green, Celia. *Out-of-the-Body Experiences*. UK: Oxford University Press, 1968.

Green, Marian. *A Witch Alone: Thirteen Moons to Master Natural Magic*. UK: Thorsons/Harper Collins, 1991.

Green, Miranda. *The Gods of the Celts*. Totowa, NJ: Barnes & Noble, 1986.

_____. *The Sun-Gods of Ancient Europe*. UK: Hippocrene Books, 1991.

Greene, Liz. *The Astrology of Fate*. York Beach, ME: Samuel Weiser, 1984.

_____. *Saturn: A New Look at an Old Devil*. York Beach: ME: Samuel Weiser, 1976.

Grey, Sir George. *Polynesian Mythology*. UK: Whitcombe & Tombs, 1965.

Grieve, M. *A Modern Herbal*. NY: Dover, 1971. (Originally published 1931.)

Griffin, Judy. *Mother Nature's Herbal*. St. Paul, MN: Llewellyn Publications, 1997.

Griffon, T. Wynne. *History of the Occult*. Mallard Press, 1991.

Gris, Henry & William Dick. *The New Soviet Psychic Discoveries*. NY: Warner Books, 1978.

Guiley, Rosemary Ellen. *The Encyclopedia of Ghosts and Spirits*. NY: Facts On File Ltd., 1992.

_____. *The Encyclopedia of Witches & Witchcraft*. NY: Checkmark Books, 1999.

_____. *Harper's Encyclopedia of Mystical and Paranormal Experience*. San Francisco, CA: HarperSanFrancisco, 1991.

Guirand, Felix, editor. Translated by Richard Aldington & Delano Ames. *The New Larousse Encyclopedia of Mythology*. UK: Hamlyn, 1978.

Guterbock, Hans G. *Mythologies of the Ancient World*. Edited by Samuel N. Kramer. Chicago, IL: no publisher, 1961.

Hacki, Monnica. *Crystal Energy*. UK: Dorset, 1993.

Hales, Dianne & Robert E. *Caring for the Mind: The Comprehensive Guide to Mental Health*. NY: Bantam Books, 1995.

Halifax, Joan. *Shaman: The Wounded Healer*. NY: Crossroads Press, 1982.

Hall, Cally. *Gem Stones*. UK: Dorling Kindersley, 1994.

Hall, Manley P. *The Secret Teachings of All Ages*. Los Angeles, CA: Philosophical Research Society, 1977.

_____. *Reincarnation: The Cycle of Necessity*. Los Angeles, CA: Philosophical Research Society, 1956.

Hall, Nor. *The Moon and the Virgin: Reflections on the Archetypal Feminine*. San Francisco, CA: Harper & Row, 1980.

Hallam, Elizabeth, editor. *Gods & Goddesses*. NY: Macmillan, 1996.

Hamilton, Edith. *Mythology*. Boston, MA: Little, Brown & Co., 1942.

Harding, Elizabeth U. *Kali: the Black Goddess of Dakshineswar.* York Beach, ME: Nicolas-Hay, 1993.

_____. *Woman's Mysteries, Ancient and Modern*. NY: Bantam, 1973.

Harner, Michael *The Way of the Shaman*. NY: Bantam, 1982.

Harold, Edmund. *Focus on Crystals*. NY: Ballantine Books, 1987.

Harper, George Mills. *Yeat's Golden Dawn*. UK: Aquarian Press, 1974.

Harrison, Jane Ellen. *Epilegomena to the Study of Greek Religion and Themis*. UK: Merlin Press, 1980.

_____. *The Religion of Ancient Greece*. UK: Archibald Constable & Co., 1905.

Harrison, Stephanie & Barbara Kleiner. *The Crystal Wisdom Kit*. Boston, MA: Journey Editions, 1997.

Harshananda, Swami. *Hindu Gods and Goddesses*. Mysore, India: Ramakrishna Ashrama, 1981.

Hartford, Huntington. *You Are What You Write*. NY: Macmillan, 1973.

Harvey, Graham & Charlotte Hardman, eds. *Paganism Today*. UK: Thorsons/Harper Collins, 1996.

Hathaway, Nancy. *The Unicorn*. NY: Avenel, 1980.

Hauck, Dennis William. *Haunted Places, Ghostly Abodes, Sacred Sites, UFO Landings, & Other Supernatural Locations*. NY: Penguin, 1996.

Hawkes, Jacquetta. *Dawn of the Gods: Minoan and Mycenaeon Origins of Greece*. NY: Random House, 1968.

Hawkridge, Emma. *The Wisdom Tree*. Boston, MA: Houghton Mifflin, 1945.

Hay, Louise L. *Your Personal Colors and Numbers*. Santa Monica, CA: Hay House, 1987.

Hays, H. R. *In the Beginnings*. NY: G. P. Putnam's Sons, 1963.

_____. *The Dangerous Sex: The Myth of Feminine Evil*. NY: G. P. Putnam's Sons, 1964.

Hazlitt, W. Carew. *Faiths and Folklore of the British Isles*. 2 vols. NY: Benjamin Blum, 1965.

Head, Joseph & S. L. Cranston., editors. *Reincarnation: An East-West Anthology*. Wheaton, IL: Theosophical Publishing, 1990.

Healki, Thomas. *Creative Ritual.* York Beach, ME: Samuel Weiser, 1986.

Heline, Corinne. *The Sacred Science of Numbers*. Los Angeles, CA: New Age Press, 1977.

Hewitt, William W. *Tea Leaf Reading*. St. Paul, MN: Llewellyn Publications, 1989.

Higgins, Godfrey. *The Celtic Druids*. UK: Rowland Hunter, 1829.

Highland Seer. *Reading Tea Leaves*. NY: Clarkson Potter/Publishers, 1993.

Hill, Douglas & Pat Williams. *The Supernatural*. UK: Bloomsbury Books, 1989.

Hill, Douglas. *Witches & Magic Makers*. NY: Alfred A. Knopf, 1997.

Hillman, James. *Dream Animals*. San Francisco, CA: Chronicle Books, 1997.

_____. *The Soul's Code: In Search of Character and Calling*. NY: Random House, 1996.

Hinnels, John. *Persian Mythology*. NY: Peter Bedrick Books, 1985.

Hipskind, Judith. *Palmistry: the Whole View*. St. Paul, MN: Llewellyn Publications, 1994.

Hirsh, Udo, et al. *The Goddess of Anatolia*. Milan: Eskenazi, 1989.

Hitchcock, Helyn. *Helping Yourself With Numerology*. West Nyack, NY: Parker Publishing, 1972.

Hoffman, Enid. *Huna: A Beginner's Guide*. Gloucester, MA: Para Research, 1976.

Holmes, Ronald. *Witchcraft in History*. Secaucus, NJ: Citadel Press, 1974.

Holzer, Hans. *Born Again: The Truth About Reincarnation*. Garden City, NY: Doubleday, 1970.

_____. *The Psychic Side of Dreams*. St. Paul, MN: Llewellyn Publications, 1992.

Hooke, S. H. *Babylonian and Assyrian Religion*. UK: Hutchinson, 1953.

_____. *Middle Eastern Mythology*. UK: Penguin, 1963.

Hopcke, Robert H. *There Are No Accidents*. NY: Riverhead Books, 1997.

Hope, Jane. *The Sacred Language of the Soul*. San Francisco, CA: Chronicle Books, 1997.

Hope, Murry. *The Way of Cartouche*. NY: St. Martin's, 1985.

Howard, Michael. *Candle Burning: Its Occult Significance*. NY: Samuel Weiser, 1980.

_____. *Finding Your Guardian Angel*. UK: Thorsons, 1991.

_____. *The Magic of the Runes: Their Origins and Occult Power*. NY: Samuel Weiser, 1980.

_____. *The Prediction Book of Practical Magic*. NY: Sterling Publishing/Javelin Books, 1988.

_____. *The Runes and Other Magical Alphabets*. UK: Aquarian Press, 1981.

Huang, Kerson & Rosemary. *I Ching*. NY: Workman Publishing, 1987.

Hubbs, Joanna. *Mother Russia: The Feminine Myth in Russian Culture*. Bloomington: Indiana University Press, 1988.

Huber, Bruno & Louise. *Moon-Node Astrology*. York Beach, ME: Samuel Weiser, 1995.

Huber, Richard. *Treasury of Fantastic and Mythological Creatures*. NY: Dover, 1981.

Hunt, Stoker. *Ouija: The Most Dangerous Game*. NY: Harper & Row, 1985.

Huson, Paul. *Mastering Herbalism*. NY: Stein & Day, 1983.

_____. *Mastering Witchcraft*. NY: G. P. Putnam's Sons, 1970.

Huygen, Wil. *Gnomes*. NY: Peacock Press, 1977.

Innes, Brian. *The Tarot: How to Use and Interpret the Cards*. UK: Orbis, 1979.

Ions, Veronica. *Indian Mythology*. NY: Paul Hamlyn, 1973.

Isaacs, Thelma. *Gemstone and Crystal Energies*. Black Mountain, NC: Lorien House, 1989.

Ishbel. *The Secret Teachings of the Temple of Isis*. St. Paul, MN: Llewellyn Publications, 1989.

Jacobson, Helen. *The First Book of Legendary Beings*. NY: Franklin Watts, 1962.

Jacoby, Kathleen. *Where You Live is What You Learn*. Palo Alto, CA: Mouse the Publisher, 1995.

James, E. O. *The Ancient Gods*. NY: G.P. Putnam's Sons, 1960.

_____. *The Cult of the Mother-Goddess: An Archaeological & Documentary Study*. NY: Frederick A. Praeger, 1959.

Janus-Mithras, Nuit-Hilaria & Mer-Amun. *Wicca: The Ancient Way*. Ontario, Canada: Isis Urania, 1981.

Jayakar, Pupul. *The Earth Mother: Legends, Ritual Arts and Goddesses of India*. San Francisco, CA: Harper & Row, 1989.

Jobes, Getrude. *Dictionary of Mythology, Folklore & Symbols*. NY: Scarecrow Press, 1962.

Jobes, Gertrude and James. *Outer Space*. NY: Scarecrow Press, 1964.

Johari, Harish. *Numerology With Tantra, Ayurveda and Astrology*. Rochester, VT: Destiny Books, 1990.

Johnson, Buffie. *Lady of the Beasts: Ancient Images of the Goddess and Her Sacred Animals*. San Francisco, CA: Harper & Row, 1981.

Jones, Wendy & Barry. *The Magic of Crystals*. Australia: Harper Collins, 1996.

Jong, Erica. *Witches*. NY: Harry N. Abrams, 1997.

Judith, Anodea. *Wheels of Life: A User's Guide to the Chakra System*. St. Paul, MN: Llewellyn Publications, 1993.

Jung, Carl G. Translated by R.F.C. Hull. *The Archetypes & the Collective Unconscious*. NJ: Princeton University Press, 1990.

————. *Dreams*. Princeton, NJ: Princeton University Press, 1991.

————. *Man and His Symbols*. NY: Anchor Press/Doubleday, 1988.

————. *The Myth of the Divine Child*. Princeton, NJ: Princeton University Press, 1973.

Kaplan, Stuart. *The Encyclopedia of Tarot*. 2 vols. Stamford, CT: U.S. Games, 1994.

————. *The Tarot of the Witches Book*. NY: U.S. Games Systems, 1973.

Kapleau, Philip. *The Wheel of Life and Death: A Practical and Spiritual Guide*. NY: Doubleday, 1989.

Karagulla, Shafica and Dora van Gelder Kunz. *The Chakras and the Human Energy Fields*. Wheaton, IL: Theosophical Publishing Co., 1989.

Karcher, Stephen. *The Illustrated Encyclopedia of Divination*. NY: Barnes & Noble, 1997.

Kargere, Audrey. *Color and Personality*. York Beach, ME: Samuel Weiser, 1979. Originally published 1949.

Kaser, R.T. *Tarot in 10 Minutes*. NY: Avon Books, 1992.

Kaster, Joseph. *The Wisdom of Ancient Egypt*. NY: Barnes & Noble, 1993.

Katzeff, Paul. *Full Moons: Fact and Fantasy About Lunar Influence*. Secaucus, NJ: Citadel Press, 1973.

————. *Moon Madness and Other Effects of the Full Moon*. Secaucus, NJ: Citadel Press, 1981.

Kautz, William H. and Melanie Branon. *Channeling: The Intuitive Connection*. San Francisco, CA: Harper & Row, 1987.

Keightley, Thomas. *The World Guide to Gnomes, Fairies, Elves & Other Little People*. NY: Avenel Books, 1978. (Originally published 1880.)

Kelly, Aidan A. *Crafting the Art of Magic*. St. Paul, MN: Llewellyn Publications, 1991.

Kerenyi, Karl. *Eleusis: Archetypal Image of Mother & Daughter*. NY: Schocken Books, 1967.

_____. Translated by Murray Stein. *Goddesses of the Sun & Moon*. Dallas, TX: Spring Publications, 1979.

Ketch, Tina. *Candle Lighting Encyclopedia*. 2 vols. No publisher, 1991.

Kilner, W. J. *The Aura*. York Beach, ME: Samuel Weiser, 1973. (Originally published 1911.)

King, Frances & Isabel Sutherland. *The Rebirth of Magic*. UK: Corgi Books, 1982.

King, Serge. *Kahuna Healing*. Wheaton, IL: Theosophical Publishing House, 1983.

King, Stephen. *Nightmares in the Sky*. NY: Viking Studio Books, 1988.

Kipling, Rudyard. Edited by John Beecroft. In "Puck of Pook's Hill," *Kipling: A Selection of His Stories and Poems*. Garden City, NY: Doubleday & Co., 1956. (Originally published 1892.)

Klimo, John. *Channeling: Investigations on Receiving Information from Paranormal Sources*. Los Angeles, CA: Jeremy P. Tarcher, 1987.

Knight, Gareth. *Knight's Practical Guide to Kabalistic Symbolism*. UK: Helios, 1970.

_____. *The Practice of Ritual Magic*. NY: Samuel Weiser, 1976.

Knight, Richard Payne. *The Symbolical Language of Ancient Art & Mythology*. NY: J. W. Bouton, 1892.

Knightly, Charles. *The Customs and Ceremonies of Britain*. UK: Thames & Hudson, 1986.

Konraad, Sandor. *Classic Tarot Spreads*. West Chester, PA: Whitford Press, 1985.

Kors, Allan C. & Edward Peters. *Witchcraft in Europe, A Documentary History 1100–1700*. Philadelphia, PA: University of Pennsylvania Press, 1972.

Kozminsky, Isidore. *The Magic and Science of Jewels and Stones*. 2 vols. San Rafael, CA: Cassandra Press, 1988.

Kraig, Donald. *Modern Magick: Eleven Lessons in the High Magickal Arts*. St. Paul, MN: Llewellyn Publications, 1989.

Kramer, Samuel N. *The Sacred Marriage Rite: Aspects of Faith, Myth & Ritual in Ancient Sumer*. Bloomington, IN: Indiana University Press, 1969.

Krippner, Stanley and David Rubin. *The Kirlian Aura*. NY: Doubleday/Anchor Press, 1974.

Kryder, Rowena Pattee. *The Faces of the Moon Mother: An Archetypal Cycle*. Mt. Shasta, CA: Golden Point Productions, 1991.

Krystal, Phyllis. *Cutting the Ties That Bind*. Los Angeles, CA: Aura Books, 1982.

Kummer, Adolf. Translated by DuWayne Fish. *Rune Magic*. Austin, TX: Rune-Gild, no date.

Kunz, George F. *The Curious Lore of Precious Stones*. NY: Dover, 1971. (Originally published 1913.)

_____. *The Mystical Lore of Precious Stones*. No. Hollywood, CA: Newcastle Publishing, 1986.

Kwok, Man-Ho. *Chinese Astrology*. Boston, MA: Tuttle Publishing, 1997.

Lady Cunningham. *Study Wicca Craft*. Glendale, CA: The Magical Way, no date.

Lady Sabrina. *Reclaiming the Power: The How & Why of Practical Ritual Magic*. St. Paul, MN: Llewellyn Publications, 1992.

Lady Sara. *The Book of Light*. NY: Magickal Childe, 1974.

Lagerquist, Kay & Lisa Lenard. *The Complete Idiot's Guide to Numerology.* NY: Alpha Books, 1999.

Lammey, William C. *Karmic Tarot.* No. Hollywood, CA: Newcastle Publishing, 1993.

Lamy, Lucie. *Egyptian Mysteries: New Light on Ancient Knowledge.* UK: Thames & Hudson, 1981.

Lang, Andrew. *Myth, Ritual & Religion.* 2 vols. UK: no publisher, 1901.

Langton, E. *Essential of Demonology.* UK: Epworth Press, 1949.

Larrington, Carolyne, editor. *The Feminist Companion to Mythology.* UK: Pandora, 1992.

Lautie, Raymond and Andre Passebecq. *Aromatherapy: The Use of Plant Essences in Healing.* UK: Thorsons, 1979.

Lawrence, Shirley Blackwell. *Behind Numerology.* San Bernardino, CA: Borgo, 1989.

Lawson, David. *The Eye of Horus: An Oracle of Ancient Egypt.* NY: St. Martin's, 1996.

Lea, Henry Charles. *The Inquisition of the Middle Ages.* NY: Macmillan, 1961.

Leach, Maria, editor. *Funk & Wagnall's Standard Dictionary of Folklore, Mythology & Legend.* NY: Funk & Wagnalls, 1972. (Originally published 1949.)

Lederer, Wolfgang. *The Fear of Women.* NY: Harcourt Brace Jovanovich, 1968.

Leek, Sybil. *The Complete Art of Witchcraft.* NY: New American Library, 1971.

_____. *Diary of a Witch.* Englewood Cliffs, NJ: Prentice-Hall, 1968.

_____. *Moon Signs: Lunar Astrology.* NY: G.P. Putnam's Sons, 1977.

_____. *The Sybil Leek Book of Fortune Telling.* NY: Collier-Macmillan, 1969.

Legge, James. *The I Ching* (translation). NY: Dover, 1963.

Lehner, Ernst. *Symbols, Signs & Signets.* NY: Dover, 1950.

Leibel, Charlotte P. *Change Your Handwriting, Change Your Life.* NY: Stein & Day, 1972.

Leland, Charles Godfrey. *Aradia: Gospel of the Witches.* Custer, WA: Phoenix Publishing, 1990. (Originally published 1889.)

Lenormant, F. *Chaldean Magic.* UK: Bagster, 1877.

Leonard, Gladys Osborne. *My Life in Two Worlds.* UK: Two Worlds Publishing, 1931.

Lethbridge, T. C. *Witches: Investigating an Ancient Religion.* UK: Routledge & Kegan Paul, 1962.

Levi, Eliphas. *The Book of Splendours.* UK: Aquarian Press, 1981.

_____. *The Mysteries of the Qabalah.* UK: Aquarian Press, 1981.

_____. *Transcendental Magic.* York Beach, ME: Samuel Weiser, 1981.

Levy, G. Rachel. *The Gate of Horn: A Study of the Religious Conceptions of the Stone Age & Their Influence upon European Thought.* UK: Faber & Faber, 1946.

Lewis, H. Spencer. *Mental Poisoning.* Supreme Grand Lodge of the Ancient & Mystical Order of Rosa Crucis, 1981.

Lewis, James R. & Evelyn Dorothy Oliver. *Angels A to Z.* NY: Visible Ink, 1996.

Lewis, Naphtali. *The Interpretation of Dreams and Portents in Antiquity.* Wauconda, IL: Bolchazy-Carducci Publishers, 1996.

Lindsay, Jack. *The Origins of Astrology*. NY: Barnes & Noble, 1971.

Line, David & Julia. *Fortune-Telling by Runes*. UK: Aquarian Press, 1984.

Line, Julia. *The Numerology Workbook: Understanding and Using the Power of Numbers*. NY: Sterling Publishing, 1985.

Linn, Denise. *Past Lives, Present Dreams*. NY: Ballantine Books, 1997.

_____. *Sacred Space*. NY: Ballantine, 1995.

_____. *The Secret Language of Signs*. NY: Ballantine Books, 1996.

Lip, Evelyn. *Chinese Geomancy*. NY: Times Books International, 1979.

Lippman, Deborah & Colin Paul. *How to Make Amulets, Charms, & Talismans*. NY: M. Evans & Co., 1974.

Loewe, Michael & Carmen Blacker. *Oracles and Divination*. Boulder, CO: Shambhala, 1981.

Lonegren, Sig. *The Pendulum Kit*. NY: Simon & Schuster, 1990.

Long, Max Freedom. *Recovering Ancient Magic*. UK: Rider Publishers, 1936.

_____. *The Secret Science Behind Miracles*. Los Angeles, CA: Kosmon Press, 1948.

Lowe, Sheila. *The Complete Idiot's Guide to Handwriting Analysis*. NY: Alpha Books, 1999.

Lucian. Translator, Harold W. Attridge & Robert A. Oden. *The Syrian Goddess*. Scholars Press, 1976.

Luck, Georg. *Arcana Mundi: Magic and the Occult in the Greek and Roman Worlds*. Baltimore, MD: Johns Hopkins University Press, 1985.

Luke, Helen M. *Woman, Earth & Spirit: The Feminine in Symbol & Myth*. NY: Crossroads, 1981.

Lum, Peter. *Fabulous Beasts*. NY: Pantheon Books, 1951.

Lurker, Manfred. *Dictionary of the Gods & Goddesses, Devils and Demons*. NY: Routledge & Kegan Paul, 1987.

_____. *The Gods and Symbols of Ancient Egypt*. UK: Thames & Hudson, 1991.

Luscher, Dr. Max. *The Luscher Color Test*. NY: Pocket Books, 1971.

MacKenzie, Norman. *Secret Societies*. NY: Holt, Rinehart & Winston, 1967.

_____. *Palmistry for Women*. NY: Warner, 1973.

Manning, Al. *Helping Yourself With White Witchcraft*. West Nyack, NY: Parker Publishing, 1972.

_____. *The Miracle of Universal Psychic Power: How to Pyramid Your Way to Prosperity*. West Nyack, NY: Parker Publishing, 1974.

_____. *Moon Lore & Moon Magic*. West Nyack, NY: Parker Publishing, 1980.

Markham, Ursula. *Fortune-Telling by Crystals and Semiprecious Stones*. UK: Aquarian Press, 1987.

_____. *The Crystal Workbook: A Complete Guide to Working With Crystals*. UK: Aquarian Press, 1988.

Marlbrough, Ray T. *Charms, Spells and Formulas*. St. Paul, MN: Llewellyn Publications, 1986.

Marron, Kevin. *Witches, Pagans & Magic in the New Age*. Toronto: Seal Books/McClelland-Bantam, 1989.

Marshall, Chris. *The Complete Book of Chinese Horoscope.* NY: Stewart Tabori & Chang, 1996.

Martello, Leo. *Witchcraft: The Old Religion.* Secaucus, NJ: University Books, 1973.

Massa, Aldo. *The Phoenicians.* Geneva: Editions Minerva, 1977.

Massey, Gerald. *Moon Worship: Ancient & Modern.* Edmonds, WA: Sure Fire Press, 1990.

Mathers, S. L. MacGregor. *The Book of Sacred Magic of Abramelin the Mage.* NY: Dover, 1975.

_____. *The Grimoire of Armadel.* UK: Routledge & Kegan Paul, 1980.

Matteson, Barbara J. *Mystic Minerals.* Seattle, WA: Cosmic Resources, 1985.

Matthews, Caitlin. *The Celtic Tradition.* UK: Element Books, 1989.

_____. *The Elements of the Celtic Tradition.* UK: Element Books, 1989.

_____. *The Elements of the Goddess.* UK: Element Books, 1989.

Matthews, John & Caitlin. *The Aquarian Guide to British & Irish Mythology.* UK: Aquarian Press, 1988.

Matthews, John. *The Celtic Shaman's Pack.* UK: Element Books, 1995.

Matthews, W. H. *Mazes & Labyrinths: Their History & Development.* NY: Dover, 1970. (Originally published 1922.)

Maven, Max. *Max Maven's Book of Fortunetelling.* NY: Prentice-Hall, 1992.

McClain, Florence Wagner. *A Practical Guide to Past Life Regression.* St. Paul, MN: Llewellyn Publications, 1994.

McCoy, Edain. *A Witch's Guide to Faery Folk.* St. Paul, MN: Llewellyn Publications, 1994.

McEvers, Joan, editor. *Web of Relationships.* St. Paul, MN: Llewellyn Publications, 1992.

McFarland, Phoenix. *The Complete Book of Magical Names.* St. Paul, MN: Llewellyn Publications, 1996.

McGrath, Sheena. *The Sun Goddess: Myth, Legend and History.* UK: Blandford, 1997.

McLean, Adam. *A Treatise on Angel Magic.* Grand Rapids, MI: Phanes Press, 1990.

_____. *The Triple Goddess: An Exploration of the Archetypal Feminine.* Grand Rapids, MI: Phanes Press, 1989.

Meadows, Kenneth. *Rune Power.* Boston, MA: Element Books, 1996.

Mellaart, James. *Catal Huyuk: A Neolithic Town in Anatolia.* UK: Thames & Hudson, 1967.

Melody. *Love Is In the Earth.* Wheat Ridge, CO: Earth-Love Publishing House, 1998.

_____. *Love Is In the Earth: Mineralogical Pictorial.* Wheat Ridge, CO: Earth-Love Publishing House, 1997.

Merivale, Patricia. *Pan the Goat-God.* Cambridge, MA: Harvard University Press, 1969.

Mestel, Sherry, editor. *Earth Rites.* 2 vols. Brooklyn, NY: Earth Rites Press, 1981.

Meyer, Marvin W., editor. *The Ancient Mysteries: A Sourcebook.* San Francisco, CA: Harper & Row, 1987.

Michael, Russ. *Finding Your Soul Mate.* York Beach, ME: Samuel Weiser, 1992.

Mickaharic, Draja. *A Century of Spells*. York Beach, ME: Samuel Weiser, 1988.

Miller, Anistatia R & Jared M. Brown. *The Complete Astrological Handbook for the Twenty-First Century*. NY: Schocken Books, 1999.

Monaghan, Patricia. *The Book of Goddesses & Heroines*. St. Paul, MN: Llewellyn Publications, 1990.

Monroe, Robert A. *Journeys Out of the Body*. NY: Doubleday, 1971.

Moody, Raymond. *Coming Back: A Psychiatrist Explores Past-Life Journeys*. NY: Bantam Books, 1992.

_____. *Life After Life*. NY: Bantam Books, 1988.

Mookerjee, Ajit. *Kali: The Feminine Force*. Rochester, VT: Destiny Books, 1988.

_____. *Kundalini: The Arousal of the Inner Energy*. NY: Destiny Books, 1983.

Moorey, Teresa. *A Beginners Guide to Witchcraft*. UK: Hodder & Stoughton, 1999.

Moran, Victoria. *Shelter for the Spirit*. NY: HarperCollins, 1997.

Morgan, Chris. *Fortune Telling: How to Predict Your Own Future*. UK: Quintent Publishing & Random House, 1992.

_____. *The Fortune Telling Kit*. NY: Barron's, 1996.

Morgan, Keith. *The Horned God*. UK: Pentacle Enterprises, 1992.

_____. *How to Use a Ouija Board*. UK: Pentacle Enterprises, 1992.

Morley, Sylvanus. *An Introduction to the Study of the Maya Hieroglyphs*. NY: Dover, 1975.

Morris, Desmond. *Body Guards*. UK: Element Books, 1999.

Morrison, Sarah Lyddon. *The Modern Witch's Spellbook, I*. Secaucus, NJ: Citadel Press, 1971.

_____. *The Modern Witch's Spellbook, II*. Secaucus, NJ: Citadel Press, 1986.

Moss, Robert. *Conscious Dreaming: A Spiritual Path for Everyday Life*. NY: Crown Trade Paperbacks, 1996.

Motoyama, Hiroshi, Ph.D. Translator, Rande Brown Ouchi. *Karma and Reincarnation*. NY: Avon, 1992.

Mottram, E. *The Book of Herne*. UK: Arrowspire Press, 1981.

Muldoon, Sylvan & Hereward Carrington. *The Projection of the Astral Body*. York Beach, ME: Samuel Weiser, 1989. (Originally published 1929.)

Murray, Alexander S. *Who's Who in Mythology*. NY: Bonanza Books, 1988.

Murray, Grace A. *Ancient Rites & Ceremonies*. UK: Senate, 1996. (Originally published 1929.)

Murray, Liz & Colin. *The Celtic Tree Oracle*. NY: St. Martin's Press, 1988.

Murray, Margaret A. *The God of the Witches*. UK: Oxford University Press, 1981.

_____. *The Witch Cult in Western Europe*. UK: Oxford University Press, 1921.

Murray, Rose. *Moving to Success*. St. Paul, MN: Llewellyn Publications, 1999.

Mylonas, George. *Eleusis & the Eleusinian Mysteries*. Princeton, NJ: Princeton University Press, 1961.

Nahmad, Claire. *Earth Magic*. Rochester, VT: Destiny Books, 1994.

Naparstek, Belleruth. *Your Sixth Sense: Activating Your Psychic Potential*. San Francisco, CA: HarperSanFrancisco, 1997.

National Geographic. *Everyday Life in Ancient Times*. Washington, D.C.: National Geographic Society, 1955.

Nau, Erika S. *Huna Awareness: The Wisdom of the Ancient Hawaiians*. York Beach, ME: Samuel Weiser, 1990.

Neiman, Carol & Emily Goldman. *AfterLife: The Complete Guide to Live After Death*. NY: Viking Books, 1994.

Netherton, Morris & Nancy Shiffrin. *Past Lives Therapy*. NY: Wm. Morrow & Co., 1978.

Neumann, Erich. Translated by Ralph Manheim. *The Great Mother: An Analysis of the Archetype*. Princeton, NJ: Princeton University Press, 1963.

New Age Fellowship. *Candle Burning Rituals*. UK: Finbarr International, 1983.

Newall, Venetia, editor. *The Witch in History*. NY: Barnes & Noble, 1996.

Newhouse, Flower A. *The Kingdom of the Shining Ones*. Escondido, CA: The Christward Ministry, 1955.

_____. *Rediscovering the Angels*. Escondido, CA: The Christward Ministry, 1976.

Newton, Michael. *Journey of Souls: Case Studies of Life Between Lives*. St. Paul, MN: Llewellyn Publications, 1995.

Nicholson, Irene. *Mexican and Central American Mythology*. NY: Peter Bredrick Books, 1985.

Nielsen, Greg & Joseph Polansky. *Pendulum Power*. Rochester, VT: Destiny Books, 1987.

Nielsen, Greg. *Beyond Pendulum Power*. Reno, NV: Conscious Books, 1988.

Nivedita, Sister. *Kali the Mother*. Calcutta, India: Advaita Ashrama, 1986.

Norvell, Anthony. *Amazing Secrets of the Mystic East*. West Nyack, NY: Parker Publishing, 1980.

Norvell, Anthony. *Meta-Psychic: New Dimensions of the Mind*. West Nyack, NY: Parker Publishing, 1972.

_____. *Miracle Power of Transcendental Meditation*. West Nyack, NY: Parker Publishing, 1972.

_____. *The Mystical Power of Pyramid Astrology*. NY: Frederick Fell Publishers, 1978.

Noteskin, Wallace. *A History of Witchcraft in England*. NY: Cromwell, 1968.

O'Boyle, S. *Ogam, the Poet's Secret*. Dublin, Ireland: Gilbert Dalton, 1980.

O'Brien, Joanne, with Kwok Man Ho. *The Elements of Feng Shui*. UK: Element Books, 1991.

O'Gaea, Ashleen. *The Family Wicca Book*. St. Paul, MN: Llewellyn Publications, 1993.

O'Rush, Claire. *The Enchanted Garden*. UK: Trafalgar Square Publishing, 1996.

O'Suilleabhain, Sean. *Folktales of Ireland*. UK: Routledge & Kegan Paul, 1966.

Olson, Carl, editor. *The Book of Goddess Past & Present*. NY: Crossroad, 1989.

Ophiel. *The Art and Practice of Astral Projection*. York Beach, ME: Samuel Weiser, 1992.

Opie, Iona and Moira Tatem. *A Dictionary of Superstitions*. UK: Oxford University Press, 1992.

Ostrander, Sheila & Lynn Schroeder. *Psychic Discoveries Behind the Iron Curtain*. NY: Bantam, 1971.

Ouseley, S. G.J. *Colour Meditations*. UK: L. N. Fowler & Co., 1974.

_____. *The Power of the Rays: The Science of Colour-Healing*. UK: L. N. Fowler & Co., 1976.

_____. *The Science of the Aura*. UK: L. N. Fowler & Co., 1973.

Page, Michael & Robert Ingpen. *Encyclopedia of Things That Never Were*. NY: Viking, 1987.

Pajeon, Kala & Ketz. *The Candle Magic Workbook*. Secaucus, NJ: Carol Publishing, 1996.

Palmer, Martin, Joanne O'Brien, and Kwok Man Ho. *The Fortune Teller's I Ching*. UK: Century, 1986.

Parfitt, Will. *The Living Qabalah*. UK: Element Books, 1988.

Parker, Derek and Julia. *The Power of Magic: Secrets and Mysteries, Ancient and Modern*. UK: Mitchell Beazley Publishers, 1992.

_____. *The Power of Magic: Secrets and Mysteries, Ancient and Modern*. UK: Mitchell Beazley Publishers, 1992.

_____. *Parker's Prediction Pack*. NY: DK Publishing, 1999.

Parrinder, Geoffrey. *African Mythology*. UK: Paul Hamlyn, 1975.

Paul, Haydn. *Gate of Rebirth: Astrology, Regeneration and Eighth House Mysteries*. York Beach, ME: Samuel Weiser, 1993.

Paulson, Genevieve L. & Stephen J. *Reincarnation: Remembering Past Lives*. St. Paul, MN: Llewellyn Publications, 1997.

Paulson, Genevieve Lewis. *The Kundalini and Chakras*. St. Paul, MN: Llewellyn Publications, 1993.

Pennick, Nigel. *The Complete Illustrated Guide to Runes*. UK: Element Books, 1999.

_____. *Magical Alphabets*. York Beach, ME: Samuel Weiser, 1992.

_____. *The Pagan Book of Days*. Rochester, VT: Destiny Books, 1992.

_____. *Practical Magic in the Northern Tradition*. UK: Aquarian Press, 1989.

_____. *Secret Games of the Gods: Ancient Ritual Systems in Board Games*. York Beach, ME: Samuel Weiser, 1992.

Perowne, Stewart. *Roman Mythology*. UK: Paul Hamlyn, 1973.

Perrottet, Oliver. *The Visual I Ching*. Boston, MA: Charles E. Tuttle Co., 1997.

Peters, Cash. *Instant Insight*. NY: Warner Books, 1998.

Pierce, Marilyn Seal. *Secrets of Egypt for the Millions*. Los Angeles, CA: Sherbourne Press, 1970.

Pliskin, Marci & Shar L. Just. *The Complete Idiot's Guide to Interpreting Your Dreams*. NY: Alpha Books, 1999.

Pollack, Rachel. *Teach Yourself Fortune Telling*. NY: Henry Holt & Co., 1986.

Poltarnees, Welleran. *A Book of Unicorns*. La Jolla: Green Tiger Press, 1978.

Ponce, Charles. *Kabbalah: An Introduction and Illumination for the World Today*. Wheaton, IL: Theosophical Publishing House, 1973.

Powell, A. E. *The Astral Body*. Wheaton, IL: Theosophical Publishing, 1982. (Originally published 1927.)

———. *The Etheric Double, the Health Aura of Man*. Wheaton, IL: Theosophical Publishing, 1983. (Originally published 1925.)

Powell, Tag & Judith. *Taming the Wild Pendulum*. Pinellas Park, FL: Top of the Mountain Publishing, 1995.

Purce, Jill. *The Mystic Spiral: Journey of the Soul*. NY: Thames & Hudson, 1974.

Rae Beth. *Hedge Witch: A Guide to Solitary Witchcraft*. UK: Robert Hale, 1990.

Ralphs, John. *Exploring the Fourth Dimension*. St. Paul, MN: Llewellyn Publications, 1992.

Ramacharaka, Yogi. *The Science of Psychic Healing*. Chicago, IL: Yogi Publication Society, 1937. (Originally published 1909.)

Ransome, H. M. *The Sacred Bee in Ancient Times and Folklore*. UK: Allen & Unwin, 1937.

Raphael. *Raphael's Ancient Manuscript of Talismanic Magic*. Chicago, IL: The deLaurence Co., 1916.

Raphaell, Katrina. *Crystal Enlightenment: The Transforming Properties of Crystals and Healing Stones*. NY: Aurora Press, 1985.

Ravenwolf, Silver. *Hexcraft: Dutch Country Pow-Wow Magick*. St. Paul, MN: Llewellyn Publications, 1995.

———. *To Light a Sacred Flame*. St. Paul, MN: Llewellyn Publications, 1999.

———. *To Ride a Silver Broomstick*. St. Paul, MN: Llewellyn Publications, 19

———. *To Stir a Magick Cauldron*. St. Paul, MN: Llewellyn Publications, 1995.

Reed, Ellen Cannon. *The Witches' Qabala*. St. Paul, MN: Llewellyn Publications, 1985.

Reed, Henry. *Dream Solution*. San Rafael, CA: New World Library, 1991.

———. *Your Mind: Unlocking Your Hidden Powers*. Virginia Beach, VA: A.R.E. Press, 1989.

Regardie, Israel. *A Garden of Pomegranates*. St. Paul, MN: Llewellyn Publications, 1978.

———. *The Golden Dawn*. St. Paul, MN: Llewellyn Publications, 1982.

———. *How to Make & Use Talismans*. UK: Aquarian Press, 1981.

———. *The Middle Pillar*. St. Paul, MN: Llewellyn Publications, 1970.

Reid, Lori. *The Art of Hand Reading*. NY: DK Publishing, 1996.

Renee, Janina. *Playful Magic*. St. Paul, MN: Llewellyn Publications, 1994.

———. *Tarot Spells*. St. Paul, MN: Llewellyn Publications, 1990

Richardson, Alan. *Gate of Moon*. UK: Aquarian Press, 1984.

Richardson, Wally & Lenora Huett. *Spiritual Value of Gem Stones*. Marina del Rey, CA: DeVorss & Co., 1983.

Riggs, Maribeth. *The Healing Bath*. NY: Penguin, 1996.

Ritsema, Rudolf & Stephen Karcher, translators. *I Ching: The Classic Oracle of Change*. UK: Element Books, 1994.

Riva, Anna. *Candle Burning Magic*. Toluca Lake, CA: International Imports, 1980.

_____. *Golden Secrets of Mystic Oils.* Toluca Lake, CA: International Imports, 1978.

_____. *Magic With Incense and Powders.* No. Hollywood, CA: International Imports, 1985.

_____. *Modern Herbal Spellbook.* Toluca Lake, CA: International Imports, 1974.

_____. *Spellcraft, Hexcraft & Witchcraft.* No. Hollywood, CA: International Imports, 1977.

Robbins, Rossel Hope. *Encyclopedia of Witchcraft and Demonology.* NY: Crown Publishers, 1959.

Roberts, Alison. *Hathor Rising.* Rochester, VT: Inner Traditions, 1997.

Roberts, Henry C. *The Complete Prophecies of Nostradamus.* NY: American Book–Stratford Press, 1969.

Robertson, R. MacDonald. *Selected Highland Folktales.* UK: David & Charles, 1977.

Robinson, Lynn A. and LaVonne Carlson-Finnerty. *Being Psychic.* NY: Alpha Books, 1999.

Robinson, Rita. *The Palm: A Guide to Your Hidden Potential.* No. Hollywood, CA: Newcastle, 1988.

Roehrig, Catharine. *Fun With Hieroglyphs.* NY: The Metropolitan Museum of Art, 1990.

Rogo, D. Scott. *Our Psychic Potentials.* Englewood, NJ: Prentice-Hall, 1984.

Roman, Clara. *Handwriting: A Key to Personality.* NY: Noonday Press, 1966.

Roman, Sanaya & Duane Packer. *Opening to Channel: How to Connect With Your Guide.* Tiburon, CA: H. J. Kramer, 1987.

Rose, Donna. *Love Spells.* Hialeah, FL: Mi-World, no date.

_____. *The Magic of Astrology.* Hialeah, FL: Mi-World, 1978.

_____. *Magic of Candle Burning.* Hialeah, FL: Mi-World, 1981.

_____. *The Magic of Herbs.* Hialeah, FL: Mi-World, 1978.

_____. *Money Spells.* Hialeah, FL: Mi-World, 1978.

_____. *Unhexing and Jinx Removing Spells.* Hialeah, FL: Mi-World, 1978.

Rose, Jeanne. *The Aromatherapy Book.* Berkeley, CA: North Atlantic Books, 1992.

_____. *Herbs and Things: Jeanne Rose's Herbal.* NY: Perigee, 1987.

_____. *Jeanne Rose's Modern Herbal.* NY: Perigee, 1987.

Rosetree, Rose. *Aura Reading Through All Your Senses.* Sterling, VA: Women's Intuition Worldwide, 1996.

Ross, Anne. *The Pagan Celts.* Totowa, NJ: Barnes & Noble, 1986.

Rush, Anne Kent. *Moon, Moon.* NY: Random House, 1976.

Russel, J. B. *Witchcraft in the Middle Ages.* Ithaca, NY: Cornell University Press, 1972.

Ryall, Rhiannon. *Symbols of Ancient Gods.* UK: Capall Bann Publishing, 1998.

_____. *West Country Wicca.* Custer, WA: Phoenix Publishing, 1989.

Ryan, Donald P. *The Complete Idiot's Guide to Lost Civilizations.* NY: Alpha Books, 1999.

Sams, Jamie. *Medicine Cards: The Discovery of Power Through the Ways of Animals.* Santa Fe, NM: Bear & Co., 1988.

_____. *Sacred Path Cards*. San Francisco, CA: Harper & Row, 1990.

San Souci, Robert S, retold by. *The Firebird*. NY: Dial Books for Young Readers, 1992.

Sanders, Pete A., Jr. *You Are Psychic*. NY: Fawcett Columbine, 1989.

Sarris, Arian. *Healing the Past*. St. Paul, MN: Llewellyn Publications, 1997.

Sasportas, Howard. *The Gods of Change: Pain, Crisis and the Transits of Uranus, Neptune and Pluto*. UK: Arkana/Penguin Books, 1989.

Saunders, Nicholas J. *Animal Powers: An Illustrated Guide to the Souls of Animals*. UK: Duncan Baird Publishers, 1997.

Schaya, L. *Universal Meaning of the Kabbalah*. Secaucus, NJ: University Books, 1971.

Schirner, Markus. *Pendulum Workbook*. NY: Sterling Publishing, 1999.

Schmaker, Wayne. *The Occult Sciences in the Renaissance*. Los Angeles, CA: University of California Press, 1972.

Scholem, Gershom. *Origins of the Kabbalah* (translation). Princeton, NJ: Jewish Publication Society, 1987.

Schueler, Gerald J. *Enochian Magic: A Practical Manual*. St. Paul, MN: Llewellyn Publications, 1985.

Schwei, Pricilla. *The Solomon Manual of Divination and Ritual Spells*. St. Paul, MN: Llewellyn Publications, 1988.

Serith, Ceisiwr. *The Pagan Family: Handing the Old Ways Down*. St. Paul, MN: Llewellyn Publications, 1994.

Shapiro, Robert & Julie Rapkin. *Awakening to the Animal Kingdom*. San Rafael, CA: Cassandra Press, 1988.

Sharkey, John. *Celtic Mysteries: the Ancient Religion*. NY: The Crossroad Publishing Co., 1975.

Sharman-Burke, Juliet & Liz Greene. *The Mythic Tarot*. NY: Fireside Book/Simon & Schuster, 1986.

Shaw, Eva. *Divining the Future*. NY: Gramercy Books, 1995.

Shaw, S. Indries. *The Secret Lore of Magic*. NY: Citadel Press, 1958.

Shepard, Odell. *The Lore of the Unicorn*. NY: Harper & Row, 1979.

Shepard, Paul & Barry Sanders. *The Sacred Paw: The Bear in Nature, Myth and Literature*. NY: Penguin Books, 1985.

Shepherd, A. P. *Rudolf Steiner: Scientists of the Invisible*. Rochester, VT: Inner Traditions International, 1983.

Sher, Barbara. *Wishcraft: How to Get What You Really Want*. NY: Ballantine Books, 1979.

Shine, Norman. *Numerology: Your Character and Future Revealed in Numbers*. NY: Simon & Schuster, 1994.

Showers, Paul. *Fortune Telling For Fun and Profit*. NY: Bell Publishing, 1985.

Silberer, Herbert. *Hidden Symbolism of Alchemy & the Occult Arts*. NY: Dover, 1971.

Silbey, Uma. *Crystal Ball Gazing*. NY: Fireside, 1998.

_____. *The Complete Crystal Guidebook*. NY: Bantam Books, 1987.

Simek, Rudolf. Translated by Angela Hall. *Dictionary of Northern Mythology*. UK: D. S. Brewer, 1993.

Sjoo, Monica & Barbara Mor. *The Great Cosmic Mother: Rediscovering the Religion of the Earth*. San Francisco, CA: Harper & Row, 1987.

Skelton, Robin. *Talismanic Magic*. York Beach, ME: Samuel Weiser, 1985.

Slater, Herman, editor. *The Magickal Formulary*. NY: Magickal Childe, 1981.

Smith, C. F. *John Dee*. UK: Constable, 1909.

Smith, Mark. *Auras: See Them in Only Sixty Seconds*. St. Paul, MN: Llewellyn Publications, 1997.

Smith, Michael G. *Crystal Power*. St. Paul, MN: Llewellyn Publications, 1985.

Smith, Michael G. & Lin Westhorp. *Crystal Warrior: Shamanic Transformation and Projection of Universal Energy*. St. Paul, MN: Llewellyn Publications, 1992.

Smith, Steven R. *Wylundt's Book of Incense*. York Beach, ME: Samuel Weiser, 1989.

Sofianides, Anna S. & George E. Harlow. *Gems, Crystals and Minerals*. NY: Simon & Schuster, 1990.

Somerville, Neil. *Your Chinese Horoscope*. UK: Aquarian Press, 1992.

Sophia. *Fortune in a Coffee Cup*. St. Paul, MN: Llewellyn Publications, 1999.

Sorrell, Roderic & Amy Max. *The I Ching Made Easy*. San Francisco, CA: HarperSanFrancisco, 1994.

South, Malcolm, editor. *Mythical and Fabulous Creatures*. NY: Peter Bedrick Books, 1988.

Sparrow, Lynn Elwell. *Reincarnation: Claiming Your Past, Creating Your Future*. NY: St. Martin's, 1988.

Spence, Lewis. *British Fairy Origins*. UK: Watts, 1946.

————. *The Encyclopedia of the Occult*. UK: Bracken Books, 1994.

————. *The Fairy Tradition in Britain*. UK: Rider, 1948.

————. *The Magic Arts in Celtic Britain*. NY: Dorset Press, 1992.

————. *The Mysteries of Britain: Secret Rites and Traditions of Ancient Britain*. UK: Rider & Co., 1979.

————. *The Occult Sciences in Atlantis*. UK: Aquarian Press, 1978.

Spicer, Dorothy Gladys. *The Book of Festivals*. NY: Woman's Press, 1937.

Spretnak, Charlene. *Lost Goddesses of Early Greece*. Berkeley, CA: Moon Books, 1978.

Squire, Charles. *Celtic Myth & Legend, Poetry & Romance*. NY: Newcastle Publishing, 1975.

Squire, Elizabeth. *The New Fortune in Your Hand*. NY: Fleet Press, 1960.

St. Christopher, Michael. *How to Use a Ouija Board*. Los Angeles, CA: International Imports, 1995.

Stallone, Jacqueline. *Star Power: An Astrological Guide to Supersuccess*. NY: New American Library, 1989.

Starhawk. *The Spiral Dance*. NY: Harper & Row, 1979.

Stearn, Jess. *Edgar Cayce: The Sleeping Prophet*. NY: Bantam, 1968.

Steiger, Brad. *Returning From the Light*. NY: Penguin, 1996.

Stein, Diane. *Healing With Gemstones and Crystals*. Freedom, CA: The Crossing Press, 1996.

_____. *The Kwan Yin Book of Changes*. St. Paul, MN: Llewellyn Publications, 1989.

_____. *Psychic Healing With Spirit Guides and Angels*. Freedom, CA: The Crossing Press, 1996.

_____. *Stroking the Python*. St. Paul, MN: Llewellyn Publications, 1988.

_____. *The Women's Book of Healing*. St. Paul, MN: Llewellyn Publications, 1993.

_____. *The Women's Spirituality Book*. St. Paul, MN: Llewellyn Publications, 1987.

Stein, Sandra Kovacs. *Instant Numerology*. No. Hollywood, CA: Newcastle Publishing, 1986.

_____. *The Power of Alpha-Thinking: Miracle of the Mind*. NY: New American Library, 1976.

_____. *Soul Mates*. NY: Bantam, 1984.

Stewart, R. J. *Living Magical Arts*. UK: Blandford Press, 1987.

_____. *The Living World of Faery*. UK: Gothic Image, 1995.

_____. *The Merlin Tarot*. UK: Aquarian Press, 1988.

_____. *Robert Kirk: Walker Between Worlds: A New Edition of the Secret Commonwealth of Elves, Fauns & Fairs*. UK: Element Books, 1990.

Stewart, W. Grant. *Popular Superstitions of the Highlanders of Scotland*. UK: Ward Lock, 1970. (Originally published 1823.)

Stone, Merlin. *Ancient Mirrors of Womanhood*. Boston, MA: Beacon Press, 1984.

_____. *When God Was a Woman*. NY: Harcourt Brace Jovanovich, 1976.

Strayhorn, Lloyd. *Numbers and You*. NY: Ballantine Books, 1987.

Sullivan, Kevin. *The Crystal Handbook*. NY: Signet, 1987.

Sun Bear and Wabun. *The Medicine Wheel*. Englewood Cliffs, NJ: Prentice-Hall, 1980.

Sun Bear, Crysalis Mulligan, Peter Nufer & Wabun. *Walk in Balance*. NY: Prentice Hall Press, 1989.

Sutphen, Tara. *Blame It on Your Past Lives*. Malibu, CA: Valley of the Sun, 1993.

Swanhild. *Holiday Folklore*. Green Man Press, 1990.

Symonds, John and Kenneth Graham, editors. *The Confessions of Aleister Crowley: An Autobiography*. UK: Routledge & Kegan Paul, 1979.

Talbot, Michael. *Your Past Lives*. NY: Harmony Books, 1987.

Tannahill, Reay. *Flesh and Blood: A History of the Cannibal Complex*. NY: Stein & Day, 1975.

Tarostar. *The Spiritual Worker's Handbook*. Toluca Lake, CA: International Imports, 1985.

_____. *The Witch's Formulary & Spellbook*. NY: Original Publications, no date.

Thierens, A. E. *Astrology and the Tarot*. Los Angeles, CA: Newcastle, 1975.

Thomas, William & Kate Pavitt. *The Book of Talismans, Amulets and Zodiacal Gems*. No. Hollywood, CA: Wilshire Book Co., 1970.

Thompson, C. J. S. *The Mysteries and Secrets of Magic.* NY: Barnes & Noble, 1993.

Thompson, William Irvin. *The Time Falling Bodies Take to Light: Mythology, Sexuality & the Origins of Culture.* NY: St. Martin's Press, 1981.

Thorsson, Edred (Stephen Flowers). *Runelore.* York Beach, ME: Samuel Weiser, 1987.

Thorsten, Geraldine. *God Herself: The Feminist Roots of Astrology.* Garden City, NY: Doubleday, 1980.

Thurston, Mark. *Discovering Your Soul's Purpose.* Virginia Beach, VA: A.R.E. Press, 1989.

Time-Life. *Ancient Wisdom and Secret Sects.* Alexandria, VA: Time-Life, 1989.

_____. *Dreams and Dreaming.* Alexandria, VA: Time-Life, 1990.

_____. *Hauntings.* Alexandria, VA: Time-Life, 1989.

_____. *The Magical Arts.* Alexandria, VA: Time-Life, 1993.

_____. *Mind and Beyond.* Alexandria, VA: Time-Life, 1991.

_____. *Mysteries of the Unknown.* Alexandria, VA: Quality Paperback Book Club, 1997.

_____. *Phantom Encounters.* Alexandria, VA: Time-Life, 1988.

_____. *Psychic Powers.* Alexandria, VA: Time-Life, 1987.

_____. *Search For the Soul.* Alexandria, VA: Time-Life, 1989.

_____. *Spirit Summonings.* Alexandria, VA: Time-Life, 1989.

_____. *Visions and Prophecies.* Alexandria, VA: Time-Life, 1991.

Tisserand, Maggie. *Aromatherapy for Women.* UK: Thorsons, 1985.

Tisserand, Robert. *Aromatherapy to Tend and Heal the Body.* Wilmot, WI: Lotus Light, 1989.

_____. *The Art of Aromatherapy.* NY: Destiny Books, 1977.

Todeschi, Kevin J. *Edgar Cayce on the Akashic Records.* Virginia Beach, VA: A.R.E. Press, 1998.

Tognetti, Arlene & Lenard, Lisa. *Tarot and Fortune-Telling.* NY: Alpha Books, 1999.

Torrens, R. G. *The Golden Dawn: The Inner Teachings.* NY: Samuel Weiser, 1973.

Torres, Katherine. *The Sacred Path Wheel.* Carlsbad, CA: Two Feathers Soaring Lightly, 1991.

Tresidder, Jack. *The Dictionary of Symbols.* San Francisco, CA: Chronicle Books, 1998.

Trevor-Roper, H. R. *The European Witch-craze.* NY: Harper & Row, 1957.

Troyer, Patricia. *Crystal Personalities.* Peoria, AZ: Stone People Publishing, 1995.

Tuitéan, Paul & Estelle Daniels. *Pocket Guide to Wicca.* Freedom, CA: The Crossing Press, 1998.

Turville-Petre, E. O. G. *Myth & Religion of the North: The Religion of Ancient Scandinavia.* Westport, CT: Greenwood Press, 1975.

Tyson, Donald. *How to Make and Use a Magic Mirror.* St. Paul, MN: Llewellyn Publications, 1990.

_____. *The New Magus: Ritual Magic as a Personal Process.* St. Paul, MN: Llewellyn Publications, 1988.

_____. *Scrying For Beginners.* St. Paul, MN: Llewellyn Publications, 1997.

_____. *The Truth About Runes.* St. Paul, MN: Llewellyn Publications, 1989.

Underhill, Callia. *The Witch's Book of Divination*. St. Paul, MN: Llewellyn, 1996.

Uyldert, Mellie. *The Magic of Precious Stones*. UK: Turnstone Press, 1981.

Valiente, Doreen. *An ABC of Witchcraft Past and Present*. NY: St. Martin's Press, 1973.

_____. *Natural Magic*. Custer, WA: Phoenix Publishing, 1985.

_____. *Witchcraft for Tomorrow*. UK: Robert Hale, 1983.

van den Eerenbeemt, Noud. *Divination by Magic*. York Beach, ME: Samuel Weiser, 1985.

Verner, Alexander. *Table Rapping and Automatic Writing*. Minneapolis, MN: Marlar Publishing, no date.

Vinci, Leo. *Incense: Its Ritual Significance, Use and Preparation*. NY: Samuel Weiser, 1980.

Viney, Geoff. *Surviving Death: Evidence of the AfterLife*. NY: St. Martin's, 1993.

Wainwright, F.T. *Scandinavian England*. UK: Phillimore & Co., Ltd., 1975.

Waite, Arthur Edward. *The Pictorial Key to the Tarot*. NY: Samuel Weiser, 1973.

Walker, Barbara G. *The Woman's Dictionary of Symbols and Sacred Objects*. San Francisco, CA: Harper & Row, 1988.

_____. *The Woman's Encyclopedia of Myths and Secrets*. San Francisco, CA: Harper & Row, 1983.

Walker, Dael. *The Crystal Book*. Sunol, CA: Crystal Col, 1983.

Walker, Morton. *The Power of Color*. Garden City, NY: Avery Publishing, 1989.

Walters, Derek. *Chinese Astrology*. UK: Aquarian Press, 1987.

Walters, Raymond J. L. *The Power of Gemstones*. NY: Chartwell Books, 1996.

Wang, Robert. *The Qabalistic Tarot*. York Beach, ME: Samuel Weiser, 1983.

Warlick, M. E. *The Philosopher's Stones*. Boston, MA: Journey Editions, 1997.

Watlington, Cindy. *Crystal Deva Cards*. Boulder, CO: Inner Quest, 1996.

Watson, Donald. *Far Journeys*. Garden City, NY: Dolphin/Doubleday, 1985.

Wauters, Ambika. *Chakra Oracle*. Berkeley, CA: Conari Press, 1996.

Webb, Marcus & Maria. *Healing Touch*. NY: Sterling Publishing, 1999.

Webster, Richard. *Omens, Oghams, and Oracles*. St. Paul, MN: Llewellyn Publications, 1995.

_____. *Revealing Hands: How to Read Palms*. St. Paul, MN: Llewellyn Publications, 1995.

Wedeck, Harry E. *A Treasure of Witchcraft*. Secaucus, NJ: Citadel Press, 1964.

Weigle, Marta. *Spiders & Spinsters: Women and Mythology*. Albuquerque, NM: University of New Mexico Press, 1982.

Weinman, Ric. *Your Hands Can Heal: Learn to Channel Healing Energy*. NY: E. P. Dutton, 1988.

Weinstein, Marion. *Positive Magic*. Custer, WA: Phoenix Publishing, 1981.

Westcott, W. W., translator. *Sepher Yetzirah*. NY: Occult Research Press, no date.

Whitcomb, Bill. *The Magician's Companion: A Practical and Encyclopedic Guide to Magical and Religious Symbolism*. St. Paul, MN: Llewellyn Publications, 1993.

White, Suzanne. *The New Astrology*. NY: St. Martin's Press, 1986.

White, T. H., translator. *The Book of Beasts: Being a Translation from a Latin Bestiary of the 12th Century*. NY: Dover, 1984.

Whitehead, Willis F. *The Magic Mirror*. The Lumen Press, no date or place.

Whitmont, Edward C. *The Return of the Goddess*. NY: Crossroads, 1982.

Whittick, Arnold. *Symbols: Signs & Their Meaning & Uses in Design*. Newton, MA: Charles T. Branford, 1971.

Wilde, Lady. *Irish Cures, Mystic Charms & Superstitions*. NY: Sterling Publishing, 1991.

Wilder, Louise Beebe. *The Fragrant Garden*. NY: Dover, 1972.

Wilhelm, Richard and Cary F. Baynes. *The I Ching* (translation). Princeton, NJ: Princeton University Press, 1969.

Williams, Jean. *Winning With Witchcraft*. UK: Finbarr Books, 1982.

Williamson, John. *The Oak King, the Holly King, and the Unicorn*. NY: Harper & Row, 1986.

Wilson, Colin. *The Occult: A History*. NY: Random House, 1971.

Wimberly, Lowry Charles. *Folklore in the English & Scottish Ballads*. NY: Dover, 1965.

Windsor, Joan. *The Inner Eye*. Englewood Cliffs, NJ: Prentice-Hall, 1985.

Wolfe, Amber. *Elemental Power*. St. Paul, MN: Llewellyn Publications, 1997.

_____. *In the Shadow of the Shaman*. St. Paul, MN: Llewellyn Publications, 1990.

_____. *Personal Alchemy: A Handbook of Healing and Self-Transformation*. St. Paul, MN: Llewellyn Publications, 1993.

Wolfe, Frankie Avalon. *The Complete Idiot's Guide to Reflexology*. NY: Alpha Books, 1999.

Wombwell, Felicity. *The Goddess Changes*. UK: Mandala, 1991.

Wood, Robin. *When, Why…If*. Dearborn, MI: Livingtree Book, 1996.

Woods, William. *A History of the Devil*. NY: Putnam, 1974.

Woodward, Mary Ann. *Edgar Cayce's Story of Karma: God's Book of Remembrance*. NY: Coward, McCann & Geoghegan, 1971.

Woolfork, Joanna Martine. *The Only Astrology Book You'll Ever Need*. Landham, MA: Scarborough, 1992.

Worthington, Vivian. *A History of Yoga*. UK: Routledge & Kegan Paul, 1982.

Worwood, Valerie Ann. *The Complete Book of Essential Oils and Aromatherapy*. San Rafael, CA: New World Library, 1991.

Wosien, Maria-Gabriel. *Sacred Dance: Encounter With the Gods*. UK: Thames & Hudson, 1974.

Zed, Sara. *The Complete Guide to Coffee Grounds and Tea Leaf Reading*. Israel: Astrology Publishing House, 1998.

Zerner, Amy & Monty Farber. *The Alchemist*. NY: St. Martin's, no date.

Zimmerman, J. E. *Dictionary of Classical Mythology*. NY: Bantam Books, 1978.

INDEX

OTHER BOOKS BY D.J. CONWAY

Advanced Celtic Shamanism

By D. J. Conway

D. J. Conway uses the four paths of shamanism (healer, bard, warrior, and mystic) to translate Celtic spirituality into a usable form for today's seekers.

Paper • ISBN 1-58091-073-4

Crystal Enchantments: A Complete Guide to Stones and Their Magical Properties

By D. J. Conway

This book will help guide you in your choice of stones from Adularia to Zircon, by listing their physical properties and magical uses.

Paper • ISBN 1-58091-010-6

Laying on of Stones

By D. J. Conway

D. J. Conway supplies forty detailed diagrams showing exactly where to place a variety of stones to help heal your body or enrich your life.

Paper • ISBN 1-58091-029-7

A Little Book of Altar Magic

By D. J. Conway

D. J. Conway shows you how to create a sacred space in your home, with information from historical and modern approaches on the use of colors, elements, objects, and symbols.

Paper • ISBN 1-58091-052-1

A Little Book of Candle Magic

By D. J. Conway

Learn the purpose of candle and other fire rituals; the meanings of candle types and colors; and candle spells for healing, love, protection, and success.

Paper • ISBN 1-58091-043-2

A Little Book of Healing Magic

By D. J. Conway

D. J. Conway introduces some of the most effective and commonly practiced magical means of restoring good health: easy-to-use spells and rituals, affirmations, visualizations, meditation, music, herbs, talismans and amulets, saints and deities, auras, long-distance healing, color, altars, and runes.

Paper • ISBN 1-58091-146-3

A Little Book of Pendulum Magic

By D. J. Conway

Learn how to use pendulum power to make the right decisions and expand your psychic abilities through tarot cards, crystals, and astrology.

Paper • ISBN 1-58091-093-9

OTHER BOOKS BY THE CROSSING PRESS

Apprentice to Power: A Wiccan Odyssey to Spiritual Awakening
By Timothy Roderick

Sharing enchanting tales, meditations, rituals, and magical techniques, neopagan Timothy Roderick weaves a colorful introduction to Wicca, Old Europe's earth-centered mystical tradition. Demonstrating how to build a relationship with the divine in all things and access the power of spirit in everyday life, *Apprentice to Power* offers an accessible path toward greater fulfillment, profound change, and mystical insight.
Paper • ISBN 1-58091-077-7

A Complete Guide to Magic and Ritual: Using the Energy of Nature to Heal Your Life
By Cassandra Eason

Cassandra Eason, a world-renowned psychic, explains how magic can change your life, from attracting love and improving family relationships to encouraging good health and prosperity. Learn how to tap in to the magic of plants, flowers, and essential oils and harness the energy of the sun, moon, and seasons to reverse bad luck, rekindle hope and passion, and trust instinct and inspiration—the most important magic of all.
Paper • ISBN 1-58091-101-3

Essential Wicca
By Paul Tuitéan and Estelle Daniels

Focusing on earth, nature, and fertility, the religion embraces the values of learning, sexual equality, and divination. While most books on Wicca address either the solitary practitioner or those in covens, Essential Wicca covers all the bases — from core beliefs and practices, basic and group rituals, to festivals and gatherings, holy days, and rites of passage. A glossary with more than 200 entries and over 100 illustrations extends the meaning of the text.
Paper • ISBN 1-58091-099-8

Spinning Spells, Weaving Wonders: Modern Magic for Everyday Life
By Patricia Telesco

This essential book of over 300 spells tells how to work with simple, easy-to-find components and focus creative energy to meet daily challenges with awareness, confidence, and humor.
Paper • ISBN 0-89594-803-6

The Wiccan Path: A Guide for the Solitary Practitioner
By Rae Beth

This is a guide to the ancient path of the village wisewoman. Writing in the form of letters to two apprentices, Rae Beth provides rituals for the key festivals of the wiccan calendar. She also describes the therapeutic powers of trancework and herbalism, and outlines the Pagan approach to finding a partner.
Paper • ISBN 0-89594-744-7

For a current catalog of books from The Crossing Press
visit our Web site: www.crossingpress.com

www.crossingpress.com

BROWSE through the Crossing Press Web site for information on upcoming titles, new releases, and backlist books including brief summaries, excerpts, author information, reviews, and more.

SHOP our store for all of our books and, coming soon, unusual, interesting, and hard-to-find sideline items related to Crossing's best-selling books!

READ informative articles by Crossing Press authors on all of our major topics of interest.

SIGN UP for our e-mail newsletter to receive late-breaking developments and special promotions from The Crossing Press.